Romantic Interactions

Social Being and the Turns of Literary Action

SUSAN J. WOLFSON

The Johns Hopkins University Press

Baltimore

© 2010 The Johns Hopkins University Press
All rights reserved. Published 2010
Printed in the United States of America on acid-free paper
9 8 7 6 5 4 3 2 1

The Johns Hopkins University Press
2715 North Charles Street
Baltimore, Maryland 21218-4363
www.press.jhu.edu

Library of Congress Cataloging-in-Publication Data
Wolfson, Susan J., 1948–
    Romantic interactions : social being and the turns of literary action / Susan J. Wolfson.
        p. cm.
    Includes bibliographical references and index.
    ISBN-13: 978-0-8018-9473-2 (hardcover : alk. paper)
    ISBN-10: 0-8018-9473-5 (hardcover : alk. paper)
    ISBN-13: 978-0-8018-9474-9 (pbk. : alk. paper)
    ISBN-10: 0-8018-9474-3 (pbk. : alk. paper)
    1. English literature—19th century—History and criticism. 2. Romanticism—
Great Britain. 3. Social interaction in literature. 4. Women and literature—
England—History—19th century. 5. Gender identity in literature. I. Title.
    PR468.R65W655   2010
    820.9′355—dc22   2009033012

A catalog record for this book is available from the British Library.

Special discounts are available for bulk purchases of this book. For more information,
please contact Special Sales at 410-516-6936 or specialsales@press.jhu.edu.

The Johns Hopkins University Press uses environmentally friendly book materials,
including recycled text paper that is composed of at least 30 percent post-consumer
waste, whenever possible. All of our book papers are acid-free, and our jackets and
covers are printed on paper with recycled content.

The social sympathies, or those laws from which as from its elements
society results, begin to develop themselves from the moment that two
human beings coexist; the future is contained within the present as the
plant within the seed; and equality, diversity, unity, contrast, mutual
dependence become the principles alone capable of affording the motives
according to which the will of a social being is determined to action . . . the
manner in which the imagination is expressed upon its forms.

—P. B. Shelley, *A Defence of Poetry* (1821/1840)

CONTENTS

III. A Public Attraction

ILLUSTRATIONS

ACKNOWLEDGMENTS

I have been fortunate in material resources and support at Princeton University, which supplied a dream of an office, expert technical support, a richly stored library, the gift of time with sabbaticals, and students with whom to share work and ideas, and from whom to learn.

Grateful acknowledgment for the use of some illustrations is given in the legends. Though I retain my affection for, interest in, and scholarly reliance on the material book, my research has been greatly assisted by on-line access to page-image reproductions of many, many out of print and otherwise rare books. I am particularly grateful for Eighteenth-Century Collections Online (ECCO), for Google Books and all its institutional partners, and the Romantic Circles website, especially the electronic editions of *Lyrical Ballads* prepared by Bruce Graver and Ronald Tetreault. For expert help in preparing my visual images, I am happy to thank my colleague Kevin Mensch.

Material in some of my chapters has been auditioned at cordial conferences, panels, invited talks, and publication. I am pleased to thank my hosts, sponsors, and editors for their interest and support, and my attentive and stimulating audiences everywhere: Anne Mellor, the William Andrews Clark Memorial Library, and UCLA; Adam Potkay and the College of William and Mary; Michael Macovski and Fordham University; Harvard Center for Literary and Cultural Studies, Seminar in Romanticism, especially Alan Richardson and Sonia Hofkosh; Clare Cavanagh and the Association of Literary Scholars and Critics; University of Western Ontario and Douglas Kneale; Jacqueline Labbe and the British Association for Romantic Studies; Peter Manning and the graduate students at the State University of New York at Stony Brook; Bill Galperin and the Center for the Critical Analysis of Culture at Rutgers University; the West Virginia Colloquium in Literary Study and Adam Komisaruk; University of West Virginia and Morgantown Public Library; the American Conference in Romanticism and Ray Fleming; Michael Sinatra, Jason Camlot, and University of Montreal and Concordia University; James Engell and Harvard University; Tom Mole and the Byron Society of America; the Eighteenth-century and Romantics colloquium at Princeton University, including my valued colleague Starry Schor.

Careful editors of essays that have contributed to some chapters include Claudia Johnson, Anne Mellor, and Thaïs Morgan. I'm also fortunate in friends and colleagues who read and commented on various present chapters, or answered questions: Andy Elfenbein, Doucet Fischer, Barry Qualls, Susan Levin, Karen Swann, Linda Dowling, Garrett Stewart, Frances Ferguson, Paul Kellerman, Jack Cragwall, Terry Hoagwood, Billy Galperin, Jerry McGann, Caroline Franklin, Peter Manning.

And, always, Ron Levao: Romantic, Interactive, and beyond compare. It's a redundancy, but also a fresh and happy pleasure, to dedicate *Romantic Interactions* to him.

When the author is evident, I use standard general abbreviations for the sources, without clutter, to indicate the author. Hence, *CW* for *Collected Works,* or *W* for *Works; L* for *Letters; PW* for *Poetic Works; PrW* for *Prose Works; P&P* for *Poetry and Prose.* Full information on such items as well as for works identified by short titles appears in Works Cited. Other abbreviations for frequently cited works are below.

AN	*Alfoxden Notebook* of Dorothy Wordsworth
AR	*Analytical Review*
B&G	James Butler and Karen Green's edition of *Lyrical Ballads*
BCB	*Blessington's Conversations of Byron,* ed. Lovell
BL	*Biographia Literaria,* by Coleridge, ed. Engell and Bate
BLJ	*Byron's Letters and Journals,* ed. Marchand
BPW	*Byron's Poetical Works,* ed. McGann
BW	*Byron's Works* (ed. Thomas Moore; published by John Murray, 1833)
DCMS(S)	manuscript(s) at Dove Cottage Archives, Grasmere, England.
DWL	*Dorothy Wordsworth: A Longman Cultural Edition,* ed. Levin
EY	(Wordsworths, *Letters*) *Early Years,* ed. de Selincourt and Shaver
FN	Fenwick note: William Wordsworth's notes on his poems, dictated in 1843 to friend and neighbor Isabella Fenwick; in Jared Curtis's edition, the first to publish Fenwick's notebook (DCMS 153) entire.
GJ	*Grasmere Journals* of Dorothy Wordsworth
HVSV	(Byron), *His Very Self and Voice,* anthology, ed. Lovell

LSR	(Wollstonecraft) *Letters Written During a Short Residence in Sweden, Norway, and Denmark*
LY	(Wordsworths, *Letters*) *Later Years,* ed. de Selincourt and Hill
MCB	Medwin's *Conversations of Byron,* ed. Lovell
MY	(Wordsworths, *Letters*) *Middle Years,* ed. de Selincourt, Moorman and Hill
Nb	*Coleridge's Notebooks,* ed. Coburn
OED	*Oxford English Dictionary*
PL	*Paradise Lost* by John Milton; 2nd edition, 1674, by book and line
RM	*Vindication of the Rights of Men* (Wollstonecraft)
RW	*A Vindication of the Rights of Woman* (Wollstonecraft)

NOTE ON TEXTS

Because *Romantic Interactions* is, among other commitments, a work of historicizing criticism, when possible, I follow lifetime editions, or ones with historical pertinence. Attempting to represent these texts as they would have been read in their first eras of publication, reading, and reception, I have not standardized or modernized (unless indicated). My only exceptions are quotation-mark convention and typography. All ellipses signify my own elisions of text.

Romantic Interactions

Introduction

"The will of a social being"

A FAMED MYTH of "Romanticism" is its generative, even revolution-ary, literature of single perspectives, solitary converse, stark differentiation of self and world, highly signaled subjective agency. Though frequently dismantled, the myth remains arresting—iconic even, for poets as various (and given to ridiculing one another) as, say, William Wordsworth and Lord Byron and for cultural interpreters such as Charlotte Smith and Mary Wollstonecraft. All speak at times as if in alienated solitude, socially and existentially, even as they are aware of bringing into being an audience, one often made up of other authorial voices—whether allied or oppositional.

Romantic Interactions at once acknowledges the power of this myth in the prestige of "Romanticism" and refracts it through a countervailing dynamics of interaction. That a solitary consciousness seeks expression in words, sometimes in the illusion of speech, suggests a social investment, if only on a minimal level of imagining audition by another. Before I take stock of this investment, it will help to desynonymize (to use S. T. Coleridge's term) my interest in its dynamic from near cousins. By *interaction*, I don't mean the webs of "intertextuality" that would capture and consume the illusion of author; nor do I intend Helen Vendler's subtly tuned story of volitional, imaginative "lyric intimacy" with invisible, sometimes historically or metaphysically remote, listeners; nor Jeffrey Cox's recovery of an avant garde School ("Cockney," in his case) whose literary production is professionally collective, collaborative, and communal; nor the events of knowing, close collaboration of author, friendly readers, editors, and publisher that shape Jack Stillinger's report on Romanticism, and much else, in *Multiple Authorship and the Myth of Solitary Genius*. While all these paradigms are brilliant, proximate, and rel-

1

evant, my interest homes in on cases of a writer coming to self-definition as "author" in connection with other authors—whether on the bookshelf, or in the embodied company of someone else writing, or in relation to literary celebrity. Refraining from claims (on the one hand) for autonomous self-determination and (on the other) authorless intertextuality or broad, social determinism, I turn to distinctive instances where a Romantic "author" gets created, as a literary consciousness, in a web of reciprocally transforming and transformative creative subjects—in what I term *interaction*.

The word itself comes into print in the Romantic age, most visibly, with Romantic philosophical and metaphysical investments. In *Saturday Evening* (1833), Isaac Taylor—born the year before Byron—proposes that there are

> influences or principles of interaction, which, though absolutely imperceptible to the senses of man, and far remote from the reach of his philosophy, . . . bind together all the solid masses of the universe, and impart to each sphere an agency that extends itself to all others.
>
> (125)[1]

In 1876, in a "long-Romantic" version of such cosmology, Ralph Waldo Emerson gives a literary—more particularly, poetic—spin to the vision of elemental interaction:

> the poet sees the horizon, and the shores of matter lying on the sky, the interaction of the elements,—the large effect of laws which correspond to the inward laws which he knows, and so are but a kind of extension of himself. (37)

For both him and Taylor, the principle of interaction is a cosmic one because it is also personally registered, not just within the self but in connection to the world. Emerson's essay, tellingly, is housed in a volume titled *Letters and Social Aims* (1876).[2]

Such visions project vast and eventual harmonies of interaction. Yet as even the Poet Laureate of poetically achieved harmonies, Coleridge, knows, a shadow-story lies in interactions that agitate and alienate. Taylor concedes this ambivalence within the word *interaction* itself:

> Excellence of all kinds, physical, intellectual, and spiritual, is the product, not of the single operation of some one principle; but of the

oppugnant forces of two or more powers. . . . exalted and resplendent qualities have always become what they are, by the vehement interaction of conflicting elements. (161)

While this is metaphysics and cosmic physics in a vast, dynamic harmony, the force field might be otherwise.

For Thomas Hardy, it is the darker processes that come to the fore in a bleak naturalism. In *Tess of the D'Urbervilles*, Hardy summons the word *interaction* for a projected dream—a remote, utopian epoch of benevolence that would, if only it could, redeem the purblind hap that dooms his fictive worlds:

In the ill-judged execution of the well-judged plan of things . . . [w]e may wonder whether at the acme and summit of the human progress these anachronisms will become corrected by a finer intuition, a closer interaction of the social machinery than that which now jolts us round and along. (Ch. V; 78–79)

For the most harmonious interaction, Hardy hopes for the acme and summit of human progress, while Taylor looks to the exalted state of the human soul—the one achieved over and against grinding social fate, the other in the refinement of metaphysical antagonism.

Both these broad visions might model the world of writing, as Taylor assessed it in the early 1830s (some pages earlier in *Saturday Evening*), using the word *interaction,* in italics, to describe the activity: "the reaction, or rather *interaction,* which at present is going on between readers and writers" (86). He wasn't sure whether this reciprocity was a cause for celebration or concern, but he did recognize that writers and readers were "stimulated" by the exercise. *Interaction* is the word to which other Romantic-era literary artists could turn to describe the tensions of both individual character and social reality: "that complexity and interweaving of qualities, that interaction of moral and intellectual powers, which we moderns understand by a character," said De Quincey in 1840 to readers of *Blackwood's,* theorizing Greek drama as this kind of psychological play (and psychology as this kind of drama) (150). In 1856, George Eliot, with her interest tuned to modern sociology, uses the word in a now famous essay in *Westminster Review,* urging a study of "the interaction of the various classes on each other" ("Natural History" 57).

Both psychological and social dynamics are involved in Percy Bysshe

Shelley's *Defence of Poetry*. Set doubly in its compositional moment—the political turmoils of the early 1820s—and in its reception and public discussion in the 1840s and onward, the *Defence* was sparked as a polemical reply to the oppugnant force of another author, Thomas Love Peacock, whose "Four Ages of Poetry" (*Olliers Literary Miscellany*, 1820) had issued a bristling, satirical attack on poetry as a useless profession for the modern age. It was, moreover, by the agency of yet another author that Shelley's polemic, left uncompleted in manuscript at his death, reached publication. Mary Shelley—posthumous editor of Shelley's poetry, then prose—brought this elaborate, contradictory, electrifying document to light for Victorian eyes. In its second paragraph—from beyond the grave, as an author newly alive for readers—Shelley issues this proposal:

> The social sympathies, or those laws from which as from its elements
> society results, begin to develop themselves from the moment that
> two human beings coexist.   (3–4)[3]

This is not a sentimental story of sympathy trumping rivalry; it is the impulse of "principles and motives," Shelley suggests (even insists), "according to which the will of a social being is determined to action"—determined in individual motive and will and, in punning complement, determined by social situations, social forces (4).[4]

Even Wordsworth—the aspiring poet who is willing to say of himself to his dearest sister as he is relating his walking tour in 1790, "I find I have again relapsed into Egotism" (*EY 37*)—is capable in this same letter of proving Shelley's point:

> At the lake of Como my mind ran thro a thousand dreams of happiness which might be enjoyed upon its banks, if heightened by conversation and the exercise of the social affections. . . . I have thought of you perpetually and never have my eyes burst upon a scene of particular loveliness but I have almost instantly wished that you could for a moment be transported to the place where I stood to enjoy it.
>
> (*EY* 34–35)

More than a friendly wish for shared transport, these sentences express social being as twin to heightened personal experience: "I" enhanced and excited by the company of "you"—not just in the event of seeing, either, but in the thousand dreams simultaneously activated.

For his immediate purpose of advancing a "defence of poetry," Shelley proposes to "dismiss those more general considerations which might involve an enquiry into the principles of society itself, and restrict our view to the manner in which the imagination is expressed upon its forms" (4). This dismissal doesn't really hold as the *Defence* unfolds, however: Shelley keeps confronting formal principles in society that generate forms of writing, forms of writing that he himself cannot but help imagine as generating principles of society. For all the solitary singing of the Romantic poet—that star of *A Defence*—it is poet-author Shelley who feels (like Wordsworth at Lake Como) compelled to theorize writing as a social rhetoric, at once intimate and interactive, making solitude itself into a moment of social reflection in the medium of its form. This is a view of authorial self as a co-existence, constantly entertaining "equality, diversity, unity, contrast, mutual dependence" (4) in the resources, and at times, pressures, of others.

In developing *Romantic Interactions* I have profited from the critical adventures that have, in recent years, reshaped study of the Romantic decades. As the census of writers expanded (even old canonicals acquiring new casts), new theories of interaction have added to the complication: Michel Foucault's relations of power; Roland Barthes' society of texts; Harold Bloom's anxious influences, the canny and uncanny misreadings, the filial strategies against literary fathers. Yet these male-invested paradigms, however instructive, are restricted by their own assumptions about what kinds of relations mattered. Since one conduit of my argument flows from women as political and cultural interpreters (Smith and Wollstonecraft), thence to a woman interpreted by and then interpreting the century's most honored Romantic poet (Wordsworth and Wordsworth), and finally to how several women poets interpret the other most celebrated poet of the Romantic era (Byron), it will help, too, to review some key perspectives in gender criticism, and to indicate my own position.

Elaine Showalter was a pioneer in 1977, uncovering "The Female Tradition" in a history of British women novelists from the 1840s to the 1960s, which she described in three primary, sometimes overlapping phases: the "feminine," imitating the modes of a dominant (male-authored) tradition; the "feminist," pressing against this tradition with a concentration on women's rights and socially conditioned values; and finally, a liberated "female" mode of self-discovery.[5] Caroline Franklin took up the arc of poetry, mapping a conspicuous gap: "a separate and specifically feminine tradition of both poetic subject-matter and style, which developed largely from Augustan into Victorian verse, while very largely eschewing Romanticism."[6] Whether by inclusion or exclusion, both she and Showalter reflect the deep received history of "Romanticism" as an archive of brilliant male exponents, mostly poets.

In other discussions, however, this history was being revised, with a fresh recovery of women's poetry in the Romantic era, involving forceful, searching analyses of local sites and stimulating theories of the general stakes. Margaret Homans's *Women Writers and Poetic Identity* (1980) concentrated on three socially isolated, scarcely publishing poets—Dorothy Wordsworth, Emily Brontë, and Emily Dickinson—to analyze the traditions that put the two categories in her title into inhibiting, at times defeating opposition, and at a remove from any vivid sense of audience beyond the domestic sphere. Mary Poovey's *The Proper Lady and the Woman Writer* (1984) then measured the ideology of styles in the better known, publicly oriented female prose writers and novelists of the Romantic age (Wollstonecraft, Shelley, and Austen). Although poets were not in her survey, the patterns she described were applicable. It was not long after, in 1988, that a path-breaking essay by Stuart Curran showed how a turn to many less known women poets in the age could alter our sense of the poetic "I" habituated from the male canon. Meanwhile, Marlon Ross's *The Contours of Masculine Desire: Romanticism and the Rise of Women's Poetry* (1989) was dislodging the received history of this canon to account for the importance of a wide and active culture of women's poetry for both male and female writing. In the next decade, Anne Mellor identified two main currents in women's poetry: a celebrated but delimited cult of the "poetess" ("feminine" themes and writing practices that survived well into the nineteenth century), and a contrary "tradition of the female poet"—"explicitly political," "self-consciously and insistently [in] the public sphere," and pressing issues not limited to women.[7] She soon went on to array Romanticism itself, not only in habits of imagination but also in national self-expression: first, in distinct "masculine" and "feminine" characters; then, in a contrast of institutional patriarchy and activist mothers. With a vigorous and careful archival investigation,

Stephen Behrendt cast strong illumination on Romantic women poets as a widespread and politically various British writing community, engaged with public issues, private matters, and shared genres.[8]

These critical reviews of Romanticism along lines of gender—whether tending to polarities, complementarities, or provocative confusions— echo a brave nineteenth-century writer, born in, though not borne by, the man's world of Romanticism, and always hopeful of social transformation, especially through the agency of writing. Here are a few paragraphs from this writer's casting of one modern man's "history," describing an educational culture of which we are the heirs, and using the keyword of my study:

> There is a tendency now in society to open the college course equally to women—to continue through college life that interaction of the comparative influence of the sexes which is begun in the family.
>
> To a certain extent this experiment has been always favorably tried in the New England rural Academies, where young men are fitted for college in the same classes and studies with women.
>
> In these time-honored institutions, young women have kept step with young men in the daily pursuit of science, not only without disorder or unseemly scandal, but with manifestly more quietness and refinement of manner than obtains in institutions where female association ceases altogether.

The chapter at hand is titled "My Dream Wife," and it is from Harriet Beecher Stowe's *My Wife and I: or, Harry Henderson's History* (53–54)— the antithesis of the other famous wife and husband under her signature, Lord and Lady Byron, subjects of her notorious *Lady Byron Vindicated*. These two books (published 1870–71) tell very different stories of interaction, the one a romance of new forms of relationship, the other, a bitter polemic on domestic and discursive abuse, the men winning, female vindication notwithstanding. It's a dilemma that would imprint feminist criticism when it emerged a century later, in the 1970s. By the 1980s, when "women's studies" programs and departments were being advocated, Myra Jehlen reviewed the first decade of professional feminist literary criticism, to argue (controversially then) that criticism, to change anything, could not be a unilateral activism, but had to engage "radical comparativism" (585).

By force of these interventions and adventures, literary studies has transformed since 1980, not only with new resources, but even the traditions of male writing (including its most canonical works) seeming less uniform, more fissured, internally contradictory. Gender criticism has made "gender" itself a question. Yet the appeal of binaries has proven hard to resist, with some of the most durably influential critical paradigms deriving their force from differentials: men and women, "masculine" and "feminine," masculinist and feminist. It is telling that for all of Jehlen's methodological savvy—her call for "focusing on relations between situations rather than on the situations themselves" (585) and her alertness to contradictions—she could still view male Romanticism as monolith: "the great Romantic poets conned us into believing that to be a great poet was to tell *the* absolute truth, to be the One prophetic voice for all Mankind" (her italics). It was up to feminist criticism, as "the philosophy of the Other" (she insisted) to "reject the very conception of such authority" (579).

It is worth remembering, however, that it was among male Romantic poets and essayists that this conception was opposed, satirized, rejected. Keats's speculation about "Negative Capability" is an obvious reference, but even poster-boys for the figure of the great poet—Wordsworth and Byron, in different poses—wrote of truths less in the absolute than in the multiple, variable, doubtful, and wrote of themselves with more questions than certainties about the origins and stability of poetic authority. The opposition that Jehlen attributes to post-Romantic feminism emerges in the Romantic age itself as part of its own dialectics, its own historical conditioning, in the "equality, diversity, unity, contrast, mutual dependence" that Shelley articulated as soon as he conceded the social being and social existence of writing. Although Shelley was not without complicity in gender binaries, his brief sociology contains a theory of representation, of language as a social and a literary production, without insisting that one determines the other.

My argument in *Romantic Interactions*, then, is that authorial self-recognition takes shape as a reciprocal formation in a society of formations, that it is continuously challenged by this field, and that it is best revealed not in categorical rhetorics, but in specific sites and textual reflections of complex interaction. Correspondingly, proof emerges from the fine grain of reading, and reading against the grain—reflecting my conviction, from my first publications on, that irreducible events of language, as these are read and debated, written and revised, reviewed and received, constitute our most fundamental resource for describing Romantic culture.

My book begins in the 1790s with two women's political perspectives on male literary traditions (and their social consequences): Charlotte Smith keenly tuned to the poetry of war, and Mary Wollstonecraft, a self-crafted female "philosopher" taking a long view of the poetry of "female character." Immersed in personal and historical complications, both women discover their authority in politically sharpened, methodologically complicated engagements with male literary traditions and male authorial voices. Constituting a virtual seminar on interactions, Smith's polemic in blank verse, *The Emigrants*, previews my interests across the book. Writing as a long war with France was emerging, and caught in conflicts of compassion and political censure as she regarded the waves of desperate aristocratic and clerical French refugees from the Terror, Smith summons traditionally masculine epic authority to advance her strongest, most passionate claims: that whatever the conflict, whatever the historical moment, women are never agents but always victims, and that victims compel figuration as female. To forge this perspective, Smith fashions her authorial persona from a series of critical alliances and realignments with Virgil, Shakespeare, Milton, Pope, Thomson, Collins, Burns—and nowhere more forcefully than with her political refraction of the most famous epic simile (in the Romantic era, anyway) of *Paradise Lost:* Satan's pained siege of unexpected enchantment by and reflexive alienation from Eden, "As one who long in populous City pent. . . ." (IX.445*ff*).

Smith's critical reading of poets' language is Wollstonecraft's explicit project, honed as a thematic interest and pointed as a theoretical intervention. Addressing the social wrongs and rational "rights of woman" against the long cultivated, "prevailing opinion of sexual character" (i.e., "female" character), *A Vindication of the Rights of Woman* invents what we now recognize as feminist criticism by textualizing received opinion (reified as "authority") as a vast, and revisable, epic poem. At the same time, for all this pungent ideological critique, Wollstonecraft remains a close reader of poetry, not just to sharpen her analytical instruments, but also, surprisingly perhaps, to shape her own most heartfelt expression, frequently in sympathy with Shakespeare's Hamlet and Milton's Satan as partners in alienation, opposition, and melancholy. So forceful and foundational a critique, and so candid a self-display, made it inevitable that Wollstonecraft herself would be figured into a text for gender-fraught cultural debates. My double focus here—placing women's readings of tradition and received understandings in relation to their own reception history—is a methodology I use throughout this study.

Smith and Wollstonecraft, women who went public with their authority, open the path to a fresh perspective on William and Dorothy Wordsworth, who embody questions of gender difference in close proximities of imagination. Their interactions are all the more compelling, given the radical asymmetry of their fame: the one, a poet of self-advertised "powerful feeling" (claimed for "manly" poetry), who would emerge as England's national poet, then its Poet Laureate; the other, a woman who frequently struggled against feeling, who kept protesting she was no poet, but who kept writing poetry, and much else, in contexts of domestic affection, domestic service, and domestic labor—all averse to public scrutiny, but with a sharp sensitivity to the world around the domestic shelter. Nurtured by domestic intimacy but sensitive to cultural stricture and social anxiety, the two Wordsworths instance a local reception history with each other, relayed in the complexities of the writing they shared with each other, and sometimes with others.

My first Wordsworthian scene is the poetics of "common feeling" wielded by William Wordsworth to launch *Lyrical Ballads* as a revolution, "a man speaking to men" in a language of "ordinary conversation." Such rhetoric constituted the front line to Francis Jeffrey's testy notice in the *Edinburgh Review* of 1802 of the second edition (now signed by Wordsworth) of this poetry and the revolution it was taken to feed: lower social orders advanced as subjects for mature poetic sympathy. Jeffrey's stance was no less political, no less social, than it was literary. He meant to stem the insurgency. At the same time, Wordsworth's democracy of sympathy, for all its revolutionary promise and provocation, was strangely pressured: he not only hewed to a male rhetorical circuit ("a man speaking to men"), but monitored this circuit against strangely affective sympathies in the poetry itself, replete with figures of male hysteric passion and fraught with female bodies, female histories, female voices, and female authority.

This unexamined fascination of male poetics with female formations vexes "William" and "Wordsworth" in close interaction with the "Sister" who figures into his poetry (variously) as native simplicity, peculiar muse, suppressed authority, and source of arresting conceptual and verbal power. Meanwhile, the empirical Dorothy Wordsworth was experiencing her own angles of vision on the world she shared with her brother, and the world into which she ventured without him. Revisiting to revise a story familiar in feminist criticism—of Dorothy inhibited to the point of silence and self-cancellation by the allied force of William's modes and cultural strictures—I show her testing alternatives to some of his most cherished, constitutive values, particularly the solitary self-concentration that (paradoxically) generates his social prestige as inspired, instructive "Poet." Across this process, Dorothy experiments with her own, variant authority as she tracks her routes into some of William's darkest terrains, shadowed by her concerns about female social experience.

Smith's embattled selfhood in man's literary (and political) culture; Wollstonecraft's alternately critical and sentimental interactions with the poets; William Wordsworth's vacillating engagements with female figures and feminine configurations; Dorothy Wordsworth's ambivalent regard of his imaginative forms: all these involve a sense of self, for better or worse, with a public identity, and with it the risks of a public's authority over (its writing about) the socially legible self. What happens when the wide orbit of society—its currents of publication, reading, conversation, scandal, and gossip—gets magnetized by a scandalous figure, flagrantly self-styled?

The most explosively centrifugal field of Romantic interaction, in a riot of authorities, stars Byron and his publics. It is with Byron and "Byron" that I round off my story of Romantic interactions. If William Wordsworth struggled with gender in a poetry determined to be the rhetoric of "a man speaking to men," Byron's poetry seemed to speak more widely than even he could have anticipated, issuing a hot challenge to the self-possession and autonomy of just about everyone, including the self-possessed author, Byron himself. His poetry propelled him into a celebrity synonymous with a pervasively decentered author, playing at home and abroad, on the page and in society, to turn "Byron" into a text of popular imagination. "We opened this new volume of poetry, bearing the noble name of Byron as it's passport to celebrity . . ."—so *The Euro-*

pean Magazine and London Review could begin a notice in 1822, as a calm matter of cultural fact, of the latest publication event (81: 58). The link of noble name to the terra incognita of celebrity was anyone's game. If Walter Benjamin proposes (in a much reproduced essay) that "that which withers in the age of mechanical reproduction is the aura of the work of art," as a plurality of copies "depreciate[s]" the quality of unique presence (221), Byron's celebrity had the effect of rejiggering depreciation into a multiplicity of appreciations. It was not just that he consciously staged himself in plural Byrons, an array in which the question of authenticity is either beside the point or part of the performance, but that these spectacles initiated the phenomenon of "Byronism" (a word coined in his lifetime), in which serial reproductions became (and still become) new works of cultural art, generating new auras, even new registers of authenticity, beyond any aura under Byron's management.

In the first part of this last act, "Gazing on Byron," I show how this Byronic romance is both amplified by and also fractured across the public drama of Lady Byron's self-removal from a marriage about which all were speculating. In the drama soon known as The Separation, "Lord Byron occupied the eyes, and interested the feelings of all"—so said Walter Scott, with no little understatement, as he rushed to play his own part in the fray, with an article in the *Quarterly* that was more love letter than sober review. In the wide arena of interaction, "The enthusiastic looked on him to admire, the serious with a wish to admonish, and the soft with a desire to console" (16: 178). The law of sympathy that produces society for Shelley becomes in the social text of The Separation a new, publicly aired test of affection for the charismatic author of this catastrophe. "Byron" stimulated and gave public sanction to rapture, spawned the inevitable parodies from cool observers, stirred venom in the disaffected. Across the world in which "Byron" whirled into factions and refractions, *Byronism* writes a new book on Romantic interactions that forecasts the electric circuits of individual genius and celebrity today.

Romantic Interactions closes by drawing its argument into the conflicts of Byronism for female poets, for whom interaction is inspiration to self-declaring, sometimes self-destructive, literary authority. The images tendered by Byron-smitten men (Scott, Coleridge, John Wilson) became a creative stimulus for women writing to and about Byron: Anne Isabella Milbanke (who would not, then would, then would not, be Lady Byron), her friend, erstwhile Byronist Joanna Baillie, her cousin (Byron's ex-lover) Caro Lamb, a sorority of Regency fans eager to read themselves into the drama, and then, at further remove, but in a close affective connection of enamored readers and Byronic writers, Felicia Hemans, Elizabeth Barrett, and L.E.L.—thence and then into the long Romanticism of later Landon, M. J. Jewsbury, Emily Brontë, Lady Blessington, Caroline Norton, and Harriet Beecher Stowe. Stowe's Wollstonecrafted *Lady Byron Vindicated* amounted to a return to the now-despised *Vindication of the Rights of Woman,* recalled from the 1790s and refreshed in 1870 for a transatlantic modern world (and subjecting Stowe, too, to scathing reactions from a world of hostile counterauthors).

The practices and possibilities of cultural criticism that my readings advance, locally and cumulatively, are meant to continue the project launched by Wollstonecraft's approach to the social through the literary, highlighting the circumstances, circuits, and textures of vital interactions.

Two Women
& Poetic Tradition

CHAPTER ONE

Charlotte Smith's *Emigrants* and the Politics of Allusion

Epic Interactions in a Crisis of Sympathy

Unfolding across Charlotte Smith's two-book epic *The Emigrants* (1793) are interactions so conspicuously literary as to seem metaliterary. Its dynamic is a conflict of humanitarian sensibility and political outrage—a conflict not just in the pressures of the historical present, the advent of war in 1792–93, but in the depths of literary history. Smith's verse, fraught with contrarieties and sympathies evoked or attenuated, generates its largest claim to authority from a trans-national, trans-historical identification of female historical experience amid men's wars. To develop this claim, however, Smith indulges no poetic binaries, but finds her energy in a series of critical engagements with the texts and voices of male literary tradition. In some views, such a practice can look dependent and derivative: a female poet's internalization and imitation of male canonical authority and prestige, by which she hopes to pass muster in its garb, to pay a daughterly tax to progenitors and influences, or display cultural capital in the absence of the credit of formal education.[1] Yet Smith vexes her textual field to effects more disruptive and confrontational: a sustained interaction with tradition and history that issues a politics of literary form.

The occasion is a mirror scene of social interaction, compelled as English shores witnessed a tide of refugees from revolutionary France, desperate abjects from the disestablished first and Second Estates, the clergy and the nobility. The patent literariness of *The Emigrants*—from its epic cast to its assembly of citations, quotations, allusions—magnetizes the textual field for conflicts of vision and sympathy in all forms of representation. The "scene" of Book I is "*November, 1792*": three years after Church lands were nationalized; two years after the clergy were ordered to swear loyalty to Civil Constitution and the Constitutional Church; six months after *réfractairs* were declared traitors; three months after the decree for their expulsion and the arrest of the royal family at the Tuileries; two months after the September massacres (among the victims, 3 bishops and 220 priests), the abolition of the monarchy, and the confiscation of emigrants' property; one month after a death penalty was decreed for returnees. By November 1792, Robespierre had risen to power and would soon oversee the Terror, Saint-Just was calling Louis XVI "a foreign enemy" of national "independence and unity" (he had tried to flee the country in June 1791), and Smith, hardly flush, was sheltering emigrants in her home, one to become her son-in-law by the next July.[2] She sets Book II in "April, 1793," after the execution of Louis (January 26), England's declaration of war against France (February 1), with Marie Antoinette and her children in prison. Smith completed it all in May, published it that summer, after the Girondins fell and Charlotte Corday assassinated Marat, and when Smith's daughter had married that emigrant nobleman. She read its first reviews as the queen went to trial and then the guillotine (October 16).

Forged amid turmoil, *The Emigrants* shapes no consolidated tract on these events; it is a dynamo of strained, often contradictory sympathies and judgments, built up, so one review called the genre at hand, into an epic "soliloquy."[3] This mode, in tandem with Smith's already famous persona as fortune's exile (launched with *Elegiac Sonnets* in 1784), would seem primed to meditative pity for the emigrants.[4] Yet a political view presses at their complicity with the ancien régime and at the Anglo-reflections of it. For a language to express this division, Smith turns to male literary tradition. She closes Book I with a plea to treat the "ill-starr'd Exiles" with a "just compassion" of "pure humanity" (354–68), but not without enlisting male tradition to admonish any swelling of British "pride" (378) in

> the deafening roar
> Of Victory from a thousand brazen throats,
> That tell with what success wide-wasting War
> Has by our brave Compatriots thinned the world.   (379–82)

Tolling her blank verse with a rare nonce (masculine) rhyme, *roar/War*, Smith does not so much echo as audit male epic tradition. The referent of these rhyming repetitions is the repetition of history itself. Literary form is cast in manifest mimesis. In the vast audit is Pope's patriarchal Jove bidding "the brazen throat of war to roar" (*Iliad* X.8), itself historically resounding the tale that Milton's warrior Archangel conveys to Adam: a world where the "brazen Throat of Warr had ceast to roar," but only in a fall to "luxurie and riot, feast and dance" (*PL* 11.713–15)—an ancient ancien régime. Smith's relay of these war cries is no call to male epic authority to amp up her own; she sounds history itself, and its epic poetry militant, as a horrific repetition of roaring war.

Given such mordant allusion, can we release Smith from secondary repetition into a proactive tradition of "female" protest against "patriarchal militarism"—surging from *Lysistrata* to Sally Field's Fox-censored maternal rant at the 2007 Emmys? *The Emigrants* makes such a case to Anne Mellor ("Female Poet" 266), gender not only imprinting its acid view of man-wars but also scarring Smith's lived experience, as a mother with a son in the war abroad and in prolonged conflict with the legal system at home. Even so, a venture in gender allegory is nothing if not tricky for the 1790s—a decade when both men and women invoked traditions of "British Liberty" to support the French Revolution, then to oppose the civil war and the Terror; a decade of stark class inequality, which men suffered with women, as poor men were called up to fight and die for the interests of the rich, and women were left bereft at home.[5] In this welter, Smith contends with the male canon to work through, if not work out, her conflicts about the emigrants—not as poignant victims of the times but as political signifiers, caught between an ancien régime with which she has no sympathy, and her hope for a new reign of "Reason, Liberty" (II.444). These ideals mark the last line of her epic, in the company of a third, which seems scarcely imaginable, "Peace." Here evoked, reconfigured, is the Revolution's male-marked slogan, "Liberty, Fraternity, Equality," an agenda that had taken a hard turn in the Terror-devoured year of 1793. How might a female poet, in test of epic dimension, formulate a hope for rational, liberal peace and use men's voices to do so?

"tho not on politics on a very popular & interesting subject"

It wasn't just the political complications of French emigration that pressed on Smith, nor the cultural regard of epic as a man's genre. It was also, and fundamentally, her signed entry into a hot public debate. Even a conservative Hannah More worried about putting her name to a fairly unobjectionable pamphlet denouncing the atheist French Republic and urging Christian charity to the fleeing clergy.[6] Whatever their views, public debate was no place for decent women. As she was writing *The Emigrants*, Smith was reading James Thomson's midcentury play *Coriolanus*, with an *Epilogue Spoken by Mrs. Woffington*—that is, Peg Woffington, the celebrated, scandal-tinged actress who played Coriolanus's monstrous, politically involved mother. The address begins:

> WELL! Gentlemen! and are you still so vain
> To treat our sex with arrogant disdain;
> And think, to you alone by partial heaven,
> Superior sense and sovereign power are given   (4: 287)

If such a greeting promises proto-feminist satire, it proves a setup by the male playwright. Within two dozen lines, the script turns reassuringly antifeminist (Kate lecturing the wives at the end of *The Taming of the Shrew* is so transparent a precedent as to seem an allusion):

> Be not alarm'd: I will not interfere
> In state affairs, nor undertake to steer
> The helm of government,—as we are told
> These female politicians did of old:
> Such dangerous heights I never wish'd to climb—
> Thank Heaven I better can employ my time—   (288)

This "anti-female stage female" was no model for Smith.[7] Although no female politician, across 1791 Smith was writing a political novel, *Desmond*, the first English novel set in the Revolution era, June 1790 to February 1792. It was published in early July 1792,[8] as dark clouds were looming across bright ideals. The date that Smith affixed to the Preface in the second edition, "June 20, 1792," is the very day that a crowd invaded the Tuileries to compel Louis XVI to replace his crown with the revolutionary cockade. Training "sensibility" to political sympathy with the victims of husband, church, and state, and making that eighteenth-century innovation, the man of feeling, into a man of political feeling, *Desmond* staged the Edmund Burke/Tom Paine debate in the voices of its characters, investing the hero with revolutionary ideals and principles and linking the heroine's plight in an oppressive marriage to a hope for her "proper spirit of resistance against usurped and abused authority."[9]

Though not with novels, other female politicians preceded Smith into Revolution-marked publication, out to steer, if not the helm of government, then the tides of public opinion. In November 1790 Helen Maria Williams issued the first installment of her enthusiastic *Letters from France*, and Wollstonecraft fired off *A Vindication of the Rights of Men*, which beat Paine, by a couple of months, to the punch against Burke's *Reflections on the Revolution in France*. The heat drawn by these publications left Smith in a bit of a jam: Burke's publisher James Dodsley had also published the first four editions of her lucrative *Elegiac Sonnets* (1784–86).[10] Alert to the backlash against Republican polemics (and the female pen) and loath to alienate a public on whom she depended for her livelihood, Smith did not want to distress her new publisher George Robinson. She had met Williams in France in 1791 and had been linked with her.[11] So she takes the opportunity of the Preface for the second edition of *Desmond* to address the "apprehension" of readers "to whom the political remarks . . . may be displeasing" (i), and points out that "imaginary characters" voice "the arguments I have heard on both sides" (iii). At the same time, she won't dodge behind this artifice, but tells readers that if the arguments "in favour of one party have evidently the advantage, it is not owing to my partial representation, but to the predominant power of truth and reason" (iii). To name *reason* is not disinterested; it's a keyword in Republican polemic.

No impartiality was discerned by Wollstonecraft when she reviewed *Desmond* (one of her longest reviews ever): "the cause of freedom is defended with warmth, whilst shrewd satire and acute observations back the imbodied arguments."[12] She saw an ally for her own irritation in *A Vindication of the Rights of Woman* (published just months before) at the censure of female politicians—say, the finger-wagging in Reverend James Fordyce's ever popular *Sermons to Young Women*. Identifying "war, commerce, politics—abstract philosophy" as unfit subjects for women (only "masculine women" would say otherwise), he preached: "It is not the argumentative but the sentimental talents, which give you that insight and those openings into the human heart, that lead to your principal ends as Women" (Sermon VII; 1: 272–73). So Wollstonecraft wanted to give Smith's Preface entire; "the author shall speak for herself," she says, springing Smith from any feint of dramatic voicing (428–29). In the Preface, Smith takes direct aim at the sermonizers—"women it is said have no business with politics"—with her own interrogation:

> Why not?—Have they no interest in the scenes that are acting around them, in which they have fathers, brothers, husbands, sons, or friends engaged!—Even in the commonest course of female education, they are expected to acquire some knowledge of history; and yet, if they are to have no opinion of what *is* passing, it avails little that they should be informed of what *has passed*, in a world where they are subject to such mental degradation; where they are censured as affecting masculine knowledge if they happen to have any under-standing; or despised as insignificant triflers if they have none. (iii–iv)

By *interest* Smith means both rational attention and rational sympathy; domestic affection and education form a *feminine* knowledge sufficient for "business with politics." It is not any dereliction of "domestic virtues" and "domestic duties," Smith makes clear, but her own degradation in male systems of justice that has sharpened her politics (iv). She will enlist Hamlet's sarcasm on the regime-change that has left him out:

> it was in the *observance*, not in the *breach* of duty, *I* became an Author; and it has happened, . . . that I am too well enabled to describe from *immediate* observation,
>
> > 'The proud man's contumely, th' oppressors wrong;
> > The laws delay, the insolence of office.' (iv–v)

This is alliance by revision, the italics reversing Hamlet's sigh about Danish dissolutions. As Smith echoes his world-weariness, she implies her better claim. University-educated Prince Hamlet is free of marriage, children, and fear of starvation. Smith, mother of nine, harassed by a deadbeat husband with whom she could no longer bear to live, indicts a legal system in which "the affairs of my family" are "most unhappily in the power of men" (v). Yet another ally, Shakespeare's banished man, Duke Senior, whom she quotes, too (vi), is still better off than she.[13]

Before the violent reprisals in France, erupting in August and horrifically waged across September 1792, it was possible for an English subject to publish Republican views. *Desmond* is full of this language, with England transparent in the ancien régime.[14] Wollstonecraft gave three-quarters of her review to quoting its inset account of the brutal oppression of a Breton peasant (based on documented case).[15] Other reviews not only did not bristle at Smith's political material but admired it. She "certainly vindicated the cause of French liberty with much acuteness," said the *London Review* (22). The *Monthly Review* reiterated the preface on the logic of women's business with politics,[16] and praised Smith for bringing "a higher and more masculine tone" to the genre of the novel (406), for describing "the improved condition of the people of France" ("earnestly asserted and eloquently") and for not stinting to note "the present defects of the British government" (408–9). Even though the Tory *Critical Review* was cool to the politics, it would say that "Mrs. Smith has spoken as she thought, and represented the conduct and sentiments of the democrats as they appeared to her. History may confirm her sentiments, and confute ours" (100).

With the looming violence of late summer 1792, however, "History" was weighing in. The Revolution was embarrassing its supporters and confirming its critics, and female politicians were especially prone to rebuke. One of the "worst effects" of these recent "dreadful" events, Smith laments in the preface to *The Emigrants*, is their conflation with "the original cause" (viii). So in late 1792 she wrote to Dodsley to pitch a poem "not on politics" but "on a very popular & interesting subject," not neglecting to cite her commercial and critical credits. She promises a pre-publication scouring of the poetry "by the very first of our present Poets—Cowper," and gamely projects a likely "very considerable profit of it," from printing "on my own account—first in Quarto—& then in a small volume to make a companion to the Sonnets." The volume would be enhanced "with a portrait"—a token of her confirmed celebrity:

It will consist of about twelve hundred verses of which near half are done—As I honour your decline all farther dealing with me, I only mention this to beg the favor of you to let me know what you think may be the value of such a work, of which I am not a judge, since it is quite unlike in its nature any I have printed—& is, tho not on politics, on a very popular & interesting subject; mingled with descriptions and characteristic excursions—in the way of the Task—only of course inferior to it. Yet of what is done my friends with their usual partiality think very highly—.[17]

Smith means to rehearse her appeal to Thomas Cadell, the liberal publisher who, though loyal to *Elegiac Sonnets*, had refused *Desmond*. He did agree to publish *The Emigrants* (but with Britain and France at war by early 1793, there could be no second edition: the official case had been decided).

It is a wonder that with three well-received she-novels to her name (*Emmeline, Ethelinde, Celestina*) and growing fame as *the* "Laureate of Lachrymose," Smith wanted to write *The Emigrants* at all.[18] French emigrants were no easy purchase: their plight was political and fraught with a long history of English contention with Catholic France.[19] In a scornful Republican judgment, the emigrants were the backwash of the ancien régime, complicit with a selfish, luxurious aristocracy that still enjoyed connections and property in England. Also suspicious, for different reasons, were the Tories, mistrusting both the aristocratic cover and the sentimental spectacle: "Under the appellation of Fugitives, a multitude of insidious and evil designing persons" bear "the intention of raising a . . . disturbance in this kingdom," warned the *Times* (14 September 1792). Not the least of these agents were those refractory priests (there would be two thousand by 1793), and there was no little concern that they either fronted a Catholic insurgency or were Jacobin spies in masquerade.[20]

In the wake of the September 1792 massacres, however (a nightmare to eyewitness William Wordsworth for decades), there arose appeals to set aside national and religious differences, rescue the helpless, and demonstrate the proud British virtues of compassion and charity. The Lord Chief Justice's son, John Eardley Wilmot, called on pan-Christian sympathies and headed a committee "for the Relief of the Suffering Clergy of France in the British Dominions." More than half of the nearly 100,000 emigrants to England were Third Estate (commoners), but the more pathetic narrative (and for fund-raising, the more compelling) was the precipitous fall of the first two Estates, the clergy and then, if a romance narrative could be spun, the nobility.[21]

Spinning such a romance wasn't much of a stretch for Smith. Herself fallen from wealth and luxury by the profligacy of that husband, and in 1784–85, an emigree to France with this debt-escaper, she had ready sympathy for abject aristocrats, advertising in the preface to *The Emigrants* a "heart, that has learned, perhaps from its own sufferings, to feel with acute, though unavailing compassion, the calamity of others" (vi). While the advertisement models a general moral sympathy, it voices a personal grievance, waged in an appeal to readers against a legal system indifferent to the theft of her children's inheritances and Benjamin Smith's relentless, legally sanctioned raids on her income and property. The reviews liked to complain of Smith's "egotism" in these serial rants across the prefaces to her publications;[22] yet from another perspective, publication was not only Smith's only court of appeal, but was the media that enabled her to theorize a politics of melancholy across a plane from the personal to the national. This melancholy heart beat with political blood.

The Emigrants is situated as a public performance, both of representative female grievances and on behalf of wider principles of justice. Even as her preface states her "utmost respect for the integrity of [the] principles" of the emigrant clergy (vii), *principles* chimes Republican themes: the only actions to admire, Wollstonecraft insisted in *A Vindication of the Rights of Men,* are ones of "principle" (6); for Tom Paine and Helen Maria Williams, *principle* was a byword of faith amid the Revolution's calamities.[23] On principle, Smith's preface laments that English champions of "Liberty," who saw the Revolution as "the demolition of regal despotism in France," have been "stigmatized as promoters of Anarchy, and enemies to the prosperity of their country"—an enemies-list that could enroll even William Cowper, Esq., to whom she addresses her preface, honoring him not just for the "infinite consolation" of his poetry (v) but also for his voice of "Liberty" (viii). She closes with praise of Whig leader Charles James Fox for citing Cowper in his plea in the House of Commons against counter-revolutionary war (viii–ix). (Fox set his hopes on the moderate French Girondins.) Smith may have opened her preface with the gender decorum that she addressed to Dodsley—"I am perfectly sensible, that it belongs not to a feeble and feminine hand to draw the Bow of Ulysses" (v)—but she closes it with no feeble hand. The first sentence of the *London Review*'s notice marked the honors to Cowper "as a Patriot and a Poet" and quoted Smith's most political remarks (41).

Smith's frank Republicanism contrasts the appeals deployed by the relief effort, which addressed the establishment—Parliament, the Anglican clergy, the nobility—without challenging its complacency. Burke's exhortation in the *Times* on 18 September 1792, fueled by news of the first massacres, cannily replayed themes and tropes from his celebrated *Reflections.*[24] Working one of his signature rolls of anaphoric syntax, Burke urged a Christian brotherhood to redeem the victims of that new French fraternity:

> It is confidently hoped, that a difference in religious persuasion will not shut the hearts of the English Public against their suffering Brethren, the Christians of France; but that all true Sons of the Church of England, all true subjects of our Saviour Jesus Christ, who are not ashamed in this time of apostasy or prevarication, to confess their obedience to and imitation of their divine Master in their Charity to their suffering Brethren of all denominations—it is hoped, that all persons who from the inbred sentiments of a generous nature, cultivate the virtues of humanity—it is hoped that all persons attached to the cause of religious and civil Liberty, as it is connected with Law and Order—it is hoped that all these will be gratified in having an opportunity of contributing to the support of these worthy sufferers in the cause of Honour, Virtue, Loyalty and Religion. (3)

Swelling the anaphora on this line of "Honour," Burke evokes the most famous passage in his *Reflections*, on the rapacious arrest of Queen Marie Antoinette:

> A band of cruel ruffians and assassins . . . rushed into the chamber of the queen, and pierced with an hundred strokes of bayonets and poniards the bed, from whence this persecuted woman had but just time to fly almost naked, and through ways unknown to the murderers had escaped to seek refuge at the feet of a king and husband, not secure of his own life for a moment. (105–6)

Here is the hallmark reprise in the *Times:*

> Several women, of whom some were of rank, dedicated to religion, in the peculiar exercise of a sublime charity, by an attendance upon the sick in hospitals, have been stripped naked, and in public barbarously scourged.—Thousands of other respectable religious women, mostly engaged in the education of persons of their own sex, and other laudable occupations, have been deprived of their estates, and expelled from their houses. . . . by the cruelty of the philosophic faction, are now . . .

obliged to fly their country, or are reduced to almost an equal degree
of penury with those they had been accustomed to relieve.   (3)

In this horribly democratic "persecution," privileges of rank and sex are
no more.

Recognizing and echoing Burke's potent appeal to Christian chivalry,
two Englishwomen writing for the relief effort, Hannah More and Frances Burney, exhorted women to a chivalry of maternal compassion and
"female benevolence." The pamphlet that More produced in April 1793
for Wilmot's committee (milking the scandal of Dupont's ringing declaration of atheism to the National Convention of France in December
1792) appeals simultaneously to Christian solidarity and to nonpartisan
traditions of English liberty:

> What English heart did not exult at the demolition of the Bastile?
> What lover of his species did not triumph in the warm hope, that one
> of the finest countries in the world would soon be one of the most
> free? Popery and despotism, though chained by the gentle influence
> of Louis the sixteenth, had actually slain their thousands. Little was it
> then imagined, that anarchy and atheism, the monsters who were
> about to succeed them, would soon slay their ten thousands.
>
> (*Remarks* 7)

More will have no commerce with Republican antidotes, however. What
she wants is liberal generosity, not a political revolution.[25] The original
title of her preface, *An Elegant and Pathetic Address to the Ladies of
Great Britain*, was pitched to a privileged class, with no design to ruffle
"Luxurious habits of living" (v). She means merely to exhort charity.[26]
Appealing to these very habits as a ground of sympathy, More superimposes its French loss on a happy British present:

> Let her who indulges such habits, and pleads such excuses in conse-
> quence, reflect, that by retrenching *one* costly dish from her abundant
> table, by cutting off the superfluities of *one* expensive desert, omit-
> ting *one* evening's public amusement, she may furnish at least a
> week's subsistence to more than one person, as liberally bred perhaps
> as herself, and who, in his own country, may have often tasted how
> much more blessed it is to give than to receive —— to a minister of
> God, who has been long accustomed to bestow the necessaries he is

now reduced to solicit. . . . the gay and prosperous would do well to
recollect, how suddenly and terribly those for whom we plead, were,
by the surprising vicissitudes of life, thrown from equal heights of
gaiety and prosperity.   (v–vii)

Holding in check her Evangelical distaste for luxury, More takes no aim
at class privileges, habits, and entitled social routines. In More's romance
narrative, the change in France is a sudden vicissitude of fate rather than
a consequence of radical political inequality and injustice.

In this key, she sets *noblesse oblige* against *noblesse manquée* as counter-
Revolutionary action. As French clergy once ministered to their poor, so
now English ladies may minister to fallen ministers, demonstrating a
maternal ethic superior to that "most unaccountable perversion of language" that the French "are pleased to call by the endearing name of
fraternization" (41). With maternal guidance, minor female sacrifices
can enter into the ledgers of Christian virtue:

> Even your young daughters, whom maternal prudence has not yet
> furnished with the means of bestowing, may be cheaply taught the
> first rudiments of charity . . . to sacrifice a feather, a set of ribbons, an
> expensive ornament, an idle diversion . . . for the suppression of one
> luxury for a charitable purpose, is the exercise of two virtues, and this
> without any pecuniary expense.   (vi)

More writes a maternal chapter in a national history of patriarchal conquest that will be the glory of Christian Britain, a "she" to be famed for
mothering the orphans of France:

> all the boasted conquests of our Edwards and our Henrys over the
> French nation, do not confer such substantial glory on our own coun-
> try, as she derives from having received, protected, and supported,
> among multitudes of other sufferers, at a time and under circum-
> stances so peculiarly disadvantageous to herself, *three thousand*
> *priests*, of a nation habitually her enemy, and of a religion intolerant
> and hostile to her own. This is the solid triumph of true Christian-
> ity . . . quietly performed without effort or exertion.   (38)

The commercial triumph was respectable, too: More's pamphlet brought
profits of about £240 to the fund (Roberts 1: 420).

Burney amplified More's cue in a pamphlet she published in November 1793, just weeks after Marie Antoinette was executed. Her *Brief Reflections Relative to the Emigrant French Clergy: Earnestly Submitted to the Humane Consideration of the Ladies of Great Britain* not only echoed Burke's *Reflections* but reprised its theatrics. Like More, she issues a call for "FEMALE BENEFICENCE" (4), and like More, she projects a transnational fraternity in rebuke of the new French formation: "O let us be brethren with the good, wheresoever that may arise," she urges her Christian sisters. She surpasses sober More in the Burkean drama, propelling the Ladies' imagination into the immediacy of a gothic horror. Suppose yourselves (Burney entreats her readers)

> for a moment only, placed in *l'Eglise des Carmes*, in Paris, on the 2d of September, 1792, in full sight of the hapless assemblage of this pious fraternity, who there sought sanctuary—not for the crimes they had committed, but for the duty they had discharged to their consciences, not from just punishment of guilt, but from fury against innocence.
>
> Here, then, behold these venerable men, collected in a body, enclosed within walls dedicated to holy offices, bewailing the flagitious actions of their country-men, yet devout, composed, earnest in prayer, and incorruptible in purity.
>
> Now, then, in mental retrospection, witness the unheard-of massacre that ensued! Behold the ruffians that invade the sacred abode, each bearing in his hand some exterminating weapon; in his eye, a more than fiend-like ferocity. Can it be you they seek, ye men of peace? unarmed, defenceless, and sanctuarised within the precincts of your own religious functions!—Incredible!—
>
> Alas, no!—behold them reviled—chaced—assaulted. They demand their offence? They are answered by staves and pikes. They fly to the altar . . .
>
> Here, at least, are they not safe? At this sanctified spot will not some reverence revive? some devotion rekindle? . . . No!—the murderers dart after them: the pious suppliants kneel—but they rise no more! . . . Groans resound through the vaulted roof—mangled carcases strew the consecrated ground—derided, while wounded; insulted, while slaughtered—they are cleft in twain—their savage

destroyers joy in their cries—Blood, agony, and death close the fatal
scene!   (22–24)

Amid the vogue of the gothic novel, Burney writes the latest installment
and signs it not with her name but her fame as novelist of sensibility: *"By
the Author of Evelina and Cecilia."* She casts the "pious fraternity" (this
phrase, too, rebuking Republican *fraternité*) not just as martyrs—their
former "affluence" now a "penury . . . wrought through the exaltation of
their souls" (6)—but in the figure of imperiled females.

She urges her countrywomen to chivalry, asking them to use their
powers to "protect" and "save" the "banished men now amongst us":
"Come forth, then, O ye Females, blest with affluence!" (26). In this exertion, women may even feel a bit manly, for "charity . . . is a virtue as manly
as it is gentle" (7). The rearrangements of gender in this "unheard of"
historical crisis—helpless fathers reduced to trembling suppliants, potent mothers poised for manly action—is no revolutionary eruption,
however. It is keyed to Burkean veneration. One "should approach to the
faults of the state as to the wounds of a father, with pious awe and trembling sollicitude" (urged Burke) and "look with horror on those children
of their country who are prompt rashly to hack that aged parent in pieces"
(*Reflections* 143). Burney concludes her tract in this ethic, with chari-
table ladies as proper daughters, whom she urges, in her closing words,
to "hold in heart and mind that, when the awful hour of your own disso-
lution arrives, the wide-opening portals of heaven may present to your
view these venerable sires, as the precursors of your admission" (26–27).

In the political conception of *The Emigrants*, however, it is the sires—
in the figure of a trans-historical, global, patriarchal war machine—who
ultimately stand to account. And it is not the emigrant clergy, but the
mothers left in France, who are its most desperate victims.

Classing The Emigrants

What sympathy do these refugees require? In early 1794 *Critical Review*
(not prone to any sympathy for the refugees of the ancien régime) felt its
heart quickened by Burney's "animated charity sermon," and urged her,
in its closing words, *"Write on"* (321).[27] Smith opens *The Emigrants* not
with the eponyms but with a display of herself as a victim of "proud op-

pression," not in France but in England, a country "where the vain boast/ Of equal Law is mockery" (1.37–38). Although this looks like cause for that reviewer-complaint of egoism, Smith has calculated this collation of the personal and the political. The domestic "legal crimes" (1.36) chime a rhyme across her blank verse with "regal crimes" abroad (2.88). Whether or not a reader can hear this, for Smith's poetic ear it is the chord of an attenuated, even alienated, patriotism. "I have neither naturally nor artificially the least partiality for my native country, which has not protected my property by its boasted Laws," she declared to her friend, Rev. Joseph Cooper Walker (25 March 1794); "if Death or Justice or any other decisive personification, should happen to interfere on my poor childrens behalf, so as that I could get their property out of the tenacious talons of the worthy Gentlemen who keep it 'All for their good,' I w^d not hesitate a moment . . . to bid to 'the Isle Land that from her pushes all the rest' a long & last Adieu!"[28] For these ironized quotations of the languages of law and sentiment, *The Emigrants* is the forecast. When the eponyms emerge, they are cast both as Burke-Burney martyrs to "conscience" and as Smith-forged victims of "lawless Anarchy" (97–100), fellow-travelers in epic misery. The indictment is of systemic tyranny, not party, not nation.

On this pulse Smith appealed, in early November 1792, to Joel Barlow, having "read with great satisfaction" his (Joseph-Johnson published) *Advice to the Privileged Orders, in the Several States of Europe, Resulting from the Necessity and Propriety of a General Revolution in the Principle of Government* (February 1792) and his *Letter to the National Convention of France on the Defects in the Constitution of 1791* (September 1792). The star poet in the cult of sensibility was "sensibly hurt" by "the hideous picture which a friend of mine, himself one of the most determined Democrates I know, has given of the situation of the Emigrants . . . more deplorable even than their crimes seems to deserve" (*L* 49). In this aesthetic frame, the conflict of sympathy and justice is just too sharp to reconcile to Painite "principle." Smith wants to insist on the political interest—even principle—of sympathy:

> The magnitude of the Revolution is such as ought to make it embrace
> every great principle of Morals, & even in a Political light (with which
> I am afraid Morals have but little to do), it seems to me wrong for the
> Nation entirely to exile and abandon these Unhappy Men. . . . They

should suffer the loss of a very great part of their property & all their
power. But they should still be considerd as Men & Frenchmen . . .
& not be turnd out indiscriminately to perish in foreign Countries
and to carry every where the impression of the injustice and ferocity
of the French republic—— (*L* 49)

Smith shifts the Painite rigor of 1791–92 into a long historical trajectory:
the "magnitude" of this Revolution for the new political possibility heralded by the emergent "glorious Government" (*L* 49). Appealing to Barlow as honorary citizen in the National Convention, she sets the picture
of "the Emigrants" before him as a potent broadcast: their treatment will
be widely communicated, a scandal to discredit the new Republic.

Yet Smith wavers in the shaping of *The Emigrants*. As Book I unfolds,
the victims begin to bear another impression, a political light trained on
"the prejudice they learn'd / From Bigotry (the Tut'ress of the blind)"
(1.101–2). Her sympathy now strained along a British Protestant bias,
Smith even manages a retro-swerve: surmise that the exiles may have
their own ferocity in harboring a "hope" that

> German spoilers, thro' that pleasant land
> May carry wide the desolating scourge
> Of War and Vengeance . . . (1.103–6)

Taking a beat, Smith corrects the course of the sentence underway: "yet
unhappy Men, / Whate'er your errors, I lament your fate" (106–7). But
she has no patience to prevent the murmur of Republican ambivalence.
Once uttered, the charge of *errors* sticks, to indict this Bigotry and its
social consequences. Soon on Smith's scene is one of the wretched clergy.
He is amazed by the compassion of the English,

> Because these strangers are, by his dark creed,
> Condemn'd as Heretics—and with sick heart
> Regrets[2] his pious prison, and his beads.— (1.122–24)

Primed for Smithian sensibility, the progressive *Analytical Review* didn't
quite register the acid in passages such as this, describing a poem that
"calls forth her powers of interesting description and pathetic sentiment"
and promises to please "every friend of humanity":

Without attempting the entire justification of the political conduct of the French emigrants, she draws several interesting and affecting pictures of their misfortunes, and applauds that generous sympathy, which ministers relief to a brother in distress, without listening to the chilling remonstrance of national or political prejudice.

(17 [September 1793] 91)

But poet Smith, feeling her sympathy wax ungenerous, thought it best to attach an endnote [2] to "Regrets" (124; the sense is *mourns the loss of,* not *is sorry about*) to deny any gloating:

Lest the same attempts at misrepresentation should now be made, as have been made on former occasions, it is necessary to repeat, that nothing is farther from my thoughts, than to reflect invidiously on the Emigrant Clergy, whose steadiness of principle excites veneration, as much as their sufferings compassion. (*Emigrants,* p. 35)

Yet she lets the poetry stand unrevised and not only distances the note-text eighteen pages on[29] but ends it in cool, if not chilling, remonstrance: "Adversity has now taught them the charity and humility they perhaps wanted, when they made it a part of their faith, that salvation could be obtained in no other religion than their own" (35). Like the medieval dance of death, adversity is a democrat, the great leveler.

Very little in Smith's verse proper excites veneration or compassion for this crowd:

Another, of more haughty port, declines
The aid he needs not; while in mute despair
His high indignant thoughts go back to France,
Dwelling on all he lost—the Gothic dome,
That vied with splendid palaces;[3] the beds
Of silk and down, the silver chalices,
Vestments with gold enwrought for blazing altars,
Where, amid clouds of incense, he held forth
To kneeling crowds the imaginary bones
Of Saints suppos'd, in pearl and gold enchas'd,
And still with more than living Monarchs' pomp
Surrounded. (1.125–36)

Nowhere in the tracts of More and Burney can one read such a critique of aristocratic clergy.[30] Smith is after bigger game than French pomp, however, as her next endnote ([3]), signaled at "palaces" (130), makes clear:

> Let it not be considered as an insult to men in fallen fortune, if these luxuries (undoubtedly inconsistent with their profession) be here enumerated—France is not the only country, where the splendour and indulgences of the higher, and the poverty and depression of the inferior Clergy, have alike proved injurious to the cause of Religion.
>
> (*Emigrants* 35)

Reading some justice in the fall of the higher clergy, Smith also implies British situations no less culpable. A few lines on, she turns to the situation of the lesser parochial clergy in France:

> perhaps, unknown
> Each to the haughty Lord of his domain,
> Who mark'd them not; the Noble scorning still
> The poor and pious Priest . . .   (1.183–86)

The terms level with the landscape aesthetics of the British noble, designed to mask poor churchyard graves, lest these "mar the smiling prospect" from his "manorial residence" (1.83–86) or remind him that his luxury is sustained by their "honest Poverty" (2.179–204).

Burns picked up this last phrase in 1794 to open a song on universal brotherhood, "Is there for honest poverty." The reactionary *British Critic* was quick to censure Smith for sounding such lines: "when fine talents descend to propagate popular cant against order, tending to excite discontent . . . treating with petulant and unseasonable scoffs the institutions of religion," this can only be trafficking in "a criminal singularity," a "sneer at usages manifestly tending to public utility and general piety" (405). It is telling of the political indecision of the times, however, that the *Critical Review*, which had censured the political insurgency of Wollstonecraft's *Vindication of the Rights of Woman*, could take a different view of Smith, willing to note that she "takes occasion . . . to threaten those of this country, whose consequence is derived from political corruption with a similar catastrophe" (301).

Such rebuke of consequence lays claim to a sensibility-primed focus for personal as well as general sympathy in *The Emigrants:* the "softer form" of a destitute, wretched mother (1.202), a standout against, or even displacement of, the predominantly male census of emigrant nobles (about 85%; Greer 91, 113), and existential kin to the iconic poet of the *Elegiac Sonnets,* an adult in rueful regard of clueless youth. She-shading the tones and terms of Gray's *Ode on a Distant Prospect of Eton College,* Smith will soon sigh of her own "hours of simple joy, / When, on the banks of Arun . . . / . . . I play'd; unconscious then of future ill!" (2.330–34). The Emigrant mother here sighs at her children in "gay unconscious" play on the seashore, "Unmindful of the miseries of Man" (1.204–13). Warming to this sentiment at least, the *British Critic* (404) quoted the inset portrait up to, but not past, the exile's yielding "awhile / To kind forgetfulness, while Fancy brings, / In waking dreams, that native land again" (1.219–21). It then juxtaposed to this passage the "striking apostrophe to the Infant King of France," excerpted from Book II—in effect redacting its own poem of poignant collation, the abject dauphin and the seaside children. The *Critical Review* reprised this collation in 1794, to clinch the claim of pity, what "we should naturally feel for those overwhelming and uncommon distresses" (2s 9: 299–302).

If it seems, however, that Smith's appeal to natural feeling prevails over political bias, these review-manipulations cast into relief, by evading, the challenging critical arc of her verse, which moves the melancholy mother's "waking dreams" into a scenario of sharp political import—a class-privileged, sympathy-straining paradise lost:

> Versailles appears—its painted galleries,
> And rooms of regal splendour, rich with gold,
> Where, by long mirrors multiply'd, the crowd
> Paid willing homage—and, united there,
> Beauty gave charms to empire—Ah! too soon
> From the gay visionary pageant rous'd,
> See the sad mourner start! (1.222–28)

The mirroring of the ancien régime and the entranced crowd is staged in an ostentation of mirrors, a gay visionary pageant, shimmering from transcendence to phantasm. Unlike the "gay unconscious children" at seashore play (204), gay visionary Versailles is a tainted worldliness. Not only are the aesthetics—"Beauty" giving "charms to empire"—reviewed as state mystification, but Smith's setting of the sad mourner on the beach at Brighton brings into play a site reeking with royal excess in the 1790s. There, at taxpayers' expense, the Prince of Wales had developed his lavish resort, including the Marine Pavilion that had become a hub of south-shore royal society and its international peers—a kind of junior Versailles: "Shut up . . . the Pavilion, / Or else 'twill cost us all another million," Byron protested in 1824 of the continuing upkeep (*Don Juan* 14.83).

In *Desmond*, which Smith was writing in late 1791, she skewers Burke's romance of the ancien régime with remarks mordantly transparent about the Prince of Wales. If, as Burke maintains, any "alteration" in the compact of government, is "impossible," it must follow that

> if at any remote period it should happen, what cannot indeed be immediately apprehended, that the crown should descend to a prince more profligate than Charles the Second, without his wit; and more careless of the welfare and prosperity of his people than James the Second, without his piety; the English must submit to whatever burthens his vices shall impose.   (*Desmond*, vol. 2, Letter VI, p. 67)

It didn't take too much wit to see that this "remote period" is the 1790s.

Unlike the *British Critic*, the *London Review* did quote the emigrant mother's nostalgia but, not catching the critical edge, fussed only about the logic of "by long mirrors multiply'd, the crowd / Paid willing homage": this was "a false image," it grumped too literally, "for the repetition in the glasses of Versailles has no connection with the willingness of the people's obedience" (43). Deciding that Smith's preposition *by* means literal agency, and not the stationing of flattering self-regard, it missed her satire of the imperial gaze. No less than Burke, though with a different spin, Smith conveys the political aesthetics of self-aggrandizing dazzle.

Smith's political shades thicken, and male authors come into play, when the mournful mother is joined by another melancholy aristocrat, this one full of

> that high consciousness of noble blood
> Which he has learn'd from infancy to think
> Exalts him o'er the race of common men:
> Nurs'd in the velvet lap of luxury,
> And fed by adulation—could *he* learn,
> That worth alone is true Nobility?

And that *the peasant* who, "amid[5] the sons
"Of Reason, Valour, Liberty, and Virtue,
"Displays distinguish'd merit, is a Noble
"Of Nature's own creation!"   (1.235–44)

The quotation that Smith imports into her blank verse is from Thomson's *Coriolanus* (III.iii), staged in 1749 and Smith-tuned for the 1790s. Heading a delegation to appeal to exiled Coriolanus to end his war of vengeance, Roman general Cominius chastises the arrogant refusal: it ill suits "one who sits / In the grave senate of a free republic, / To talk so high, and as it were to thrust / Plebeians from the native rights of man.——" (p. 250). Then follow (251) the lines that Smith quotes, with her own note ([5]) that such phrases "when used by living writers" are not called "common-place declamation, but sentiments of dangerous tendency" (*Emigrants*, p. 36). After July 1789, and again in 1792, John Philip Kemble barred performances of *Coriolanus* in the legitimate theater of Covent Garden, fearing the effect on British plebeians.

Braving danger, Smith will recall the phrase "rights of Man" in a bitter poem she added to the eighth edition of *Elegiac Sonnets* (1797), *The Dead Beggar*. It is "Addressed to a LADY, who was affected at seeing the Funeral of a nameless Pauper," an event set on the very scene of *The Emigrants*, "Brighthelmstone, in November 1792." In tones that More would never address to her "Ladies," Smith sarcastically gives this affected Lady a valediction against mourning over a place "Where even the houseless wanderer finds an home" (8):

Rather rejoice that *here* his sorrow cease,
    Whom sickness, age, and poverty oppress'd;
Where Death, the Leveller, restores to peace
    The wretch who living knew not where to rest.

Rejoice, that tho' an outcast spurn'd by Fate,
    Thro' penury's rugged path his race he ran;
In earth's cold bosom, equall'd with the great,
    Death vindicates the insulted rights of Man.   (13–20)

Not just this last modern phrase but the traditional trope of "Death the Leveller" voices Smith's Republican sarcasm. She is not shy about putting a note in *Elegiac Sonnets* on the "blame" she has incurred "for having used in this short composition, terms that have become obnoxious" (vol. 2: 104).[31]

Smith's quotation of Thomson, both in the poem of 1797 and in *The Emigrants*, sets modern arrogant nobles in exile in the lineage of Coriolanus. Are they susceptible to Cominius's instruction, or are they unwilling pupils of the levelling times? Tuning the question more sharply, Smith's verse scorns the pride in both Britain and France of all those

> Men, who derive their boasted ancestry
> From the fierce leaders of religious wars,
> The first in Chivalry's emblazon'd page.   (1.248–50)

In their fixation on "splendid trophies / Of Heraldry," Smith sees only "Gorgons and Hydras, and Chimeras dire" (1.253–56)—summoning Milton's cast (with a Virgilian imprint) for the feigned, fabled horrors against which the outland of Satan's Hell is measured.[32] The riff on *Paradise Lost* draws on the figures for Satan's sublime discovery:

> Shades of death
> A Universe of death, which God by curse
> Created evil, for evil only good,
> Where all life dies, death lives, and Nature breeds,
> Perverse, all monstrous, all prodigious things,
> Abominable, inutterable, and worse
> Than Fables yet have feign'd, or fear conceiv'd,
> Gorgons and Hydra's, and Chimera's dire.   (2: 621–28)

Universe, curse, perverse, worse is the embedded chord of Milton's verse, across which *death* unrolls from shape to shade, from verb to agent, from miscreation to inutterability. By allusion, Smith signals a refusal of glory to what warmongering men have made of human history.

The horror of Milton's Satan is not just this but the pain of its antithesis, forever lost. It is this agonized consciousness, unfolded in the most famous epic simile of *Paradise Lost*, that Smith summons for the taints of modern imagination:

> As one who long in populous City pent,
> Where Houses thick and Sewers annoy the Aire,
> Forth issuing on a Summers Morn to breathe
> Among the pleasant Villages and Farmes

Adjoynd, from each thing met conceaves delight,
The smell of Grain, or tedded Grass, or Kine,
Or Dairie, each rural sight, each rural sound;
. . . .
Such Pleasure took the Serpent to behold
This Flourie Plat, the sweet recess of *Eve* . . .   (9.445–56)

Milton's epic narrator brings a severe moral turn to the simile. Satan's city is never escapable, except in the brief suspense of illusory delight.

But the hot Hell that alwayes in him burnes,
Though in mid Heav'n, soon ended his delight,
And tortures him now more, the more he sees
Of pleasure not for him ordain'd . . .   (9.467–70)

Coleridge, Wordsworth, and Keats would summon the simile for urban miseries or suburban-rural vacations, making it a hallmark of (male) Romantic alienation, rehabilitating its bearer, Satan, from moral villain to modern psychological hero. Smith puts Milton's simile to political work, emphasizing class arrogance and culpability. Her version joins the haughty noble, fallen from his seat of glory, to a bewildered consciousness of sudden exposure (273*ff*), then, more damnably, to a Satanic consciousness of deserved, irrevocable exile.[33]

      —As one, who long
Has dwelt amid the artificial scenes
Of populous City, deems that splendid shows,
The Theatre, and pageant pomp of Courts,
Are only worth regard; forgets all taste
For Nature's genuine beauty; in the lapse
Of gushing waters hears no soothing sound,
Nor listens with delight to sighing winds,
That, on their fragrant pinions, waft the notes
Of birds rejoicing in the trangled copse;
Nor gazes pleas'd on Ocean's silver breast,
While lightly o'er it sails the summer clouds
Reflected in the wave, that, hardly heard,
Flows on the yellow sands: so to *his* mind,   273
That long has liv'd where Despotism hides

His features harsh, beneath the diadem
Of worldly grandeur, abject Slavery seems,
If by that power impos'd, slavery no more:
For luxury wreathes with silk the iron bonds,
And hides the ugly rivets with her flowers,
Till the degenerate triflers, while they love
The glitter of the chains, forget their weight.
But more the Men,[7] whose ill acquir'd wealth   282
Was wrung from plunder'd myriads, by the means
Too often legaliz'd by power abus'd,
Feel all the horrors of the fatal change,
When their ephemeral greatness, marr'd at once
(As a vain toy that Fortune's childish hand
Equally joy'd to fashion or to crush),
Leaves them expos'd to universal scorn
For having nothing else; not even the claim
To honour, which respect for Heroes past
Allows to ancient titles; Men, like these,
Sink even beneath the level, whence base arts
Alone had rais'd them;—unlamented sink,
And know that they deserve the woes they feel.   (1.260–95)

Smith's intensifying rant is a massive political recasting of Milton's grand epic simile for Satan's self-torture. Her unfolding not only Satanizes "Men like these" but even supplements this casting with an edge of English Protestant-Republican antipathy to Continental Catholic-monarchal decadence, as if she were also working the satire of Milton's Pandemonium into this account.

The republican voice of Smith's simile-tenor ("But more the men"; 282*ff*) inspires another endnote ([7]), this one unequivocal:

In the present moment of clamour against all those who have spoken or written in favour of the first Revolution of France, the declaimers seem to have forgotten, that under the reign of a mild and easy tempered Monarch, in the most voluptuous Court in the world, the abuses by which men of this description were enriched, had arisen to such height, that their prodigality exhausted the immense resources of France: and, unable to supply the exigencies of Government, the

Ministry were compelled to call Le Tiers Etat; a meeting that gave
birth to the Revolution, which has since been so ruinously conducted.

(*Emigrants* p. 36)

Smith's political shaping of Milton's simile contrasts not only with later
Romantic uses but also, sharply, with eighteenth-century uses. In *Night
Thoughts IV* (1743), Edward Young exalts the form and figure of Milton's
simile into a salvational quest for "Providence! an After-State!" (557):

> As when a Wretch, from thick, polluted Air,
> Darkness, and Stench, and suffocating Damps,
> And Dungeon Horrors, by kind Fate, discharg'd,
> Climbs some fair Eminence, where Ether pure
> Surrounds him, and Elysian Prospects rise,
> His Heart exults, his Spirits cast their Load,
> As if new-born, he triumphs in the Change;
> So joys the Soul, when from inglorious Aims,
> And sordid Sweets, from Feculence and Froth
> Of Ties terrestrial, set at large, she mounts,
> To Reason's Region, her own Element,
> Breaths Hopes immortal, and affects the Skies.   (563–74; pp. 32–33)

Smith's simile reverses both the trajectory and the spiritual economy of
this well-known text.[34] She's also involving Cowper's turn (also under-
pinned by Young) on Milton's simile at the opening of *The Task* Book III
(1785), *The Garden*. Cowper's tenor is psychological:

> As one who, long in thickets and in brakes
> Entangled, winds now this way and now that
> His devious course uncertain, seeking home;
> Or having long in miry ways been soiled
> And sore discomfited, from slough to slough
> Plunging, and half despairing of escape,
> If chance at length he find a green-swerd smooth
> And faithful to the foot, his spirits rise,
> He chirrups brisk his ear-erecting steed,
> And winds his way with pleasure and with ease;
> So I, designing other themes . . .
>
> . . . .

Have rambled wide. . . .

. . . .

But now with pleasant pace, a cleanlier road
I mean to tread. I feel myself at large,
Courageous, and refresh'd for future toil,
If toil await me, or if dangers new.   (1–20; pp. 91–92)

Cowper bends Milton's simile from its tenor of moral damnation, Satanic misery and alienation, into a heroic story of emotional, creative, psychological restoration—ready to undertake a modern epic. Steeped in Milton and Cowper, Smith casts the protagonists in her version of the simile (a layered interaction) as only degenerate, with no claim to heroic narrative, no claim to pathos.[35]

Shaping her political voice from but not in this train of men's heroic similes, Smith ventures an even riskier allusion for the exiled nobles, especially in the 1790s:

> Poor wand'ring wretches! whosoe'er ye are,
> That hopeless, houseless, friendless, travel wide
> O'er these bleak russet downs; where, dimly seen,
> The solitary Shepherd shiv'ring tends
> His dun discolour'd flock (Shepherd, unlike
> Him, whom in song the Poet's fancy crowns
> With garlands, and his crook with vi'lets binds);
> Poor vagrant wretches! outcasts of the world!
> Whom no abode receives, no parish owns;
> Roving, like Nature's commoners, the land
> That boasts such general plenty.   (1.296–306)

Against the Poet's pastoral fancy (kin to Beauty's giving charm to empire), Smith sounds the shock of Shakespeare's newly banished Lear confronting the world outside the castle walls:

> Poor naked wretches, wheresoe'er you are,
> That bide the pelting of this pitiless storm,
> How shall your houseless heads and unfed sides,
> Your loop'd and window'd raggedness, defend you
> From seasons such as these?   (3.4.28–32)

Smith makes *houseless* the existential name for all nameless beggars (so, too, in that other Brighton-sited poem written in 1792, *The Dead Beggar*). When Wordsworth uses this word in *Lines written a few miles above Tintern Abbey* (1798), it appears in an oblique conjecture about what may (or may not) abide beneath the "pastoral" landscape: smoke that might be a "notice . . . / Of vagrant dwellers in the houseless woods" (17–21). Smith's *houseless* is a confrontational sociology for the 1790s.

Moreover, to activate the context of Lear's sudden leveling—"Take physic, pomp; / Expose thyself to feel what wretches feel"—is to venture an indictment of royal arrogance, not omitting the British king, whose madness in 1788 and spendthrift luxurious sons had made him politically vulnerable. By 1795, Prime Minister William Pitt's Treasonable Practices Acts would extend actionable offenses to the mere imagining of a king's overthrow and death. Smith's summoning of Lear's comeuppance ventures a Republican critique of pompous royalty, *un*exposed to the wretchedness of its subjects. On a vista of wretchedness, Smith might seem to plea for sympathy for the "exil'd Nobles, from their country driven," the sudden change even a "more poignant anguish" than the inured misery of the poor (1.310–14). But her allusion to *King Lear* pivots against the nobles. If they find themselves now "like Nature's commoners" (305), the simile recalls a world of British commoners, whose lot was worsening in the 1790s with each new enclosure law, exiling them from their own country lands and casting them on mere nature.[36]

In just such a tenor Smith summons *Lear* into *Desmond*. To a friend who had given him Burke's *Reflections* out of pride in British government, Desmond replies: "I cannot pronounce it to be without imperfections, where I observe such dreadful contrasts in the condition of the people under it," and he cites the "shocking inequality" evidenced in any daily newspaper:

> To-day, we see displayed in tinsel panegyric, the superb trappings, the gorgeous ornaments, the jewels of immense value, with which the illustrious personages of our land amaze and delight us— To-morrow, we read of a poor man, an ancient woman, a deserted child, who were found dead in such or such alley or street, "supposed to have perished through want, and the inclemency of the weather"; and is it possible to help exclaiming,

　　　　　　　—"Take physic, pomp—
Expose thyself to feel what wretches feel;
So shalt thou shake the superflux to them,
And shew the heavens more just*!"

*Shakespeare.

(Vol. 2, Letter 10 [125–26])

In the preface to *The Emigrants,* Smith hoped that French emigrants might help allay "that reciprocal hatred so unworthy of great and enlightened nations" (vii); Desmond reports a damning reciprocity already in place, a mirror of England in the ancien régime. The urgent divisions are not of nation but of class: rich and outcast, despot and slave, unfeeling arrogance and wretched pain.

The allusion to *Lear* in *The Emigrants* primes Smith for a rant against "Fortune's worthless favourites" (1.315) and all those "pamper'd Parasites! whom Britons pay / For forging fetters for them" (330–31). This is a "lesson," on the example of France, that "if oppress'd too long,"

The raging multitude, to madness stung,
Will turn on their oppressors; and, no more
By sounding titles and parading forms
Bound like tame victims, will redress themselves! 　　(1. 334–37)

Edged by the rhyme-work of *sounding/Bound,* this is classic 1790s Republican rhetoric, echoing from Blake to Paine to Wollstonecraft.[37]

In contradictory impulses of sympathy and political principle, Smith takes the emotive force of Book I through male literary traditions to shape her turns. Her epigraph for Book II—set after the execution of Louis XVI and after the declaration of war between England and France—advertises a deepening spiral of interactions. Drawn from Virgil's *Georgics* (1.505–11), the final words of Smith's epigraph are *saevit toto Mars impius orbe:* "vicious Mars savages the whole globe."

Gendering War

In Book II the poet claims the Bow of Ulysses she had declined in the preface and lets fly a bitterly gendered critique of "War, wide-ravaging" (73). Her affective front, "the Widow's anguish and the Orphan's tears"

(318), demolishes the Burkean argument of chivalry, of men going to war to protect the women of hearth and home.[38] Not only was Smith one of the first poets of the 1790s to collapse the separate spheres of "male" warfare and "female" home into fatal continuity, but she did so in early 1793, when Prime Minister Pitt's regime of prosecution made it unwise to speak against a war with regicidal France, even within a frame of "female" values.[39] Sarah Spence's antiwar pamphlet, "written about 28 Jan. 1793," on the eve of war, didn't see print until 1795, when its plea for patrician sympathy for the large domus of state could be seen as a kind of sentimental patriotism. It is "the Poor," Spence urges, who bear the fullest wartime penalty:

> *Their* lot at *best* is too frequently distressing: let them then have to bless that benign and mild Government which leaves to them their *only* enjoyment;—domestic happiness. Wring not the sighs and tears of agonizing distress from the Widow and Fatherless; bring not down to the Grave the grey hairs of the aged mourning Parent: but, in mercy to the worthy poor, avert the impending War; and thus secure to the Rulers of this prosperous Nation the prayers and blessings of a grateful and happy People. (88)

Spence's gender-cast, iconic Man and Woman, is carefully tempered with propriety:

> But alas! blind and erring Man!—How often dost thou spurn thy choicest blessings: and suffer Pride, Passion, or Revenge, to rob thee of that portion of felicity which the beneficent and wise Creator has mingled in the cup of Life.
> As a Woman, I would seek Peace and domestic felicity; relying on the Judgement of my Husband in all political affairs; conscious that it is not the province of my sex to investigate the various sources from which political information may be derived. (91)[40]

Smith's own husband is a sorry joke for such reliance, and her province was necessarily otherwise. Yet as she and Spence knew, official policy was hardening not only against France but also against agitation at home, especially over the wrongs of woman and the wrongs of the poor.[41]

One publication that did issue, on 29 January 1793 in a nice quarto from radical publisher Joseph Johnson, was by a young poet, William

Wordsworth. He had visited Smith on his way to France in 1790, a trip undertaken to witness the transformations of the Revolution. *Descriptive Sketches [in Verse, Taken during a Pedestrian Tour in the . . . Alps]* was one product. Negotiating questions of liberty and slavery, Wordsworth wavers between moods of revolutionary hope and anxiety about France at war and England about to be drawn in. He concludes with a prayer to "great God" to propel "Freedom's waves" over "Conquest, Avarice, and Pride," "dark Oppression," "Persecution," "mad Ambition," and "Discord" (791–800). Mindful of England's history of warfare with France and its heroizing of war-mongering kings, Wordsworth writes his prayer against the famous prologue to *Henry V,* the world of his day transparent in Shakespeare's historical setting,

> Where Discord stalks dilating, every hour,
> And crouching fearful at the feet of Pow'r,
> Like Lightnings eager for th'almighty word
> Look up for a sign of havoc, fire, and Sword;*

> *   And at his heels,
> Leash'd in like hounds, should Famine, Sword, and fire,
> Crouch for employment.

With a bit of Julius Caesar crying "havoc!" for the dogs of war (3.1), and a nonce sight rhyme conveying how almighty *word* becomes instrumental *Sword,* Wordsworth echoes and footnotes the Prologue (6–8, "his" in the first line refers to Henry V).

Smith also has the contemporary force of this Prologue in mind. Just months after Bastille, on 1 October 1789, Kemble mounted a revival at Drury Lane titled *Henry V; or, the Conquest of France,* and acted the title role across the next five seasons—generating a public theater for Britain heading to yet another war with France. Smith sets Book II in "*April 1793,*" a springtime, but no season of hope for the Emigrant-exiles, blasted by news of France, a land where

> . . . War, wide-ravaging, annihilates
> The hope of cultivation; gives to fiends,
> The meager, ghastly fiend of Want and Woe,
> The blasted land—There, taunting in the van
> Of vengeance-breathing armies, Insult stalks;

And, in the ranks, "[1]Famine, and Sword, and fire,
Crouch for employment."   (73–79)

Writing Shakespeare's meters into her own, Smith endnotes the source
as just "SHAKSPEARE" (p. 67), as if the text and context were common
knowledge. Like Wordsworth, she quotes the Prologue not for the sublimity of "a kingdom for a stage, princes to act, / And monarchs to behold
the swelling scene"—all that a "Muse of fire" might body forth (Prologue
1–4)—but to rue the war-torn world, a horror that Book II genders, increasingly, as the work of "Man," with allegorical females Freedom and
Liberty (57–58, 87–89) the victims. Man with a capital M becomes her
refrain—"Woes such as these does Man inflict on man"; "the variety of
woes that Man / For Man creates" (319, 413–14)—picking up the opening
of the poem as a whole as its now ringing keynote:

> . . . Man, misguided Man,
> Mars the fair work that he was bid enjoy,
> And makes himself the evil he deplores.   (1.32–34)

In the translinear poetics of *Man/Mars* flickers an anticipatory pun on
Mars impius, the icon of Book II's epigraph. In Book I, the victims are
nature and general humanity; by Book II, Smith is specifying the male
agency of warfare.[42]

Reviling war as a "black scroll, that tells of regal crimes" (2.88), too
often a "disputed claim / Between anointed robbers: [2]Monsters both!"
(92–93), Smith keys an endnote ([2]) to Shakespeare's historical scenes:
"Such was the cause of the quarrel between the Houses of York and Lan-
caster; and of too many others, with which the page of History reproaches
the reason of man" (p. 67). The apprenticeship of Henry V enters the verse
itself as Smith again incorporates into her iambic pentameter (just fifteen lines after inweaving the Prologue to *Henry V*) Prince Hal's ambivalent regard of his destined crown (*2 Henry IV* 4.5.23; also endnoted):

> "[3]Oh! Polish'd perturbation—golden care!"
> So strangely coveted by feeble Man
> To lift him o'er his fellows;—Toy, for which
> Such showers of blood have drench'd th' affrighted earth—
> Unfortunate *his* lot, whose luckless head
> Thy jewel'd circlet, lin'd with thorns, has bound.   (2.94–99)

This head is doomed to a "headless corse of one, whose only crime / Was being born a Monarch" (54–55), Louis XVI. As she was writing this verse, Smith was urging Joel Barlow to consider "amnesty" for this "wretched victim" of accident, an "unfortunate Man who could not help being born the Grandson of Louis 15th" (3 November 1792, *L* 49–50).

This fate falls also on the "imperial Boy" and his "wretched Mother, petrified with grief" (2.148, 152). It was the fatal imprisonment of the family in 1792 that domesticated and sentimentalized the French King and Queen for British eyes. The fallen family could now be reconfigured as a text to broadcast the inhumanity and "unnaturalness of republican government."[43] In early 1793, the British conservative press teemed with sympathetic verses of Burkean pathos.[44] Smith, as in her letter to Barlow, argues that the cause of progress has more to gain from compassion than from a policy of "Vengeance" or "Fear": such impulses are "unworthy" of "Freedom's cause"; an "innocent" dauphin bears the "crimes and follies of [his] race"; his mother's amply penalized "errors" ought to be "no more remember'd" (127–29, 160–69). Her argument confronts the rigor of Painite principle, Burns-anger, even Wollstonecraft vindication. Burns held to the big picture, seething:

> What is there in the delivering over a perjured blockhead & an un-principled prostitute to the hands of the hangman, that it should arrest for a moment, attention, in an eventful hour, when . . . "the welfare of Millions is hung in the scale."[45]

Yet Smith, a mother many times over, couldn't set this identification aside. So poignantly did her tableau of doomed Queen and Dauphin transcend partisan politics that even such "Church & King" magazines as the *Universal* (August 1793) could print a set piece from Book II under the title "On the present unhappy Situation of the QUEEN of FRANCE, and her Son."[46]

It is a short step in Book II to the war-hell of all mothers, from a royal "wretched Mother" to a poor "wretched Woman" doomed by battle's "driving tempest" (2.254–91)—more desperate than the Brighton beach "wretches" (1.296). So much for the cult of prolific maternity enlisted to produce troops for war.[47] To render the French mother's futile flight with her baby—"Fear, frantic Fear, / Wing'd her weak feet" (2.268–69)—Smith recruits William Collins's *Ode to Fear* (1747), not just for its allusive dimension, but also to render a critical reading of his psycho-melodrama, especially its genderings. Here is how Collins hails the haggard "mad nymph" (47):

> THOU, to whom the World unknown
>   With all its shadowy Shapes is shown;
> Who see'st appall'd th' unreal Scene,
> When Fancy lifts the veil between:
>   Ah *Fear!* Ah frantic *Fear!*
>   I see, I see Thee near.
> I know thy hurried Step, thy haggard Eye!
> Like Thee I start, like Thee disorder'd fly.
> For lo, what *Monsters* in thy Train appear!
>
> . . . .
>
> Whilst *Vengeance*, in the lurid Air,
> Lifts her red Arm, expos'd and bare:
> On whom that rav'ning Brood of Fate,
> Who lap the Blood of Sorrow, wait;
> Who, *Fear,* this ghastly Train can see,
> And look not madly, wild like Thee?   (1–9, 20–25, pp. 5–6)

This *Fear* (and fear) is a mythic hysteric of unoriginated madness, regendered from a long tradition of red-armed male Vengeance.[48] That this politics of misogyny mattered to Smith is clear in the way her war scene revises not only Collins's she-Fear but also the twin in his visionary train, Pope's phallic female, "purple *Vengeance* bath'd in Gore" (*Windsor-Forest*, 417–18, p. 18). In *Rights of Woman*, Wollstonecraft subordinated gender to system: it is royal tyranny that is "the pestiferous purple" (30). Writing against Pope, Smith genders system and historical agency: "the purple Tyrant's rod" is the enemy of lady Liberty (2.282–87), and the "purple Pestilence, that to the grave / Sends whom the sword has spar'd" is yet another woe that "Man inflict[s] on Man" (315–19).

Smith's inset tale of a desperate mother's fear in the current war derives much of its power from her revision of the gendered psychic imaginary of Collins and Pope, and it gains depth and dimension from epic history—a famous scene in the *Aeneid*, where Aeneas, fleeing the sack of Troy with his father and son, is gripped by unaccustomed fear. This is Dryden's rendering:

by choice we stray
Thro' ev'ry dark and ev'ry devious way.
I, who so bold and dauntless, just before,
The Grecian darts and shock of lances bore,
At ev'ry shadow now am seiz'd with fear,
Nor for myself, but for the charge I bear;
Till, near the ruin'd gate arriv'd at last,
Secure, and deeming all the danger past,
A frightful noise of trampling feet we hear.[49]

In place of Virgil's male family (Aeneas's wife is lost during the escape),
Smith focuses on a terrified mother as the locus of fearful consciousness:

A wretched Woman, pale and breathless, flies!
And, gazing round her, listens to the sound
Of hostile footsteps——No! it dies away:
Nor noise remains, but of the cataract,
Or surly breeze of night, that mutters low
Among the thickets, where she trembling seeks
A temporary shelter—clasping close
To her hard-heaving heart her sleeping child,
All she could rescue of the innocent groupe
That yesterday surrounded her—Escap'd
Almost by miracle! Fear, frantic Fear,
Wing'd her weak feet: yet, half repentant now
Her headlong haste, she wishes she had staid
To die with those affrighted Fancy paints
The lawless soldier's victims—   (2.258–72)

In Collins's scene, a general psychology (revelatory or hysteric) summons
Fancy to lift the veil on an "unreal" world of shadows and monsters.
Haunted by Aeschylus, Sophocles, Shakespeare, and Milton, Collins's
theater is patriarchal poetics, to which he seeks admission via histrionic
inspiration, in struggle with the arrest of writerly power.

It is against his casting of Fancy as the unveiler of an "unreal scene" of
fear, self-wrought in the midnight storms of the mind and its phantasmic
Danger (3, 10, 13), that Smith recovers Virgil's Aeneas, writing his fear
into the theater of latest modern warfare:

The driving tempest bears the cry of Death,
And, with deep sullen thunder, the dread sound
Of canon vibrates on the tremulous earth;
While, bursting in the air, the murderous bomb
Glares o'er her mansion.   (2.273–77)

In this universe of death, Smith replaces Collins's monstrous mother, lurid Vengeance, with a mother who is the victim of a warfare that is forever Man-wrought:

True to maternal tenderness, she tries
To save the unconscious infant from the storm
In which she perishes; and to protect
This last dear object of her ruin'd hopes
From prowling monsters.   (2.282–86)

If Collins's deep agenda is a petition of admission to the patriarchal canon, in Smith's war-tale no patriarchy survives. The mother's perishing is followed by a feudal Chief's return to his castle, to find his family slaughtered and its only historian a "wild raving Maniac" (2.292–311).[50]

The war that comes home, or rather to the home that can't be saved from war, is the urgency on which Smith brings *The Emigrants* to its close:

O Power Omnipotent! with mercy view
This suffering globe, and cause thy creatures cease,
With savage fangs, to tear her bleeding breast:
Restrain that rage for power that bids a Man,
Himself a worm, desire unbounded rule
O'er beings like himself.   (2.421–26)

The *London Review* wanted to cavil at this trope of horrific predation: "To transmute the neutral noun *globe* into a female, and tear *her* breast, is a *licentia* not *sumpta pudenter*" (43; *license*, not *modesty*). But Smith's figure, involving a rage for power that bids a Man to "consign / To tears and anguish half a bleeding world" (2.320–24), insists on the gendering of globalized suffering—an anguish in which *tears* sounds double: as wound and as sorrow. The only savior is "Power Omnipotent." It is with potent icons of female alliance that Smith infuses her summary visionary hope:

May lovely Freedom, in her genuine charms,
Aided by stern but equal Justice, drive
From the ensanguin'd earth the hell-born fiends
Of Pride, Oppression, Avarice, and Revenge.   (2.431–34)

It is a plea, however, not a program. Although Smith closes her vision in a hope that the "ill-starr'd wanderers" of her occasion will "regain their native country" in a new era of "Reason, Liberty, and Peace!" (2.436–44), its largest arc of historical imagery arrays a sequel to Adam's vision of history as warfare in *Paradise Lost* XI: one "ensanguined field" after another (654). Changing *field* to *earth*, Smith not only renders a global totality, but gains the potent phonemic slide into *ensanguin'd dearth*. It is a sign of her dilemma in the 1790s that her prayer is invested all in allegorical abstractions.

The opening of Book II sets the mythic stage, evoking both the sorry exit from Eden into history, and Helen Maria Williams's Milton-inflected reverse emigration to new liberty, *A Farewell . . . to England* (Smith read it in the summer of 1791).[51] "Pensive I took my solitary way," Smith writes (5), inhabiting both Milton's great closing lines, where Adam and Eve "with wandring steps and slow, / Through Eden took their solitarie way" (12.648–49), and the afterlife in Williams's farewell: "ALBION! far from Thee, my cherish'd home, / To foreign climes my pensive steps must roam" (5–6). Smith's "Pensive I" stands for a world of exiles. For all its hope for a world at peace, *The Emigrants* subsides with its visionary company suspended between lone spiritual determination and lonely melancholy relapse. Echoing Milton again, she is grateful for "unwearied" friends who minister to her "wearied spirit" and "bid [her] go / 'Right onward'" (2.364–68). Or, in relapse, she summons the end of Gray's *Elegy* (123) to plead, "I gave to misery all I had, my tears" (2.386).[52] The trajectory of *The Emigrants* is "the rugged path, / That leads at length to Peace"—but not in this world: "Peace will at last be mine; for in the Grave / Is peace" (2.371–73). Smith's allusions are her argument. No Christian soldier, no retro-graveyardist, the poet of *The Emigrants* projects grave-peace as a critical figure: in the failure of political hope (and the history of which it is the latest instance), peace is only in the grave, out of this world, not only for this poet but for all. The utopian no-place recoils as a bitter critique of the here and now of "April 1793."

It is visionary pathos that is also political pathos. By 1797—when the rise of Napoleon issued the latest discredit to the Revolution, and the founding of the *Anti-Jacobin Review* stoked domestic reaction—Smith seemed to be losing political nerve and retreating into her melancholy habits. She extracted the mother pining for Versailles from the equivocations of 1793 to craft charmingly beautiful set-piece lyrics for the magazines and for the (second) subscription volume of the eighth edition of *Elegiac Sonnets.*[53] Here the verse redaction is a set of quatrains, titled simply and mythically *The Female Exile* (2: 29–32), about a mother's pained regard of "her innocent children, unconscious of sorrow." Save a subtitle date ("Nov. 1792"), there is no historical referent. "Versailles" is effaced, and the past is remade into a Hannah More romance: the sad exile was "to fair fortune born" (25). This refashioning was partly the prompting of those reviews (of which Smith was always conscious) that elided the sigh for Versailles and linked the exiled children to the pathos of the imprisoned, fatherless dauphin.[54] While an endnote does mention that "a sketch" for this "little Poem . . . first appeared in blank verse in a Poem called 'The Emigrants'" (2: 105), the immediate reference is an engraving from "a Drawing by the Right Hon. Countess of Bessborough."[55] This More-like play to aristocracy (the Countess was a subscriber to this edition) coincides with Smith's claim to affiliation: "like thine, my hard fate has of affluence bereft me," the poet says to the Exile (35). The pathos of the Countess's sketch twins the illustration for Sonnet XII in volume 1 (*Written on the Sea-shore—October 1784*), imaging the poet herself as a fatally "exhausted sufferer," "On some rude fragment of the rocky shore."[56]

The novel that appeared between *Desmond* (1792) and the 1797 *Elegiac Sonnets,* and just after *The Emigrants* (1793), was *The Banished Man* (1794). This narrative consolidates sympathy for the emigrants against an historically conditioned, more pessimistic view of the French Revolution. In the last paragraph of its preface, dated "July 30, 1794," Smith introduces to her public "the emigrant gentleman who now makes part of my family"—a Catholic aristocrat of "merit" whom she had sheltered in the winter of 1792–93, and who married her favorite daughter the next August. In the paragraph just before, she execrates the new state, for which only horrific Roman history can supply an adequate gloss: "a people who, in place of a mild and well-meaning monarch, have given themselves up to the tyranny of monsters, compared with whom,

Engraved by J.Neagle from a Drawing by the Right Hon. the Countess of Besborough –

"The Female Exile," engraved for Charlotte Smith's *Elegiac Sonnets,* 8th edition, 1797 (vol. 2, facing p. 31). By kind permission of Rare Books Division, Department of Rare Books and Special Collections, Princeton University Library.

Stothard del.   *Neagle sculp.*

Published January 1st 1789. by T. Cadell Strand.

On Some rude fragment of the rocky shore.

"On Some rude fragment of the rocky shore," engraved as an illustration for "Sonnet XII: Written on the Sea Shore.—October, 1784," Charlotte Smith's *Elegiac Sonnets*, 5th edition (London: T. Cadell, 1789); republished in *Elegiac Sonnets*, 8th edition, 1797 (vol 1., facing p. 12). Subscribers included William Wilberforce, Thomas Warton, Horace Walpole, Mrs. Siddons, Samuel Rogers, William Pitt, William Hayley, and later, a Cambridge undergraduate, William Wordsworth. This plate was reprinted in the 8th edition of 1797, with the same sonnet (vol 1., opposite p. 12). By kind permission of Rare Books Division, Department of Rare Books and Special Collections, Princeton University Library.

Nero and Caligula are hardly objects of abhorrence" (xi). The female novelist in this novel (transparently Smith) now affiliates with the exiled emigrants: "Alas, Sir, my children and I have also been wanderers and exiles, . . . banished from the rank of life where fortune originally placed us" (vol. 2, chap. IX; 205).

The conservative press hailed the author of *The Banished Man* a penitent enthusiast, returning to the fold of monarchy.[57] Welcoming her hero as "a young and noble foreigner; an emigrant from his country in the royal cause," the *British Critic* triumphed in Smith's reform (621):

> We must not close this article without congratulating the lovers of their King and the constitution, in the acquisition of an associate like Mrs. Charlotte Smith. Convinced by observation, that the changes in France have only produced rapine and murder, and that the most worthy among the French have been forced to quit their country to avoid inevitable slaughter, she makes full atonement by the virtues of the Banished Man, for the errors of Desmond. Such a convert, gained by fair conviction, is a valuable prize to the commonwealth.   (623)

Sighing at the apparent forfeiture, the *Analytical Review* could only lament that the author of *Desmond* has made an "*amende honorable* for her past political transgressions by writing a novel on contrary principles," its French chivalry signing Smith over to the party of Burke: "As commonly happens to new converts, she is beyond all measure vehement in her exclamations against the late proceedings of the French" (20: 254). The *Analytical* would fold four years later, when publisher Joseph Johnson was jailed for sedition—the same year, 1798, that Rev. Richard Polwhele, ranting against "unsex'd" females of Jacobin views, would cut Smith some gentlemanly slack. Although he was sorry that in the early 1790s "charming SMITH resign'd her power to please, / Poetic feeling and poetic ease," and that for a lost weekend she suffered "the Gallic mania," he could now hope that "she is completely recovered from [this] disorder" (having "observed only a few slight symptoms"; pp. 17, 18n).

Yet *The Banished Man* registers a dubious conversion. It conspicuously lacks the ritual "retrospective re-evaluation of old convictions" that is the generic contract of recantation (Grenby, *Anti-Jacobin* 33), and the preface remains unstinting in its indictment of the tyrannies of the English legal system (107–8) and its fidelity to the principles of 1789.[58] As for other Republicans, the principles were only betrayed, not undone, by the events of 1792–93. The sentences that precede Smith's indictment of the French "tyranny of monsters" were sheared off in the Tory reviews, because there is (*pace* the *British Critic*) no evident atonement:

> If I had been convinced I was in an error in regard to what I formerly wrote on the politics of France, I should without hesitation avow it. I still think, however, that no native of England could help *then* rejoicing at the probability there was that the French nation would obtain, with very little bloodshed, that degree of freedom which we have been taught to value so highly.   (108–9)

The onset of war was the real, international bloodshed that possessed Smith's imagination and her family (her son Charles lost a leg at Dunkirk in 1793).

Even as the eighth edition of *Elegiac Sonnets* redeemed the French mother from Versailles stigma, it also revived Smith's antiwar passion, right in the teeth of Pitt's Gagging Acts. Smith would not be suppressed. "Ah! thus man spoils Heaven's glorious works with blood!" closes one of the new sonnets, *The Sea View* (LXXXIII); a vista of "purple radiance" turns "fierce and red" as "war-freighted ships . . . pollute the flood" with "mangled dead / And dying victims." This followed another new poem, a sonnet *To the Shade of Burns* (LXXXII). Also on board were *The Dead Beggar* and *The Forest Boy*. This last had a long note attached to its title and a final stanza of bitter reproach to statesmen happy to send young men to war for dubious cause. Smith's title-note recruits a famous poem by pacifist William Crowe:

> *I*, who have been so sad a sufferer in this miserable context, may well *endeavour* to associate myself with those who apply what powers they have to deprecate the horrors of war. Gracious God! will mankind never be reasonable enough to understand that all the miseries which our condition subjects us to, are light in comparison of what we bring upon ourselves by indulging the folly and wickedness of those who make nations destroy each other for *their* diversion, or to administer to their senseless ambition.
>
> —If the stroke of war
> Fell certain on the guilty head, none else—

If they that make the cause might taste th' effect,
And drink themselves the bitter cup they mix;
Then might the Bard (the child of peace) delight
To twine fresh wreaths around the conqueror's brow;
Or haply strike his high-toned harp, to swell
The trumpet's martial sound, and bid them on
When *Justice* arms for vengeance; but, alas!
That undistinguishing and deathful storm
Beats heaviest on the exposed and innocent;
And they that stir its fury, while it raves,
Safe and at distance send their mandates forth
Unto the moral ministers that wait
To do their bidding!————Crowe

Smith gives these words as if they could be her own, interacting with Crowe by putting her own italics at *Justice*. Crowe's poem, an intended oration for a formal occasion at Oxford University, was suppressed by the vice-chancellor for "the *too free* sentiments which they conveyed" (so Coleridge told readers of *The Watchman* when he published most of it).[59]

Republishing these incendiary lines in 1797, Smith closes her own poem in sympathetic concert, placing this last stanza on its own page (2: 67):

Ah! such are the miseries to which ye give birth,
    Ye cold statesmen! unknowing a scar;
Who from pictured saloon, or the bright sculptured hearth,
Disperse desolation and death thro' the earth
    While ye let loose the demons of war.   (*The Forest Boy* 131–35)

Hitting the sound from *birth* to *hearth* to *death thro' the earth* to *demons of war*, Smith spares no heat to cold statesmen. Viscount St. Cyres certainly felt it, commenting, "Mrs. Smith was no sounder than her brother-poet William Wordsworth on the subject of the French Revolution. . . . she could deal very severely with Mr. Pitt and all the Statesmen"; he quotes the final lines as the voice of "irresponsible treason" (691). By 1797, this famous poet and novelist had a voice equal to the men's—if not in the courts of law, then in the courts of poetry.

Just a few pages on in volume II, she redacts the passage from *The Emigrants* Book II which the radical *Analytical Review* had cited for praise and given full quotation: the frantic mother trying to save her children; the feudal chief returning to a devastated home, a murdered family, and a raving maniac. Smith's redaction is titled *Fragment, Descriptive of the Miseries of War; from a Poem called "The Emigrants," Printed in 1793.*[60] As Smith watched the Terror and war with France unfold, her conflicting reactions—sentimental, political, visionary—turned to men's texts and traditions, sometimes in affiliation, sometimes in opposition. *The Emigrants* interacts with the authors of this tradition not only by taking men's words into a woman's poetry but also by demonstrating how a woman's "historical sense" (T. S. Eliot's phrasing in 1917, in the wake of another war) works upon, to alter, the "relations, proportions, values" of what she reads. If, as Eliot wryly proposed in *Tradition and the Individual Talent,* it is not "preposterous that the past should be altered by the present as much as the present is directed by the past," Smith managed at least one "supervention of novelty" (4–5) that did not occur to his wit—a drama of gender criticism, set within literary tradition and history, that is inseparable from political reflection.

This is the mode of supervention that would constitute Mary Wollstonecraft's brilliant invention of feminist literary criticism, written from the interactions of her reading against the grain of a long history of masculine formations taken as gospel, taken from gospel.

CHAPTER TWO

Mary Wollstonecraft
Re:Reading the Poets

What Poetry Makes Happen

"A taste for rural scenes, in the present state of society, appears to me to be very often an artificial sentiment, rather inspired by poetry and romances, than a real perception of the beauties of nature," begins a letter from "W. Q." to the editor of the *Monthly Magazine* April 1797. W. Q. goes on to propose that "poetry, written in the infancy of society is most natural," seeming a "transcript of immediate emotions" (279). This is the durable genealogy of "the poet, the man of strong feelings," his words conveying "a picture of his mind when he was actually alone, conversing with himself, and marking the impression which nature made on his own heart" (279–80). The culture of modern poetry, issuing from "a more advanced state of civilization," W. Q. indicts as a degradation: the language of "spontaneous feelings and ideas" is now an "unnatural, . . . remote and disgusting" confection, "servilely copied . . . selected from books" in a bid for "elegance of diction" by a writer more "the creature of art, than of nature" (280).

These sentences could be a draft toward the Preface to *Lyrical Ballads* (1800), signed by W. Wordsworth, steady reader of the *Monthly Magazine*, host to one of the more favorable notices of the 1798 *Ballads*. The new Preface called for a revolution in poetic manners: a refusal of artificial diction and taste, a turn from urbane culture to nature, an insistence on spontaneous feeling. The romance of social primitivism could well have been Percy Shelley's draft, too, for his *Defence of Poetry*, its Wordsworth-inflections amplified into a macro-historic vision: "in the infancy of society" and "the infancy of art," the language of poetry, contended Shelley, is "vitally metaphorical" (4–5). This is the sociology of speech itself: "In the infancy of society, every author is necessarily a poet, because language itself is poetry," with no rupture "between existence and perception, . . . between perception and expression." (6). Because such vitality "marks the before unapprehended relation of things, and perpetuates their apprehension" (5), it might even herald a revolution of values, from the epistemic to the political to the metaphysical.

For the poetic theory advanced by Wordsworth, then by Shelley, W. Q.—alias Wollstonecraft Questioner—was a probable inspiration.[1] For Mary Wollstonecraft the critique of decadent artifice even relaxes her otherwise firmly held reins of reason. True poetry, she had proposed in her fame-making *Vindication of the Rights of Men,*

> naturally addresses the fancy, and the language of passion is with
> great felicity borrowed from the heightened picture which the imagi-
> nation draws of sensible objects concentred by impassioned reflec-
> tion. And, during this "fine phrensy," reason has no right to rein-in
> the imagination.   (60–61)

The "poet's eye, in a fine frenzy rolling" (says Shakespeare's Theseus) is one with the "seething brains" of lovers and madmen, all far from what "cool reason ever comprehends" (*Midsummer Night's Dream* 5.1). The rational vindicator of the rights of man and woman sees no problem in such passion. The problem is a "modern poetry" that likes to "fabricate the pretended effusions of the heart," and *"Poets"* (her italics) such as Edmund Burke who "often cloud the understanding, whilst they move the heart by a kind of mechanical spring" (*Rights of Men* 60–63).

Poets were nothing if not a dilemma for a woman in the age of Enlight-enment. If the best of them give "the language of truth and nature with resistless energy" (W. Q. 280), the readers of poetry were another ques-tion. It wasn't just prim conduct monitors who worried about nonsense and danger stoking sensibility with fantastic or libidinous fare; it was also those whose political hopes were premised on a rationally capable citizenry. "This overstretched sensibility naturally relaxes the other pow-ers of the mind, and prevents intellect from attaining that sovereignty which it ought to attain to render a rational creature useful to others," writes Wollstonecraft, in another mood, targeting poetry, in *A Vindica-tion of the Rights of Woman* as one collaborator in forming "the *fair* sex" into a "mixture of madness and folly" (130). Such disdain is on the same page as Wordsworth's serial rants, from the 1800 Preface onward:

Away, then with the senseless iteration of the word, *popular,* applied to new works in Poetry, as if there were no test of excellence in the first of the fine arts but that all Men should run after its productions, as if urged by an appetite, or constrained by a spell!—The qualities of writing best fitted for eager reception . . . are chiefly of a superficial kind . . . the fancy amused without the trouble of thought.

> (*Essay, Supplementary* [1815] 372–73)

This alluring spellbinder of "all Men" is the antagonist of truly "manly" poetry. Although this gendering is not without complication (as we'll see in a later chapter), for now it is enough to note the chime with Wollstonecraft's critique of "feminine" culture. To scientist, Dissenter, and Rights-of-Man advocate Joseph Priestley, poetry was no friend to any "confirmed consciousness of the *strength of our faculties*": "in mere reading of this kind we are little more than passive," left "sleeping" (143–44). About this effect, Wollstonecraft could scarcely quarrel.

Yet *Rights of Woman* reflects an author who is a wide-ranging reader of poetry, impressed by the mental strength of the "great men" who wrote it. Even if these men could get "lost in poetic dreams" when

> fancy has peopled the scene, and the soul has been disturbed, till it shook the constitution, by the passions that meditation had raised; whose objects, the baseless fabric of a vision, faded before the exhausted eye, they must have had iron frames. Shakspeare never grasped the airy dagger with a nerveless hand, nor did Milton tremble when he led Satan far from the confines of his dreary prison.—These were not the ravings of imbecility, the sickly effusions of distempered brains; but the exuberance of fancy, that "in a fine phrenzy" wandering, was not continually reminded of its material shackles.   (76–77)

This appreciation of manly iron involves casually literate riffs on the poetry of Prospero in *The Tempest,* of *Macbeth,* of *Paradise Lost* Book II, and Theseus (again)—all, moreover, immune to what the vindicator of the *Rights of Woman* indexes among the wrongs of woman: imbecility, distemper, overheated fancy.

In the vast wrongs of woman, poetry would seem a minor culprit. It might, moreover, even supply an antidote or solace to oppressed souls. Wollstonecraft's mirror-named heroine of *Mary* (1788) finds refuge from misery in a nook of a ruined castle where she curls up to "read Thomson's Seasons, Young's Night-Thoughts, and Paradise Lost" (ch. IV; 1: 25). She proudly takes lessons from them all, and quotes or claims their verses to signify her cultured, refined sensibility.[2] In *The Wrongs of Woman; or Maria*, the political novel Wollstonecraft drafted ten years on, wrongly incarcerated Maria (another self-imprint) finds comfort, even liberation, in poetic romance:

> She took up a book on the powers of the human mind; but, her atten-
> tion strayed from cold arguments on the nature of what she felt,
> while she was feeling, and she snapt the chain of the theory to read
> Dryden's Guiscard and Sigismunda.   (ch. II; 1:33–34)

It's a telling choice. Defying a tyrant father, Sigismunda speaks a passionate poetry on behalf of erotic liberty. And for Maria to have seen this poetry of female love embodied heroically on the living stage—by Sarah Siddons in one of her signature roles, no less—was sheer intoxication:

> My delighted eye followed Mrs. Siddons, when, with dignified deli-
> cacy, she played Calista; and I involuntarily repeated after her, in the
> same tone, with a long-drawn sigh,
>
>   "Hearts like our's were pair'd—not match'd."   (ch. IX; 1:5–6)

Poetry solicits ennobling identification, a dignified solidarity of matched hearts. In Nicholas Rowe's *The Fair Penitent*, Calista's cry for true love (vs. being marriage-matched) sounds even like a rights-of-woman anthem: "How hard is the condition of our sex, / Thro' ev'ry state of life the slaves of man," Calista sighs (1795 text; 3.1.40–41). William Godwin recruited the second line for his praise of Wollstonecraft "standing forth in defence of one half of the human species, labouring under a yoke"; "She regarded her sex, in the language of Calista, as 'In every state of life the slaves of men'"(*Memoirs* 79–80).

Yet to anyone who knows (everyone did) the story of that century-long favorite (*The Fair Penitent* had been performed by Siddons as recently as 1796),[3] Maria's sigh of poetic identification is a caution. "Such hearts as ours were never pair'd above: / Ill-suited to each other; join'd not match'd," Rowe's Calista advises Altamont about their prospects (2.1.102–3), rejecting this good man, chosen by her father, to embrace heart-throb Lothario, a cad (destined for an eponym) who seduces and abandons her (in shame she commits suicide). Calista-smitten Maria is already marriage-joined to a man whom her sentiments have mistaken for better, and now faces prison death-in-life. On a peculiar line of sympathy with the un-wisely spurned suitor, Godwin, in the midst of reflecting (posthumously) on the suicidal passion of Wollstonecraft for her faithless lover Gilbert Imlay, again summons *Calista:* "fraught with imagination and sensibil-ity, with all, and more than all, 'that youthful poets fancy, when they love,' she returned to England, and, if he had so pleased, to the arms of her former lover" (130). Quoting Altamont in deluded rapture about the "all" of Calista (who's already given herself to Lothario),[4] Godwin twins love-struck Wollstonecraft to Altamont's poetry of delusion, as well as (by force of the narrative arcs of both *Memoirs* and *Calista*) to suicidal Ca-lista. In a "corrected" edition, he decided, for Wollstonecraft's sake, to cancel this second reference to Calista (133).

The enchantment of poetry is precisely the cue to rational suspicion, its power-play to sensibility over sense (or as Wordsworth will write it, appetite over thought). Maria, mad-housed by her husband-from-hell, is courted by a fellow inmate (Imlay-patterned Henry Darnford), first by proxy of his stash of books, including Rousseau's novels and Dryden's fables. Maria responds with an "affectionate heart . . . loving, as poets love" (ch. II; 1:33), imagining a lover out of the patterns of poetry. Within a few weeks they meet, and within a few days

> paradise bloomed around them; or they, by a powerful spell, had
> been transported into Armida's garden. Love, the grand enchanter,
> "lapt them in Elysium," and every sense was harmonized to joy and
> social exstacy.   (ch. IV; 1:75)

Against this spell, the novelist taps her own store of poetic warning: Ar-mida's garden (in Tasso's *Gerusaleme Liberata*) is a temptress-trap; to "take the prison'd soul, / And lap it in *Elysium*" is the artfulness (in Mil-ton's *Comus*) of Circe and her Sirens, wielding "Potent hearbs, and bale-full drugs" that "lull'd the sense, / And in sweet madness robbed it of it self" (253–61). With a tacit half-allusion to this poetry, Wollstonecraft had written to a "dear friend" (Imlay, unnamed) of the "extreme affection of [her] nature," the disorderly, "impetuous tide" of her feelings—"tokens of love which I have received have rapt me in elysium," she confesses, with "rapt" usurping "lapt" (Letter VIII, *LSR* 95). The novelist of *The Wrongs of Woman* is a cautious disenchanter, allied with the vindicator of the Rights of Woman in seeing the romance of poetry everywhere complicit on "the historic page" of the wrongs of woman (*RW* 1).[5]

As the anthology arraigned in *Rights of Woman* may testify, poetry is one of the prime pushers of "THE PREVAILING OPINION OF A SEXUAL CHARACTER" (the title-language of chapter II), conning consent with its aura of sensibility, praise, gentle instruction, jesting satire, or urbane misogyny—all proffered in sure "knowledge" of "the sex." It may seem no big deal now to bust this nefarious poetic traffic, rife in *Paradise Lost* (and its Mosaic base); Pope's epistle *To a Lady: Of the Characters of Women;* the poetic fabric of fictions such as Richardson's wildly popular *Clarissa* and Rousseau's "progressive" novel, *Émile, ou de l'education;* and the authority of poets (especially Milton) in such household helps as Rev. Fordyce's *Sermons to Young Women* and its generic twin, Dr. Gregory's *A Father's Legacy to His Daughters.* But it was a big deal in 1792, and Wollstonecraft had her sights on even bigger game, for which such poetry was synecdoche: the vast cultural poetics wrought by "the male prejudice, which deems beauty the perfection of woman," a "male prejudice that makes women systematically weak," fueled with a poetry-polished lexicon—*innocent, delicate, beautiful, feminine, angel*—and claiming the authority of divine design or "natural" order.[6]

In cherishing poetry "most natural," W. Q. concedes that "natural is a very indefinite expression" (279). *Rights of Woman* magnetizes this expression for an unforgiving review: "the effect of habit is insisted upon as an undoubted indication of nature" (179).[7] Rousseau, champion of progressive educational and political philosophy, irritates Wollstonecraft with his retrograde stress on the "natural" order of male power and its instrumental female training. She will reeducate her readers in the teeth of his tract. If this "philosopher" contends that "a state of dependence being natural to the sex, [women] perceive themselves formed for obedience," she exposes an argumentation that is "begging the question" (182). Where Rousseau declares, "Such is the order of nature" of Émile's "claims" to the "obedience" of Sophy (who "naturally" directs his heart), Wollstonecraft mocks the "unintelligible paradoxes": this is poetry perhaps, but no logic (198).[8] "Dr. Gregory fell into a similar error" in advising his daughters to "cultivate a fondness for dress" because this "is natural to them." "I am unable to comprehend what either he or Rousseau mean, when they frequently use this indefinite term," she murmurs archly, inviting her reader to comprehend the politics of "nature" (53). If Rousseau "pretends to draw" his "arguments . . . from the indications of nature," she shows him contradicting himself when (for example) he says, "with respect to the female character, obedience is the grand lesson which ought to be impressed with unrelenting rigour" (47). A character forged by impress and unrelenting rigor is scarcely any "natural" formation. If by now we handily deconstruct "nature" as culture, in Wollstonecraft's day such a critique (let alone critical practice) was unlikely: it was the appeal to nature over society that was the countercultural, modern gesture, "poetic" in the true sense; hence, Rousseau's prestige. The new knowledge was called "Natural Philosophy": objective, progressive.

Wollstonecraft's critical skills were honed by her work at the *Analytic Review*, on assignments that had her constantly reading (widely, comparatively) and then writing analyses. Across her reviews she shapes the method that will drive her two *Vindications:* a view of "history" as a contingent narrative, and of narratives as productions of contingent history—a chiasmus that she exercises with deconstructive genius. In *Rights of Woman*, again and again, she exposes a motivated social-text, the frailties not in the name of woman but in a questionable construction "woman." For this mode of oppositional review, Wollstonecraft likes the term *animadversion;* she titles Chapter V "ANIMADVERSIONS ON SOME OF THE WRITERS WHO HAVE RENDERED WOMEN OBJECTS OF PITY, BORDERING ON CONTEMPT" (170). Women, she is sorry to say, collaborate and "act contrary to their real interest on an enlarged scale" in habits of complicit reading, "when they cherish or affect weakness under the name of delicacy" (96).

She renders a re-reading lesson, in poetry and, more foundationally, in cultural poetics. Where "sensualists have planted" these names of delicacy in the culture-text, her animadversion, written in the very semiotic of "nature," is to "eradicate the firmly rooted prejudices" (96). When Rev. Fordyce coaches a wife to indulge a husband by giving "*soft* answers to hasty words, complaining as seldom as possible" (see Sermon XII; 2:300), Wollstonecraft italicizes the offense to prompt a review. "Such a woman ought to be an angel," she sums the cant, then reads the dark workmanship of the angel in the house: "or she is an ass—for I discern not a trace of the human character, neither reason nor passion in this domestic drudge, whose being is absorbed in that of a tyrant's" (*RW* 214). Another toxic term is *innocence:* "why should they be kept in ignorance under the specious name of innocence?" (32). If "innocence, as ignorance is courteously termed" (90), solicits chivalry, the entailment of its negative construction (*in-nocent:* unharmed) is mental weakness; when men tell women to "remain, it may be said, innocent; they mean in a state of childhood" (132).[9]

A co-conspirator is the poets' romance of innocent childhood, no more resonant than in the famous climax of Gray's *Ode on a Distant Prospect of Eton College:* "where Ignorance is Bliss, / 'Tis Folly to be wise" (p. 8; 99–100). Yet those Eton lads are getting an education, while their sisters are preserved in ignorance. "Thus Milton describes our first frail mother," is Wollstonecraft's headline for her reading lesson on this creature of beauty and ignorance, with a dash of Hamlet's misogyny. She then turns the question:

> Though when he tells us that women are formed for softness and sweet attractive grace, I cannot comprehend his meaning, unless . . . he meant to deprive us of souls, and insinuate that we were beings only designed by sweet attractive grace, and docile blind obedience, to gratify the senses of man when he can no longer soar on the wing of contemplation. (*RW* 33)

She is referring to Milton's paradise-paradigm, "For contemplation hee and valour formd, / For softness shee and sweet attractive Grace" (*PL* 4.297–98), the scheme Reverend Fordyce happily endorses, quoting these very lines in *Sermons to Young Women* following these remarks:

> Meekness cultivated on Christian principles, is the proper consummation, highest finishing of female excellence. . . . in his admired work of Paradise Lost [Milton] has with equal judgment and delicacy marked, throughout, the separate characters of the first Pair, so he has, in two lines, happily expressed the principal objects of their respective destinations. (Sermon XII; 2d edition, 2:260–61)[10]

Wollstonecraft, mindful that it is "with attractive graces" that Milton's Sin impresses rebel angels and enamors her father Satan (the epic's first instance of this phrase; 2.762–65), exposes the gross "insult" to woman:

for a man, "grace" is not to be measured by adjectives such as "sweet attractive" and "gentle" is not linked to the helpless compliance of or to be found in "domestic brutes" (33). Poets may plot a fall into error, but reading them against the grain can serve an education in error.

Yet for all the deliberate, ironic confusion of Milton's purposes,[11] Wollstonecraft knows that poetry is a gordian twine: natural and unnatural; a lover's "poetical licence" and "empty words" of "delusive flattery" (*RW* 211); a culture of misogyny or specious praise; a source of pleasure or resource for expression. Her interactions with the poets are diverse, even divergent; she may use poets to voice her thoughts, or to elevate and amplify her passions; she may put their words in revisionary frame or work the words against the grain; or indict the complicity of poetry with the social-text. She can league with Hamlet's melancholy, Macbeth's fateful anxiety, or Lear's agony on the heath (all as if her own soul); with Satan's energetic contempt (if not his moral temptation), with Pope's remarks (if not his theses), with the crazed despair of the lovelorn swain in Gray's *Elegy*, with Edward Young's laments for humanity. Poetry vibrates with a world of references, tones, and tropes; it is a medium to "see or feel poetically" (261), a gleaming "poetical fiction" to enhance a virtue (293), to lend a tragic dignity to passions that know no gender, and—not least— to give a voice to vindication.

All About Eve; or, the Genesis of Feminist Literary Criticism

Looking at Milton's "pleasing picture of paradisiacal happiness" in *A Vindication of the Rights of Woman*, Wollstonecraft recoils in Satanic dislocation, not along lines of moral alienation but from pride in her mental power. She ventures a higher Satanism: "instead of envying the lovely pair, I have, with conscious dignity, or Satanic pride, turned to hell for sublimer objects"—a poetry for "exercise of mind or stretch of thought" (46). "Whenever I read Milton's description of paradise," she confided to her sister in 1790, her pleasure conflicts with moral self-reflection: "the happiness, which he so poetically describes fills me with benevolent satisfaction"; yet it all seems the happiness of two "inferiors"—a "mistaken pride" maybe, or maybe a "conscious dignity . . . whispering me that my soul is immortal & should have a nobler ambition" than complete "happiness in a world like this" Eden (*CL* 179–80). As she was writing *Rights of Woman*, she was happy to sense a sympathy in Henri Fuseli's illustrations of *Paradise Lost:* "like Milton he seems quite at home in hell—his Devil will be the hero of the poetic series; for, *entre nous*," she hints to William Roscoe (another champion of the French Revolution), "I rather doubt whether he will produce an Eve to please me . . . unless it be after the fall" (*CL* 194).

On the text of Milton's Eve, Wollstonecraft invents what we now call feminist literary criticism: a resistant reading of argument and its ideological grain; sharp attention to language and its cultural information; and a reflection on herself as both victim and theorist of male prejudice. Milton is her chief quarry because, like Rousseau, his republican principles were celebrated by British liberals, including those in her own circle. One effect, as with *Émile*, has been that the gender hierarchy in *Paradise Lost* (the most celebrated of English poems) not only has slipped critique but could be iterated across otherwise sharp political divisions. Moreover, where Rousseau attributed the weakness of woman to "nature," Milton argued divine design. At the same time, however, for all this enmity to the rights of woman, *Paradise Lost* was a monumental convenience to the vindicator of the Rights of Woman: contesting Scripture was risky business, but one could contend with a poet and a poetic artifact. Sagely limiting her animadversion to the Old Testament, Wollstonecraft treats it not as scripture but as a script of dubious poetry: "the prevailing opinion, that woman was created for man" is "Moses's poetical story" (*RW* 49). Milton's poetical story is implied: "were an angel from heaven to tell me Moses's beautiful, poetic cosmogony, and the account of the fall of man, were literally true, I could not believe what my reason told me was derogatory to the character of the Supreme Being" (173–74). Wielding this sublime satire as "a suggestion of reason," Wollstonecraft at once sets the Mosaic foundation as a frangible fiction and presses the epithet "Supreme Being" into continuity with rational human being. It's a brilliant double play, saving the vindicator's character as God-fearing and indicting the poets as fallible fabulists. This measure of reason also distinguishes her from counter-Enlightenment modern poets (such as Blake) who cast "Reason" as the enemy of imaginative liberty and, in this venture, attempt to redeem poet Milton from high-argument Milton.[12] For Wollstonecraft, the problem with Milton is not any theology of reason; it's the degraded female investment.[13]

This critique of Eve is all the more notable because just a few years before the French Revolution, she was using Eve by the book.[14] Adam's sigh of Eve, "Those thousand decencies that daily flow / From all her words and actions" (*PL* 8.601–2), imprints the advice on matrimony in her *Thoughts on the Education of Daughters: With Reflections on Female Conduct, in the more important Duties of Life* (1787): "there are a thousand nameless decencies which good sense gives rise to" (97). In *The Female Reader* (1789) Wollstonecraft blithely purveys a selection from the *Spectator* (no. 631) that climaxes in Adam's first raptures:

> When Adam is introduced by Milton describing Eve in Paradise, and relating to the angel the impressions he felt upon seeing her at her first creation, he does not represent her like a Grecian Venus, by her shape or features, but by the lustre of her mind, which shone in them, and gave them their power of charming.
>
> > Grace was in all her steps, heav'n in her eye,
> > In all her gestures dignity and love!
> >
> > (*Reader* 59; cf. *PL* 8.488–89)

Mind-luster is still linked to the power of charming. Even more remarkably, the lines that will launch the animadversion on Eve in *Rights of Woman* sit in this *Reader* (273–76) without a critical blink, in a centaine dose with a nonce title, "Conversation Between Adam and Eve on Going to Rest" (*PL* 4.598–690).

In *Rights of Woman* Wollstonecraft revisits a part of this conversation, 4.634–38, to mine a mother-lode of "THE PREVAILING OPINION." One nugget is that already-interrogated keyword, *innocent*, "but a civil term for weakness" (34):

> For if it be allowed that women were destined by Providence to acquire human virtues, and by the exercise of their understandings, that stability of character which is the firmest ground to rest our future hopes upon, they must be permitted to turn to the fountain of light, and not forced to shape their course by the twinkling of a mere satellite. Milton, I grant, was of a very different opinion; for he only bends to the indefeasible right of beauty. . . .
>
> > "To whom thus Eve with *perfect beauty* adorn'd.
> > My Author and Disposer, what thou bidst

Unargued I obey; so God ordains;
God is *thy law, thou mine:* to know no more
Is Woman's *happiest* knowledge and her *praise."*

These are exactly the arguments that I have used to children; but I
have added, your reason is now gaining strength, and, till it arrives at
some degree of maturity, you must look up to me for advice—then
you ought to *think,* and only rely on God. (34–35)

Where Eve lisps as Adam's text (*PL* 4.634–38), disposed by and obedient
to this regent Author, author Wollstonecraft italicizes the specious names
and her own *think* to fissure Milton's opinion. She takes like aim at Swift's
sarcasm in the opening of "The Furniture of a Woman's Mind," ridiculing
women "for repeating 'a set of phrases learnt by rote'" or for bubbling (as
Dr. Gregory might prompt) in "passion for a scarlet coat": "nothing could
be more natural," she sighs, "considering the education they receive, and
that their 'highest praise is to obey, unargued'—the will of man" (264).

Anti-Wollstonecraftian Hannah More grasped the stakes: if one admitted a flaw in the poet's Eve, God's ways to man might fall apart. More's
strategy in her *Strictures on . . . Female Education* (1799) is to co-opt
Wollstonecraft by reading Milton's Eve not against Milton's Adam, but
against the figure of "woman" in the fatuous poetry that Wollstonecraft,
too, despises—and to do so, moreover, with the very lines from *Paradise
Lost* that Wollstonecraft had admired in *Education of Daughters:*

I would make it the criterion of true taste, right principle, and genuine feeling, in a woman, whether she would be less touched with all
the flattery of romantic and exaggerated panegyric, than with that
beautiful picture of correct and elegant propriety, which Milton
draws of our first mother, when he delineates

"Those thousand *decencies* which daily flow
From all her words and actions." (*Strictures* 5)

Yet in representing Milton/Adam as this better poet, More manages to
expose the limit: she has had to suppress Milton's ensuing gender split in
the flow of decencies. In Adam's full delineation, recall, Eve's love is
"sweet compliance" (8.603), while his is "half abash't" (595) by the well-
ing of passion from which misogyny (his in book 10, thence in literary
iteration and reiteration) will erupt.

That More is still worrying Wollstonecraft's animadversion is registered in her reprise of the debate in her conduct-novel *Cœlebs in Search of a Wife* (1808), with no few telling slips of representation. Its first chapter, titled *Milton on Eve—Opinions of the Ladies not correct*, is an address by the hopeful Eve-enamored bachelor to perversely Wollstonecrafted women:

> I have been sometimes surprised, when in conversation I have been expressing my admiration of the character of Eve in her state of innocence, as drawn by our immortal poet, to hear objections raised by those, from whom of all critics I should have least expected it—the ladies. . . . I never formed an idea of conjugal happiness, but my mind involuntarily adverted to the graces of that finished picture.   (9)

Yet this More-scripted "idea" is taxed not just by the equation of grace to aesthetic finishing, rather than relationship to God, but also by historical complications; neither Milton nor More was a legend of conjugal happiness. More was jilted, gaining a settlement that enabled her independent career as author. Silent on this point, she does try to spin Milton's famed failure on behalf of Cœlebs's suit:

> The ladies, in order to justify their censure, assert that Milton, a harsh domestic tyrant, must needs be a very inadequate judge, and of course a very unfair delineator, of female accomplishments. These fair cavilers . . . insist that it is highly derogatory from the dignity of the sex, that the poet should affirm, that it is the perfection of the character of a wife,
>
> > To study household good,
> > And good works in her husband to promote.
>
> Now, according to my notion of "household good," which does not include one idea of drudgery or servility, but involves a large and comprehensive scheme of excellence, I will venture to affirm that, let a woman know what she may, yet, if she knows not this, she is ignorant of the most indispensable, the most appropriate branch of female knowledge. . . . the offence taken by the ladies against the uncourtly bard, is chiefly occasioned by his having presumed to intimate that conjugal obedience
>
> > Is woman's highest honour and her praise.

... I would point out to them that the supposed harshness of the observation is quite done away by the recollection, that this scrupled "obedience" is so far from implying degradation, that it is connected with the injunction to the woman "to promote good works" in her husband; an injunction surely inferring a degree of influence that raises her condition, and restores her to all the dignity of equality.

(9–10)

The argument slips on the elision of a complicated context for first inset quotation: Adam's indulgent praise of, then chiding of Eve's labor-efficient proposal for working separately (*PL* 9.232–34), then his concession to her—the situation that canny, watchful Satan springs to exploit, playing on Eve's restless ignorance. No less slippery is the way More tries to manage (or misrecalls) Eve's rote lesson that her ignorance is "womans happiest knowledge and her praise" (4.638). More elevates this to highest honors, the *summa* evading the educated knowledge that matters even to More herself.

If "a degree of influence" confesses but a qualified raise, More puffs the stock of "dignity." Cœlebs concludes his homage by asking any "fair objector" to "take the trouble" to observe that Milton,

is so far from making Eve a mere domestic drudge . . . that he pays an invariable attention even to external elegance, in his whole delineation, ascribing grace to her steps, and dignity to her gesture. He uniformly keeps up the same combination of intellectual worth and polished manners:

For softness she, and sweet attractive grace.   (ch. I, 11–12)

More is sure of a triple coup, refuting Wollstonecraft's animadversion on these lines and her gloss of the good wife as "domestic drudge" (*RW* 214) and reclaiming Dr. Gregory's assurance to his daughters that he means to honor their sex "not as domestic drudges, or the slaves of our pleasures, but as our companions and equals" (*Legacy* 6). Yet More may overplay her hand. It is not Eve who is Wollstonecraft's drudge but her lineal descent in the "house slave" (213), and Cœlebs's logic bids fair for Wollstonecraft's roster of unintelligible paradoxes: to describe softness and sweet attractive grace as "intellectual" is the "delusive flattery" of logical contradiction (211).

About the verse that follows in *Paradise Lost* just after "For softness shee, and sweet attractive Grace" (4.298), moreover, there is some scandal. "A shameful error to have pass'd through all the Editions," said infamous eighteenth-century emender Richard Bentley: "The Author gave it, *He for God only, She for God* AND *Him*" (117n; cf. 4.299). In her introduction to *Epistles on Women* (1810), a very learned Lucy Aikin (Anna Letitia Barbauld's niece) called out Milton's she-theology as a "blasphemous presumption" (vi–vii), even as she thought "absurd" the "idea that the two sexes ever can be, or ever ought to be, placed in all respects on a footing of equality" (v)—no Wollstonecraft, but no More either. Line 299 provokes such comments in no small part because it was being cited with approval. "That line in Milton is very striking—'He for God only, she for God in him.' Such is the order of nature and providence," exclaimed William Hazlitt, to readers of the radical weekly the *Examiner* (12 February 1815) no less, certain that "Women are what they were meant to be": creatures of "no ideas, except personal ones," answering only to "their senses, their vanity, or their interest" (108).[15]

About Milton's unequal footing of "grace," More is evidently uneasy. As severe a critic of "female accomplishments" as Wollstonecraft, she gives Cœlebs, in conclusion, a script to address the figure of "accomplisht *Eve*" (*PL* 4.660) with an historicizing excuse:

I will not, however, affirm that Adam, or even Milton, annexed to the term *accomplished* precisely the idea with which it is associated in the mind of a true modern-bred lady.
    If it be objected to the poet's gallantry, that he remarks,

Her beauty is excelled by manly grace,
And wisdom, which alone is truly fair;

let it be remembered that the observation proceeds from the lips of Eve herself, and thus adds to her other graces, the crowning grace of humility.   (ch. I; 12)

Yet in the gambit to co-opt Eve, More forgets that Eve herself strains the defense. Her full sentence (recalling Adam's coaxing of her to his side) is "thy gentle hand / Seisd mine, I yielded, and from that time see / How beauty is excelld . . ." (4.488–91)—a coercion strangely dissonant with the epic poet's cheers for her "meek surrender" and "submissive Charms"

(494–98). Woman is given "all the 'submissive charms,'" Wollstonecraft remarks dryly of the "received opinion" (*RW* 65); her favorite bugbear theorist, Burke, had written, "we love what submits to us" in a treatise on beauty that writes *we* as masculine prerogative and *what* as its female subject (*Inquiry* 97). More's elision of the political vectors of aesthetic ideology is conspicuous—communicating, in effect, what hasn't been, can't be, said.

Wollstonecraft is smartly alert to the deconstructive lever of contradiction. In *Rights of Men* she proposes a method of refuting Burke's "sophisms": "putting the numerous contradictions" that she has observed "in opposition to each other"—and so producing, with this counteractive rhetorical analysis, "an effectual refutation" of Burke's political bias (153). On a similar critical axis, she collates in *Rights of Woman* what has now become a *locus classicus* in feminist criticism of *Paradise Lost*—"two passages" that "it would be difficult to render . . . consistent"—this dyad assembled with a dig at Milton in the terms Hazlitt likes for women: "into similar inconsistencies are great men often led by their senses" (35).[16] The first passage is Eve's address to Adam as her "Author and Disposer" (4.634–38; *RW* 35). The second is Adam's petition to his Maker for equal society in Paradise, which Wollstonecraft presents, with italics, as an honorary page for her own vindication: "Yet in the following lines Milton seems to coincide with me . . ."

Hast thou not made me here thy substitute,
And these inferior far beneath me set?
Among *unequals* what society
Can sort, what harmony or true delight?
Which must be mutual, in proportion due
Giv'n and receiv'd; but in *disparity*
The one intense, the other still remiss
Cannot well suit with either, but soon prove
Tedious alike: of *fellowship* I speak
Such as I seek, fit to participate
All rational delight—   (35–36 [*PL* 8.381–91])

Milton can imagine Adam's rational wish for an equal, and then a God who refuses it.[17] Eve's reining by a "line of subordination in the mental powers" prompts Wollstonecraft to a footnote in chapter 4 animadvert-

ing on Milton's "fall" into "inconsistencies," with a poke at another pernicious figure, *angel:* "Women, weak women, are compared with angels;
yet, a superiour order of beings should be supposed to possess more intellect than man; or, in what does their superiority consist?" She stays to
answer:

> Only "absolute in loveliness," the portion of rationality granted to
> woman, is, indeed very scanty; for denying her genius and judgment,
> it is scarcely possible to divine what remains to characterize intellect.
>
> (*RW* 110)

This is a nice play on *divine*, against the gushing of Adam (8.547), which
even Arch Angel Raphael hastens to chastise (560*ff*). With *Paradise Lost*
as her primer, Wollstonecraft gives a brisk reading lesson on the ideology
of poetic compliment.

A bit into the chapter that hosts this last critique ("OBSERVATIONS ON
THE STATE OF DEGRADATION TO WHICH WOMAN IS REDUCED . . ."), Wollstonecraft animadverts more fully on the verse just after "absolute in
loveliness," scoring Adam's raptures to expose the insidious insult. She
summons another Adam, Adam Smith, for his scathing critique (in *The
Theory of Moral Sentiments*) of Louis XIV, Sun-king creator of Versailles,
esteemed "the most perfect model of a great prince" but in actual case, a
confection of "frivolous accomplishments, supported by his rank," de-
void of "knowledge, industry, valour, and beneficence." Figurally, he is
"woman"—as Smith's own scathing quotation of Voltaire's praises in *Siè-
cle de Louis XIV* draws the figure, too: "the gracefulness of his shape, and
the majestic beauty of his features" (quoted in *RW* 125–27). Wollstonecraft reads the frivolous blazon back into Milton's iconic Eve:

> Woman also thus "in herself complete," by possessing all these
> *frivolous* accomplishments, so changes the nature of things
>
> ———"That what she wills to do or say
> Seems wisest, virtuousest, discreetest, best;
> All higher knowledge in *her presence* falls
> Degraded. Wisdom in discourse with her
> Loses discountenanc'd, and, like Folly, shows;
> Authority and Reason on her wait."———
>
> And all this is built on her loveliness!   (*RW* 127; [*PL* 8.549–54])

In an Adamic rapture in which Folly usurps Wisdom and Reason is side-lined, Wollstonecraft tracks the fault lines of misogyny: no surprise that post-lapsarian Adam will gripe about this same "Feminine" novelty as a "fair defect/Of Nature," the perversity of a "Creator wise" who didn't keep to the Heaven-plan of "Spirits Masculine" and find "some other way to generate/Mankind" (10.888–95).

Across *Rights of Woman,* Wollstonecraft animadverts on his epithet "fair defect" as a contradiction speaking volumes on female morals and manners:

> Inheriting, in a lineal descent from the first fair defect in nature, the sovereignty of beauty, they have, to maintain their power, resigned the natural rights, which the exercise of reason might have procured them, and chosen rather to be short-lived queens than labour to ob-tain the sober pleasures that arise from equality. (116)

To any reader in the 1790s, "Reason" is an ideology. It was a keyword in the French Revolution and in the principles of English progressives, and was branded by reactionaries as a proxy for everything Godless, anti-patriotic, immoral, and inimical to female virtue. Linking Reason and Rights, Wollstonecraft makes her political point. Heirs neither of "natural rights" nor of rational respect, but rather of a lineal descent into multiple "fair defects in nature" (145), women, in Wollstonecraft's narrative, figure a sorry travesty of Adam's original petition, seeming, instead, to have been "created not to enjoy the fellowship of man, but to save him from sinking into absolute brutality, by rubbing off the rough angles of his character; and by playful dalliance to give some dignity to the appetite that draws him to them" (*RW* 145–46). It was Adam's late grievance—and the misogyny stirred by sexual passion—far more than his encomi-ums to prelapsarian Eve, that distressed women and, correspondingly, honed men's satires.

Mary Wray opened *The Ladies Library* (1714) with a melancholy "musing" on the "general and undistinguished Aspersions" cast by "the most polite Writers of the Age" on the "Composure" of women, including the rant that Milton scripts for Adam. Pondering the possibility that "the Character of those that speak" might "circumstantiate the thing so as not to make it a Reproach upon Women as such," Wray rather doubted it (1: 2–4).[18] Even better than Wray, Wollstonecraft could report the uncircumstantiated credit in "the present modification of society" (*RW* 116): if "women every where appear a defect in nature," the pervasive fiction, she remarks, is a "determinate effect" of a pervasive culture: "the enervating style" of their education and "subordinate state in society" (259). Only if they prove incapable of reason should they "submit to be a *fair defect* in creation," she contends; "But to justify the ways of Providence respecting them, by pointing out some irrefragable reason" for making women "not accountable" to reason "would puzzle the subtlest casuist" (93)—her satire honed on Milton's claim to "assert Eternal Providence, / And justifie the wayes of God to men" (*PL* 1.25–26).[19] And to women?

> As a philosopher, I read with indignation the plausible epithets which men use to soften their insults; and, as a moralist, I ask what is meant by such heterogeneous associations, as fair defects, amiable weaknesses, &c.?   (*RW* 67)

Among the men is Pope, whose oft-quoted phrase "Fine by defect, and delicately weak" (*To a Lady* 44) has Adamic fingerprints all over it.

Pope's full sentence displays the pernicious binding of fineness and defect in female culture:

> Ladies, like variegated tulips, show;
> 'Tis to their changes that their charms they owe;
> Fine by defect, and delicately weak . . ."   (41–43)

'Tis to viruses that tulips owe their charming variety, a horticulture of mutant defects that guarantees constitutional weakness. Wollstonecraft reads *variegated* with a difference:

> It would be an endless task to trace the variety of meannesses, cares, and sorrows, into which women are plunged by the prevailing opinion, that they were created rather to feel than reason, and that all the power they obtain, must be obtained by their charms and weakness:
>
> "Fine by defect, and amiably weak!"
>
> And, made by this amiable weakness entirely dependent, excepting what they gain by illicit sway, on man, not only for protection, but advice, is it surprising that, neglecting the duties that reason alone points out, and shrinking from trials calculated to strengthen their

minds, they only exert themselves to give their defects a graceful covering, which may serve to heighten their charms in the eye of the voluptuary, though it sink them below the scale of moral excellence?

(*RW* 132)

Her slight misremembering of Pope's phrase aptly registers the social value to men (amiability: attractiveness for marriage) that sustains the culture of female deficiency.

As Wollstonecraft suggests in other quotations of Pope, faint praise is kin to damning judgment and uncivil leers.[20] In the same paragraph of *To a Lady* that praises fine defects,

Pope has said, in the name of the whole male sex,

> "Yet ne'er so sure our passion to create,
> As when she touch'd the brink of all we hate."
> (*RW* 50 [Pope, lines 51–52])

This pithy couplet summary, Wollstonecraft observes, renders women merely "females," forever "degraded by being made subservient to love or lust" (50).[21] To drive the point home a little further along the trajectory of man-made degradation, after the brink has been crossed, she summons a couplet, this from another of Dryden's *Fables* (*RW* 269):

> —————"Where love is duty, on the female side,
> On theirs mere sensual gust, and sought with surly pride."[22]

So laments Emily in *Palamon and Arcite*, pleading to Cynthia, goddess of chastity, to take her out of this worldly fate, and accept her as a votress in a world elsewhere:

> Like Death, thou know'st, I loath the Nuptial state,
> And Man, the Tyrant of our Sex, I hate,
> A lowly Servant, but a lofty Mate.
> Where Love is Duty, on the Female side;
> On theirs meer sensual Gust, and sought with surly Pride.
> (p. 46; III.227–31)

State/hate/Mate: this is one of those eruptive triplets in Dryden that tropes hyper-bondage.[23] On the same hard lesson of the "pernicious tendency of those books, in which the writers insidiously degrade the sex whilst they are prostrate before their personal charms," Wollstonecraft quotes the postlapsarian lament of Eve in Dryden's opera, *The State of Innocence: and Fall of Man:*

> ———"Curs'd vassalage,
> First idoliz'd till love's hot fire be o'er,
> Then slaves to those who courted us before." (V.1; *RW* 204)

The full first line is actually "Curs'd Vassalage of all my future Kind"—the long view of the lineal descent. Inspired by *A Vindication of the Rights of Woman,* Blake etched ENSLAV'D as the first bold word of *Visions of the Daughters of Albion.*

Wollstonecrafting Poetry

In letters written to her friend Jane Arden, a teenage Wollstonecraft volleys the poetry of Dryden, Pope, Gray, William King, Henry Baker, and others—all untagged, as if a "commonplace book" parody played in the wit of the signatory, with a flair of decorum, "your friend / & humble Servant / Mary Wollstonecraft" (*CL* 3).[24] Fifteen years on, adventures with poetry beckon in *The Female Reader,* an anthology compiled in 1788 and published in the politically turbulent spring of 1789. Presented as the labor of "Mr. Cresswick" and subtitled *for the Improvement of Young Women,* the *Reader* promises a kind of courtesy-conduct resource to "imprint some useful lessons on the mind, and cultivate the taste" (Preface iv) with the assembly of Milton (*Paradise Lost*), Cowper (*The Task, A Fable, Alexander Selkirk*), Dr. Johnson (*The Natural Beauty*), Thomson (a biblical paraphrase), Edward Young (*Dying Friends*), Charlotte Smith (sonnets), Swift (*Stella* poems), Percy's folk anthology, *Reliques,* Barbauld, Shenstone, Steele, Edward Moore, Merrick, Gay, Elizabeth Carter —as well as ample verse from the poet esteemed as "English Poetry" itself, Shakespeare. Mr. Cresswick's preface offers assurances that in choosing works "addressed to the imagination," the aim has been "to awaken the affections and fix good habits more firmly in the mind than cold arguments and mere declamation" (vi).

But the fix is unfixed by the double grammar of "The Female Reader": the book, and its peruser, its reading agent. Not just a curriculum, Wollstonecraft's text is a field for the female reader as an active imaginer, especially with poetry, especially Shakespeare's. Under the cover of Shakespeare's cultural prestige and of service to the "desirable attainment" of reading "with propriety" (v), his poetry (Wollstonecraft knew) could license improper adventures and desires. "Reader" here does not designate a sequestered, silent encounter with a book (though it can mean this); it refers, primarily, to a script for reading out loud, for elocutionary exercise in a social situation, in interaction with other readers. So while a female reader can voice the polite-culture poetry of Rosalind, Cordelia, Imogen, and Miranda, she can also audition the more turbulent male voices of Orlando (*As You Like It*); Lear, Kent, Gloucester, Edgar, and Edmund (*Lear*); Hubert, Arthur, Executioner, Bastard, and Philip (*King John*); Ferdinand, Ariel, and Prospero (*Tempest*)—and both regicidal Macbeths.[25] Although Milton is mined only for Eden-happy Adam and Eve (no Satan), a female reader might try on Adam for size, or some Dissenting (even proto-Revolutionary) voices in passages from Cowper's *The Task* (titled herein *On Slavery, The Bastile*, and *Humanity*); or from Goldsmith's *The Deserted Village* (nonce-titled *Poverty and Luxury Contrasted*).[26] Fronted as an exercise in elocution, a sympathetic identification, an inhabiting of another subjectivity, may take place. "It is the individual manner of seeing and feeling, pourtayed by a strong imagination in bold images that have struck the senses, which creates all the charms of poetry," Wollstonecraft remarks in "Hints" (notes toward a sequel to *Rights of Woman*): "A great reader is always quoting the description of another's emotions" (#31; 194–95). In liberal reading, quotation can lead to appropriations, identifications, and extravagant inspirations.

Loyalist expatriot (from the Revolutionary United States) Lindley Murray had only young men in mind when he assembled *The English Reader* (1799), urging a practice of dramatic "expression, in such a way as to show that the student has minutely perceived the ideas, and entered into the feelings of the author" (74)—an assumed male circuit. Wollstonecraft is alert to the potential of female inhabitings and adventures. She herself quotes poetry, theatrically, not just to reflect learning and taste, but also to sound allegiances, political and affectional. She hails Hamlet's world-weary soliloquy into *Rights of Men* to rail against the tracks of advancement in which talent is "either bent or broken by the high man's contumelies" (51; *Hamlet* 3.1.71). In *The Wrongs of Woman*, mad-housed Maria channels this soliloquy-fount into female syntax:

"She descanted on 'the ills which flesh is heir to,' with bitterness, when the recollection of her babe was revived by a tale of fictitious woe" (ch. II; 1:19). She claims Hamlet's sigh of "the heart-ache, and the thousand natural shocks / That flesh is heir to" (3.1) for the "ills" of her child-robbed flesh, the shocks of male tyranny.[27] Denmark is a prison for an alienated prince; England is such for any woman.

Milton is even a perverse resource. The practice of "cramping a woman's mind, . . . in order to keep it fair" has "made it quite a blank," a fate that has Wollstonecraft, in *Rights of Woman*, thinking of Satan: "would it not be a refinement on cruelty only to open her mind to make the darkness and misery of her fate *visible?*" (196). A hopeless world of "No light, but rather darkness visible" is what hell flames reveal to Satan's defeat (*PL* 1.63)—by her lights, to any thinking woman's mind.[28] What she boldly calls "the tyranny of man" (32) is not limited to the ancien régime, but is extended to the new republicans, precisely to embarrass them with this contradiction to their liberal politics—or rather, to expose the gender status quo in liberal tradition.[29] Wollstonecraft's truest twin in *Paradise Lost* is not prelapsarian Eve, but dark-defeated Satan and his potential cousin—blanked, blinded Milton. "I discovered in myself a capacity for the enjoyment of the various pleasures existence affords," Maria writes in her memoirs; "yet, fettered by the partial laws of society, this fair globe was to me an universal blank" (*Wrongs*, ch. X; 2:34). "For the Book of knowledge fair / Presented with a Universal blanc / Of Natures works to mee expung'd and ras'd, / And wisdom at one entrance quite shut out," laments blind Milton (*PL* 3.47–50). In *Rights of Woman* the same passage is summoned to gloss the social fate that deems female purity "incompatible with knowledge": "Thus is the fair book of knowledge to be shut with an everlasting seal!" (277).

Milton's catastrophes stay in Wollstonecraft's head. Writing to Imlay from civil warring Paris, she echoes Milton's Republican despair: "'I am fallen,' as Milton said, 'on evil days;' for I really believe that Europe will be in a state of convulsion" (Letter X; *Post. W* 3: 24–25, quoting *PL* 7.25). Near in mind is Hamlet: "My head aches, and my heart is heavy. The world appears an 'unweeded garden,' where 'things rank and vile' flourish best" (25 [*Hamlet* 1.2]). She could trace Miltonic principles smuggled into Satanic grievances: in *Rights of Men* she summons Satan's sublime crabbing about how "all the Stars / Hide their diminisht heads" in the noonday sun (*PL* 4.32–35) to bolster her refusal, in light of the "continual miseries of the poor," to lament the mere "outrages of a day" against the monarchy (the assault on Versailles, 6 October 1790, by a starving mob): "Let those sorrows hide their diminished head before the tremendous mountain of woe that thus defaces our globe!" (151–52). Only self-pitying Satan could elide this magnitude (and even he is an incipient republican); royal laments pale in the darkness visible of global tyranny. At the outset of *Rights of Woman*, this Satan-voice is reiterated to subtend the argument for "natural rights" over "the utmost importance" of "rank and titles . . . before which Genius 'must hide its diminished head'" (18).

Even a little Pope can supply a theme. "A *little Learning* is a dang'rous Thing" (*Essay on Criticism* p. 12; 1.215) gives a keynote (unsigned, as if accepted general wisdom) for a chapter in *Thoughts on the Education of Daughters* (24). A phrase in *An Essay on Man* for how one "*ruling Passion*" can take over "in Body and in Soul"—"Grows with his Growth and strengthens with his Strength" (II.126–28)—is a Wollstonecraft favorite for saying how habits, for better or worse, become character: "the false notions" that canker budding virtue (*RM* 55); the habits that form "moral character" (*RW* 262); "the malady of genius" that engenders a "characteristic melancholy" (Letter XX, *LSR* 224). She can retool the opening line of the infamous *Of the Characters of Women* for opening lines of her own: "Most women, and men too, have no character at all," begins a chapter in *Education of Daughters* on the uses of adversity (111); or, "It has been sarcastically said, by a snarling poet, that most women have no character at all: we shall apply it to their production.—Novels," begins a scathing review of a "flimsy" tome "by a lady" (*AR* V [1798]: 488). The snarl can also be harnessed to new purpose: "I have frequently with full conviction retorted Pope's sarcasm on them," she says of men inclined to think that only women are given to a love of pleasure and a love of sway (*RW* 158).[30]

Or if she is inclined to concede a female "sexual character," she puts it into her own syntax and points it differently. Thus her retort to an adage from a categorical "poet" satirizing woman as no "accountable creature" (avatar of Jack Nicholson's Melvin Udall, the novelist in the film *As Good as it Gets* who, when asked by a female fan how he can "write women so well," snarks, "I think of a man, and I take away reason and accountability"):

The poet then should have dropped his sneer when he says,

"If weak women go astray,
The stars are more in fault than they."

For that they are bound by the adamantine chain of destiny is most
certain, if it be proved that they are never to exercise their own reason, never to be independent, never to rise above opinion, or to feel
the dignity of a rational will . . .   (*RW* 70–71; cf. 93)

Wollstonecraft submits the poet's *If* to a crafty *if* of her own. Poet Prior's
If issues in the indirect rationalizing discourse of the errant young wife
of "*Hans Carvel*, impotent and old" (1):

She made it plain, that human Passion
Was order'd by Predestination;
That if weak women went astray
Their Stars were more at fault than they . . .   (*Hans Carvel* 9–12)

Wollstonecraft's *if* reframes the urbane satire for analysis; the contempt
of the "poet" for star-faulting women ought to be aimed at male social
astrology, the adamantine destiny, from Adam downward, that has made
women into weak creatures of passion.[31]

If antifeminist poetry can be drafted into *Rights of Woman*, so can
Shakespeare's satirists. "But what have women to do in society? I may be
asked, but to loiter with easy grace," answers the vindicator, voicing Iago
with a protest of difference: "surely you would not condemn them all to
suckle fools and chronicle small beer!" (*RW* 337).[32] She elides Desdemona's retort to this "most lame and impotent conclusion" (*Othello* 2.1.160–
61), finding the male satirists more pungent—including Hamlet. "You jig
and amble, and you lisp, you nickname God's creatures," he sneers at Ophelia, contemptuous of her face-"painting" and hissing her off to "a nunnery"
(3.1.146–51). If Hamlet's contempt bubbles in a bile of personal melancholy, poet Burke, as Wollstonecraft is painfully aware, promotes the report to general aesthetic theory: truly "sensible" women know that "to lisp,
to totter in their walk, to counterfeit weakness, and even sickness" will
constitute "the most affecting beauty" (*Enquiry* 91; Part Three, sect. IX).

Rights of Men satirizes this Burked Hamlet: "to be loved, women's
high end and great distinction! they should 'learn to lisp, to totter in their

walk, and nick-name God's creatures' . . . that Nature, by making women *little, smooth, delicate, fair* creatures, never designed that they should exercise their reason" (80). Introducing *Rights of Woman*, Wollstonecraft enlists Hamlet's tirade to lament "the present conduct of the sex" (abetted by Burke's aesthetics): "they dress; they paint, and nickname God's creatures—Surely these weak beings are only fit for a seraglio!" (9).[33] Reviewing a book on Shakespeare's women that tendered "cordial praise" to Ophelia, she allies with Hamlet's anger at her collusion with her father and her king: "Her conduct was mean and unjust; if she acted like a female we pity her weakness, but should not either praise or palliate a fault that no mistaken notion of duty could justify without confounding the distinction between virtue and vice" (*AR* II [1788], 460). Mindful of the recruitment of Shakespeare's female characters for lessons in conduct, she holds Ophelia to a sex-neutral judgment.

The allegiance with Hamlet, as may be apparent, can draw the vindicator of woman's rights into bitter satires that set her apart from, and against, her sex: Hamlet's she-hating *you* compounds with her alienated *they*. That Wollstonecraft felt the strain of this alienation is reflected in a slight alteration in her next voicing of Hamlet in *Rights of Woman*, in exasperation with Dr. Gregory's *Legacy*-advice to his daughters to hide their intelligence. "It is this system of dissimulation . . . that I despise": "Women are always to *seem* to be this and that—yet virtue might apostrophize them, in the words of Hamlet—Seems! I know not seems!— Have that within that passeth show!" (220–21). She refracts Hamlet's self-defining alienation from a corrupt court, "*I* have that within . . ." (1.2.76–86)—into an imperative of virtue, set against male strictures on amiable accomplishments.[34]

But poetry is a various field for Wollstonecraft: satire jostles with sentiment, critique with surprising identification, reservation with respect. Cool to the intellectual and moral temper of the First Pair's innocence, Wollstonecraft can warm to their intimacy. When she writes to her lover Imlay the year after the publication of *Rights of Woman*, she alludes to Eve's retreat from Raphael's seminar in favor of a sequel, "Adam relating, she sole auditress" (this is the very run of verse that will supply Cœlebs' rebuke to the objections of "some sprightly lady, fresh from the Royal Institution"; 11):

... hee, she knew, would intermix
Grateful digressions, and solve high dispute
With conjugal Caresses, from his Lip
Not Words alone pleas'd her.   (*PL* 8.54–57)

"Mary" will hold some news until she sees her beloved because "I like to
see your eyes praise me; and, Milton insinuates, that, during such recit-
als, there are interruptions, not ungrateful to the heart, when the honey
that drops from the lips is not merely words" (spring 1793; *CL* 223). It is
with a taste for honey that she anticipates a philosophy seminar with
Godwin: "You are to give me a lesson this evening—And, a word in your
ear, I shall not be very angry if you sweeten grammatical disquisitions
after the Miltonic mode" (15 September 1796; *CL* 365).[35]

"[T]hose who feel lively emotions wish to know if the same string vibrates in another bosom—if they are indeed tied to their species by the
strongest of all relations, fellow-feeling," opens an essay Wollstonecraft
wrote for *Analytical Review* back in 1788 (II, 431). The poetry of the
heart was one way to know this. In the same year that she issued the
rational-principled *Rights of Woman,* she could despise two poets' versions of Eloisa for their inadequacy to the "passionate sorrow and tender
melancholy, delicately though forcibly expressed" in Eloisa's own letters
to Abelard (*AR* XIII, 59–60). "The following Letters may possibly be
found to contain the finest examples of the language of sentiment and
passion ever presented to the world." This is not Wollstonecraft on Eloisa's letters to Abelard; it is the opening sentence of Godwin's preface to
her letters to Imlay (*Post. W,* v. 3). That the language of passion and sentiment could bear fatal as well as enlivening feeling, Wollstonecraft
would admit: "on examining my heart, I find that it is so constituted, I
cannot live without some particular affection—I am afraid not without a
passion," she writes to fading lover Imlay in 1795, in a precipitously dark-
ening state of mind.[36] Across this summer of despairing exile from this
"beloved," poetry is her resource for sympathy. The first of her *Letters
Written During a Short Residence in Sweden, Norway and Denmark*
(1796), addressed to but not naming Imlay, tells of seeing "some heart's
ease," adding, "If you are deep read in Shakspeare, you will recollect that
this was the little western flower tinged by love's dart, which 'maidens
call love in idleness'" (10). She implies the lore of *A Midsummer Night's*

Dream: the western flower, "purple with love's wound," has a power to pain women with men's inconstancy.[37]

In publishing the private letters to Imlay, Godwin plays to the poetic aura and commercial appeal of a famous literary type, the fatal sensation of the 1770s: "They bear a striking resemblance to the celebrated romance of Werter. . . . Probably the readers to whom Werter is incapable of affording pleasure, will receive no delight from the present publication," he advises, advertising the cache as "the offspring of a glowing imagination, and a heart penetrated with the passions it essays to describe" (*Post. W,* v. 3). Godwin's simultaneously issued *Memoirs* dubbed Wollstonecraft "a female Werter" (112).[38] If, for Wollstonecraft herself, suicidal Werter was too intimate an identification, in Denmark she could vibrate to Hamlet as the genius loci. On wartime business there in 1795, she laments the perpetual life-wasting "war, and 'the thousand natural ills which flesh is heir to'" (Letter XXII; *LSR* 241), and loads Hamlet's voice with her own heartache:

my oppressed heart too often sighs out,

'How dull, flat, and unprofitable
Are to me all the usages of this world—
That it should come to this!'—

Farewell! Fare thee well, I say—if thou can'st, repeat the adieu in a different tone. (Letter XXI; *LSR* 231–32)

Betrayed by Gertrude's hasty remarriage, Hamlet is suicidal, a mood Wollstonecraft channels into her miserable communication to faithless lover Imlay.

In the years before this desperate imitation, her *Analytical* reviews of Werterism had waxed increasingly satiric about female investments, especially in the Werter-romance on which a market-savvy Charlotte Smith was not shy to capitalize.[39] Even so, Smith's poetic talents continued to interest Wollstonecraft. She thought Smith a better poet than novelist, and thought the best passages of the novels were the poetry or moments when "she looks at nature with a poet's eye" (a review of *Ethelinde, or the Recluse of the Lakes; AR* V, 484). Wollstonecraft's affection for the poet's eye, like Wordsworth's, is deeply involved with her sense of the humanity of the natural passions. In the essay that opens with those comments on ties of strong fellow feeling (*AR* II [1788]), she proposed that whatever the "dissimilitude of forms" in material cultures, a "degree of uniformity" could be discerned in all human passions.[40] These passions come to vivid aesthetic life in

> the glowing minds that concentrate pictures for their fellow-creatures; forcing them to view with interest the object reflected from the impassioned imagination, which they passed over in nature. . . . The generality of people cannot see or feel poetically . . . but when an author lends them his eyes they can see as he saw.

So writes the author of *A Vindication of the Rights of Woman* (261), ten years ahead of the Preface to *Lyrical Ballads*.[41] "I am more and more convinced," Wollstonecraft wrote in her "Hints" for a sequel to this vindication, "that poetry is the first effervescence of the imagination, and the forerunner of civilization" (#23; 189). To see her add "The passions speak most eloquently, when they are not shackled by reason" (#25; 189) is to see the continuing attachment to imaginative power that reason has no right to rein in (*RM* 61).

Yet the polemics of these vindications embarrass such convictions because in the history of civilization poetry can prove the enemy of reason. *Rights of Woman*, ruing and satirizing the civilized deformation of "woman" as a homology of poetic artifice, indicts a conspiracy of "novels, music, poetry, and gallantry" for producing these "creatures of sensation" (130). W. Q. concludes *On Poetry* chiming with this thesis: "when sensation, rather than reason, imparts delight," it "frequently makes a libertine," leading a man "to prefer the tumult of love, a little refined by sentiment, to the calm pleasure of affectionate friendship, in whose sober satisfactions, reason" holds sway (282).[42] It's Eve everywhere. So exquisitely is Wollstonecraft tuned to the real language of men in this senseless respect that it pains her to hear the "same sentiments" voiced by such "women of superiour sense" as Barbauld (*RW* 113), a rare sister in the progressive circles of 1790s London.[43]

Back in 1787, in *Thoughts on the Education of Daughters*, Wollstonecraft was happy to recommend Barbauld's *Hymns in Prose for Children* as a great help from this "ingenious author" in "mak[ing] the Deity obvious to the senses" (16–17).[44] Even in *Rights of Woman*, she finds occasion to admire Barbauld's good moral sense and to enlist her poetry for cautions about the shallow praise accorded to women's beauty:

"In beauty's empire is no mean,
And woman, either slave or queen,
Is quickly scorn'd when not ador'd."

But the adoration comes first, and the scorn is not anticipated.   (119)

The poetry is the voice of an "aged Shepherd" advising lovelorn Araminta of this cold truth (*Song V; 1773 Poems*)—Barbauld's quick near rhyme of *scorn'd* to *ador'd* giving the lie to Pope's oft-cited claim that "ev'ry Lady would be Queen for life" (*To a Lady* 218). Wollstonecraft also rather liked this couplet from Barbauld's complement to her friend, Joseph Priestley's wife, *To Mrs. P—, with some Drawings of Birds and Insects:*

Pleasure's the portion of th' *inferior* kind;
But glory, virtue, Heaven for *man* design'd.
                                    (*RW* 113 [*Poems* 1773])

Barbauld uses *man* to denote the categorically human being, superior to the birdbrain. So when Barbauld endorses Beauty's empire, Wollstonecraft is sorry, very sorry.[45] "After writing these lines, how could Mrs. Barbauld write the following ignoble comparison?" she exclaims. The stinging offence is *To a Lady, with some painted flowers* (*Poems*, 1773), a piece of post-Pope botany that Wollstonecraft quotes full in a note (*RW* 113), scoring the offenses with her own capitals and italics:

"Flowers to the fair: to you these flowers I bring,
And strive to greet you with an earlier spring.
Flowers SWEET, *and gay, and* DELICATE LIKE YOU;
Emblems of innocence, and beauty too.
With flowers the Graces bind their yellow hair,
And flowery wreaths consenting lovers wear.
Flowers, the sole luxury which nature knew,
In Eden's pure and guiltless garden grew.
To loftier forms are rougher tasks assign'd;
The sheltering oak, resists the stormy wind,
The tougher yew repels invading foes,

And the tall pine for future navies grows;
But this soft family, to cares unknown,
Were born for pleasure and delight ALONE.
Gay without toil, and lovely without art,
They spring to CHEER *the sense, and* GLAD *the heart.*
Nor blush, my fair, to own you copy these;
Your BEST, *your* SWEETEST *empire* is—to PLEASE."

"So the men tell us," Wollstonecraft dryly remarks, with this dose of moral reason: "but virtue, says reason [this authority added in the second edition], must be acquired by *rough* toils, and useful struggles with worldly *cares*" (113; cp. 1st ed. 113). Degendering both Milton-manned reason and male-rooted *virtue (vir)*, she refutes the florid lexicon that "nips reason in the bud,"—thus she exfoliates the metaphor (118). In the measure of reason, Barbauld is a sad ally with that species of poetic *"courtesy"* by which women, "commonly called Ladies," figure as repositories of "the negative virtues only . . . incompatible with any vigorous exertion of intellect" (123).

Wollstonecraft's adroit textual tactics with the poet's inventory would recoil in a textualizing of "Wollstonecraft" herself in poems designed to praise or bury her. How she was read and read into the social-text of 1790s feminism is a scene of volatile interaction, with consequences for "woman" across the next two centuries.

CHAPTER THREE

The Poets' "Wollstonecraft"

P RAISED SHE WAS, by sentimental and political allies; but the stronger reflux was the acid wave that crested just after her death, thanks to Godwin, who in grieving devotion to the full story, rushed into print his *Memoirs of the Author of the Vindication of the Rights of Woman* (1798). Notwithstanding his intent to honor Wollstonecraft as "Author" and honor her *Vindication*, the revelations he tendered within, on principles of candor (suicide attempts, unmarried cohabitation and childbirth), cast forth a "Wollstonecraft" that balked admirers and gave enemies ears to rapture. So lavishly did Richard Polwhele quote the scandals of *Memoirs* in footnotes to *The Unsex'd Females* (1798), that one might think his couplets were crafted just as convenient scaffolding.

The attacks on Wollstonecraft and her principles had remarkable longevity. It was still possible in 1947 to describe her philosophy as psychopathology and sexual deviance.[1] In the 1970s, the mainstream press could chirp schoolboy misogyny. Open the pages of the *New York Review of Books* in 1972, and you'll find David Levine's cartoon of an angry, sour, glowering Wollstonecraft. Two years on, Oxford don Richard Cobb lectured on the front page of *TLS* that Wollstonecraft was "always silly: she was almost always egotistical; and she was generally envious, rancorous, and meddlesome." "Mary's very surname [he sagely advised] has about it an unmistakable ring of crankiness, ungainliness, and discomfort, a promise of puritanism and serious intent"[2] (so pleased was he with his unmistaking ear, that he was deaf to the joke-potential of his own surname.) Reprising the late 1790s rants against all women's rights (modest as the terms were), the misogynist sniggers of the 1970s wielded a "Wollstonecraft" to impugn the (then-called) "women's liberation movement."

The demographic that she would vindicate also had problems. "There is no bond of union among literary women," Anna Barbauld curtly replied when Maria Edgeworth proposed in 1804 that they edit a periodical of this community (Le Breton 86–87). Barbauld cited "different sentiments," a divergence that Wollstonecraft had made evident in her remarks on several literary women in *Rights of Woman,* including Barbauld. By 1804, Barbauld had retaliated with a rebuke, which she did not publish but which she probably circulated. Pointedly titled *The Rights of Woman,* Barbauld's poem treated the "vindication" as simply vengeful power politics.

> Yes, injured Woman! rise, assert thy right!
> Woman! too long degraded, scorned, opprest . . .   (1–2)[3]

In a mocking distortion of Wollstonecraft's logic, Barbauld does the voice of vindication in sarcasm, and she counters with retro-Rousseauvian principles:

> O born to rule in partial Law's despite,
> Resume thy native empire o'er the breast!   (3–4)

Across the next five stanzas she hisses an agenda in militant coquetry. "Go forth arrayed in panoply divine" (5), urges Lieutenant Barbauld for a reconquest on the field of the heart: "Make treacherous Man thy subject, not thy friend" (19). It's the language of conduct advice with a vengeance, as if Rousseau's Sophie were being coached by Machiavelli.

All this turns out to be rhetorical foreplay for an assault, not on Man but on Wollstonecraft-Woman. In the serious advice of her final two stanzas, Barbauld not only judges the social revolution called for by "The Rights of Woman" a poor nurture to the heart, but celebrates the heart as the only vanquisher of tyranny:

> Then, then, abandon each ambitious thought,
> Conquest or rule thy heart shall feebly move,
> In Nature's school, by her soft maxims taught,
> That separate rights are lost in mutual love.   (29–32)

Under Barbauld's management, the school of "Nature" is no cover term for culture; it is counterculture, a separate peace outside the partialities of "Law."

In Barbauld's review of Wollstonecraft, Anne Mellor reads a seriously modest proposal: a moderate's correction of a radical opposition.[4] But Barbauld's poetry represents a *Vindication* that is more aggressive, more radical than Wollstonecraft's *Rights of Woman* is. Like conservative contemporaries such as More, Wollstonecraft disdains coquetry as conquest. She shares Barbauld's ideal of mutual love, aligning it to the principles of democratic, progressive education that Anna Laetitia Aikin imbibed in the dissenting culture of Warrington Academy. Here is Wollstonecraft animadverting on the master philosophy of education in *Emile:*

> "Educate women like men," says Rousseau, "and the more they resemble our sex the less power will they have over us." This is the very point I aim at. I do not wish them to have power over men; but over themselves.
>
> In the same strain have I heard men argue against instructing the poor. (*RW* 134)

From the sarcasm about power politics to a return to "Nature's School" that seems like tweaked Rousseau, Barbauld seems to get wrong the argument of *Rights,* perversely misreading it, or just plain misrepresenting it. Such warping registers the deepest challenge of *A Vindication of the Rights of Woman, with Strictures on Political and Moral Subjects* for the 1790s: its conceptual impossibility. Even as Barbauld recognizes "partial Law" (3), she can't envision legal reform: "Law" seems as immutable as "Nature." Wollstonecraft drives her polemic to a call for "A REVOLUTION IN FEMALE MANNERS" (414). Barbauld issues less a refutation of than a testimony to the radical ideal; reform can't be imagined except in monstrous form. Chastened by her own disappointments of agency in the public sphere, Barbauld figures a "Wollstonecraft" that serves to exorcise her political impulses, and to find a settlement of apolitical privacy as the higher wisdom.

Even Wollstonecraft's admirers were uncomfortable with Wollstonecraft's politics. John Henry Colls signals a warmly inspired tribute in his title, *A Poetical Epistle Addressed to Miss Wollstonecraft Occasioned by Reading her Celebrated "Essay on the Rights of Woman" and Her "Historical and Moral View of the French Revolution"* (1795). But the opening sentence of his lengthy "Dedication" makes it clear that his admiration of her "mental acumen and logical definition" should not be "understood as including [any] approbation" of her views on the French Revolution. From a post-Terror gloom, Colls voices the distress of many initial idealists (including Wollstonecraft herself):

Callous indeed must have been the heart, that did not exult in the emancipation of twenty-five millions of men, from the tyranny of a despotic Government; but, how much *more* callous must be the heart, that does not shrink with horror at the enormities resulting from a licentious abuse of their liberty. (vi–vii)

"I can admire your abilities without subscribing myself a proselyte to your political creed," he closes (ix). Thus immunized, thus differentiated, Colls can advocate the rights of woman.

In his sequel to her celebrated tract, Colls unfurls a handsome homage of nearly a hundred heroic couplets, beginning with an endorsement of her argument for education:[5]

> Shall men with men each social blessing share,
> And doom to mean servility the fair?
> Unjustly claim an arbitrary sway,
> And reign the petty monarchs of a day? (9–12; pp. 11–12)

What follows could be *Rights of Woman* in heroic couplet verse:

> ... form'd by nature for the self same ends,
> *Each* on the *whole*, for social bliss depends;
> That, *Sex* to *Sex*, for mutual succor clings,
> And all our diff'rence from our treatment springs.
> What then is *Woman* on the *present plan?*
> The splendid plaything of tyrannic man—
> His equal, only in a wanton hour,
> When lawless lust subdues the tyrant's pow'r;
> *Then*, in fervor of illicit love,
> He deems the fair an angel from above,
> Enraptur'd gazes on her form and face,
> And thinks each blemish a superior grace;
> At length, all blushing from the traitor's arms
> She springs, divested of her wonted charms,
> Condemn'd to bear, for having been too kind,
> A frame polluted and a wounded mind. (61–76; pp. 14–15)

The verse is crafted and calculated to refute Pope in his own favorite measure. On behalf of Wollstonecraft and women in general, Colls summons Pope's satires and redirects their aim:

"Curst be the verse, how well so e'er it flows,"
That gives a death-wound to the mind's repose,
And may contempt obscure the *Poet's fame,
Who brands the guiltless with a guilty name;
Gives truth the lie unmanly freedom takes,
And says "all women at their hearts are rakes;"
Yet such *his merit,* and *his failings* such,
We scarce can *praise* or *censure* him too much . . .   (89–96)

---

* "*Some* MEN to *business, some* to *pleasure* take,
"But *ev'ry* WOMAN is at *heart* a *rake.*
                                                  POPE.

His goodness of heart must surely be very problematical, who
could prefer such an infamous charge against the fair sex, and that
too without excerpting even his own mother.   (pp. 15–16)

Colls re-verses Pope's invectives to stab Pope himself for his wrongs to
women. In his *Epistle to Dr. Arbuthnot* Pope complained of his imitators
and impersonators,

Curst be the Verse, how well soe'er it flow,
That tends to make one worthy Man my foe,
Give Virtue scandal, Innocence a fear,
Or from the soft-ey'd Virgin steal a tear!   (279–82)

Colls puts the curse on Pope for making woman the foe of "Man." With a
Wollstonecraft twist, he compounds Pope with the sex he would slander
as *rake*—a nod to her own sarcasm on the line from *Of the Characters of
Women* (216; *RW* 264). With Wollstonecraft, Colls suggests that marriage by English custom is tantamount to a death sentence:

What time the fair-one, in the bloom of life,
Resolves "to be, or not to be"—a wife—
Parental force subverts her fix'd intent,
And gives her hand against her heart's content:
Hence many a female, from her nuptial hour,
Becomes the victim of oppressive pow'r . . .   (113–18; p. 17)

At one with Wollstonecraft's Maria in this echo of Hamlet's suicide-
soliloquy, Colls converts it into the sentence of wedlock.

Alert to the power of poetic signs in stating a public case, Colls lets fly anti-Popean zest in his summary character of a woman excluded from Pope's noble seat of thought:

> Thus WOLLSTONECRAFT, by fiery genius led,
> Entwines the laurel round the female's head;
> Contends with man for equal strength of mind,
> And claims the rights estrang'd from womankind.
> Dives to the depths of science and of art,
> And leaves to fools the conquest of the heart . . .   (147–52; pp. 18–19)

This is a heroic Wollstonecraft who benefits from the image of physical vigor and an equal contest for the prestige of heroic couplets.

But turn the political sympathies from disclaimer to distress, and Wollstonecraft's vigor is a revolt against "Nature." This is the banner, unfurled in the still radiant heat of the French Revolution at the end of the 1790s, that Reverend Polwhele shuddered at and broadcast in *The Unsex'd Females* (1798)—a satire cheered in anti-Jacobin quarters for its disciplinary zeal:

> Survey with me, what ne'er our fathers saw,
> A female band despising NATURE's law,
> As "proud defiance" flashes from their arms,
> And vengeance smothers all their softer charms.
>   *I* shudder at the new unpictur'd scene,
> Where unsex'd woman vaunts the imperious mien.   (11–16; p. 6)

"NATURE's law" is held against Wollstonecraft's *Vindication,* her "Woman" unknown in Nature's books, unpictured in art, truant from any poet's lexicon—except the lists of monstrosity. The conjured ghost is that gothic star, Shakespeare's ambitious regicide, Lady Macbeth, crying "unsex me here" to her dark spirits and abjuring all natural womanhood: "come to my woman's breasts, / And take my milk for gall" (*Macbeth* 1.5.42–49). To disdain "Nature," Polwhele contends, is to extinguish with a vengeance the "softer charms" that, from Eve downward, have distinguished the poets' woman.[6]

It's not just Wollstonecraft but, as the plural *Females* advertises, all those poetic sisters who have "caught the strain" (91–106; pp. 15–19): "SMITH," "ROBINSON," "HELEN" (Williams), "YEARSELEY," "flippant HAYS," "veteran BARBAULD" (91; p. 15), the last lamented as a poet who "deem'd her songs of Love, her Lyrics vain" (92) to publish "several political tracts" (p. 17 n.). "BURNEY" escapes this censure by cover of the "Delicious feelings and the purest taste" in her novels of female manners (196–97). Not for nothing did she leave her political *Reflections* unsigned, except as "the Author of Evelina and Cecilia" (both praised by Polwhele; p. 34 n.), and strained to assure the "Ladies" to whom she submitted her appeal that "the cause of tenderness and humanity" allowed their exertions "without the charge of presumption, or forfeiture of delicacy . . . without rivality or impropriety . . . without a blush" (prefatory "Apology" iv–v)—without, that is, being mistaken, in 1793, for the party of Wollstonecraft, not only an acerbic critic of feminine "delicacy" but the implied binary of all those *withouts*.

Polwhele's "Wollstonecraft" is set in play as both bold author and a horrific cultural signifier. So fixated is he on Godwin's *Memoirs*, that Polwhele even seems innocent of the *Vindication*, which had insisted on sexual modesty and chastity as rational, moral behavior. Anticipating Barbauld's translation of animadversion as aggression, Polwhele reports the force field gathering to transfigure Rationalist Wollstonecraft into Radical Wollstonecraft, liberal politics into libertine promiscuity:

> See Wollstonecraft, whom no decorum checks,
> Arise, the intrepid champion of her sex;
> O'er humbled man assert the sovereign claim,
> And slight the timid blush of virgin fame.
>   "Go, go (she cries) ye tribes of melting maids,
> Go, screen your softness in sequester'd shades."   (63–68; p. 13)

In the front line of his satire is Wollstonecraft's rupture of what the poets write of "her sex"—here summed as "the rapt Bard" of Rousseauvian sexual politics in a Wollstonecraft lecture:

> "Tho' the rapt Bard, your empire fond to own,
> Fall prostrate and adore your living throne,
> The living throne his hands presum'd to rear,
> Its seat a simper, and its base a tear;
> Soon shall the sex disdain the illusive sway,
> And wield the sceptre in yon blaze of day;

Ere long, each little artifice discard,
No more by weakness winning fond regard;
Nor eyes, that sparkle from their blushes, roll,
Nor catch the languors of the sick'ning soul,
Nor the quick flutter, nor the coy reserve,
But nobly boast the firm gymnastic nerve;
Nor more affect with Delicacy's fan
To hide the emotion from congenial man;
To the bold heights where glory beams, aspire,
Blend mental energy with Passion's fire,
Surpass their rivals in the powers of mind
And vindicate *the Rights of womankind."* (73–90; pp. 14–15)

Yet a strange counter-effect of this scandal-sheet is its inadvertent vindication of Wollstonecraft. Polwhele's list—"artifice discard," "no more of
weakness" or affected "Delicacy," "gymnastic" pride, aspiring for "mental
energy," "powers of mind"—iterates Wollstonecraft's basic argument.

The surest assault is launched from Powhele's surge of footnotes on
the scandals—Wollstonecraft's "love-sick" infatuation with Fuseli and "licentious love" for Imlay, her suicide attempts ("Poor maniac!"), and her
refusal of established religion (pp. 25–30). Further verses mock her failure, in "licentious love" (156; p. 26), to live by her principle of reason:

Hast thou no sense of guilt to be forgiv'n,
No comforter on earth, no hope in heaven?
Stay, stay—thine impious arrogance restrain—
What tho' the flood may quench thy burning brain,
Rash woman! can its whelming wave bestow
Oblivion, to blot out eternal woe? (163–68)

The forty-four lines (125–68) of versified scandal rival in page space the
voluminous footnote-retail of the *Memoirs* scandals (pp. 28–30). Bran-
dishing "the dire apostate, the fell suicide" (174), Polwhele even gloats
over Wollstonecraft's childbed death, discerning in the event the "visible"
"Hand of Providence" correcting her critique of "the destiny of women"
(pp. 28–30).

Polwhele dedicated his bile to T. J. Mathias, whose Preface to the
Fourth Dialogue of *The Pursuits of Literature* (1797) gave him his title,

an inspiration which Polwhele featured on his title page: "Our unsex'd female writers now instruct, or confuse, us and themselves, in the labyrinth of politics, or turn us wild with Gallic frenzy—Pursuits of Literature, Edit. 7. P. 238." (Mathias had even italicized *unsexed*, the sole instance of this alarming denomination in his entire tract.) "Gallic frenzy" is an anti-Jacobin brand name for the ideas and events of the French Revolution. Its superstructure is that icon of the gothic novel, the labyrinth, a counterworld in which proper distinctions of nation (English/Gallic), gender (females unsex'd), and decorum (wild frenzy) all conspire to contaminate and corrupt "us." Universal catastrophe looms: "the understanding and affections are either bewildered, darkened, enervated," driven on "fatal paths which would lead us all to final destruction, or to complicated misery" (7th ed., p. 5). Wollstonecraft, on the wings of her two Vindications, is the leader of this frenzy, threatening to transform the map of modern life into the architecture of a vast gothic novel.[7]

To complement Polwhele's compliment to his epithet, Mathias spewed some equally venomous anti-Wollstonecraft stanzas in a subsequent satire (*The Shade of Alexander Pope*) published the next year, and as replete as Polwhele's with such lengthy notes on Godwin's *Memoirs* as to make the verse seem a mere pretext for the annotations:

> Fierce passion's slave, she veer'd with every gust,
> Love, Rights, and Wrongs, Philosophy, and Lust.[8]

The *Anti-Jacobin Review* piled on in 1801 with *The Vision of Liberty*, a satire in dream-allegory Spenserian stanzas.[9] The visionary poet, after a sad survey of the headless corpses of the French royal family, enters "The house of liberty" (VIII), den of Voltaire, Paine, and various Jacobin criminals:

> XV
> Then saw I mounted on a braying ass,
> William and Mary, sooth, a couple jolly;
> Who married, note ye how it came to pass,
> Although each held that marriage was but folly?—
> And she of curses would discharge a volley
> If the ass stumbled, leaping pales or ditches:
> Her husband, sans-culottes, was melancholy,

For Mary verily would wear the breeches—
God help poor silly men from such usurping b-----s.

XVI

Whilom this dame the Rights of Women writ,
That is the title to her book she places,
Exhorting bashful womankind to quit
All foolish modesty, and coy grimaces;
And name their backsides as it were their faces;
Such licence loose-tongued liberty adores,
Which adds to female speech exceeding graces;
Lucky the maid that on her volume pores,
A scripture, archly fram'd, for propagating w----s.

XVII

William hath penn'd a waggon-load of stuff,
And Mary's life at last he needs must write,
Thinking her whoredoms were not known enough,
Till fairly printed off in black and white.—
With wondrous glee and pride, this simple wight
Her brothel feats of wantonnness sets down,
Being her spouse, he tells, with huge delight,
How oft she cuckolded the silly clown,
And lent, O lively piece! herself to half the town!   (p. 518)

The vision evokes *Anti-Jacobin Review and Magazine*'s debut issue (July 1798), which indexed "Prostitution" for the sake of a gleeful cross-reference, "*See* Mary Wollstonecraft" (859).

Adrienne Rich took this libel to heart in her stanza on Wollstonecraft in *Snapshots of a Daughter-in-Law* (1963), snapshots taken just as a re-invigorated Anglo-American feminism was emerging. Her epigraph is poeticized from *Thoughts on the Education of Daughters* (34):

> "*To have in this uncertain world some stay*
> *which cannot be undermined, is*
> *of the utmost consequence.*"
>   Thus wrote
> a woman, partly brave and partly good,
> who fought with what she partly understood.

Few men about her would or could do more,
hence she was labeled harpy, shrew and whore.   (section 7)

Rich is only partly right, however, for there were a few good men in Wollstonecraft's own day, in addition to Colls, who contested the labeling, adhesive though it was.

William Roscoe's satirical *The Life, Death and Wonderful Atchievements of Edmund Burke: a new ballad* (1791) was one of the first, praising Wollstonecraft's attack on Burke's *Reflections on the Revolution in France* in *Vindication of the Rights of Men*—a tribute for which she thanked Roscoe as she was finishing her next *Vindication* (3 January 1792; *CL* 194). The news that this first *Vindication* was a woman's writing had roiled the initial reviews,[10] and Roscoe hails this extraordinary event of female confrontation:

An lo! an Amazon stept out,
    One Wolstoncraft her name,
Resolv'd to stop his mad career,
    Whatever chance became.

An oaken sapling in her hand,
    Full on the foe she fell,
Nor could his coat of rusty steel
    Her vig'rous strokes repel.

When strange to see, her conq'ring staff,
    Returning leaves o'erspread,
Of which a verdant wreath was wove,
    And bound around her head.   (7)

In Roscoe's baroque image, the oaken weapon that figures pen generates Wollstonecraft's honors: it sprouts the leaves (punning pages) for the head wreath that designates a (usually male) laureate. This was John Opie's serious woman of letters, too: a level gaze, a book, and no frills.

To similar gender-bending praise, in the wake of *Rights of Woman*, George Dyer, a poet of Wollstonecraft's London circle, was inspired. His *Ode on Liberty* (1792) hails Liberty for having chosen "to warm / With more than manly fire the female breast," fueling "Wollstonecraft to break the charm, / Where beauty lies in durance vile opprest" (36). Dyer appends a lengthy note:

Mary Wollstonecraft, engraving by Timothy Cole, from an oil
painting by John Opie, 1792. *Century Magazine* vol. 57/4, February
1899. This issue contains an article on Cole. The image conveys an
unfussy woman of letters, the Enlightenment Rationalist for the
1790s, and just the icon for the "new woman" of the 1890s, when it
was possible to talk about and write about Wollstonecraft again,
without stigma or scandal.

*Author of the Rights of Woman.——I have observed, that the most sensible females, when they turn their attention to political subjects, are more uniformly on the side of liberty than the other sex. This may be accounted for without adopting the sentiments or the language of gallantry. The truth is, that the modes of education and the customs of society are degrading to the female character; and the tyranny of custom is sometimes worse than the tyranny of government. When a sensible woman rises above the tyranny of custom, she feels a generous indignation; which, when turned against the exclusive claims of the other sex, is favourable to female pretensions; when turned against the tyranny of government, it is commonly favourable to the rights of both sexes. Most governments are partial, and more injurious to women than to men. (36)

Where Rich will reiterate *partly* to mean "incompletely" and "with a bias," Dyer locates all fault in a system of injurious "partial" privileges—what even Barbauld concedes in "The Rights of Woman" is a system of "partial Law."

Dyer puts Wollstonecraft in impressive female company, including Barbauld, Williams, Smith, and Catharine Macaulay, the sorority that Polwhele will indict. Robert Southey summons a different company, heroic women from the page of history. Rebuking Horace Walpole for a famously poor opinion of women, Southey argues a "directly opposite conclusion":

I find purer & more affection and more constancy — take this last word not in its general confined sense — but in a more extensive signification. were I a heathen I would build a temple & worship the Maid of Orleans— Charlotte Corde— & the wife of Roland. by the by it were better to distinguish him as the husband of such a woman, than her as the wife only of even so excellent a man. she was indeed a wonderful woman. I repent me of saying so little of her in Joan of Arc — & I repent me more of omitting to speak of Charlotte Corde. these women ought to be mentioned in another edition & the edition to be dedicated to Mary Wollstonecraft. of this last woman you may perhaps not know the miserable situation. she married Imlay- — who used her wickedly & left her. she struggled with calamity awhile — but it is not many weeks since she attempted to drown herself! — she is an

excellent woman — of mild — feminine & unassuming manners. & xx
whose character calumny cannot blacken.   (12 June 1796; *CL* #160)

Southey admired *Rights of Woman* (12 June 1796; *CL* #159), and he
would soon go public with praise of Wollstonecraft's unique excellence.
In some elegiac verses of 1797 (*To A. S. Cottle, from Robert Southey*), he
honors her as one

> Who among women left no equal mind
> When from this world she pass'd; and I could weep,
> To think that *She* is to the grave gone down!   (90–92)

Southey had already written *To Mary Wolstoncraft* (1795–97), a dedication for *The Triumph of Woman* (in *Poems*, 1797), tuned to restore to this
nonpareil some of the usual poets' praises:

> The lilly cheek, the 'purple light of love,'
> The liquid lustre of the melting eye, —
> Mary! of these the Poet sung, for these
> Did Woman triumph! with no angry frown
> View this degrading conquest. At that age
> No MAID OF ARC had snatch'd from coward man
> The heaven-blest sword of Liberty; thy sex
> Could boast no female ROLAND's martyrdom;
> No CORDE's angel and avenging arm
> Had sanctified again the Murderer's name
> As erst when Caesar perish'd: yet some strains
> May even adorn this theme, befitting me
> To offer, nor unworthy thy regard.[11]

Despite the heroic company (political martyrs Jeanne d'Arc, Mme.
Roland, Charlotte Corday), the phrase quoted in line 1 is red meat for
Wollstonecraft-animadversion: "O'er her warm cheek and rising bosom
move / The bloom of young desire and purple light of love," sighs Gray in
The Progress of Poetry (40–41). Southey had not yet met Wollstonecraft,
but, admiring her passion, he hoped a "Poet" might proffer some of the
old tributes, seasoned with modern consciousness.[12] His revisions of this
near-sonnet (a form curtailed for his modern praise) relay conflicts of
admiration and unease about an unpoetic "feminine" figure: "angry

frown" loses the intensifying adjective from 1815 on, and so is softened a bit; but from 1808 to 1823, "heaven-blest sword of Liberty" becomes a more Tory-honed "avenging sword of Freedom"; by 1837, Roland is not a martyr, nor Cordé an "angel," just a "self-sacrificing" zealot. Zigzagging more than consolidating, Southey's revisions reflect the force of Wollstonecraft in unsettling even a Tory poet laureate, during decades when it was fairly routine to disparage her, if mention her at all.[13]

Coleridge had talked over the codes of praise with his brother-in-law Southey, and then wrote an essay to lead off the 17 March 1796 *Watchman*, in which he spoke back to Gibbon's disdain of "the dignity" of women in ancient Germany:

> "heroines of such a cast may claim our admiration; but they were most assuredly neither lovely, nor very susceptible of love. Whilst they affected to emulate the stern virtues of *man,* they must have resigned the attractive softness in which principally consists the charm and weakness of *woman.*" Of this I must say with Mary Woolstonecraft, "that it is the philosophy of sensuality." The women of Germany were the free and equal companions of their husbands; they were treated by them with esteem and confidence, and consulted on every occasion of importance. What then, is this love which woman loses by becoming respectable? (90–91)[14]

Godwin's *Memoirs* met the question in 1798, by insisting that the polemicist was "feminine" at heart (83). Registering the static that Polwhele electrifies, he admits that some phases of *Rights of Woman* display a "rigid, and somewhat amazonian temper" but ascribes this to the "character of [a] performance," insisting that this character was distinct from "the person of the author," which he renders with poetic resourcefulness: "a luxuriance of imagination, and a trembling delicacy of sentiment, which would have done honour to a poet, bursting with all the visions of an Armida and a Dido" (81–82)—women (in the poetry of Tasso and Virgil) who, for all their powers, commit suicide when abandoned by the men they love. He revised *bursting* to *burning* in the second edition.

Coleridge's former pupil Charles Lloyd, though an anti-Godwinian and an anti-Jacobin pack-runner in the late 1790s (especially in his novel *Edmund Oliver*), was enchanted. Fresh from reading Godwin's *Memoirs, The Wrongs of Woman,* and the letters to Imlay, he wrote *Lines to Mary*

Wollstonecraft Godwin, an elegy as fervent in affection for her as in disaffection from her polemics. "I am happy in being able to offer this imperfect tribute to the memory of a woman, whose undeserved sufferings have excited my indignation and pity; and whose virtues, both of heart and mind, my warmest esteem," begins a headnote, which proceeds to "avow a complete dissent from Mrs. Godwin with regard to almost all her moral speculations"—by which he meant *The Wrongs of Woman,* which he quotes with incredulity:

> so far from convincing me that "the misery and oppression peculiar
> to women arise out of the partial laws of society"[15] . . . the source of
> the miseries she complained of must rather be sought for in the brute
> turbulencies of human nature, than in the operation of any laws,
> conventional or positive.   (64–65)

Having said this, he also wants to say that "the heart and upright dignity of this excellent woman have much interested me" (65). For an epigraph, he taps a lonely heartfelt letter to absent Imlay:

> "On examining my heart, I find that it is so constituted, I cannot live
> without some particular affection. I am afraid not without a passion;
> and I feel the want of it more in society than in solitude." *Mary Woll-*
> *stonecraft Godwin's Letters, vol. i. p.* 178.   (66)[16]

Elevating passion over politics, Lloyd writes his ode as an elegiac valentine to "MARY":

> Amid the trials of this difficult world,
> Surely none press so sorely on the heart
> As disappointed loves, and impulses
> (Mingling the lonely insulated soul
> With all surrounding and external things)
> Sever'd from nature's destined sympathies!
> This was thy lot on earth! . . .
>   Therefore thou,
> Though here tormented, shalt in better worlds
> Be greatly comforted!   (pp. 67–68)

Shearing the social surnames "Wollstonecraft Godwin," Lloyd shapes his "Mary" as a tragic type, bereft of sympathy and love—a plight felt on his own troubled pulse, too.

So, too, a poet in the Joseph Johnson circle saw in the abuse of Wollstonecraft, especially after the *Memoirs,* a mirror of his own felt persecution for heterodoxy. In *Mary* (1802–3, published in 1866), Blake celebrates a martyr: an unembarrassed, radiant beauty (9–12) with a bountiful hand (23) (the work of her pen), meeting hostile reception and vile representation: "Some said she was proud some calld her a whore / And some when she passed by shut to the door" (16–17). Blake's calumniated "Mary" is a martyr to her ideals:[17]

> She went out in Morning in plain neat attire
> And came home in Evening bespatterd with mire
>
> . . . .
>
> With Faces of Scorn & with Eyes of disdain
> Like foul fiends inhabiting Marys mild Brain
> She remembers no Face like the Human Divine
> All Faces have Envy sweet Mary but thine
>
> And thine is a Face of sweet Love in Despair
> And thine is a Face of mild sorrow & care
> And thine is a Face of wild terror & fear
> That shall never be quiet till laid on its bier.   (35–36; 41–48)

With few exceptions, nineteenth-century British culture laid Wollstonecraft on a bier, burying her challenges in the scandal of her name.

Yet for some radical poets she remained a living light. In the Dedication of *Laon and Cythna* (1818) to his new wife, Mary Wollstonecraft Godwin, Percy Shelley eulogizes her mother, one of her "glorious parents" (101), as both a lost light and a continuing inspiration to his own political idealism:

> One then left this Earth
> Whose life was like a setting planet mild,
> Which clothed thee in the radiance undefiled
> Of its departing glory; still her fame
> Shines on thee, through the tempests dark and wild
> Which shake these latter days . . .   (stanza 12)

In the shining light is Wollstonecraft's rational enlightenment: "a fine woman, who inspires more sublime emotions by displaying intellectual beauty," she sighed in *Rights of Woman,* "may be overlooked or observed

with indifference, by those men who find their happiness in the gratification of their appetites" (160). This lament was redeemed by Godwin's
praise of her "intuitive perception of intellectual beauty" (*Memoirs* 196),[18]
then by Shelley, who found a title for a poetic declaration he wrote in
1816: *Hymn to Intellectual Beauty.*

Even Eve-admiring William Hazlitt could be derailed by Wollstonecraft. She could halt his usual tendency across a question about the suffi-
ciency of Pope's aphorism:

> The character of women (I should think it will at this time of day be
> granted) differs essentially from that of men, not less so than their
> shape or the texture of their skin. It has been said indeed, "most
> women have no character at all,"—and on the other hand, the fair and
> eloquent authoress of the Rights of Women was for establishing the
> masculine pretensions and privileges of her sex of a perfect quality
> with ours. I shall leave Pope and Mary Wolstonecraft to settle that
> point between them.   ("On Personal Character" 294)

Two years on, in 1823, Hazlitt turns the point a bit by producing a Wollstonecraft imbued with the poetic faculty of "imagination." Coleridge
had asked him if he had ever seen her,

> and I said, I had once for a few moments, and that she seemed to me
> to turn off Godwin's objections to something she advanced with quite
> a playful, easy air. [Coleridge] replied, that "this was only one in-
> stance of the ascendancy which people of imagination exercise over
> those of mere intellect."   ("My first Acquaintance" 30–31)

And hence, a poet's intellectual beauty.

In the textual imaginary of *The Wrongs of Woman*, the beauty of poetry is less decided, however, still involved with Wollstonecraft's hesita-
tions. In the madhouse, Maria hears another inmate, said to be "a lovely
maniac," singing "the pathetic ballad of old Robin Gray with the most
heart-melting falls and pauses." It's Anne Lindsay's popular ballad (first
published in the 1770s): the pathetic singer has been compelled by dire
economic hardship to accept the hand of good kind old Rob, forsaking
her beloved Jamie, gone to sea to earn enough to marry her. Jamie returns, alas too late, and the lovers part, miserably. Wangling a visit to the
maniac's chamber, Maria expects to encounter a soul sister in the "lovely

warbler," only to be appalled when "a torrent of unconnected exclamations and questions burst from her, interrupted by fits of laughter, so horrid, that Maria shut the door" (ch. II; 1:38). She learns that the maniac was deranged by the darkest version of the ballad-fable: a loveless marriage to a brutally jealous, rich old husband. The poetry enchants Maria in delusion; the material performance is a shocking demystification.

Yet if the narrative question about Maria is how securely she ever shuts the door on poetic delusion, the novel *Maria* can linger in poetic pleasure off to the side of the narrative arc and its potential ironies. In novelist Wollstonecraft's report of the trove of books that Maria receives from Darnford, one affection is imprinted:

> Dryden's Fables, Milton's Paradise Lost, with several modern productions, composed the collection. It was a mine of treasure. Some marginal notes, in Dryden's Fables, caught her attention: they were written with force and taste. (ch. II; 1:31–32)

While in the arc of narrative there are perils to Maria (the mine of books is Darnford's proxy to her), as a representation, the treasure is a Wollstonecraft poetry shelf, a site for thinking with force and taste in the margins of poetry. Maria reads, reperuses, speculates (32–33). This engagement is no passive, uncritical impressment by opinion, but an interactive dynamic: unmaking, remaking, making opinion anew—ultimately, in the root sense—"making" another poet.

Wollstonecraft's essay on reading poetry, wavering back and forth about its force in refining and in corrupting sensibility, first appeared in *Monthly Magazine*, April 1797. The next year *Lyrical Ballads* issued forth, then, in a second, expanded edition, greeted the new century with a Preface advancing the revolutionary claim that "the Poet" is a "man speaking to men." Yet it gathered in its turns not only the poetic theory that W. Q. had articulated, but also an unappeasable fascination with female passions, mad and vibrant—and, ultimately, a strange but not estrangeable recognition of female authority over poetic imagination.

II

Gender Interactions, Generative Interactions

TWO WORDSWORTHS

CHAPTER FOUR

Lyrical Ballads and the Pregnant Words of Men's Passions

Engendering Passion

"It was my wish in this poem to show the manner in which such men cleave to the same ideas, to follow the turns of passion . . . by which their conversation is swayed . . . while I adhered to the style in which such persons describe, to take care that words, which in their minds are impregnated with passion, should likewise convey passion to Readers who are not accustomed to sympathize with men feeling in that manner or using such language." So wrote William Wordsworth, in a long defensive note in the back pages of the second edition of *Lyrical Ballads* (1800), with some exasperation, but also with explicatory candor, about *The Thorn*, one of the most rebarbative experiments of the first, anonymous edition, two years before. He also took pains to explain a denaturalized formal analogue to this apparent deformation: "It seemed to me that this might be done by calling in the assistance of Lyrical and rapid Metre . . . the Poem, to be natural, should in reality move slowly; yet . . . by the aid of the metre . . . it would appear to move quickly" (1: 212). Slow gestation of passion conveyed by a quick delivery?

Eighteen years on, Coleridge was gathering notes for a public lecture in which he wanted to argue that poetry is not just impregnated words, but the impregnating force: "*N.b.* by excitement of the Associative Power passion itself imitates Order, and the *order* resulting produces a pleasurable *Passion* (whence Metre)." This involute of passion for order and order for passion, by another name, is poetic impregnation: "recalling the Sights and Sounds that had accompanied the occasions of the original passion [Poetry] impregnates them with an interest not their own by means of the Passions, and yet tempers the passion."[1]

Pope may have had good sport in *The Rape of the Lock* (1712) with an epidemic of the vapors in which "Men prove with Child, as pow'rful Fancy works" (33 [4.53]). But for these two later theorists of poetic power, the pregnancy of impassioned words is a risky affair: an inspiration, yet a problem for orderly management; a language to communicate, yet a challenge to sympathetic hearing; a force to quicken writing, yet apt to deaden on delivery. The basic poetic signifier, meter, is not even certain force: midwife to passion, or tempering counteragent? Wordsworth said his very intent was to confront poetic custom and reader-habits, to solicit unaccustomed routes of sympathy, to mobilize strangely pregnant words. No fan of the experiment, yet still mulling over the venture, Coleridge labored to theorize the force of *impregnates* not as primary passion but as a return through poetic art and order. Drawing from separate etymologies—*preindre, to press* into consciousness, and *praegnus*, generative—Wordsworth enlists the action for poetic creation and communicative power; Coleridge turns it to the art of poetry in giving sense-memory new vitality. Yet whatever the divergent theoretical vectors, a common anxiety is the proximity of the trope to the female condition and, perforce, to a field of interaction with female passions that may compromise male poetic identity.

Wordsworth seems to intuit as much by cordoning off the extravagant verbal effects as an experiment in dramatic "character" (1: 211). But across *Lyrical Ballads* such turns of voice and verse—conveying (variously) compulsion, possession, aberrant or unassignable sways of imagination—come to seem the character of poetry itself. No wonder, then, that by the 1802 *Preface* this poet is fortifying the "Poet" as "a man speaking to men" (xxviii).[2] Manning up hardly settles the question, however. Not only does one differentiation after another from "qualities that are supposed to be common among mankind" (xxviii) pile onto a qualifying elaboration, but the terms of difference—the heightened sensibility, tenderness, feeling, susceptibility to excitement in the Poet—might well describe the figures of female passion (especially maternal) populating *Lyrical Ballads*. In this aspect, the *Preface* looks like a belated defense of a poetry already in contradiction: men impregnated and perhaps unmanned by passion, and (as some reviewers said, with no approbation) apt to convey this to readers not accustomed to sympathize with men feeling in that manner or using such language. Strong passion is a potential confusion to proper sexual identifications.

The problem is containable in some cases—say, where men manly in all local lore gain a feminine complement from domestic affection or their passions focus social values. In *The Brothers*, a village priest recalls Walter Ewbank, toiling in generations "from sire to son" with a pace that "was never that of an old man" (207–23), caring for his orphan grandchildren with a mother's love:

> . . . if tears
> Shed, when he talk'd of them where they were not,
> And hauntings from the infirmity of love,
> Are aught of what makes up a mother's heart,
> This old Man in the day of his old age
> Was half a mother to them. (234–39)

Old mountain-man Michael, toiling in and for the land of his "Forefathers" (378), nurtures baby Luke with "female service" and rocks his "cradle with a woman's gentle hand" (164–68). In an essay for the *Tatler*, Sir Richard Steele half-rues his "unmanly Gentleness of Mind," mother-fed from early childhood and still breaching "defenses from my own judgment,"[3] but Wordsworth's programmatic poetics of feeling unapologetically enlists female gentleness into "the essential passions of the heart" in a man (xi).

Still, Michael and Walter are old men, in remote Lakeland. A young man in the modern world, aspiring to profession as a "Poet," has no such cover, and so hazards more in a display of female passions. The *Advertisement* for the unsigned *Lyrical Ballads* of 1798 indicated only an experiment against social prejudice: "how far the language of conversation in the middle and lower classes" might supply "a natural delineation of human passions, human characters, and human incidents" (i–ii). While class-liberal manly dignity was implied,[4] the poet who signed the *Preface* of 1800 seems to have felt some gender discriminations to be in order, to distinguish male from female passion in "the fluxes and refluxes of the mind when agitated by the great and simple affections of our nature." He indicates a "maternal passion" in *The Idiot Boy* and *The Mad Mother* and something more elevated for the men—"the strength of fraternal, or to speak more philosophically, of moral attachment" in *The Brothers* (xv–xvi).[5]

Even so, *Lyrical Ballads* has a traffic in men philosophically embarrassed by weakness. *The Last of the Flock* opens with a speaker disturbed at seeing "a healthy man, a man full grown/Weep in the public roads" (3–4); when the weeper is queried, his first words are "Shame on me, Sir!" (17). A poignant tale unfolds, but shame lingers. In *The Brothers,* Leonard's tears on learning of his brother's death strike a village priest (who doesn't recognize him) as unseemly:

> —If you weep, Sir,
> To hear a stranger talking about strangers,
> Heaven bless you when you are among your kindred!   (239–41)

A weeping man has something to answer for, to others and to himself. Though aching with fraternal attachment, Leonard regards his tears as a "weakness of his heart" (446). "Luke had a manly heart; but at these words/He sobb'd aloud," writes the poet of this filial throb (*Michael* 367–68), in syntax that pivots on *but* to turn *manly* against *sobb'd aloud.* Wordsworth's *Preface* may calibrate a manly poetics of feeling, but poetry such as this registers, and communicates, social rules that disconnect "the passions of men" (xi) from the manliness of men.

Two centuries on, gender critics would see no softie in the poet "Wordsworth," at least. He was all male discursive power, in the world, in the text. Notwithstanding the difference he urged in poetic taste, the gender hierarchy of his poetry, noted Anne Mellor, was ancien régime. Marlon Ross saw an iconic quest for "poetic identity" relying on "distinctive masculinist postures and premises"—an "aggressive male" formation "inscribed in each of the lyrics and tales that has determined Wordsworth's status in our literary canon and his influence in our cultural history." If there was a "feminine" inscription, it was a resource to be "colonized," Alan Richardson argued, for new forms of male subjectivity.[6] Thanks to these critics, such designs are part of our discussion, but what may have sunk below sight is how Wordsworth struck his contemporaries. In severest reviews, the poetry of *Lyrical Ballads* seemed fantastic, undisciplined, childish, infantile—in a word, unmanly.

Crack open the *Duties of the Female Sex,* a primer for the late 1790s and decades on, and you'll find Thomas Gisborne indexing "the dispositions and feelings of the heart" and "sympathising sensibility" as the "native worth of the female character" (23). In the first of his *Sermons to Young Women* (1765, and still strong in the 1790s, as Wollstonecraft's

Rights of Woman testifies), Rev. Fordyce felt it necessary—as he praised the influence of female conversation on men's manners (by which their "sentiments and deportment will contract a grace")—to allay a concern that men "will become feminine" from the contact (1: 23). If in his 1800 *Preface* Wordsworth put forward a poetry where "feeling . . . gives importance to the action" (xvii), by 1842 Mrs. Ellis would be gendering poetry for the Daughters of England in exactly these terms. A man has to "sacrifice" poetry "for the realities of material and animal existence"; but "for woman, whose whole life, from the cradle to the grave, is one of feeling, rather than action . . . to cast away the love of poetry, is to pervert from their natural course the sweetest and loveliest tendencies of a truly feminine mind" (73).

The "overflow of powerful feelings" that carries Wordsworth's cause (*Preface* xiv) would become a feminized current by the time he was Poet Laureate. The course was being charted even in his young manhood. If it was Burke's politics that fired Wollstonecraft's ire in *A Vindication of the Rights of Men*, it was the unmanly, too impassioned, too poetic prose that sparked her satire.[7] Sentimental manhood did gain prestige from Burke's impassioned conservatism—one could love one's country, its institutions, its royal family. But it was not as clear that poets could indulge the excesses without risks. Toward the end of his Preface, Wordsworth confesses that he has been "apprehensive" (cognizant and anxious) that his poetry may have exposed too much of this sentimental imprint,

> may frequently have suffered from those arbitrary connections of feelings and ideas with particular words, from which no man can altogether protect himself. Hence I have no doubt that in some instances feelings even of the ludicrous may be given to my Readers by expressions which appeared to me tender and pathetic.   (xxxvii)

The boldest gambit of *Lyrical Ballads*, I argue in this chapter, was the wild card of gender in the poetry of feeling.[8]

The Gender of "The Poet"

"Mr. Wordsworth, in . . . the Lyrical Ballads, gave considerable testimony of strong feeling and poetic powers, although like a histerical schoolgirl he had a knack of feeling about subjects with which feeling had no proper concern," was the divided verdict of *Le Beau Monde* in 1807 (2: 138). The liability magnetizes the satires on Burkean sentiment honed by Wollstonecraft and Paine, but its grammar is latent even in the benevolent anatomy of Adam Smith's *Theory of Moral Sentiments* (1759) and Henry Mackenzie's *Man of Feeling* (1771).[9] While advancing an ethic of manhood in distinction to the anti-sentimental masculinity of the captains of industry and war, such discourse also is a kind of free radical because affective generosity can (and often does) act across, and so confuse, sexual difference. Take, for instance, Smith's first paragraph, which urges (what Mackenzie's novel dramatizes) the moral import of one man's "pity or compassion" (1) for another man, and allies it with the imaginative dynamics of sympathetic reading:

> By the imagination, we place ourselves in his situation, we conceive ourselves enduring all the same torments, we enter as it were into his body and become in some measure him, and thence form some idea of his sensations and even feel something which, though weaker in degree, is not altogether unlike them. (2-3)[10]

But what if we enter as it were into *her* body and become in some measure *her?*

We can see why Coleridge, Wordsworth's collaborator on the 1798 *Lyrical Ballads,* wanted to desynonymize moral sentiment from sensibility, denigrating the latter as female: the thrilling of "the fine lady's nerves" as she reads and "weep[s] over the refined sorrows" of fictional characters while remaining insensitive to real atrocities. "Sensibility is not Benevolence," he railed as he wrote "On the Slave Trade" in 1796 for *The Watchman,* a newspaper for "Men of Letters" (so said the Prospectus, 4). "Nay, by making us tremblingly alive to trifling misfortunes, it frequently prevents it, and induces effeminate and cowardly selfishness" (139). Even women could voice the critique. "Where is the dignity, the infallibility of sensibility, in the fair ladies" who affect horror at slavery, and then—asks "manly" reasoner Wollstonecraft—"after the sight of flagellation, compose their ruffled spirits and exercise their tender feelings by the perusal of the last imported novel?" (*Rights of Men* 111). In her next vindication, *Rights of Woman* (on Wordsworth's bookshelf),[11] she derided fiction-fanned sensibility. Coleridge may even have drawn his hiss of contempt, "tremblingly alive," from her very first review for the

Analytical (June 1788), which satirized "the *cant* of sensibility" gushing from young women who, having battened on the latest "Sentimental Novel. By a Lady," "boast of being tremblingly alive all o'er, and faint and sigh as the novelist informs them they should" (I: 208). Although Hannah More reviled *Rights of Woman*, she could find common cause here, writing a lengthy chapter for *Strictures on Female Education* titled "On the danger of an ill-directed Sensibility,"[12] with hot censures on "young women in whom feeling is indulged to the exclusion of reason" (2: 115). Such indictment was all too trainable on the passion principle of poetry.

Coleridge was sensitive not only to this but also to the artifice of gender difference. Writing his own chapter "On Sensibility" in *Aids to Reflection, in the Formation of a Manly Character* (1825), he replaces his she-cartoon in the 1796 *Watchman* essay—that blood-sugared, tea-sipping, novel-reading lady—with self-chastising lines from his *Reflections on Having Left a Place of Retirement*, about the moral necessity to resume a manly life of political activism:

> Sensibility is not necessarily Benevolence. Nay, by rendering us tremblingly alive to trifling misfortunes, it frequently prevents it, and induces an effeminate Selfishness instead,
>
> ————————pampering the coward heart,
> With feelings all too delicate for use.
>
> .   .   .   .
>
> But even . . . *cold* benevolence,
> Seems Worth, seems Manhood, where there rise before me
> The sluggard Pity's vision-weaving Tribe,
> Who sigh for Wretchedness yet shun the wretched,
> Nursing in some delicious Solitude
> Their Slothful Loves and dainty Sympathies.
>   *Sibylline Leaves*, p. 180 (53)[13]

For the Reflector of *Aids to Reflection*, the self-indictment is a past chapter of a recovery narrative now served as exemplum for the "over-stimulated age" of the 1820s (53). In the same decade, M. J. Jewsbury could spoof the line as a Young Author's cant of sensibility: "he became possessed (as if by magic) of nerves and sensibilities . . . 'feelings all too delicate for use'" (*Young Author* 191). Coleridge's verse, merely sardonic, first appeared in the decade of Revolutions, in *Monthly Magazine* 1796, as "Reflections on Entering into Active life, *A Poem which affects Not To Be* POETRY"—i.e., not the poem of a vocational Poet. By 1797 it had the new title, from the surety of "Having Left." With this past tense, even the 1790s Reflector gets immunized, boosted by his forward march to "honourable toil" (63). Wordsworth will capture this last phrase in an early draft of *The Prelude* as he hopes for power that "May spur me on, in manhood now mature, / To honorable toil"—the epic on which he had been dallying to the disappointment of Friend-Coleridge.[14]

Yet both poets can't help but lodge "honorable toil" in ambivalent syntax. Wordsworth's guarded *May* relays the tug of "weakness" in his fond recollection of childhood days (MS. *V:* 10ᵛ), the haunt and main region of his poem so far; and Coleridge's *Reflections* is a poem of nostalgia, never doubting that "oft when after honourable toil / Rests the tir'd mind," it will "revisit" that place of retirement, still being apostrophized with an affectionate "thee" (63–65 and *ff*). He is always worrying about an unmanly sensibility, especially as a reader of passionate-pregnant poetry. He famously "wept over" Bowles's sonnets,[15] the gender effects amply indexed in the sonnet to Bowles he published in the *Morning Chronicle,* 26 December 1794. If in a footnote he admired the "manly Pathos" of Bowles's twenty-fifth sonnet, in his verse it was the "soft strains / That . . . tremblingly / Wak'd in me Fancy, Love, and Sympathy!" (1–3) that he adored. He saw the problem and, for his 1796 *Poems,* he canceled the girly *tremblingly* (worsened by a feminine-rhyme with *Sympathy!*) and inserted a new line to honor Bowles's's "mild and manliest melancholy" (8) in the insistent superlative. By the time he was writing *Biographia Literaria* (1817) Coleridge would be hailing *Tintern Abbey* as a poem of "manly reflection" (1: 79) and citing both Wordsworth and Bowles as instances of how a "contemporary *poet*" may excite the mind "in youth and commencing manhood" (2: 144).

As the Bowles-site makes clear, sonnetry, or any genre of "little songs," activates the gender question. A routine apprenticeship for a higher-minded male poet, sonnets had acquired a female imprint by the 1790s in the pathos-saturated success of another Smith, Charlotte Smith.[16] Epic was more than ever the he-genre, its themes manly strife in the world, and its compositional labors proof of manly poetic power. "The lofty Epic," More advised young women in 1777, is "reserved for the bold adventurers of the other sex" (*Essays* 7). Those of this other sex plying lesser forms had, at least, to venture bold style. When in 1796 William Taylor introduced his versions of Bürger's ballads to readers of the *Monthly Magazine,* he hit the right marks: here is a poet "every where distinguished for manly sentiment and force of style," "extraordinary powers of language," "hurrying vigour"—all "fitted to become national popular song" (1: 118).[17] Reader Wordsworth was paying attention.[18] His Preface gives the poet a heroizing capital *P,* and professional parity with the active producers and investigators of knowledge in the modern world. By the 1802 Preface, this is the front line. If female poetry was invading the magazines and bookstores with "gaudiness and inane phraseology" (vi) and truckling to "amusement and idle pleasure" (xxxii), Wordsworth's Poet is "a Man" who will entertain no "unmanly despair" (xxxi), whose task is no "degradation" (xxxiii). His style is "manly" (xxx); he writes "for men" and "thinks and feels in the spirit of the passions of men"; he expresses himself "as other men express themselves" (xli–xlii).

This 1802 Preface installs the "Poet" in "a body of men," with the "Man of Science, the Chemist and Mathematician," the "Anatomist, the Botanist, or Mineralogist" (xxxiv–viii). From the get-go in 1800, power is his byword: "all good poetry" draws on "powerful feelings" (xiv) "forcibly communicated" (xi) and continuous with "powers" in the world (xix). Such feelings, by 1802, "excite rational sympathy" (xlii), not the gushing she-kind. An Appendix endows this Poet's language with a trans-historical lineage and a "natural" sanction:

> The earliest Poets of all nations generally wrote from passion excited
> by real events; they wrote naturally, and as men: feeling powerfully as
> they did, their language was daring. (II: 237–38)

In this long historiography, passion is no trembling sentiment. It is the epic dimension of the "real": writing "as men" is a project infused with the force of nature; inspirations are heroic; language is "daring." A man-poet is also known by his skilled artistry. A Mad Mother's voice may be deranged, but the man-poet arranges ten orderly dexains. A Female Vagrant has an "artless story" (2); the poet gives it the manly treatment of thirty Spenserian stanzas—a complex "structure of verse" (Wordsworth will lecture a clueless poetess who had attempted the form) "almost insurmountably difficult" (*LY* 2: 58).

The Gender of Passion

Yet for all this manly exertion, across the poetic structuring of *Lyrical Ballads* issue affinities of impregnated passion that press against any sure artifice of gender difference. A really strange case of a man speaking to men enters in the newly Prefaced 1800 volume: an untitled confession, beginning "Strange fits of passion I have known" and recounting one such fit—or "fit occasion" as Wordsworth would have it, for the Poet's powers of judgment (1802 *Preface* xxv–xxvi).

Off to visit his beloved one evening, this "I" is agonized by a sense of ominous signifying in the moon upon which he "fix'd" his eye: "Towards the roof of Lucy's cot / The moon descended still" (15–16). The moonset, already impregnated with intention (*descended*, not set) provokes a passionate association of ideas in a state of excitement:

> When down behind the cottage roof
> At once the planet dropp'd.
>
> What fond and wayward thoughts will slide
> Into a Lover's head—
> "O mercy!" to myself I cried,
> "If Lucy should be dead!"   (23–28)

Wordsworth lets us see that language as much as anything generates this cry: the Latin linking of *Lucy* to "light" underwrites the sudden drop into a fate feared of her. The brief self-ironizing at 25–26 would make light of it all with a sigh of predictability, *will slide*—any Lover's lunacy, or superstition, especially in tandem with *Lucy*, a hallmark name of eighteenth-century love elegies.[19] But literate self-satire is not the mode of the quiet cry that follows, the fit that compels telling:

> Strange fits of passion I have known,
> And I will dare to tell,
> But in the lover's ear alone,
> What once to me befel.   (1–4)

It is not passion per se that makes this telling "daring"; it is its perpetual pregnancy, delivering the declared "once" into apparently serial "fits."[20]

Wordsworth's words propose this as an operation of the poetry itself: *fits* are psychic spasms but also a "fitting to metrical arrangement" (*Pref-*

ace v);[21] *to tell* is to recount but also to re-count, mark out again. On a pulse of meter, in accretions of *and,* telling seems enchanted into reliving: "I to her cottage bent my way," "I fix'd my eye" (7–9); "My horse trudg'd on, and we drew nigh" (11); "And now we reach'd the orchard plot, / And, as we climb'd the hill" (13–14); "And all the while" (19); "My horse mov'd on, hoof after hoof / He ras'd, and never stopp'd" (21–22). In a letter-draft Wordsworth made that presencing *And now* a present event: "And now I've reached the orchard-plot,"[22] a tense-form continuous with the preamble "I have known." "What once to me befel" emerges as the pattern from, or for, "at once the planet dropp'd." On this slide, "'O Mercy!' to myself I cried, 'If Lucy should be dead!'" is a powerful overflow of feeling in no recollective tranquility. It is a fresh recurrence in the throes of a passion that all but kills—at the very least, hallucinates—an already allegorized Lucy into a phantasm of death.

The anecdote could find a good fit with the diagnosis of "love-sickness" in J. M. Good's *Study of Medicine* (1822): "from the exalted state of the imagination and the increased sensibility of the body, it may transpose the reality of life into a kind of visionary existence, and . . . produce mental derangement."[23] Or unmanly derangement: "In any man who utters the other's absence *something feminine* is declared," writes a later diagnostician, Roland Barthes, of a lover's discourse; the "man who waits and who suffers from his waiting is miraculously feminized," regendered "because he is in love" (14). Wordsworth's oblique diagnosis glints in a weird substitution: not the moon but "the planet" dropp'd, the Greek base of the word, *wanderer,* allegorizing the extravagance. For such a man and manner of speaking, Coleridge might gloss discursive impotence: a reliance on connectives, "and then," "and there," "and so," versus the intellectual power reflected in a man's "habitual arrangement of his words, grounded on the habit of foreseeing, in each integral part or . . . the whole that he then intends to communicate"—in sum, a "method in the fragments."[24] Overriding these opposites, Wordsworth's poetics of passion fit a method in the connectives, a communicated foreseeing.

Has witty Wordsworth thus written himself out of a compact with this Lover-Lunatic? Not to Francis Jeffrey, for whom such poetic "character and sentiment," in contrast to "the manly sense and correct picturing" of Crabbe, expose "fantastic and affected peculiarities in the mind or fancy of the author, into which it is most improbable that many of his readers will enter" (*Edinburgh Review* 12: 136–37). What readers may enter instead is a question about the manly sense in the auditorium of *Lyrical Ballads* itself. The rattled Lover's cry "to himself" sounds in Martha Ray ("to herself she cries"; *The Thorn* 64, 75), in helplessly afflicted Harry Gill ("Ever to himself he mutters"; *Goody Blake, and Harry Gill* 123), or in that "deranged state, in which from the increased sensibility . . . the sufferer's attention" succumbs to "one despotic thought, . . . by the blending, *fusing* power of Imagination and Passion" that Coleridge hears in the "expressive" "pathos" of *The Mad Mother* (*BL* 2: 150). Coleridge writes this in admiration, but the point could easily be turned to strange fits of male passion—or to the new poetics of feeling where gender-marking seems more like a contingency than a definitive logic.

Such proximity to female derangements may be why Wordsworth was tempted to underwrite the Lover's anxiety with hints of visionary prescience. That letter-version shows a last stanza in this key. Lucy lightly mocks her Lover's confession; then from a later narrative point, the Lover gets to imply his better clairvoyance:

> I told her this; her laughter light
> Is ringing in my ears;
> And when I think upon that night
> My eyes are dim with tears. (*EY* 238)

Now the irony is not at the Lover's expense; it's his sad discourse: his daring was to tell his fantasy to Lucy's ears; she returned laughter. His record of her laughter is now her epitaph, his vindication, in the dimming of her light. Wordsworth decided to cancel this confirmation, leaving it as an intimation of mortality in the now determinate past tense of narration:

> When she I lov'd, was strong and gay
> And like a rose in June,
> I to her cottage bent my way,
> Beneath the evening moon. (5–8)

The trope "like a rose in June," rhyming even with *moon*, looks at first like just so much sentimental cant. In retrospect, it gains the shading of a temporal portent. The difference matters, for on it pivots a reader's willingness to review hysteria as prescience. The ballad's hypnotic rhythm has this rhetorical force, too: it is a mimetic pulse of a Lover's lunacy that also paces out readerly suspense, the sympathetic measure of an inexorable determination.

A few pages on in the 1800 *Ballads,* another untitled verse, beginning in the metrical lilt of "'Tis said, that some have died for love," stages the communicative force of male love-grief. A poet musing on the lore of "wretched" lovers driven to suicide speaks of "one whom I . . . have known" (5): a manly man "of giant stature, who could dance / Equipp'd from head to foot in iron mail" (45–47), but is now so undone by the death of his "pretty Barbara" that all he can do is "moan." Though the poet exhorts "gentle Love" to spare him "kindred hours," his poem is an unsparing contradiction: its core (four of six stanzas) consists of a rehearsal of the grieving lover's "feverish complaint" so full and feeling that by the time he pleads—

Ah gentle Love! if ever thought was thine
To store up kindred hours for me, thy face
Turn from me, gentle Love, nor let me walk
Within the sound of Emma's voice, or know
Such happiness as I have known to-day   (45–50)

—it's already too late. By a sympathetic fever, the poet has wrought his imagination into "kindred hours" with the lovelorn man, whose moan he voices within, and as if, his own. The deep logic, as Barthes knows, is that Love is inextricable from imagining its devastating loss.[25]

Coleridge may underreport the "mild and philosophic pathos" of this last lyric (*BL* 2: 150). These men in love, fearing to be forlorn, sense self-loss in the very fear. Their closest company in *Lyrical Ballads* are all those forsaken women—Martha Ray, Mad Mother, Female Vagrant— whose passions possess male imaginations. *The Female Vagrant* seems, even, to earn its gender differential by force of a too proximate poetic identification: a "wanderer" whose "poor heart," so burdened by a "perpetual weight" on the "spirit" that it has "lost all its fortitude" (262–70), twins the darkest passages in Wordsworth's self-reports in the 1790s, *Tintern Abbey* and *The Prelude.*[26] In a poem written in 1802 but not published until the 1815 *Poems* Wordsworth imagines himself into the heart and voice of an emigrant mother, bereft of her own child and maternally doting, in near delusion, on an English child. The relay from chance seeing to a translation into English male imagination is so pressing that the discursive frame dissolves into an identificatory sympathy:

> Once did I see her clasp the Child about,
> And take it to herself; and I, next day,
> Wish'd in my native tongue to fashion out
> Such things as she unto this Child might say:
> And thus, from what I knew, had heard, and guess'd,
> My song the workings of her heart express'd.
>
> *(Songs of the Affections* XX, 9–14)

In several versions, manuscript to print, the poet's guess is such a heartfelt song that he lets his verse shift into the mother's voice unmarked with differentiating quotations (see Curtis, ed., 507–9.)

The poet of *The Mad Mother* actually speaks in the place of "a lady of Bristol who had seen the poor creature" (FN 11), the pathos communicated from mother to lady to poet. "While the distance removes her from us, the fact of her speaking our language brings us at once into close sympathy with her," said Wordsworth, in a late retrospect that still manages to use a present tense (*LY* 3: 293). She is "speaking our language" not just as the "English tongue" (10) but in chords of sympathy. A headnote in the *Morning Post*, 2 April 1800, confessed, "we have been so captivated with [*The Mad Mother*] that we are tempted to transgress the rule" of not publishing poetry already in print.[27] If Hazlitt is any index, all these she-voice ballads tugged at men's heartstrings:

> in the *Thorn*, the *Mad Mother*, and the *Complaint of a Poor Indian Woman*, I felt that deeper power and pathos which have been since acknowledged "In spite of pride, in erring reason's spite" as the characteristics of this author; and the sense of a new style and new spirit in poetry came over me.
>
> ("My first Acquaintance" 39, quoting the penultimate
> line of Pope's *Essay on Man*, Epistle I)

Impatient as he was with Wordsworth's egotistical transparency in all the male company of *The Excursion*, Hazlitt could surrender to Wordsworthian pathos in female dramatic form.

This may be because such ballads tap one habit of association that Wordsworth does not challenge: male impulses to chivalry, pained by social consciousness. The Female Vagrant is everywhere a victim of male forces: in the American war, "Murder . . . and Rape / Seized their joint prey, the mother and the child" (158–59); peace is found again only at sea, "Remote from man, and storms of mortal care" (141). *The Complaint of a forsaken Indian Woman* displaces this peril across the globe and in an alien culture, with a headnote about a tribal policy of abandoning those too weak for migratory treks: "it is unnecessary to add that the females are equally, or still more, exposed to the same fate" (191). Wordsworth added this anyway, as prelude to ballad in the voice of a new mother, childbirth exhausted, with no hope of male rescue except in an extravagant, pathetic fantasy:

> When from my arms my babe they took
> On me how strangely did he look!
> Through his whole body something ran,
> A most strange something did I see;
> —As if he strove to be a man,
> That he might pull the sledge for me.
> And then he stretched his arms, how wild
> Oh mercy! like a little child. (32–40)

The counterfactual fantasy "As if he strove to be a man" collapses into the simile's correction, "like a little child." Robert Langbaum's proposal that the speakers of *Complaint* and *The Affliction of Margaret* "are simply spokes*men* for an emotion" (72, my italics), though true to the lyric mode, may dispense too quickly with the drama of gender. Dorothy Wordsworth wrote out five stanzas drafted for the *Complaint* in her journal, 22 December 1800, as William was courting Mary Hutchinson.[28] Was this the only paper handy? Or did she feel this voice as her own? She knew she would not be forsaken (Mary would join their household), but she also knew the fear felt by a redundant woman.

In *The Mad Mother* (allied with *The Complaint* by its stanza form), Wordsworth infuses female grief with female grievance. As this mother indicts a renegade father, her passion imperils his surrogate, their "little boy." Even as suckling him calms her, the lullaby evokes the cad: "Thy father cares not for my breast, / 'Tis thine, sweet baby" (61–62). The chiasmus (father-breast-baby) tends toward a perilous substitution: "My love for thee has been well tried: / I've sought thy father far and wide" (86–88). Yet for all this perception about the courses of aggrieved female passion, when female retribution gets staged in one of the *Lyrical Ballads*, Wordsworth vexes the event with complicated, even contradictory, lines of sympathy. This is *Goody Blake, and Harry Gill*, shaped from a report (known "in the newspapers" and local conversation) in Erasmus Darwin's *Zoonomia; or, the Laws of Organic Life.* A poor, desperately cold old woman had been filching kindling from a farmer's hedge; when he brutally arrested her, she called down a curse on him, and he wound up cold and shivering thereafter.[29]

Lyrical Ballads' 1798 *Advertisement* cites "a well-authenticated fact which happened in Warwickshire" (iv); "it is a *fact*," insists the 1800 *Preface* (xxxvi), and the subtitle is always *A True Story.* What fascinates Wordsworth is "the power of the human imagination . . . sufficient to produce such changes even in our physical nature as might almost appear miraculous" (xxxvi). Yet what perplexes his ballad is how to array the larger power-grid: divine retribution? moral justice? social critique? witchcraft? Darwin's discourse is not of a piece. It does convey the cruel aggression of a "young farmer" on "an old woman": "He lay many cold hours under a hay-stack, . . . then springing from his concealment, he seized his prey with violent threats." Yet it also tags an alien simile to the old woman, "like a witch in a play," and the vehicle shimmers into the tenor itself when Darwin's report reaches the curse:

> she kneeled upon her bottle of sticks, and raising her arms to heaven beneath the bright moon then at the full, spoke to the farmer already shivering with cold, "Heaven grant, that thou never mayest know again the blessing to be warm." He complained of cold all the next day . . . always saying that nothing made him warm, . . . and from this one insane idea he kept his bed above twenty years for fear of the cold air, till at length he died.   (2: 359)

Wordsworth shifts this way, too. His ballad begins in lines of male pity for this woman:

> Auld Goody Blake was old and poor,
> Ill fed she was, and thinly clad;
> And any man who pass'd her door,
> Might see how poor a hut she had . . .   (21–24)

That this report of this still industrious woman goes on for forty lines more bears Wordsworth's dismay how any Englishman, let alone a neigh-

bor in his own Dorsetshire (29), could abide such a spectacle.[30] So when
in reaction to Harry's cruel "vengeance" (68), Goody Blake prays to "God
that is the judge of all" (96), a moral reckoning, in league with chivalry,
seems at hand. Yet it is just at this point that Wordsworth pivots into a
scene of witchcraft, in excess:

> She pray'd, her wither'd hand uprearing,
> While Harry held her by the arm—
> "God! who art never out of hearing,
> "O may he never more be warm!"
> The cold, cold moon above her head,
> Thus on her knees did Goody pray,
> Young Harry heard what she had said,
> And icy-cold he turned away.   (97–104)

It's not just that "icy-cold" turns from a moral cast into a physical affliction. That would be justice, making "cold and very chill" (106) Harry's
attribute as well as Goody's (62). It is the gothic staging of a conspiracy
between Goody and the cold, cold moon: the way her "wither'd" arm,
which could have evoked feeling for an "ill-fed" body, seems instead the
haglike agent and instrument of supernatural power.

The double trouble for man's sympathy is clear in two reviews. Aristarchus (Southey) wondered in the *Critical Review* if Wordsworth's "fact"
was "promot[ing] the popular superstition of witchcraft" (24: 200),
while in the *Monthly* Dr. Burney worried about a prompt to popular insurgency. Conceding a poetic power ("distress from poverty and want is
admirably described," and "the hardest heart must be softened into pity
for the poor old woman"), he focused on how the anarchy of female
"plunder" could impregnate other imaginations: "if all the poor are to
help themselves, and supply their wants from the possessions of their
neighbours, what imaginary wants and real anarchy would it not create?"
(June 1799: 206–7). "Goody Blake" is the name of an incipient threat to
an individual man's property.

If Wordsworth's ballad doesn't hit this question of property rights and
wrongs, it does turn to the orbit of male possession and dispossession in
Harry Gill's big chill:

> No word to any man he utters,
> A bed or up, to young or old;

But ever to himself he mutters,
"Poor Harry Gill is very cold."   (121–24)

Ostensibly a study of spooked imagination, this is also a poetry of female power and male anxiety: a man not speaking to men but, as an effect of a woman, left muttering "to himself," death-in-life in a body now like hers. The ballad's oscillation between hagcraft and hysteria may not have been much of a stretch: in diagnostic discourse from the Middle Ages through the seventeenth century, symptomata were similar, and not sex-differentiated.[31] Wordsworth even infects the balladeer: a shiver of ono-matopoeia, from his opening question about Harry Gill, "Oh! what's the matter? what's the matter?", to the answerable style of *chatter, chatter, chatter, chatter, chatter, chatter, chatter*.[32] This, too, seems Goody-cursed. At the close, the balladeer is carrying her speech-act, "pray," to his com-munity of men: "Now think, ye farmers all, I pray, / Of Goody Blake and Harry Gill" (102–3). If (goes one theory) the "woman in the text" makes "the text into a woman, and the circulation of this text/woman becomes the central ritual that establishes the bond between the author and his male readers,"[33] *Goody Blake, and Harry Gill* writes this bond with a difference, enforcing men, via its text, into a physical sympathy with a woman's suffering body.

One female reveled in this transformation. "I must hear 'Harry Gill,' once more," cried Hannah More to Joseph Cottle (publisher of *Lyrical Ballads*) after he had read it to a group of ladies. When he came "to the words, 'O, may he never more be warm!'" (adds Cottle), More "lifted up her hands, in smiling horror" (196). Not only does More double Goody, she happily takes her place, literally asking for "more" of Harry's misery. Her "smiling horror," Adela Pinch observes, enjoys "the power of a wom-an's curse to engender poetic pleasure" (97), doing Wordsworth's "Poet" with a difference in the circuit of speaking.

It wasn't such thrills that "irritated" Coleridge in defending Words-worth's genius in *Biographia Literaria* (this was the author of *Christa-bel*, after all), but the popular transmission of gothic passion into mere childish simplicity: "a *sweet, simple poet!* and *so* natural, that little mas-ter Charles, and his younger sister, are *so* charmed . . . that they play at 'Goody Blake'" (2: 159). Coleridge was waging his defense of Words-worth's manly poetry (not juvenile, not effeminate) in the wake of some brutal reviews of *Christabel*, which Wordsworth had deemed beyond the pale even for the experiment of *Lyrical Ballads*. When at last *Christabel* appeared in 1816 (with Byron's advocacy), the reviews ridiculed it as unmanly. To the *Anti-Jacobin*, it confounded "common sense," fit only for a Byromaniac "woman of fashion" (632, 635); the *Augustan* called it "affected and childish" (14); the *Scourge and Satirist* described it as "irregular, feeble," "abounding in affected sentiment, puerile imagery," and "imbecility of thought," the "accents of manly tenderness" forsaken for "those of the nurse . . . to sooth her babe" (61–62). The charges were consolidated, no less, by the progressive *British Lady's Magazine:* "an old woman's story of fairyism" and "witch-craft" (249), a genre that it hoped "reason has banished" even from the nursery, only to see it "rise in the pages of our bards" (251).[34]

The closest cousin in *Lyrical Ballads* to *Christabel's* gothic hysteria is *The Thorn*. Save some stanzas of mimetic garrulity, Coleridge would defend it, too—for the power of universal delight, he says in *Biographia* (2: 20), but also, I think, for retro-credit to extravagant *Christabel*.

A Man Speaking

"Of all the men I ever knew, Wordsworth has the least femineity in his mind. He is *all* man," said Coleridge sometime after 5 May 1829, as Wordsworth was emerging as the poet for the British Empire.[35] Across the century, he was weaned from his Romantic generation of "poetry." If "In great poets there is an exquisite sensibility both of soul and sense that sympathizes like gossamer sea-moss with every movement of the element in which it floats," so James Russell Lowell gave the anatomy in 1894, "Wordsworth shows less of this finer feminine fibre of organization than one or two of his contemporaries, notably Coleridge or Shelley; . . . he was a masculine thinker" (413). Yet if masculine thinking seems thus secured, this was not the guarantee of *Lyrical Ballads*, replete with fibers, even networks, not just of feminine cast but of hysteria: anarchies of voice (crying, ranting, clattering, chattering), invasion by other voices, paralytic blockage.

At once a pathology and a contagion, hysteria is a parody of poetic communication.

As she laughed I was aware of becoming involved in her laughter
and being part of it. . . . I was drawn in by short gasps, inhaled at each

momentary recovery, lost finally in the dark caverns of her throat, bruised by the ripple of unseen muscles.

This report is from *Hysteria*, the singular prose fluency in T. S. Eliot's first volume of deftly crafted poetic forms. It associates several collapses: of decorum, of self-possession, of poetry itself in the throat of an hysterical woman—or perhaps the hysterical invention of an hysterical woman to take the rap for the fantasia. The referent of Hysteria is teasingly unspecific: it is his and hers; it is a literary excursion into territory sited by Wordsworth's ballads.

Smirking at Wordsworth's Note to *The Thorn*, Byron gendered its balladeer as a type of Joanna Southcott, famous for an hysterical pregnancy, but no less famous for her powers of communication. Byron's occasion is a (suppressed) preface for *Don Juan*, where the ridicule also registers a serious complaint about the infection of hysteric poetics on the patrimony of letters: Wordsworth feeds "a System of prosaic raving that is to supersede all that hitherto by the best and wisest of our fathers has been deemed poetry" (*PW* 5: 81–82). In the poetic system of *Don Juan* hysteria is a marked she-spectacle: Donna Julia addles a suspicious husband with drama-queen "hysterics" (1.162), and her maid Antonia yields to genuine "hysterics" after Juan's narrow escape (1.187); dream-traumatized Dudù is an "hysteric of a vision" (6.80); and it is only desperate or drunk men that wax even "half hysterical" (2.50).

Hysteria is "*the* female malady," in Elaine Showalter's phrase. Both the etymology (named by Hippocrates as a disease of *hyster*, the womb) and its Englishing into "the mother" say as much. Burton's *Anatomy of Melancholy* lists it among the "maladies incident to young women" (1.303). "For centuries," comments Mark Micale, it was the term men slapped onto everything they found "mysterious or unmanageable in the opposite sex":

> The wildly shifting physical symptomatology of the sickness was thought to mirror the volatile and unpredictable nature of women. The exaggerated emotionality of the hysterical woman was understood as a pathological intensification of natural feminine sensibility.   (320)

But what men understood could waver. Contemporary to *Don Juan*, Good's *Study of Medicine* (1822) noted that "men may labour under the hysteric passion as well as women" (3: 401), as if, even, impregnated. Back in the early seventeenth century, esteemed Scots physician Robert

Whytt commented on a motivated nomenclature,[36] in a medical community that knew better:

The hypochondriac and the hysteric diseases are generally considered by physicians as the same; only in women, such disorders have got the name of *hysteric*, from the antient opinion of their seat being solely in the womb; while in men, they were called *hypochondriac*, upon the supposition that in *them* they proceeded from some fault in those *viscera*, which ly under the cartilages of the ribs.   (104)

Whytt went on for several pages about this. French physician Carolus Piso (Charles Lepois) had observed, "*hysterica symptomata omnia fere viris cum mulieribus sunt communia*" (nearly all hysterical symptoms are common to men and women; 181). In the 1680s Thomas Willis, though deeming women more susceptible, admitted that "sometimes the same kind of Passions infest Men" (69); and Thomas Sydenham noted that while it is women who are prone to hysteria, those "accustom'd to hard Labour" seem exempt, and men "who lead a sedentary Life, and grow pale over Books" are not (149). By these lights, hysteria is a situational affliction, not a naturally female one.

And so the wandering mother could appear in a man feminized by confinement, or loss of authority and power, especially over women. Ex-king Lear, dissed and ditched by two daughters, cries out, "O! how this mother swells up toward my heart; / *Hysterica passio!* down, thou climbing sorrow!" (2.4.54–55).[37] Echoing the dispossessed son in the same play ("Poor Tom's a-cold" [3.4]), Harry Gill shakes with the woman's chill: "Poor Harry Gill is very cold" (124). In 1799 Coleridge summons hysteria to slur the Ministry's warmongering cant: "men whose delicate religion is frightened into hysterics by the transient babble of Gallic infidelity."[38] What about poets? The "wayward Queen" in *The Rape of the Lock* who is "Parent of Vapors and of Female Wit" has power to "give th' *Hysteric* or *Poetic* fit" (p. 33, 4.58–60), as if a she-wit, the poet and th'hysteric were of imagination compact. No wonder that Coleridge wants, by 1817, to distinguish the "legitimate language of poetic fervor self-impassioned" from "the madness prepense of Pseudo-poesy, or the startling *hysteric* of weakness over-exerting itself, which bursts on the unprepared reader in sundry odes and apostrophes" in the anthologies "and the magazines of the day" (*BL* 2: 84–85).

Or in some of the *Lyrical Ballads*. Passion, proposes Barthes, is drawn into "that region of hysteria where language is both *too much* and too little" (99). In *The Thorn*, a spare voice of female passion agitates a balladeer into impassioned talkativeness. Burton's *Anatomy* indexed the contagion. Hysterics "cannot tell how to express themselves in words" or "what ailes them," and auditors or witnesses may get pulled in: "you cannot understand them, or well tell what to make of their sayings"; "Some think they see visions, confer with spirits"; "they will not speak, make answer to any question."[39] This is central casting for the confessor of "Strange fits," or the balladeer of *The Thorn*, who keeps saying "I cannot tell; I wish I could."

Whytt outlines discursive consequences not only in this frustration, but also in the agency of telling: among the agitations to "delicate people" (10–11), in addition to "horrible or unexpected sights," are the "strong impressions" made by "doleful or moving stories" (212). While the impression of primary interest to him is the "sympathy which obtains between various parts of the body" (v), if the term of communication is "sympathy," it has potential play outside of one body. This is the throb of Adam Smith's moral sympathy, and what Wordsworth theorizes as poetic "power" in his Preface. Writing and then annotating *The Thorn*, the poet fits out Whytt's transactions for a discursive structure: a woman's doleful story becomes a moving story for its reporter, whose report runs an hystericized rhetorical operation that collapses distinction of cause and effect. How does this unfold?

Wordsworth's balladeer, fixated on an hysteric woman, speaks a ballad that everywhere exposes symptoms in him: blocked speech, alternating with a garrulity that channels other voices—repeatedly, the woman's cry, "Oh woe is me! Oh misery!," repeatedly, an unbodied interrogative echo, "But why . . . ?" and a chorus of village gossip. The Note added in 1800 assigns all this to an experiment in how words, "impregnated with passion, should likewise convey passions to Readers." The conveyance delivers more than passion, however; it delivers an hysteriology of personification in "Martha Ray." The balladeer swears his credibility, "as I am a man" (his sole instance of the noun), in the very sentence, just words away, in which he insists that he "found / A woman" at the spot (196–98).

Well before he delivers the "tale" that names "Martha Ray" and the cad "Stephen Hill" (XI), his own story has been impregnating the spot with her history: it has a hill, as if a trace of Hill; it has an "aged . . . wretched thing forlorn" [I]), as if a remnant of Martha Ray "some two and twenty years" (115) on; it has a proto-narrative, a "mossy network . . . / As if by hand of lady fair, / The work had woven been" (IV). As his telling proceeds, that hill gets a narrative-impregnated simile, and *As if* turns into an assertion of a genius loci, a "woman in a scarlet cloak":

> For oft there sits, between the heap
> That's like an infant's grave in size,
> And that same pond of which I spoke,
> A woman in a scarlet cloak,
> And to herself she cries,
> "Oh misery! oh misery!
> Oh woe is me! Oh misery!"
>
> (VI: 60–66)

Gender makes a critical difference: he speaks, she cries; he arranges, she's deranged; her words are "to her self," his are addressed to a communal assent of "you." Yet the tendency of a voice expressing or attempting to communicate "impassioned feelings" to "cling to the same words, or words of the same character" (Note I: 213) issues in *The Thorn* not just from the woman, but also from this man speaking, perhaps only to himself, echoing question and reply in no communication but to himself: "Now wherefore . . .?"; "I cannot tell; I wish I could."[40]

Wordsworth telescopes this hysteric incapacity into a strange fit of discourse that literalizes the etymology: *hysteron proteron*. It was "Ere I had heard of Martha's name" (184), the balladeer admits, that he got caught in that horrible, unexpected mountain-top storm:

> and off I ran,
> Head-foremost, through the driving rain,
> The shelter of the crag to gain,
> And, as I am a man,
> Instead of jutting crag, I found
> A woman seated on the ground.
>
> XIX
> I did not speak—I saw her face,
> Her face it was enough for me;
> I turned about and heard her cry,
> "O misery! O misery!
>
> (193–202)

Invoking what "all the country know" (207) and could report, the balladeer asserts his chance witnessing of her prior presence, prefaced by a rhetoric of legal oath: "I will be sworn is true" (180). But Wordsworth's poetics array a fiction of *hysteron proteron* (the later earlier/first): a storm-panic, then hearing Martha's name, then a substitution of her history for his hysterics.[41] Burton's *Anatomy* actually indexes *hysteron proteron*, via the Latin phrase, as one form of hysteria: "preposterous judgement" (1: 302). In the balladeer's story, "Martha Ray" precedes and produces his own story, his passion impregnated by hers. In Wordsworth's discursive structure, his storm-hysteria gains an exculpatory rationale in delivering "Martha's name."

In an essay that he published in *The Friend* (in 1809 and again in 1818) Coleridge worked out a "Ghost-Theory" (1: 245) on these principles. He wanted to explain how

> small and remote resemblances, what mere *hints* of likeness from some real external object, especially if the shape be aided by colour, will suffice to make a vivid thought consubstantiate with the real object, and derive from it an outward perceptibility. Even when we are broad awake, if we are in anxious expectation, how often will not the most confused sounds of nature be heard by us as articulate sounds?
>
> (1: 247)

This could be an introduction to the case of hysteria (or ghost-sighting) staged in *The Thorn*. Such an analysis certainly occurred to Stephen Parrish, in a brilliant deconstruction of narrative and discourse in the poetic operation. Taking a cue from the first paragraph of Wordsworth's Note (I: 211), Parrish reads out a case-study of "superstition," in which "Martha Ray" exists only in "the narrator's imagination": in a howling storm, the sea captain ran for shelter to a mountain spot where he saw a gnarled thorn-stump overgrown with lichen and red moss; he later heard a legend (Martha Ray: pregnant, jilted, infanticidal, agonized in remorse) which he then retrojects, to "turn the tree into a woman, the brightly-colored moss into her scarlet cloak, and the creaking of the branches into her plaintive cry" (100–105).[42] The gender-structure of this turn also matters, matters deeply.

Glimpsed in the arrangement of *hysteron proteron* in *The Thorn* is a sociology of *hysteria*, for which Elaine Showalter provides valuable help.

In the "social expectations of the masculine role in war," symptoms of "hysteria" in traumatized men received the nom de guerre "shell shock."[43] Still shocked, the teller of *The Thorn*, like the lover of "Strange fits," turns "one" event (181) into general knowledge:

> And this I know, full many a time,
> When she was on the mountain high,
> By day, and in the silent night,
> When all the stars shone clear and bright,
> That I have heard her cry,
> "Oh misery! oh misery!
> "O woe is me! oh misery!"   (247–53)

But in this last stanza, Wordsworth lets us see a shared repetition, the woman's voice inside the man's tale, *heard her* in tightly bound chord, too. The final line takes this bind into a last rhyme, *her cry* of mis*ery* into which his *I* is also, and irrevocably, conscripted. It is a revenge of the traditional ballad, in which one singer/speaker channels and performs all the voices, as if relaying them afresh, or with a gothic turn, haunted and possessed by them.[44]

"Whenever we repeat any idea frequently, the mind by a sort of mechanism repeats it long after the first cause has ceased to operate," observes Burke, in the throes of his analysis of the sublimity of "Infinity" (*Inquiry* Part II, sect. IX; p. 53). Turn this mechanism against the phantasm of a first cause, and the repetitions turn into a gothic conundrum of cause and effect winding into one another in a tight sympathy. To this core of experimentation, Wordsworth leads *The Thorn*, with a haunting of the psychic sublimity that Burke shudders at in "multipli[cation] without end": "in madmen . . . in the constant repetition of some remark, some complaint, or song; which having struck powerfully on their disordered imagination, in the beginning of their phrensy, every repetition reinforces it with new strength" (54). For Burke, the sequence of repetition becomes coterminus with life itself in madness. For Wordsworth it configures the hysteria of narrative form, in which a cause personified in a woman returns as a Humean effect of the phantasmic drive for a "discoverable connexion" (1: 184). In the poetics of the ballad, the voice that possesses the mind at once beckons as cause of possession and reads out as its effect.

The "close sympathy" with the Mad Mother that Wordsworth felt as late as 1836 may have been closer in 1798, where her voice similarly takes over the poem, and with no close-quotation mark (p. 146). There is such an absence at the end of a medial stanza of *The Thorn* (XIX).[45] Even more eerily here, the missing close-quotation lets the third and last interruption by the disembodied questions seem continuous with, as if the same vocal event, of "her cry":

> She shudders and you hear her cry,
> "Oh misery! oh misery!
>
> > XX
> "But what's the thorn? And what's the pond?
> "And what's the hill of moss to her?
> "And what's the creeping breeze that comes
> "The little pond to stir?"

The voices inhabit one echo chamber. A poet may well have a lively "disposition to be affected more than other men by absent things as if they were present; an ability of conjuring up in himself passions, which are indeed far from being the same as those produced by real events" (1802 *Preface* xxviii). It may be fatal, however, to a man-poet to "bring his feelings near to those of the persons whose feelings he describes, nay, for short spaces of time perhaps, to let himself slip into an entire delusion, and even confound and identify his own feelings with theirs" (xxx), if they are female.

Reading *The Thorn*, Francis Jeffrey was quick to prick the delusion into an equation:

> A frail damsel is a character common enough in all poems; and one upon which many fine and pathetic lines have been expended. Mr Wordsworth has written more than three hundred lines on that subject: but, instead of new images of tenderness, or delicate representation of intelligible feelings, he has contrived to tell us nothing whatever of the unfortunate fair one, but that her name is Martha Ray; and that she goes up to the top of a hill, in a red cloak, and cries "Oh misery!" All the rest of the poem is filled with a description of an old thorn and a pond, and of the silly stories which the neighbouring old women told about them.   (*Edinburgh* 12 [1808], 135)

Jeffrey renders a society of female hysterics. Never mind that Wordsworth's gossips are the male narrator and an "old Farmer Simpson" (149); to Jeffrey, they're all old women. Coleridge, too, turns to gender (seconding Southey) to sigh about a lapse into imitative form in the experiment.[46] His caution is the old Nurse in *Romeo and Juliet:* "it is not possible to imitate truly a dull and garrulous discourser, without repeating the effect of dulness and garrulity," he writes in parodic imitation (*BL* 2: 49). Though he is not writing about *The Thorn* when he complains of Wordsworth's tendency to a "minute adherence to *matter-of-fact* in character and incidents," and an "*anxiety* of explanation and retrospect" that amounts to "a small *Hysteron-Proteron*" of aesthetic judgment (pleasure should come first), he could have been (*BL* 2: 129–31). So closely connected are these two faults in *The Thorn* that they seem (what Coleridge, in a coinage, terms) "congeneric":[47] the name issued in explanation is also the issue of a small *Hysteron-proteron.*

When Jeffrey says he got "nothing" on "Martha Ray," he had the right number but didn't care to do the theoretical math. Nothing is also the sum of Wordsworth's Note, where we could have expected something, given that the name was so well known as to be a marked delivery. Actress Martha Ray, mistress of the fourth Earl of Sandwich, was shot in the lobby of a playhouse by a jealous rival (awfully named Mr. Hackman) in 1779—a scandal (like that in *The Thorn*) some twenty years past, but hardly dead. Darwin's *Zoonomia* cited it as a case of a rejected lover's "furious or melancholy insanity" (2: 365). Moreover, the boy with the poet on the day he saw "a stunted thorn" in a storm and then "wrote some lines describing" it (19 March 1798; *AN* 13), was the son of Martha Ray's "natural" son, his friend Basil Montagu. Why would Wordsworth vex a friend —or embarrass the *Preface*-boast that his poems will produce excitement without catering "a craving for extraordinary incident" (xix)?[48]

"Martha Ray" is nothing if not a determined impregnation of the poetry, a powerline to passion that Wordsworth infuses from a grid of bereaved mothers and bereft females, deranged and infanticidal, bristling in the magazine-world of the 1790s, in which the "commonest of all literary associations for a thorn tree" (notes Mary Jacobus) "were illegitimate birth and child-murder."[49] In the balladeer's first figure of the spot's "woven" moss, the poet's etymological punning (*textus: woven*) hints at the connection to literary fabrications. Even the woman's refrain—

"O woe is me! oh misery!"—though it mimes the wind, intones "poetic diction" and a prefabricated lilt of rhyming iambic dimeter. This is textual impregnation, and a good enough case for Coleridge's view (in a Wollstonecraft mood) of one the liabilities of reading "Romances": "the mind *may* become credulous & prone to superstition" (*L* 1: 354). Such is the mind that Wordsworth identifies in his thorny balladeer: "credulous" and "prone to superstition" (I: 211), and in a particularly literary way. His words are impregnated with passion because the passion is impregnated with words, words, words.

But if words are the medium, the balladeer is more than one "superstitious" man. By the third paragraph of Wordsworth's Note, he is signifying "many other Poems in these volumes": "Poetry is passion"—by another name, "the history or science of feelings." This history (not hysteria), in the measure of "a Poet's words . . . in the balance of feeling," tells what "every man must know": that efforts "to communicate impassioned feelings" are rarely free of a "consciousness of the inadequateness of our own powers, or the deficiencies of language." While this sounds like Whytt's symptomology of hysteria, what Wordsworth has done, without theorizing, is to indicate hysteria as the passion-principle of poetry, wherein distinction of tenor and vehicle (signified and signifier) collapse in "the interest which the mind attaches to words, not only symbols of the passion, but as things, active and efficient which are of themselves part of the passion." Hence the poetic value of "repetition and apparent tautology" not just in a suffering woman or garrulous balladeer, but as a basic science of feeling (I: 213).

A text that Wordsworth will name at the end of his Note brings in another legend of female murder, also a mother, also a poetry of repetition: see "Song of Deborah," he advises (I: 214). This is repetition without pathology: a "tumultuous and wonderful Poem" sung in Judges 5 by prophet-judge Deborah with Israeli general Barak after a national victory. Inspired by her vision of the Canaanites' chariots balked by a flood, Barak led an army against this enemy, vanquishing all but the general Sisera, who fled, finding refuge in the tent of Jael, the wife of a Hebrew ally. She fed him milk and honey, then drove a tent nail through his head as he slept. The three verses that Wordsworth recommends (12, 27, 28) all involve politically pregnant female passion. The first, "Awake, awake, Deborah! awake, awake, utter a song!" exhorts her to celebrate the victory she had prophesied. The second sings of Sisera's fall to Jael: "At her feet he bowed, he fell, he lay down: at her feet he bowed, he fell: where he bowed, there he fell down dead." The third, half in sympathy, half in irony, is the anguished voice of Sisera's mother: "Why is his chariot *so* long in coming? why tarry the wheels of his chariots?" All communicate, with passionate repetition, female passion that is neither private nor pathetic: Deborah is called upon as a national voice; Jael secures national liberation; Deborah, "a mother in Israel," can inhabit (in a way that Charlotte Smith understands) maternal anguish across national boundaries. Wordsworth's Note closes by writing into "the history or science of feelings" this glance at female power and authority—social, political, and poetic.[50]

Female Naming

Wordsworth closes the 1800 *Lyrical Ballads* in masculine terrain. He ends volume II with *Michael* (his longest poem therein), told by a Poet to "Poets" (38–39), its world the "men" of the poet's boyhood (23); its tale, of a "Son and a Father" (99), the son "more dear" than "his Help-mate" (149–50); its crisis involving "patrimonial fields" (234), "Forefathers" (378), and a bond to a "Brother's Son" (221); its pathos, a ruined "emblem" of "the life the Fathers lived" (420). Yet the patriarchy is in radical erosion. From a world no more, its names and place-names are epitaphs, fast-fading vestiges that might, save the poet's *Michael,* remain "unnamed" or "unknown."[51]

A five-chapter unit just before presents the fore-end of such history: initiatives of place-naming, in prompts of fancy, affection, tribute, rebuke, or commemoration.[52] Wordsworth, whose name is now placed on the title-page of *Lyrical Ballads,* even gives a name to this poetic place, *Poems on the Naming of Places,* and marks it, in rare distinction, both with a recto title-page, then a recto *Advertisement:*[53]

By Persons resident in the country and attached to rural objects, many places will be found unnamed or of unknown names, where little Incidents will have occurred, or feelings been experienced, which will have given to such places a private and peculiar interest. From a wish to give some sort of record to such Incidents or renew the gratification of such Feelings, Names have been given to Places by the

Author and some of his Friends, and the following Poems written in
consequence. (177)

Noting the signposting, some critics like to amass ironies against the
presumptive place-naming, even collate it with the worst excesses of the
British Empire.[54] Wordsworth's *Advertisement* describes no dominion-
izing, however: just "private and peculiar" records of which even the poet
is not the sole agent or proprietor; no durable legislations, just "some sort
of" socially contingent gesture. Moreover, "the Poems written in consequence" expose erosions of the poet's self-possession—sometimes in interaction with a female companion, or a feminine-gendered place. The
only two poems to which this poet cares to give any name at all are dedicated to women: *II. To Joanna,* and *V. To M. H.* I'll be treating Wordsworth's chapters out of numerical order in order to foreground the inter-
play between his ironies against Adamic privilege and his willingness to
honor "incidents" of female authority.

The narrative of *IV* ("A narrow girdle of rough stones and crags") delivers a place-name earned by an event of rash misnaming. But the poetic
text records more, in imagistic and verbal doublings that trace the limited logic of the place-naming. The first doubling is a sentimental repetition of the somewhat aggrieved introductory line. On a mellow September morning, a trio of lakeside walkers (the poet, a Friend, and She),
contending with a "retir'd and difficult" path (that "narrow girdle"), encounter a native Queen *retir'd* in ease by the local lake:

> that tall plant
> So stately, of the Queen Osmunda nam'd,
> Plant lovelier in its own retir'd abode
> On Grasmere's beach, than Naid by the shore
> Of Grecian brook, or Lady of the Mere
> Sole-sitting by the shores of old Romance. (36–40)

This is the first name in the verse, and so regal that the mood of modern,
native Romance soon plays into a "noise" beyond: "the busy mirth / Of
Reapers, Men and Women, Boys and Girls" (42–44). The labor, involving
children, even, is heard by the trio as a substantive *mirth*. When, however, Wordsworth writes that they "Delighted much to listen to those
sounds, / . . . / Feeding unthinking fancies" (44–46), he presents another

double, a doubt about how we are to read the modifier *unthinking:* pastoral pleasure or complacent inattention?

This fanciful mood feeds into a scene of reading (for the trio and us) that seems to materialize from old Romance itself, a "Man" to match the native "Queen":

> Through a thin veil of glittering haze, we saw
> Before us on a point of jutting land
> The tall and upright figure of a Man. (48–50)

With that glittering veil, surely some revelation is at hand; but metaphysical expectation is ruffled by a social notation and suspect activity, "Attir'd in peasant's garb, . . . / Angling beside the margin of the lake" (51–52). And so a second naming issues, this from a *We* which a reader may well join:

> We all cried out, that he must be indeed
> An idle man, who thus could lose a day
> Of the mid harvest, when the labourer's hire
> Is ample, and some little might be stor'd
> Wherewith to chear him in the winter time. (56–60)

On surefooted Æsop-moralism, the namers shift from a marked "peasant's garb" to the class itself, "Peasant" (61). And thus their corporate chagrin on discovering the angler is no slacker: too "weak to labour in the harvest field," he is "using his best skill to gain / A pittance from the dead unfeeling lake" (69–71). From the "happy idleness of that sweet morn" the trio falls to "serious musing and to self-reproach" and a lesson to temper "all our thoughts with charity" (74–79).[55] Hence their place-name: "POINT RASH-JUDGMENT" (86).

At the same time, Wordsworth's verbal doublings have been arraying an unnamed, and so unjudged social logic: the disparity between a trio's "happy idleness" (74) and an "idle man" having to prove himself no idler; the phonic doubling in the trio's *retir'd* way (9) and the *attir'd* peasant (51). Attentive to nuances, Wordsworth briefly ratcheted up the suspect to "Idler" (1815–20), a jaded social type, as if to heighten the trio's misprisoning, which from 1827 on, is even more rash: "Improvident and reckless, we exclaimed." At the same time, he deletes *unthinking* for a spell (1815–20), as if to cut the misreaders some slack for fancy. From

Wordsworth on, indexing the ironies has become a trial for a reader's judgment—in effect, a judgment about the point of judgment.[56]

Elided is the radical abjection of this iconic "Man" from all harmonies, social, natural, romantic, and from sympathetic human communication. He "stood alone" is something the poetry says twice (51, 63). If Wordsworth's *Preface* disdains personification (xx), the figure returns here with a vengeance—Man as a disjointed blazon, starkly at odds with the blazon naturalized for stately tall Queen Osmunda:

> worn down
> By sickness, gaunt and lean, with sunken cheeks
> And wasted limbs, his legs so long and lean
> That for my single self I look'd at them,
> Forgetful of the body they sustain'd. (64–68)

The syntax of "for my single self" means to signal the poet's private reaction. But the syntax doubles to produce a doublet: the poet facing a mirror "for my single self," in a specter for self-reckoning. The poetry shimmers with metapoetic (dis)placements: "the spot where with his rod and line / He stood alone" (62–63) places *line* at the end of the poet's line, and annexes keywords in the lexicon of Wordsworthian imagination, *the spot, stood alone.* In the multiple relays of this sight, the lone angler of "the dead unfeeling lake / That knew not of his wants" (69–72) rebukes not only that unthinking reverie of a picturesque "dead calm lake" (22–23), but also the poet's deepest mythology of man in nature, the very argument of the autobiography being drafted during these same years.[57] It's not that this poet is "Therefore, unwilling to forget that day" (80), but that he cannot. "POINT RASH-JUDGMENT is the Name it bears" (86), because it bears an abstraction (as the poet of *The Prelude* would put it) that has a "mighty . . . charm" for a mind "beset / With images and haunted by itself" (*1805* 6.179–80).

The next (and last) poem in the set—*V. To M.H.*—may seem a recovery by the book of male possession and male security in nature. Its nominal tribute to "my sweet Mary" (24) has the look of a pretext for swelling the catalogue of *my.* But the text proves more a romance of dispossession than anything else: a "calm recess" (13) from Man, far from "any woodman's path" (2), a "spot . . . made by Nature for herself" (15). The allure of male retreat from the busy world attracts, by reflex, the power of self-sufficient female making:

> And if a man should plant his cottage near,
> Should sleep beneath the shelter of its trees,
> And blend its waters with his daily meal,
> He would so love it that in his death-hour
> Its image would survive among his thoughts,
> And, therefore, my sweet MARY, this still nook
> With all its beeches we have named from You.　　　　　(18–24)

Though a rhetoric of *therefore* produces the name as tribute, the poet's peculiar preposition, *from You* (not *for you*), issues from a desire so other-worldly, so death-romancing, that it has to draw *from* a woman to name this thought, and to pretend that it is not doing so.

　　I. has sensed this death in along another vector, confronting a nature indifferent to any man's presence, let alone any man's naming:

> It was an April Morning: fresh and clear
> The Rivulet, delighting in its strength,
> Ran with a young man's speed . . .　　　　　(1–3)

The actual young man is the passive one, superfluous amid the superflux, or absorbed into it. No "I" appears for 18 lines, and then just as an element of the place: "I roam'd in the confusion of my heart, / Alive to all things and forgetting all" (18–19), *I* echoing in the *Alive* of connection to a resounding auditorium of "glad sound" (23),

> Which, while I listen'd, seem'd like the wild growth
> Or like some natural produce of the air
> That could not cease to be.　　　　　(28–30)

Absorbed in this wild growth, the poet discerns a single human product:

> And on a summit, distant a short space,
> By any who should look beyond the dell,
> A single mountain Cottage might be seen.　　　　　(34–36)

The place-naming adduced by *And* bears a protest of self-presence:

I gaz'd and gaz'd, and to myself I said,
"Our thoughts at least are ours; and this wild nook,
My EMMA, I will dedicate to thee." (37–39)

The motive *I will* is a punning self-inscription for this poet (*I William*),
set in sound and meter to answer the teeming *wild*. The prelude may be
calmer than "to myself I cried" / "to himself he mutters" / "to herself she
cries," but the kinship of Lucy's Lover, Harry Gill, and Martha Ray is an
audible affiliation with these radical privacies. In a draft, the adage of
differentiation was singular and phonically linked to *I*, "My thoughts at
least are mine."[58] The first voicing of the name, "My EMMA, I will . . . ,"
reads out an act of self-possession, and self-inscription:

—Soon did the spot become my other home,
My dwelling, and my out-of-doors abode. (40–41)

Years later, Wordsworth enters into the record his own wild produce at
this local habitation: "I have composed thousands of verses" (FN 18)—including this one. In this first one, however, he composes his own erasure
more certainly than the security of his place-name:

And, of the Shepherds who have seen me there,
To whom I sometimes in our idle talk
Have told this fancy, two or three, perhaps,
Years after we are gone and in our graves,
When they have cause to speak of this wild place,
May call it by the name of EMMA'S DELL. (42–47)

"EMMA'S DELL," though it chimes with "my dwelling," is a fancy that "perhaps . . . may" or may not take, and if it does, perhaps only as an empty
name, its agent and referent unknown. The surest place for the survival
of "the name of EMMA'S DELL" is *Poems on the Naming of Places*, which
the Shepherds probably won't consult.

A challenge to male poetic self-possession in the next chapter, *II. To
Joanna*, involves a she in collusion with she-nature. Wordsworth fiction-
alizes a prologue that, for all its framing as an affectionate letter "to Joanna," pre-emptively casts her to the poem's readers as alien to the poet
and his circle, a city-bred girl "distant" from rural affections.[59] "How fares
Joanna, that wild-hearted Maid! / And when will she return to us?" we

hear from the Vicar (23–24). She returns as a poet's inscription, "Some uncouth name upon the native rock" that the Vicar sees the poet chiseling away at, "like a Runic Priest" (28–30). It turns out to be "Joanna's name" (83), and the site of the place-name, "Joanna's Rock," is the story.

It all began one day while out on a walk. Caught by the beauty of the season, the poet "stopp'd short" (43), and gazing on the scene, was arrested by the delight of "one impression" (49). But unlike the "I" in "It was an April morning," this gazer is observed:

> When I had gaz'd perhaps two minutes' space,
> Joanna, looking in my eyes, beheld
> That ravishment of mine, and laugh'd aloud.   (51–53)

The double grammar of "That ravishment of mine" blurs agent and object, ravisher and ravished, possession and dispossession: the poet's ravishment of the view with his eyes, and its of him (*mine* refers to "eyes")—all caught in a female gaze.

In a cunning fragment on male enamoration, Barthes gives a gloss for this kind of gender confusion.[60] In "the ancient myth," the ravisher is male and "active," cut from Harry Gill's cloth: "he wants to seize his prey ... a Woman"; but "in the modern myth (that of love-as-passion), the contrary is the case ... the lover—the one who has been ravished—is always implicitly feminized" (188–89). As the object of Joanna's gaze, the poet finds himself in both the ancient female place and the feminized modern place. He could be a case for the hysteric "feminine body" described by Dr. Rondibilis in *Pantagruel:* "all the senses ravished, all the passions carried to a point of repletion, and all thought thrown into confusion" (477; Rabelais himself lectured on medicine). In a later gloss on *To Joanna* Wordsworth re-enacts his surrender, in language that spells a self-feminizing, by Wordsworthian codes: "my mind partly forgets its purpose being softened by the images of beauty in the description of the rock, & the delicious morning."[61] A soft mind, forgetful of purpose, slides from masculine registers.

It's not just that Joanna's gaze catches this, but that her laughter awakens a female auditorium of choral amplification:

> The rock, like something starting from a sleep,
> Took up the Lady's voice, and laugh'd again:

That ancient Woman seated on Helm-crag
Was ready with her cavern; Hammar-Scar,
And the tall Steep of Silver-How sent forth
A noise of laughter; southern Loughrigg heard,
And Fairfield answer'd with a mountain tone:
Helvellyn far into the clear blue sky
Carried the Lady's voice,—old Skiddaw blew
His speaking trumpet;—back out of the clouds
Of Glaramara southward came the voice;
And Kirkstone toss'd it from his misty head.   (54–65)

In the retelling of his gloss, Wordsworth re-verses the effect to make his own imagination, not Joanna's voice, the agent: "& when I come to the 2 lines 'The Rock like something &c' I am caught in the Trap of my own imagination." The gloss orchestrates the confusion: the lines are "describing what for a moment I believed either actually took place at the time, or when I have been reflecting on what did take place, I have had a temporary belief in some fit of imagination, did really or might have taken place." Then it goes on to say that it's all been a "trick" played on a vicar (reader), a performed "extravagating" in prelude to a capable masculine poetics, on the template of the Preface to *Lyrical Ballads:* "I then tell the story as it happened really; & as the recollection of it exists permanently & regularly in my mind."

But more than one story abides in the verse. To Coleridge's ear, Joanna's laugh was amplified by the she-chorus in *Song XXX* of Drayton's *Poly-Olbion,* and he can't decide if this is "noble imitation" or unwitting "coincidence"—whether, that is, the poet is managing all the echoes.[62] It was Coleridge, too, who wrote to Joanna's sister, Sara Hutchinson, two years later to the month, August 1802, about his own fall into the Wordsworthian auditorium. He had been scrambling alone down a fell-side, his somatic peril alternating with magnificent prospects for the eye, when a storm sent him scurrying into some sheepfolds:

Here I found an imperfect Shelter from a Thunder-shower—accompanied with such Echoes! O God! what thoughts were mine! O how I wished for health & Strength that I might wander about for a Month together, in the stormiest month of the year, among these Places, so lonely & savage & full of sounds!

After the Thunder-storm I shouted out all your names in the
Sheep-fold—when Echo came upon Echo and then Hartley &
Derwent & then I laughed & shouted Joanna It leaves all the Echoes
I ever heard far far behind, in number, distinctness & <u>humanness</u>
of Voice—& then not to forget an old Friend I made them all say
Dr. Dodd & c. (6 August 1802; *Letters* 2: 844)

Coleridge laughs as Joanna had, and he honors her name, writing the
event up for her sister as Wordsworth-with-a-difference. Unlike rattled
Wordsworth, Coleridge himself provokes this chorus of self-echoing,
claiming no mastery beyond the joking reference to the famous forger
and anthologizer of the "Beauties of Shakespeare."[63]

Against Coleridge's gleefully forged anthology of names, Wordsworth's
poetics of mastery come into sharper relief. In the sequel, the poet not
only tames "the Lady's voice" but calls nature back into male formation.
"Now whether," says he in his best analytic mode,

> . . . this were in simple truth
> A work accomplish'd by the brotherhood
> Of ancient mountains, or my ear was touch'd
> With dreams and visionary impulses . . .   (66–71)

As the colloquy shifts from Joanna and the hills to poet and Vicar, not
only Joanna but also the "ancient Woman" in the chorus that carried "the
Lady's voice" fade from the surmise: the hills are now a "brotherhood."
And the poet reduces Joanna to, and silences her within, an image of
female fear seeking male protection—a small chivalric scene:

> . . . there was a loud uproar in the hills.
> And, while we both were listening, to my side
> The fair Joanna drew, as if she wish'd
> To shelter from some object of her fear.   (74–76)

"The fair Joanna," an epithet from England's ancient brotherhood, coincides with the *as if* that concedes the poet's wish behind the one he attributes to her: to see her vulnerable and dependent, amid a din that
evokes the "wilde uproar" of Miltonic scenes, pandemonium (*PL* 2.541)
or chaos (3.710). Wordsworth even appended a NOTE to the end of the
poem (the only such appendage in the 1800 *Ballads*) that slights the first

of the female catalogue, the ancient woman seated Helm-crag: "a Rock which from most points of view bears a striking resemblance to an Old Woman cowering" (II: 187)—twin to fearful Joanna.

The power of Joanna's laugh recedes even further in the poetic present, "eighteen moons" later, the laugher absent and the poet "alone . . . on a calm / And silent morning" (78–80). In such removal, from her and by time, he says he "chanc'd" on a means to reclaim agency from the "the hey-day of astonishment" (67), exercising it on a living stone:

> I chissel'd out in those rude characters
> Joanna's name upon the living stone.
> And I, and all who dwell by my fire-side
> Have call'd the lovely rock, Joanna's Rock.   (82–85)

Living Joanna is "call'd" back in the medium of the poet's voice. "W. . . . read us the poem of Joanna beside the Rothay by the roadside," Dorothy reports (22 August 1800; *GJ* 35). In fresh self-possession, her brother writes this up "in memory of affections old and true" (81)—"a strain of deep tenderness," he says in that gloss.

The shift from Joanna's laugh to the poet's engraving of her name and en-graving of her agency prompts Stephen Parrish to propose that *To Joanna* is not ultimately about Joanna or the place. It is the poet's "dramatic self-portrait": his imagination confronts "a wild excitation in which his sense of reality is momentarily overwhelmed, then sinks once more under rational control, leaving a current of warm emotion as the poet looks tranquilly back through the filter of memory" (29). Parrish gives this "sense of reality" priority over how much the reins of rational control and the career into tranquil memory rely on the taming of the woman: first as fearful damsel, then as a name for chiseling, then as addressee to be reproached from the onset. Yet Wordsworth's "fit of imagination" runs deeper than the strain of deep tenderness declared in the gloss. His poetry lets Joanna's laughter keep its irruptive, pregnant power.

The next in the unit (III) is a figurative sequel. Here a "She" is neither place nor signified, but the place-namer. The "Name" she proposes, moreover, unsettles its referent, the poet. "There is an Eminence,—of these our hills / The last that parleys with the setting sun," begins his record, then elaborates an iconography of pre-eminent poetic power:

> . . . this Cliff, so high
> Above us, and so distant in its height,
> Is visible, and often seems to send
> Its own deep quiet to restore our hearts. (5–8)

It seems merely anticlimactic by the time "She" bestows the poet's name on the place. And yet the poet doth protest, a chagrin that Wordsworth stages against her belated logic:

> 'Tis in truth
> The loneliest place we have among the clouds.
> And She who dwells with me, whom I have lov'd
> With such communion, that no place on earth
> Can ever be a solitude to me,
> Hath said, this lonesome Peak shall bear my Name. (12–17)

His battery of plurals (*we, us, our*) names no Titanic solitude, but a shared life in shared places. The chime of *She* and *me*, the lettering of *we* at the heart of *dwell*, issue a soft objection. Yet it's hard to measure ironies. Is *She* ironized for not getting this? Or is Wordsworth's poetry ironizing a poet's resistance to her logic, her authority?

The historical referent of this *She* (and "Emma," too) is Dorothy Wordsworth. The poetry that William Wordsworth wrote in her company, sometimes about her company, amasses an archive that exposes, at nearly every turn, interactions that vex his sense of poetic priority and thus poetic authority. If this dynamic does not add up to a revolution in male manners, its turns and counterturns are acutely attentive to what Dorothy was doing and writing, often at William's side, in pregnant alternatives to his Romanticism.

CHAPTER FIVE

William's Sister

Alternatives of Alter Ego

The "mission with which she was charged"

"There never lived a woman whom he would not have lectured and admonished under circumstances that should have seemed to require it; nor would he have conversed with her in any mood whatever without wearing an air of mild condescension to her understanding," wrote Thomas De Quincey, in a tone of documentary authority, about William Wordsworth.[1] Though De Quincey was not without his own biases on woman, Wordsworth's poetry makes the case. Even its cherished "dear Sister" is cast for mild condescension, marked with an oft-cited pattern in Romantic poetics: a hierarchical poetics of masculine/feminine. The archetype is the primal first sister, God's gift to Adam:

> Thy likeness, thy fit help, thy other self,
> Thy wish exactly to thy hearts desire.   (*Paradise Lost* 8.450–51)

That Eve is also wife does not rupture translation to the Wordsworths. Dorothy ("gift of God") played the role of wifely partner to William, right up to the eve of his marriage, and with a physical affection that, if not sexual per se, was channeling the intimacy.

Yet this very intimacy could also unsettle, with a lateral dynamic of alter-ego poetics, the masculine priority in God's gift to Adam, or its later version in what Keats satirized as the "egotistical or wordsworthian sublime."[2] The lateral interactions trouble another, cognate story about "masculine" Romanticism: its romance of nurturing female alter-egos (the Wordsworths in starring roles).[3] This may be William Wordsworth's favorite fable, but his imagination is acutely sensitive to the volatile grammar of "alter ego." As *alter* ego, his "Sister" can pose an "other" to the point of inaccessibility, vexed by gender difference; or, in the recipro-

cal relay, as alter *ego*, she can pose (sometimes impose) disquieting proximities against the poet's mode of self-defining masculine difference. The
consequences are potent, at once personal, domestic, and—not the least
—vocational.

The potency is all the more compelling, given the context of Dorothy's
devotion to her brother. She keeps house, keeps company, keeps faith;
she nurtures his poetry and tirelessly word-processes fair-copies, as one
more household labor.[4] De Quincey was even prompted to take that
"Greek meaning" of her name, *"gift of god,"* as a "prophecy" of "the relation in which she stood":

> the mission with which she was charged—to wait upon him as the
> tenderest and most faithful of domestics; to love him as a sister; to
> sympathize with him as a confidant; to counsel him as one gifted
> with a power of judging that stretched as far as his own producing;
> to cheer him and sustain him by the natural expression of her feel-
> ings—so quick, so ardent, so unaffected—upon the probable effect
> of whatever thoughts, plans, images he might conceive; finally, and
> above all other ministrations, to ingraft, by her sexual sense of beauty,
> upon his masculine austerity that delicacy and those graces, which
> else . . . it would not have had.   ("William Wordsworth" 358–59)

Such sentences could have found a home in the domestic ideal of any
conduct manual. De Quincey's rendition and the biographical pattern it
so influentially installed give the impression of a natural ("sexual") character in the subjects themselves.

William's poetry supplies the prototype, trope and true. The sister of
Home at Grasmere is a second self in experiential survival, a "younger
orphan of a Home extinct" (MS *D* 78), and an inspiration continuous
with the natural world, with the force of divine visitation:

> Where'er my footsteps turned,
> Her Voice was like a hidden Bird that sang;
> The thought of her was like a flash of light
> Or an *unseen* companionship, a breath
> Or fragrance independent of the wind.   (*D* 90–94)

In *The Prelude* this companion is not just embodied "Nature" but salvation in nature:

My soul, too reckless of mild grace, had . . .
Longer retain'd its countenance severe,
A rock with torrents roaring, with the clouds
Familiar, and a favorite of the Stars:
But thou didst plant its crevices with flowers,
Hang it with shrubs that twinkle in the breeze,
And teach the little birds to build their nests
And warble in its chambers. At a time
When Nature, destined to remain so long
Foremost in my affections, had fallen back
Into a second place . . . thy breath,
Dear Sister, was a kind of gentler spring
That went before my steps.   (*1805* 13.228–46)

This tribute becomes a citation in De Quincey's romance (359; he was one of the earliest readers of the manuscript) and a fount for his own narrative: she "humanized him by the gentler charities, and engrafted, with her delicate female touch, those graces upon the ruder growths of his nature" (272). The Dear Sister is Nature's ally and metonym, securing "a saving intercourse" for her brother with his "true self": the "Poet" under a guarantee he could be "no further changed / Than as a clouded, not a waning moon" (*1805* 10.915–17). Such mythology registers as biographic fact even for critics such as David Ferry, otherwise inclined to read William Wordsworth against the grain: "Dorothy was not so much a person to him as the symbol of nature's power, instinctive and unconscious in all her dealings with the natural scene, one with it" (156).

But what happens when this poet does apprehend a person—one, moreover, whose power of imagination and action, whose symbolic communication with nature, may issue in terms other than mild grace?

Wild Girls, Wild Boys

De Quincey's sibling romance is curiously fractured along these very lines. "I have been assured that both were, in childhood, irritable or even ill-tempered," he reports (343–44). In adulthood, too: for all her tender grace, in "Miss Wordsworth" lodges an "irritable temperament . . . all fire, and an ardor which . . . looked out in every gleam of her wild eyes (those 'wild eyes' so finely noticed in the 'Tintern Abbey')" (343). The fine notice is from the second movement of *Lines written a few miles above Tintern Abbey*. The first part of this poem, coursing through disturbances and doubts, wins its way to a climax of impassioned praise to "nature and the language of the sense" (109):

> The anchor of my purest thoughts, the nurse,
> The guide, the guardian of my heart, and soul
> Of all my moral being.   (110–12)

Such absolutes of *my* seem to say it all—especially for the capstone of *Lyrical Ballads* 1798. By rhetorical logic, *Lines*, and volume, could have ended here. But as a codicil for this insurance, the poet sends the truncated pentameter into a new verse paragraph:

>   Nor, perchance,
> If I were not thus taught, should I the more
> Suffer my genial spirits to decay:
> For thou art with me, here, upon the banks
> Of this fair river; thou, my dearest Friend,
> My dear, dear Friend . . .   (112–17)

The safeguard is a hyper-companionate "dear, dear Sister!" (122): an alter-ego repository of "my former heart," "my former pleasures," "what I was once" (118–21)—and by this proxy, an immediately present mediator of Nature's guarantees.

Yet the codicil also brings risks. For one, to recognize "Nature" in the language of anchor, nurse, guide, and guardian, is to admit into the picture of the mind the ghost of a self bereft—unanchored, nurseless, unguided, unguardianed—against which Nature's insurance is so suddenly, so passionately appealed. In the metonymic alliance with Sister, moreover, gender activates a surplus contingency: a female alter ego, far from being simply or automatically recruitable to a masculine egotistical sublime, may entail alienation in the alterity.[5] The question registers in that glance at the Sister's "wild eyes," and it radiates into the ministry of a "Nature" which this poet, for the first time in his *Lines*, is about to feminine-gender (124).

In this association, the most arresting statement in *Lines* is not the faith that "Nature" will "lead / From joy to joy" (125–26) in repair of "the many shapes / Of joyless daylight" that vex a man's life in the wide world (52–54). It is the "sad perplexity," in already confessed "recognitions, dim and faint," that in "boyish days" "nature led" otherwise: to fretful stirs of feeling "more like a man / Flying from something that he dreads" (60–73). In such retrospect, lower-case "nature" has forecast everything that a boy must lose, that a man strangely flees, that a poet can now only elegize, in the language of a newly gendered she-Nature, graced with a mythologizing capital:[6]

> . . . Nature never did betray
> The heart that loved her; 'tis her privilege,
> Through all the years of this our life, to lead
> From joy to joy: (123–26)

In a rare rhyme in this blank verse "never did betray" echoes its antonym in the processes of time: "I . . . / Suffer my genial spirits to decay," the latent confession that presses forward at line 113. Explicated across negations and denials, the path from joy to joy cannot escape knowledge of the contrary, a visible pressure on the assertion of chearful faith:[7]

> neither evil tongues,
> Rash judgments, nor the sneers of selfish men,
> Nor greetings where no kindness is, nor all
> The dreary intercourse of daily life,
> Shall e'er prevail against us, or disturb
> Our chearful faith that all which we behold
> Is full of blessings . . .   (129–35)

If the crucial player in this *us/we* is the dear Sister, summoned against the decay of the poet's genial spirits, what her figuration reports proves tenuous, even fugitive:

> in thy voice I catch
> The language of my former heart, and read
> My former pleasures in the shooting lights
> Of thy wild eyes. Oh! yet a little while
> May I behold in thee what I was once,
> My dear, dear Sister!   (117–22)

While *catch* and *behold* may sound like a voice of masculine appropriation, the verbs waver with strain: *catch* may say only *apprehend fleetingly*, and *may I behold* is pleading, fleeting.

In writing out the alter-ego logic of identifying Sister with Nature, this poet has hazarded alienation—a sensation of otherness—from both. Across the array of *my*-claims ripple signs, even signals, of a confederate wild strangeness: a "wild secluded scene" (6); those "wild eyes." De Quincey caught this in his gloss on the "irritable temperament" of the historical referent. He returns (a few pages on) to the adjective, revising it from temperament to a superlative alliance with nature: "I may sum up . . . Miss Wordsworth's character, as a companion, by saying, that she was the very wildest (in the sense of the most natural) person I have ever known" (359). The lexicon in *Lyrical Ballads* is not this companionable, however. The phrase "Her eyes are wild" is given to no alter ego, but to a madwoman, linked only in "English tongue."[8] Even the poet of *Tintern Abbey* sounds a strain to the dear Sister, imagining himself unable to "catch from thy wild eyes these gleams / Of past existence" (149–50).

A poem that Wordsworth added in 1800 to volume II does recover a wild gleam, but on a disturbingly wild trajectory, across which the gender assignments of *wild* and *gentle* are nothing if not critical, nothing if not volatile. Decades later, in 1843, he would speak of a category crisis about *Nutting:* although it "arose out of the remembrance of feelings I had often had when a boy" and was "intended as part of a poem on my own life," it was "struck out as not being wanted there" (FN 13). What was it in this *often* that rejected the memory from a self-authorizing poetic autobiography? It's striking verse to strike out, involving at its core a boy's sexually energized assault on "virgin" hazelnut trees, and concluding in a short sermon about the moral fallout—not self-directed, not given to other boys, but imposed on a suddenly present dearest Maiden.

The gender-text has not gone unespied. The boy-pulsing of this "impassioned nutter" (so William later dubbed the hero; FN 13)—was noted, forgivingly, by David Ferry and Harold Bloom.[9] Michael Cooke addressed the feminine binary, reading a salutary seminar on "the analogies and substitutions by which nature and the feminine are encountered," leading to the poet's "rectified understanding" of both "the feminine" and "through the feminine, of himself" (137–39). Feminist criticism begged to doubt the rectified understanding, pointing to a master-plot of masculine power, in action and poetry. In the double placement of "the feminine" as object of male action—that ravaged "virgin scene" and that lectured "Maiden"—Anne Mellor saw textbook masculinist poetics. Margaret Homans assessed a further accrual in that lecture:

> Then, dearest Maiden! move along these shades
> In gentleness of heart with gentle hand
> Touch,—for there is a Spirit in the woods.   (53–55)

By transmitting his experience cleansed of its pain, "sheltering her" and "interpreting these benefits for her," the poet, in Homan's reckoning, also reserves for himself "what he knows to be the true gain": the sort of experience "necessary to becoming a poet."[10]

Yet for all this, the gender-plot of *Nutting* is unstable, and the manuscripts are part of the archeology. Even the published poem exposes a strange gender imprint, a virgin bower of trees that "rose / Tall and erect" (18–19). Caught by this detail, Cooke reads a "masculine" element, which the wilding boy, in the hysteric reaction of "Then up I rose" (41), forces into a feminine submission, at once "distorting its quality and his perception."[11] But what if "Tall and erect" glimpses a preternatural feminine alternative to "natural" female subordination in the culture-text?[12]

Nutting is not pointed toward this question; it seems an accidental flicker in a chapter framed for—but, as I'll argue, not containable to—a boy's life. And not any boy: it is autobiography, as a rare, same-page footnote makes clear (2: 132).

> ———————————It seems a day,
> (I speak of one from many singled out)
> One of those heavenly days which cannot die,
> When forth I sallied from our cottage-door,*
> And with a wallet o'er my shoulder slung,
> A nutting crook in hand, I turn'd my steps
> Towards the distant woods, a figure quaint,
> Trick'd out in proud disguise of Beggar's weeds
> Put on for the occasion, by advice
> And exhortation of my frugal Dame.   (1–10)

* The house at which I was boarded during the time I was at School.

The autobiographer unfolds an adventure-anecdote: a day away from schoolmasters and frugal dames, on pretext of thrifty nutting. The sallying forth is mock-heroic, no portent of Spenserian-Miltonic trial.[13] Wordsworth even revised to heighten the fun: by 1815 the expectant wallet is "huge" (6; a cartoon retrieved from an 1800 ms); by 1827 the inspiration is "eagerness of boyish hope," and "cottage-door" becomes "Cottage-threshold" (4–5), to hyperbolize a boundary-crossing.[14]

As the adventure unfolds, a language of sexual appetite and aggression also sallies forth, perhaps still in a mock-heroic register, but manifestly invested:

> Among the woods,
> And o'er the pathless rocks, I forc'd my way
> Until, at length, I came to one dear nook
> Unvisited, where not a broken bough
> Droop'd with its wither'd leaves, ungracious sign
> Of devastation, but the hazels rose
> Tall and erect, with milk-white clusters hung,
> A virgin scene! (13–20)

By 1845 the phrase would be "tempting clusters," in key with an already libertine narrative:

> —A little while I stood,
> Breathing with such suppression of the heart
> As joy delights in; and with wise restraint
> Voluptuous, fearless of a rival, eyed
> The banquet . . . (20–24)

The winking knowingness of "such suppression" and "wise restraint" has to be one of the strangest stagings of the Wordsworthian "Poet" as "a man speaking to men."[15] The impending assault then issues in seven pounding iambics: "Then up I rose, / And dragg'd to earth both branch and bough, with crash . . ." (42–43). At the same time, the report extends to terms that seed the reproof: an action of "merciless ravage" (44), its objects "Deform'd and sullied" (46). The denouement is the moral fallout—for the boy, for the poet he is to become, and for the Maiden, taken to School after all.

Yet if this is the payoff, it gets strangely deformed in transmission:

> . . . unless I now
> Confound my present feelings with the past,
> Even then, when from the bower I turn'd away,
> Exulting, rich beyond the wealth of kings
> I felt a sense of pain when I beheld
> The silent trees and the intruding sky. —   (47–52)

The sentence drives to this last arresting image: a sky now visible behind the stripped trees, felt as a bust by a shaming, even punitive witness. The confusion is about the agency of this apprehension: a boy's pained reflux, or a poet's regulatory moral?[16] The question takes a further weird turn in *Selections from the Poems of William Wordsworth, chiefly for the Use of Schools and Young Persons* (assembled in 1836 by Surrey schoolmaster Joseph Hine), where, instead of "Even then, when . . ." (49), the text is "Ere from the mutilated bower I turned"—the phrasing Wordsworth used thereafter. While the addition of *mutilated* does intensify the moral reflux, the new chronology may contest it. To make the pain prior to the exulting turn away may not be to poison conquest with pain, but to allow exultation to succeed and suppress pain.

The revision (so often the case with Wordsworth) suggests not just present feelings confounded with the past, but present feelings confounded about the past. If Spenser and Milton might clarify the moral vectors of bower-ravaging, the heritage is dubious help, not the least because nutting excursions are not inevitable for moral allegorizing.[17] Spenser's sexually decadent Bower of Blisse brings on a "rigour pittilesse" of destruction (II.xii.83) in the police-action of Guyon and the Palmer to save Christian knights for the missions with which they are charged. Milton's bower-invading, Eve-ravishing Satan is the adversary of God and enemy of mankind. Wordsworth's impassioned nutter, though he borrows the trappings both theatrical and moral, is no secure fit with either invader, and Wordsworth decided not to pursue a providential plot that he tested out in some drafts: "They led me, & I followed in their steps"; "They led me far, / Those guardian Spirits."[18]

No wonder that the sermonizing to the Maiden has a lopsided effect for most readers. It's not just the gender shift but the imbalance of the recollection—a vividly expansive, energetic 53 lines—and its postscript, a terse tercet of gentle, humorless lessoning.[19] The chief heritage from

Spenser and Milton may be this asymmetry. Not only is Spenser's bower-episode ambivalent about the violent discipline of pleasure, luxury, and sexuality;[20] but its errant knights, once rescued, do not reflect on their lapse to learn moral self-control. And Satan bears both the dramatic excitement of *Paradise Lost* (especially in Romantic interactions) and (*vide* Wollstonecraft) a critique of knowledge-gendering in Paradise. What is unknowable in the rhetorical afterlife of Wordsworth's anecdote is how an admonished Maiden, iconic though she is, might process the sequence, and balance dramatic excitement and moral reproof.

This is a fundamental question about juvenile reading per se—and it is curiously, if inadvertently, in play in schoolmaster Hine's Preface:

> Having for many years been extensively engaged in the tuition of youth, I could not be ignorant of the great importance of good poetry in this office: whether by giving the pupil a relish for literature, in order to open, enlarge, and strengthen his mind; or by awakening in him a sympathy for all truly desirable things, and producing a clearer perception of all moral and religious, all virtuous, principle. Under these necessities I have been accustomed to read, from the volumes of our great poets, such productions as I thought were suitable to the ends I had in view; and I need scarcely say how great was the effect when Mr. Wordsworth's poems were read: the pupils were in a glow of delight, and never failed to listen with much attention; were always deeply impressed with the matter, and eager to hear more; and numbers of them would apply to me to borrow the volume to read more and again.—"Upon this hint I spake." (v)

Hence this generous selection, on behalf of all moral and religious, all virtuous, principle. Yet what is fueling that glow of delight and eager application for another encounter in private rather than schoolroom reading? The schoolmaster's self-pleased witty compact with Othello responding to Desdemona's eager ear (*Othello* 1.3.192) is a potential slip, given the catastrophe (for a proper lady) that unfolds from her seduction by exotic poetry. M. J. Jewsbury's unsigned review for *The Athenaeum* (191: 404), quoting this preface, wisely stopped short of this overloaded allusion.

Wordsworth's abrupt coda of gender-admonishment is the reciprocal of what is mysteriously indicated by the verse's initiation *in medias res:* that long dash into two iambs. The "nutting scene," explained Dorothy

Wordsworth to Coleridge of this effect, was a pendant: "the conclusion of a poem of which the beginning is not yet written."[21] When it was written, variously in MSS 15 and 16, it was meant to fill out the formal logic, with a female nutter begging for that coda-lesson:

> Ah what a crash was that   _with gentle hand
> Touch those fair hazels: my beloved Maid,
> Though tis a sight invisible to thee,
> From such rude intercourse the woods all shrink,
> As at the blowing of Astolpho's horn.
>   It is a fancy which will make thee smile
> Again - ~~while in the cave we sat, thy face~~
> ~~Was still as water when the winds are gone~~
> ~~And no one can tell whither, now, in truth~~
> Yet had I
> ~~If I had~~ met thee with those eager ~~looks~~ eyes
>   wild
> And cheeks thus ~~rich~~ with a tempestuous bloom
> In truth
>   I should have thought that I had seen ~~in thee~~
>   in
> A houseless wanderer ~~with~~ a human shape;
> An enemy of nature who comes
> From regions far beyond the Indian hills.
> While in the cave we sate this   noon
> Oh! what a countenance was thine come here
> And rest on this light bed of purple heath
>   and let me see thine eye
> As at that moment, rich with happiness
> And still as water when the winds are gone
>
>   . . . .

. . . ~~if I had met thee here unknown~~

~~Thy cheeks thus rich with a tempestuous bloom~~

~~In truth I might have thought that I had~~

                           pass'd

A houseless being in a human shape

An enemy of nature one who comes

From regions far beyond the Indian hills.

Come rest on this light bed of purple heath

And let me see thee sink to a dream

                     once again

Of gentle thoughts   till / thine eye

    the

Be like / heart of love & happiness

Yet still as water when the winds are gone

. . . .

But had I met thee now ~~those cheeks~~ with that keen look

Half cruel in its eagerness, thy cheek

Thus rich with a tempestuous bloom, in truth

I might have half believe that I had pass'd . . .   (15: 63ᵛ–64ʳ)[22]

Drafting this prequel was, clearly, no easy schematic for Wordsworth. This wilding girl does not get the tone of wry sympathy that the boy does. Her "crash" into nature relays an eagerness so wild, keen, tempestuous, and cruel as to cast her not only beyond civilization (the Indian hills) but beyond human recognition (a masquerade in human shape). It is only in dreamland that this poet can romance a female formation that is "gentle": those half-cruel eyes calmed to the stillness of windless water, at one with a "heart of love & happiness."

If that's the remedy, the coda to *Nutting* is a fiction of difference written over a knowledge of common passions. The draft-girl's ally is not calm Nature, but Ariosto's male adventurer Astolpho, replete with a horn of magical potency. In *chansons de geste*, Astolpho has a cousin Orlando, whose Shakespeare-namesake imprints another draft of the story:

Ah! what a crash was that! with gentle hand
Touch these fair hazels—My beloved Maid!
Though 'tis a sight invisible to thee,
From such rude intercourse the woods all shrink
As at the blowing of Astolpho's horn.—
Thou, Lucy, art a maiden "inland bred,"
And thou hast "known some nurture"   (16: 1–7; B&G 305–6)

Beholding a sword-wielding crasher of his sylvan feast, Shakespeare's Duke Senior wonders if this is a "rude despiser of good manners." When Orlando assures him that he's not outlandish—"I am inland bred, / And know some nurture"—the Duke finger-wags the chiasmus of polite society: "Your gentleness shall force, / More than your force move us to gentleness" (*As You Like It* 2.7.91–103). For a Maid to enact Orlando's rude extremes intensifies the gender scandal. Wordsworth even changed "beloved Friend!" to "beloved Maid!" to deepen the shock.[23]

At the same time, the reminder of breeding and nurture glimpses an understanding of gentleness as a cultural form, not a natural trait.[24] "Nature" is what culture recruits for its motivated lessons:

See those stems
Both stretch'd along the ground, two brother trees
That in one instant at the touch of spring
Put forth their tender leaves, and through nine years,
In the dark nights have both together heard
The driving storm—— Well! Blessed be the Powers
That teach philosophy and good desires
In this their still Lyceum, hand of mine
Wrought not this ruin—I am guiltless here.
For, seeing little worthy or sublime
In what we blazon with the pompous names
Of power and action, I was early taught
To look with feelings of fraternal love
Upon those unassuming things which hold
A silent station in this beauteous world.   (16: 19–33; B&G 306)

Fraternal love, fraternal amity and endurance, fraternal education—all this is set, didactically, against both a blazon of man's power and action, and a dismay at a female refusal of kinship with all things beautiful and silent. How arresting, for one so attentive to the metrical "exponent" of poetry (*Preface* ix), that this poetry sets "I am" at odds with the iambic pattern of the protest, pounding out a plenum of stress: "*Wrought not this ru*in—*I* am *guilt*less *here.*"

MS 16 allies the gentle fraternal ideal with a "general ministry" (45) continuous with the "chearful faith" of *Tintern Abbey:* a spirit in the woods intent to "interpose" (46)

> Even as a sleep, betwixt the heart of man
> And the uneasy world, 'twixt man himself,
> Not seldom, and his own unquiet heart . . . (47–49)

Ministry to the conflicts of "man" with "the uneasy world," or to the homology of "man himself" and "his own unquiet heart," requires, it seems, a feminine binary, not a female repetition. Yet even De Quincey finds himself doubting this arrangement, not only giving Wordsworth's adjective for the boyhood nutter to both brother and sister ("both, having such impassioned temperaments"), but writing of active equivalence: "they were constantly together; for Miss Wordsworth was always ready to walk out—wet or dry, storm or sunshine, night or day" (343–44). Marlon Ross's proposal that Wordsworth's male-plotted poetry "effaces the issue of the growth of the female mind" ("Naturalizing" 395) may be right about the logic, but what it elides is the wild growth of Wordsworth's unpublished drafts.

If *Nutting* does less to secure gender differentials than to produce signs of critical doubt, the remedial sequel on the obverse page in the 1800 *Lyrical Ballads* (2: 136) is so over-driven in its resolution that it can't help but re-activate the question. This is the untitled verse that begins "Three years she grew," arresting a girl in this year, under the sign of a Nature that declares, "She shall be mine, and I will make / A Lady of my own" (4–6), endowing her with all that Miss Lucy wrecks: "And hers shall be the breathing balm, / And hers the silence and the calm / Of mute insensate things" (16–18).[25] This formation of Ladyhood promises not only no voice, not only no activity, but no vitality: a "Lady" is the growth of a mind in reverse, back into an undifferentiated nature—with all the difference for the Poet's masculine vocation. But Dorothy's lively presence in William's life, and the activity of her writing argue otherwise.

William's "I" and Dorothy's "very words"

From "the pleasure which the mind derives from the perception of similitude in dissimilitude," remarks the Poet of the 1800 *Preface,* "the sexual appetite, and all the passions connected with it take their origin: It is the life of our ordinary conversation; and upon the accuracy with which similitude in dissimilitude, and dissimilitude in similitude are perceived, depend our taste and our moral feelings" (xxxii–iii). William and Dorothy's domestic life could supply a case in point: a dissimilitude of sex across the similitude of a shared life, shared adventures, shared home, and ordinary (sometimes extraordinary) conversations. This was surely William's imagination in 1793, eagerly shared with Dorothy, for their household idyll:

> How much do I wish that each emotion of pleasure and pain that visits your heart should excite a similar pleasure or a similar pain within me, by that sympathy which will almost identify us when we have stolen to our little cottage! I am determined to see you . . .
>
> (July 1793; *EY* 101–2)

How remarkable to see William, icon of the egotistical sublime, cast "I" and "me" into "your" and then "our": a sympathy that makes identification corporate, double-bound, in that play (again) on *determined* as a volition indistinguishable from fate. This union may have a sexual structure in its candid intimacy, but it is cast as a domestic utopia.[26]

The sexually configured passion gains an analogue, some years on in their life together, in the shared production frequently noted in Dorothy's Grasmere journals. "After Tea I wrote the first part of Peter Bell—William better"; "I wrote the 2nd prologue to Peter Bell. . . . After dinner I wrote the 1st Prologue"; "I wrote the Pedlar & finished it"; "wrote out Ruth—read it with the alterations"; "I wrote the Leech Gatherer for him which he had begun the night before." So she writes, her *I* not just his technological agent but also her own.[27] If to Elizabeth Hardwick, this conflation indulges a "peculiar illusion of collaboration" (4), to me these are creditable records of conversation and collaboration across a difficult period of writing, refitting, "disaster" (*GJ* 73), and anguished, then productive rewriting. The poetic work is intensely interactive: "I almost finished writing The Pedlar, but poor William wore himself & me out with labour. We had an affecting conversation"; "We sate . . . talking & William read parts of his Recluse aloud to me" (12–13 February 1802; *GJ* 67–68); "Wm & I were employed all the morning in writing an addition to the preface" (5 October 1800; *GJ* 24); "We began the letter to John Wilson" to answer to "a complimentary & critical letter" he had sent to Wm.; "we" continued "writing the letter" over the next days (5–6 June 1802; cp. 31 May; *GJ* 103, 106).

The journal is not just a record; it is also a medium of interaction. William, who sometimes wrote his poetry in its pages, was always the intended reader. Hardwick is right to see Dorothy's journal "as a sort of offering" to him (3)—and it was an urgently invested gesture: she began her Grasmere journal on 14 May 1802, the day William set off to York-shire, to begin his courtship of Mary Hutchinson. The journal, as their shared book, is her way of sustaining a relationship that had begun to feel like a marriage—intellectual, vocational, and labor-intensive. "When [Wm.] writes, she is never far away—she listens to him compose, reads to him, suggests occasions for poems, reminds him of the experience he has shared with her, delights in and repeats what he finishes," notes William Heath (120). If De Quincey could not theorize such a collaboration, he was impressed by the evident resource:

> the exceeding sympathy, always ready and always profound, by which she made all that one could tell her, all that one could describe, all that one could quote from a foreign author, reverberate . . . to one's own feelings, by the manifest impression it made upon her . . . the answering and echoing movements of her sympathizing attention.
>
> (272)

Yet in the reciprocal records of William's sororal poetry, such debts are peculiarly less than all, and this, too, is a register of a sympathy more troubled than the cottage romance of 1793.

The epic mythology of Dorothy's mission as Nature's agent that so en-chanted De Quincey, contains, for instance, a strange, even strained, no-tation on a Sister

> Who ought by rights the dearest to have been
> Conspicuous through this biographic Verse,
> Star seldom utterly concealed from view.
>
> (1805 *Prelude* 13.339–42)

Though a lovely analogue to her sustaining of his ego-ideal of a "true self . . . no further changed, / Than as a clouded not a waning moon" (10.915–17), it also concedes insufficient credit in "The Story" at hand (13.335). In the sororal lyrics that do praise her (also enchanting to De Quincey), what is most conspicuous is a figuration that scarcely reflects the intellectual vigor of a trusted collaborator, or the labor of hands and eyes in the compositional drudgery:

> She gave me eyes, she gave me ears;
> And humble cares, and delicate fears;
> A heart, the fountain of sweet tears;
>   And love, and thought, and joy.
>
> (*The Sparrow's Nest* 17–20)

If, in De Quincey's story, such verse sums up Wordsworth's "grateful acknowledgments of his own maturist retrospect" (359), it also shows a perspective of difference and dissimilitude, even determined alterity, of gifts too delicate for the growth of a mature poet's mind.

The full anecdote is hardly better. "Look, five blue eggs are gleaming there! / Few visions have I seen more fair," this poet greets us (1–2), challenging us to the vision, and for reinforcement turning his visionary gleam to a memory of himself and his Sister:

> The home and shelter'd bed,
> The Sparrow's dwelling, which, hard by
> My Father's House, in wet or dry,
> My Sister Emmeline and I
>   Together visited.   (6–10)

But the Sister's hesitation at the nest, "as if she fear'd it; / Still wishing, dreading to be near it" (11–12), is too delicate by half, starkly dissimilar to another memory of a boy and a nest:

> Oh, when I have hung
> Above the raven's nest, by knots of grass
> Or half-inch fissures in the slipp'ry rock
> But ill sustained, and almost, as it seemed,
> Suspended by the blast which blew amain,
> Shouldering the naked crag, oh at that time,

While on the perilous ridge I hung alone
With what strange utterance did the loud dry wind
Blow through my ears, the sky seemed not a sky
Of earth, and with what motion moved the clouds   (MS V 3^r)[28]

In contrast to the sing-song metrics of *The Sparrow's Nest*, these epic pen-
tameters, both in memory and as poetry, vibrate with transgression and
fear undistinguishable from the thrill of everything slippery, perilous, unintelligible, undomestic. Wordsworth encases *The Sparrow's Nest* in the
1807 subset, "Moods of My Own Mind," rather than (say) "Imagination."

The first poem in the subset, *To a Butterfly*, gives this creature a
Dorothy-function:

A little longer stay in sight!
Much converse do I find in Thee,
Historian of my Infancy!   (2-4)

The history turns out to involve the Sister, in the similitude in this childish era:

Oh! pleasant, pleasant were the days,
The time, when in our childish plays
My Sister Emmeline and I
Together chaced the Butterfly!   (10-13)

In this nostalgia, U. C. Knoepflmacher writes, William "identified Dorothy with his own desire of arresting or reversing a process of separation
that he equates with the loss of a much coveted, presocial, Edenic one-
ness" (97–98). It also effaces Dorothy from his adult converse, her agency
as Historian. Her journal for 10 June 1800 describes two boys in an analo-
gous sibling ratio: "one about 10 the other about 8 years old at play chasing a butterfly. They were wild figures" (*GJ* 10). In a later entry that exclaims William "wrote the poem to a Butterfly!" (14 March 1802), she
gives the story of their own childhood play:

I told him that I used to chase them a little but that I was afraid of
brushing the dust off their wings, & did not catch them—He told me
how they used to kill all the white ones when he went to school because they were frenchmen.   (*GJ* 78)

William's poetry shifts this, not only depoliticizing his aggression, but hyperbolizing her girlish gentleness into a too-silly delicacy:

> A very hunter did I rush
> Upon the prey:—with leaps and springs
> I follow'd on from brake to bush;
> But She, God love her! feared to brush
> The dust from off its wings. (14–18)

Kin to the nutter, the boy is an avid predator, while "She" (no kin to MS Lucy) halts. Is this a "documentary" of William's "respect" for his sister (Frosch 630), an endorsement of "superior sororal imagination" (Knoepflmacher 98)? To me, it's hard to brush off the dust of soft condescension to her fear, or affection for the energy (if not eco-ethics) of boyish pursuit.

William's revisions of Dorothy's records could find a place in Harold Bloom's archive of "the anxiety of influence." Bloom's dramatis personae are male poets in oedipal contention with strong male precursors, for which one strategy is disappropriation, "a Counter-Sublime whose function suggests *the precursor's relative weakness*" (*Anxiety* 100). How more anxious if the precursor is a dear Sister. Even if this isn't a Bloomian sublime, it would be hard to find a paradigm more apt to Wordsworth's rhetoric of condescension, or to his classification of most of the sororal pieces in the *Poems* of 1815 under Childhood or Fancy, the domain of puerile delights.[29] It was such refractions that set the biographical, and later critical, pattern for regarding the Sister and her empirical referent as merely, sheerly "spontaneous, intuitive, emotional"—one of a gallery of "characters who are oracularly banal . . . not thoughtful"; "at twenty-six she is what William was at seven. She is splendid but rudimentary and incomplete."[30] The figure suppresses what Dorothy Wordsworth's journals and letters everywhere show: that she was full of thought, fluent in French, a reader of French, German, Italian, and English literature (*Clarissa*, Fielding, Milton, and the *Iliad*—the last two presents from her brothers[31]), and valued as an intellectual companion no less than as a successful manager of several households. Her historical and domestic intimacy with her brother is complex: she is a mirror for his self-affirmation and self-completion, but also a similitude compelling him to differentiate himself, and not always securely.

Although one critic tells us that "Dorothy's few remarks" on the "genesis and development" of William's Grasmere poems are not "materially" important, the material circumstances recorded in the journals matter in the perspective of William's determined differentiations.[32] On 13 March 1802 Dorothy records that she spent all morning taking down "stanzas &c" for *The Beggars;* by late afternoon William "warmed with the subject & had half cast the Poem." Meaning to help, she opened up her journal to 10 June 1800 and read her "account of the little Boys belonging to the tall woman" to him.[33] This proved "an unlucky thing," however, for William "could not escape from those very words, & so he could not write the poem, he left it unfinished & went tired to Bed." He "slept badly," but he knew the cure: "before he rose he had finished the Beggar Boys," as if determined to find his voice before hearing his sister's (*GJ* 77–78). *The Beggars* escapes her words by usurping her place: "I . . . before me did espy / A pair of little Boys at play, / Chasing a crimson butterfly" (19–22). William's devotion to this self-authorizing fiction is such that by 1817 he could write, "I their pastime witnessed . . . / They met me."[34] Decades later, this poet would say the boys were "Met & described by me to my Sister" (FN 14).[35]

Their conversations are typically generative this way, producing poetry, and defensive this way, too: *we* converted to *me.* William would remember *To a Butterfly* as "Written in the Orchard 1801" (FN 1), but it was written the next morning, 14 March 1802, at breakfast with Dorothy: "The thought first came upon him as we were talking about the pleasure we both always feel at the sight of a Butterfly" (*GJ* 78). Uncannily, William's late remark to Isabella Fenwick indicates, as if a necessity, their disunion: "My Sister and I were parted immediately after the death of our Mother who died in 1778" (FN 1). So, too, a month on, Dorothy records, "I saw a Robin chacing a scarlet Butterfly this morning," and the next day "William wrote the poem on the Robin & the Butterfly." William shows Dorothy his conclusion, which she reads back to him, and "We left out some lines" (17–18 April; *GJ* 88). Then he left out her presence in *The Redbreast and the Butterfly,* framing a cast of all male characters: "Father Adam" dismayed at the predation of "brother" creatures.

The pattern of inspiration by Dorothy's very words, followed by a poetry that effaces her agency, is a recurrent self-authorization. "Wm wrote two sonnets on Buonaparte after I had read Milton's sonnets to him," notes Dorothy of the event in May 1802 that fired his interest in sonnet-writing (*GJ* 101). When "I grieved for Buonaparte" appeared in the 1815

Poems, its title erased the year of Dorothy's reading: it read 1801 (and thus for decades). William was attentive to errata, so the persistence suggests a defensive formation.[36] The emphasis on the Milton-muse also elides another female influence: Charlotte Smith's sonnets. William read these as a schoolboy, and as an undergraduate he had subscribed to the fifth edition (1789).[37] But in November 1802, it is "Milton's Sonnets" that he praises, implicitly against feminine sonnetry: "manly and dignified compositions, distinguished by simplicity and unity of object and aim, and undisfigured by false or vicious ornaments" (*EY* 379).

Dorothy's journal entries across 1802 record the shared scenes that inspired the sonnets he was writing across this year: *Composed Upon Westminster Bridge, Sept. 3, 1803; Composed by the Sea-Side near Calais, August, 1802* ("Fair Star of Evening"); and "It is a beauteous Evening." In all these sonnets, William presents a poet profoundly alone, musing in solitude, even in company.[38] The date of *Westminster Bridge* is even postdated, as if the public poet wanted to efface any companionable moment with Dorothy. It wasn't until *The Sonnets of William Wordsworth* in 1838 that it would be corrected to *1802* (83). The contraction to masculine singularity in the Calais sonnets involves more than displacing Dorothy. They went there, during the Peace of Amiens, to settle affairs with William's abandoned lover, Annette Vallon, and daughter, Caroline, prior to his marriage in October. And so *Composed by the Sea-Side* is a love poem to England, from France, in the language of chivalric nationalism; and "It is a beauteous Evening" gives the "dear Child!" Caroline over to another father.[39] While Dorothy had never to fear such a sentimental rejection, it was she who was conscripted by William, in late 1800, to manage the correspondence with Annette, writing for him, in terms flattering to his self-regard: "When you are writing to France say all that is affection to A. and all that is fatherly to C" (*EY* 282). This is a double "all" of a fiction in which both were materially absent, a kind of erasure that Dorothy could ponder.

William's conversion of experience shared with Dorothy into generative solitude marks his poetry as far back as the year at Alfoxden, 1798. Dorothy records their having taken shelter "under the hollies, during a hail-shower. The withered leaves danced with the hailstones" (18 March; *AN* 13); "William wrote a description of the storm," she adds. But the poem in *Lyrical Ballads* 1800 beginning "A whirl-blast from behind the hill" gives a singular *I* that "sate within an undergrove," marveling how "where'er the hailstones drop/The withered leaves all skip and hop" (6, 13-14). Working from Dorothy's words and metaphors—a draft from 18 or 19 March 1798 twice plays her phrase, "withered leaves" (B&G 284)— William later recalls the date of writing as "Spring of 1799," distancing Dorothy's record (FN 1).

Dorothy has another record on 25 January 1798 (*AN* 6), from which William channeled her language into his "lonesome path" of inspiration. Here is Dorothy's record of their shared sight:

> The sky spread over with one continuous cloud, whitened by the light of the moon, which, though her dim shape was seen, did not throw forth so strong a light as to chequer the earth with shadows. At once the clouds seemed to cleave asunder, and left her in the centre of a black-blue vault. She sailed along, followed by multitudes of stars, small, and bright, and sharp. Their brightness seemed concentrated, (half moon).

Two days later, she describes how "in the wood the moon burst through the invisible veil which enveloped her" (6). William drafted a poem on the twenty-fifth or shortly after (B&G 453), revised it, and published it as *A Night-Piece* under "Poems of Imagination" in *Poems* of 1815, crowing about "the imaginative power displayed" as "among the best" of this group (Morley 1: 166). Whose imaginative power? Here is the draft from late January 1798, in Dorothy's hand, heavily marked by William (the high-lighting italics are mine):

> The *sky is overspread*
> With a close veil of *one continuous cloud*
> *All whitened by the moon*, that just appears,
> A *dim-seen* orb, yet *chequers* not the ground
> *With any shadow*,—plant, or tower, or tree.   [5]
> At last, a pleasant, an instantaneous light
> Startles the musing man whose eyes are bent
> To earth, He looks around, *the clouds are split*
> *Asunder*, and above his head, he views
> The clear moon, and the glory of the heavens.   [10]
> There, in *a black-blue vault she sails along*,

Followed by multitudes of stars, that small.
                                & bright
                ~~within~~   *vault*
And bright, and sharp, along the gloomy *vault*
                                chasm
Drive as she drives. How fast they wheel away!

Yet vanish not! The wind is in the trees,   [15]

But they are silent; still they roll along
                        chasm
Immeasurably distant, and the ~~vault~~
                        vault
~~The deep blue vault~~
~~And the vault built round by those white clouds~~
Built round by those white clouds, enormous clouds,

Still deepens its interminable depth.   [20]

At length the vision closes, & the mind

Not undisturbed by the deep joy it feels,

Which slowly settles into peaceful calm,

Is left to muse upon the solemn scene.   (MS 15: 2ʳ)[40]

William's poem is different from Dorothy's journal, most obviously in turning a perceptual scene into a drama of "mind," played into beautifully extended, deftly enjambed blank-verse ("bent/To earth"; "split/Asunder"). Yet across William's stage of a lone musing masculine mind and a muselike female moon falls the legible mediation of Dorothy's script, and his struggle with her words.[41] He tries out, but is not satisfied with alternatives to her sublime trope of the night sky as a "black-blue vault" (13, 17–18). In the *Night-Piece* that he finally published in 1815, her initial participle *spread* (also line 1 of the 1798 draft) is moved to line 6, and the opening revised:

————————The sky is overcast
With a continuous cloud of texture close,
Heavy and wan, all whitened by the Moon,
Which through a veil is indistinctly seen,
A dull, contracted circle, yielding light
So feebly spread that not a shadow falls,
Chequering the ground . . .   (1–7)

But it's still close to Dorothy's journal entries of 25 and 27 January 1798, and to yet another: on 31 January she noted how the closing in of late evening clouds seemed to be "contracting the dimensions of the moon without concealing her" (*AN* 7).

Heath proposes that William never frees himself of "dependence" on Dorothy until *The Leech-Gatherer*, aptly titled *Resolution and Independence* when it was published in 1807, the first volume of new poems since the 1800 *Lyrical Ballads*.[42] But if the iconic title posts attributes that a vocation-vexed poet would like to absorb from this exemplary male figure, the poem-text is inflected by Dorothy's record: "Wm & I . . . met an old man almost double" (3 October 1800; *GJ* 42). The most famous case of Wm's singularizing his sister out of poetic agency involves another journal record, her account of their coming upon "a long belt" of daffodils along a lakeshore, "about the breadth of a country turnpike road":

> I never saw daffodils so beautiful they grew among the mossy stones
> about & about them, some rested their heads upon these stones as
> on a pillow for weariness & the rest tossed & reeled & danced &
> seemed as if they verily laughed with the wind that blew upon them
> over the Lake, they looked so gay ever glancing ever changing . . .
> the simplicity & unity & life of that one busy highway.
>
> (15 April 1802; *GJ* 85)

Dorothy's racing syntax conveys a panorama of busy activity. Poet Wordsworth's untitled stanzas, beginning "I wandered lonely as a Cloud," are categorically, metaphysically different. His drama glances at the panorama of sprightly dance, but the affective arc demotes this original, shared moment to secondary importance, replaying it as resource for a solitary self "in vacant or in pensive mood," its images most vital in "the bliss of solitude" (14–17). If recollected pleasure is this poet's signature, the scheme also accrues the wealth of having vacated Dorothy's agency. Decades later, William would acknowledge a female influence, but not hers: he commented that the register of deepest value—"They flash upon that inward eye / Which is the bliss of solitude"—was written "by Mary," and to his mind, constituted the poem's "two best lines." One female coauthor is credited, another suppressed.[43]

A similar relay of effacement and substitution is reported by Aubrey de Vere (via a footnote in William Sharp's *Sonnets of this Century*):

It was to Father Faber that Wordsworth adjudged the possession of as true an eye to nature as he himself owned: "I have hardly ever known anyone but myself who had a true eye for Nature" [how eminently Wordsworthian!]; "one that thoroughly understood her meanings and her teachings—except" (here he interrupted himself, says the narrator—Aubrey de Vere, in his *Recollections*)—"one person. There was a young clergyman called Frederick Faber, who resided at Ambleside. He had not only as good an eye for Nature as I have, but even a better one, and sometimes pointed out to me on the mountains effects which, with all my great experience, I had never detected." (284)

Faber may have been true in this eye, but to delimit him as the "one person" is to satisfy a wish at the expense of a debt to another resident near Ambleside. A Father who instructs in finer sight can be acknowledged, but a sister who offers words is canceled from credit.

This recurrent suppression evokes not only Bloom's revisionary ratios, but also the paradigms of some feminist social psychologists on gender development and self-possession. In households where the primary caregiver is female, in Nancy Chodorow's story, "girls come to experience themselves as less differentiated than boys, as more continuous with and related to the external object world" (167). William surely has such moments of experience in nature; but in scenes of writing, charged with vocation, attenuated differentiation registers different pressures of relation. Carol Gilligan elaborates the asymmetry for her story of social being and self-possession:

since masculinity is defined through separation while femininity is defined through attachment, male gender identity is threatened by intimacy while female gender identity is threatened by separation. Thus males tend to have difficulty with relationships, while females tend to have problems with individuation. (8)

Skeptical of these narratives (however mythic their allure), Mary Jacobus points out that all identity is a formation by differentiation, a strong female identity no less individuated than a strong male one (*Romanticism, Writing* 220). Jacobus's correction cuts two ways for the Wordsworths: William at once cherishes and suppresses Dorothy's gift to his individuated identity as "Poet," while the gifted care-giving sister, alive to the external world and passionately related to her brother, but also writing her own poetry and much else, could never regard herself as a writer or as a poet, even in modest lowercase.

The symptoms of conflict caught De Quincey's eye. He marked Dorothy's difference—not so much from William, as from the "feminine" pattern: the way she walked "gave an ungraceful, and even an unsexual character to her appearance when out of doors. She did not cultivate the graces" (132). As we recall from Polwhele's and Mathias's "unsexed," the term means "not in accordance with the standard for her sex." De Quincey found this *un*-character at once part of Dorothy's appeal and a sign of cultural abjection, acutely internalized. In 1807—the year of William's *Poems, in two volumes*—De Quincey prefaced his romance of William's "Dorothy" with this register of conflict:

> Her eyes were not soft . . . they were wild and startling, and hurried in their motion. Her manner was warm and even ardent; her sensibility seemed constitutionally deep; and some subtle fire of impassioned intellect apparently burned within her, which, being alternately pushed forward into a conspicuous expression by the irrepressible instincts of her temperament, and then immediately checked, in obedience to the decorum of her sex and age, and her maidenly condition, (for she had rejected all offers of marriage, out of pure sisterly regard to her brother and his children,) gave to her whole demeanor and to her conversation, an air of embarrassment and even of self-conflict, that was sometimes distressing to witness . . . perhaps, from some morbid irritability of the nerves. At times, the self-counteraction and self-baffling of her feelings caused her even to stammer. (271)

Obedience to the decorum of sex and devotion to her brother, De Quincey implies, was her marriage vow. When William left to court Mary Hutchinson, Dorothy resolves to keep at her journal "because I will not quarrel with myself, & because I shall give Wm Pleasure by it when he comes home again" (14 May 1800; *GJ* 1). The coincidence of refusing a "quarrel with myself"—the very energy, says Yeats, that makes poetry—and caring for Wm's pleasure is a self-counteraction that De Quincey could have written more about, against his romance narrative.

What he would record was discipline in conflict—those eruptions of self-counteraction and self-baffling—and the consequent cultural alienation. She was "thoroughly deficient (some would say painfully deficient—I say charmingly deficient) in ordinary female accomplishments," he commented of her prospects for any marriage market (359–60), while her irregular education "exiled her from the rank and privileges of *bluestockingism*" (361). Dorothy Wordsworth was living in a no-woman's land, neither a marriageable miss nor a blue-stocking hit, neither traditional nor modern. De Quincey, for all his aversion to brainy women, wondered if it would have been "better for her happiness if she *had* been a blue-stocking" (363, his italics). She had the resources of intellect and discernment that would have made her a respectable "writer for the press," the only profession "open to both sexes alike": with "absolutely no sacrifice or loss of feminine dignity," she could "have cultivated the profession of authorship" in that "womanly and serene . . . temper . . . pursued by Joanna Baillie, by Miss Mitford, and other women of admirable genius." He even proposes that such a profession might have spared her "that nervous depression which . . . has clouded her latter days" (364–65).

He was not so much fantasizing, as projecting this prospect from his experience of Dorothy Wordsworth's lively company and conversation, as well as her poems and narratives, her journals and recollections. By this calculus, De Quincey would believe abundant recompense, "ample amends for all that she wanted of more customary accomplishments" (361). With his love of William's visionary poetry, he wouldn't deem Dorothy's gifts equal to her brother's, but he did think her a candidate for the sorority of "admirable genius." No small part of this potential was Dorothy's evident genius, for writing against, and in alternatives to, the forms and forces of her brother's imagination.

Dorothy's Conversation with William

What makes "a Poet"?

No use arguing that for Dorothy Wordsworth, William Wordsworth did not set the model of "Poet": her words may imprint his poetry, but his power of imagination haunts hers. Such is the story of another moon-scaped inspiration, elaborated in her Grasmere journal:

> —it was a grave evening—there was something in the air that compelled me to serious thought—the hills were large, closed in by the sky. It was nearly dark . . . night was come on & the moon was overcast. But as I climbed . . . the moon came out from behind a Mountain Mass of Black Clouds—O the unutterable darkness of the sky & the Earth below the Moon! & the glorious brightness of the moon itself! There was a vivid sparkling streak of light at this end of Rydale water but the rest was very dark & Loughrigg fell & Silver How were white & bright as if they were covered with hoar frost. The moon retired again & appeared & disappeared several times before I reached home. Once there was no moonlight to be seen but upon the Island house & the promontory of the Island where it stands, "That needs must be a holy place" &c—&c. I had many very exquisite feelings and when I saw this lowly Building in the waters among the dark & lofty hills, with that bright soft light upon it—it made me more than half a poet. I was tired when I reached home I could not sit down to reading & tried to write verses but alas! I gave up expecting William & went soon to bed.   (18 March 1802; *GJ* 80–81)

If, with Virginia Woolf, "one feels the suggestive power which is the gift of the poet rather than of the naturalist,"[1] one might also feel (and not here alone) a perverse gift of self-cancellation: "tried to write verses but alas! I gave up expecting William." Dorothy means that she is expecting his return home, but her syntax registers "William" as an absence in her poetic capacity.

Four years on (20 April 1806), she renders a non-vocational preface to her poems in a letter to her friend Lady Beaumont, who had been pleased by two William had read, along with his own *Benjamin the Waggoner* and the "Intimations" *Ode*. Dorothy's letter zigzags between desire and embarrassment, hope and despair, the flux of William's support and a reflux of her self-abasement against his habits of composition, his skills, his traditions, his vocation. She starts in gladness that William's poems gave "so much pleasure," then halts at their friend's encouragement:

And you would persuade me that I am capable of writing poems that might give pleasure to others besides my own particular friends!! indeed, indeed you do not know me thoroughly; you think far better of me than I deserve. (*MY* 1: 24)

Even so, she feels a persuasion to unfold a history of her impulses and activity:

I must tell you the history of those two little things which William in his fondness read to you. I happened to be writing a letter one evening . . . I laid down the pen and thinking of little Johnny (then in bed in the next room) I muttered a few lines of that address to him about the Wind, and having paper before me, wrote them down, and went on till I had finished. The other lines I wrote in the same way, and as William knows every thing that I do, I shewed them to him when he came home, and he was very much pleased; (*MY* 1: 24)

The "history" sounds vocational: Dorothy auditions some poetry composed extempore, writes it down, shows it to William; he is pleased, reads it to the Beaumonts, who are pleased, and she attempts more, in impulses that are social, domestic, situational, and occasional.

And then the psychic imaginary Poet-William weighs in. Following the semicolon after "much pleased" she pivots into an elaborate self-devaluation:

. . . but this I attributed to his partiality; yet because they gave him pleasure and for the sake of the children I venture to hope that I might do something more at some time or other. Do not think that

I was ever bold enough to hope to compose verses for the pleasure of grown persons. Descriptions, Sentiments, or little stories for children was all I could be ambitious of doing, and I did try one story, but failed so sadly that I was completely discouraged. Believe me, since I received your letter I made several attempts . . . and have been obliged to give it up in despair; and looking into my mind I find nothing there, even if I had the gift of language and numbers, that I could have the vanity to suppose could be of any use beyond our own fireside, or to please, as in your case, a few partial friends; but I have no command of language, no power of expressing my ideas, and no one was ever more inapt at molding words into regular metre. I have often tried when I have been walking alone (muttering to myself as is my Brother's custom) to express my feelings in verse; feelings, and ideas such as they were, I have never wanted at those times; but prose and rhyme and blank verse were jumbled together and nothing ever came of it. As to those two little things which I did write, I was very unwilling to place them beside my Brother's poems, but he insisted upon it, and I was obliged to submit; and though you have been pleased with them I cannot but think that it was chiefly owing to the spirit which William gave them in the reading and to your kindness for me.   (*MY* 1: 25)

With a semi-canny sibling pun on "unwilling," Dorothy exposes a negative of vocation: excuses and qualifications streaked with desire, ambition, and effort. She tries William's custom of pacing and poeticizing. By 1806 he was a published poet, and had been pacing out poetry for more than a decade. Frustration is part of his territory, as Dorothy knows. Had she wrought her struggle into epic blank verse, she might have had something like those two hundred lines of "Impediments" in the Introduction to *The Prelude* (1.68–272), the test of vocation that William had completed, provisionally, just months before. Yet lacking a "gift" that she can index only as a talent for "regular metre" and generic orderliness, she won't allow herself any adventure in "prose and rhyme and blank verse . . . jumbled together," just the self-baffling, self-counteraction that De Quincey noticed, acutely, when he visited the next year.

Thus the serial, ritual disclaimers. Pasting some 160 lines of verse on a holiday into her commonplace book, she postscripts a plea to any reader, "be in good humour & forgive—bad metre, bad rhymes—no rhymes—identical rhymes & all that is lawless" (*CP* 177). In *Lines intended for my Niece's Album*, she sighs to her namesake, niece Dora, "why should I inscribe my name,/No Poet I?" (37–38)—alienating herself from the capital. So arrested is she by the fraternity around Dora's "gifted Sire"—"A wreath for thee is here entwined/By his true Brothers of the Lyre" (27–28)—that, in the logic of alienation, she cannot mention the sisters of the lyre who also inscribed the album: Maria Jane Jewsbury, Mary Lamb, Lydia Sigourney, and, not the least, famous poet Felicia Hemans, who gave the album to Dora as a gift.[2]

Yet for all this sense of inappropriate identification, Dorothy Wordsworth (as Susan Levin's important edition shows) kept writing poems, across decades, for adults as well as children. William, "trusting in his own sense of their merit," is happy to announce that he has "*extorted* them from the Authoress" to put a few in his volumes, identifying the poet as Sister or Friend. Charles Lamb, glad to see these in the 1815 *Poems*, was sorry that the extorter had not thought to "have clapt a D. at the corner and let it have past as a printrs mark to the uninitiated, as a delightful hint to the better-instructed."[3] Seeming diminished things to D's eyes "beside" William's poems, D's poems, by their very production, have a presence that puts the "literal meaning of the poem 'beside itself.'" This is J. Hillis Miller on William's poetics of self-contradiction (68), and the double play is transferable to Dorothy's report, "I gave up," and "nothing ever came of it." This is only half her story. Under the cover of protest that she is not a Poet, nor was meant to be, her writing delivers a subgenre of poems performing what they deny, speaking unnegated desire as well as vocational negation, not projected for publication yet prized enough to title, date, and fair-copy, as late as 1840 (*CP* 211–12), and to send to a friend to leave something "that would be valuable when she was gone."[4]

An extended staging of this double story gets "tried out" in late 1829, to answer a friendly request on her Christmas-birthday. The first title she gave to a poem that she "could not make a finish of" (*LY* 2: 176), before signing it off as *A Fragment*, was *Irregular Verses*, a designation hovering between self-deprecation and generic affiliation.[5] Double-saying is the very launch, half in chagrin, half in pleasure, at Julia's friendly prompt to rhyme:

Ah Julia! ask a Christmas rhyme
Of <u>me</u> who in the golden time
Of careless, hopeful happy youth
Ne'er strove to decorate the truth . . .   (1–4)

No poet in her youth, Dorothy says she wrote to Julia's mother (her girl-
hood friend Jane Pollard) only "in simple prose / Each girlish vision, as it
rose" (9–10). Yet the adult poet rhymes, even rhymes *prose*. And so *Irregular Verses* plays the pattern of her letter to Lady Beaumont, protesting little skill, yet exercising skill for the protest.

> You ask why in that jocund time
> Why did I not in jingling rhyme
> Display those pleasant guileless dreams
> That furnished still exhaustless themes?
> —I <u>reverenced</u> the Poet's skill,
> And <u>might have</u> nursed a mounting Will
> To imitate the tender Lays
> Of them who sang in Nature's praise.   (56–63)

The underscored desire, doubles "Will" and William in the unrealized
volition.

The story that Dorothy is most confident in telling, and telling herself,
is the anatomy of her melancholy. While William's confidence as "Poet"
could waver, neither he nor Dorothy doubted the calling. Her *Verses* give
the discipline and unconsummation of her poet's mind, in everything
that stood most prominent, recollecting chastisement in the very lexicon
that *The Prelude* summons for vocation—"pride," "ambition," "confidence,"
"self-love":

> But bashfulness, a struggling shame
> A fear that elder heads might blame
> —Or something worse—a lurking pride
> Whispering my playmates would deride
> Stifled ambition, checked the aim
> If e'er by chance "the numbers came."
> —Nay even the mild maternal smile,
> That oft-times would repress, beguile
> The over-confidence of youth,

Even that dear smile, to own the truth,
Was dreaded by a fond self-love;
"'Twill glance on one—and to reprove
Or," (sorest wrong in childhood's school)
"Will <u>point</u> the sting of ridicule." (64–77)

The voice audible still in its inscription as speech plays against the other
quoted words, "the numbers came" (69), this an echo of William's "glad
preamble" (7.4) to his epic of self:

To the open fields I told
A prophesy; poetic numbers came
Spontaneously, and clothed in priestly robe
My spirit, thus singled out, as it might seem,
For holy services. (*1805* 1.59–63)

William in turn echoes the poet of *Paradise Lost,* whose verses "feed on
thoughts, that voluntarie move / Harmonious numbers" (3.37–38), whose
"Celestial Patroness . . . inspires / Easie my unpremeditated Verse" (9.21–
24). Dorothy's phrase inhabits inhibition, with its rendering in couplets
attracting an even nearer, no less self-defeating allusion to Pope's couplet-
shaped story, in *Epistle To Dr. Arbuthnot,* of his birth into poetry:

As yet a Child, nor yet a Fool to Fame,
I lisp'd in Numbers, for the Numbers came. (127–28)

This Child's father encouraged the prodigy. A footnote routine in editions
that Dorothy would have known cites a report by William Warburton:

He used to say, that he could write verses further back than he could
remember. . . . When Mr. Pope was yet a child, his father, though no
Poet, would set him to make English verses. He was pretty difficult to
please, and would often send the boy back to new-turn them. When
they were to his mind, he took great pleasure in them, and would say
These are good rhymes. (*Works* [1806] 4: 23–24)

Adult Dorothy is still impressed by a mother's discouraging return—a
memory that both forgets the lapse into doubt and despair after William's glad preamble, and confects a narrative of social repression.[6] Yet
just as telling is the fact that she doesn't stop verses here. She continues

with a wish that Julia's mother will be touched by "this poor memorial strain" (96), about which she cares enough to sum up with an adage about the double measures of life: "—The happiest heart is given to sadness; / The saddest heart feels deepest gladness" (101–2). This is a rhyme that is willing, even, to revise William's autobiographical adage: "We Poets in our youth begin in gladness; / But thereof comes in the end despondency and madness" (*Resolution and Independence* 48–49).

Critical assessment, at least up to the 1970s, sided with the discouragers: Dorothy's poems are "beguiling" but not "interesting."[7] A subsequent generation of gender critics tried to recuperate this as the effect of a disabling "masculine literary tradition" and the allied cultural strictures, some critics proposing a divergent, undervalued "feminine romanticism."[8] These revaluations brought forward important issues, but the paradigms still tended to gender polarities—"masculine" egotism, sexism, and power; diffuse and permeable "feminine" subjectivity—that seem to me to be most compelling for the Wordsworths in the aberrations. William's purchase on that "masculine tradition," insofar as it implies a dominant, consolidated ego, is not as firm as it is famed to be; it is from crises that issue the haunts and main regions of his songs. And Dorothy's "expecting William," though depleting, is not extinguishing. Her inhibitions alternate with vivid ventures of imagination that are neither abjectly nor oppositionally "feminine," but diversely—and interactively—Wordsworthian.

The Poetry That Dorothy Makes

One interaction between the Wordsworth-poets gathers to a phrase in Dorothy's moon-night journal entry, "'That needs must a holy place' & c—&c." It is likely shorthand for a run of lines in William's *Home at Grasmere*, an epic-chapter afoot in Spring 1800:

> I cannot look upon this favoured Vale
> But that I seem by harbouring this thought
> To wrong it such unworthy recompence
> Imagining, of confidence so pure
> Ah! if I wished to follow where the sight
> Of all that is before my eyes, the voice

Which is as a presiding Spirit here
Would lead me I should say unto myself
They who are dwellers of this holy place
Must needs themselves be hallow'd.   (MS B 15ʳ, 17ʳ; 358–67)

William sets "holy place" in a conditional syntax, kin to that strain in *Tintern Abbey* to believe "Abundant recompense" for raptures lost to childhood (88–89). This is a poet always worrying the ledger. To the sigh of "Ah! if . . ." this verse never secures a reversal. The doubt has been agitated by a rupture in the sign-system being tested in the uncertain home:

But two are missing, two, a lonely pair
Of milk-white Swans ah why are they not seen
To share in this day's pleasure? From afar
They came, like Emma & myself to live
Together here in peace & solitude
Chusing this Valley they who had the choice
Of the whole world: we saw them day by day

        ·   ·   ·

      their state so much resembled ours
They also having chosen this abode
They strangers & we strangers they a pair
And we a solitary pair like them
They should not have departed

        ·   ·   ·

Shall we behold them yet another year
Surviving they for us & we for them
And neither pair be broken   (B: 14ʳ, 15ʳ; 322–29, 338–42, 348–50)

In the wake of such dismay and its question, the syntax that bears "holy place" is elegiac, delusional, forlorn. Dorothy recovers the phrase in a different mood of mind and relation to its world, a passionate ecstasy that is inspirational: "'That needs must be a holy place' &c—&c. I had many very exquisite feelings . . . it made me more than half a poet."

The title of a poem in her commonplace book, *Floating Island at Hawkshead, An Incident in the schemes of Nature*, brings visionary grammar into a sense of place that proves inspiring precisely because it is autonomous, not answerable to the calls of a privileged *I*.[9] The incident teases at William's *I* and its intentional energy toward impressive events in nature:

> Once did I see a slip of earth,
> By throbbing waves long undermined,
> Loosed from its hold—<u>how</u> no one knew
> But all might see it float, obedient to the wind. (5–8)

Dorothy presents her *I* as accidental witness to what "all might see," no elected self-presence.[10] Her own scheme of rhyme (*undermined / wind*) allows an off-sound that is an apt poetic. In such difference, this poet is willing to contemplate the schemes of Nature as indifferent to human-minded, human-marked ledgers of losses, recompenses, or ministry:

> . . . Nature, though we mark her not,
> Will take away—may cease to give.
>
> Perchance when you are wandering forth
> Upon some vacant sunny day
> Without an object, hope, or fear,
> Thither your eyes may turn—the Isle is passed away. (19–25)

If one is gender-measuring, such an island might seem "a latent figure for the dissolving self"—a female *I* cast loose and becoming "similarly diffuse," even a "vanished self" that joins the isle in a disappearance of "both subject and object" (so Homans reads the figure in *Women Writers*, 85). Yet Dorothy's verses move past "passed away" to abiding possibility—if not for the self, then for others:

> Buried beneath the glittering Lake!
> Its place no longer to be found,
> Yet the lost fragments shall remain,
> To fertilize some other ground. (26–28)

She "takes a pleasure in repeating these verses," William remarked (FN 77). The pleasure is a poetic self-possession that wants to recognize "other ground."

Dorothy's island poetics converse with William's intense self-regard, whether in images of social alienation or of visionary transcendence. Recalling his Cambridge days of "loose indifference," of "duty and zeal dismiss'd," the poet of *The Prelude* writes out this trope:

Rotted as by a charm, my life became
A floating island, an amphibious thing,
Unsound, of spungy texture, yet withal,
Not wanting a fair face of water-weeds
And pleasant flowers.—   (*1805* 3.339–43)

In Book VIII, about love of nature leading to love of mankind, he shifts the trope into a sublime self-sufficiency, at a nearly mystical remove. The figures of *I* and *Island* are intimately reflective:

Along a narrow Valley and profound
I journey'd, when, aloft above my head,
Emerging from the silvery vapours, lo!
A Shepherd and his Dog! in open day:
Girt round with mists they stood, and look'd about
From that enclosure small, inhabitants
Of an aerial Island floating on,
As seem'd, with that Abode in which they were,
A Little pendant area of grey rocks,
By the soft wind breath'd forward.   (*1805* 8.92–101)

William's aerial Island floats on, not only spatially but also temporally. It is one of those phenomena (Dorothy observed elsewhere) that appeal to him as "a text" of "that visionariness which results from a communion with the unworldliness of nature."[11] Her island registers a temporal variation, where what is "lost" to her becomes a potential for others.

And so the Lake burials contrast, too. In *The Prelude* the most memorable of these is the corpse of a drowning, an event guessed by a boy and pressed into significance by the adult recollector (Book V). Across William's poetic corpus, fragments bespeak ruptures and lost possibility: the unfinished sheepfold in *Michael,* the broken bowl and ruined cottage of *The Excursion* Book 1. Dorothy's fragments "remain" in a scheme that eludes narrative desire:

our own dear Grasmere first making a little round lake of natures own
with never a house never a green field—but copses & the bare hills,
enclosing it & the river flowing out of it. Above rose the Coniston Fells
in their own shape & colour—not Man's hills but all for themselves the
sky & the clouds & a few wild creatures.   (23 Apr. 1802; *GJ* 90)

Grasmere is owned by affection, "our own dear," and contemplated as "natures own," the "own" of its shapes and creatures. This figuring of elusive figures is not the syntax of William's relays of appropriation and alienation, nor a selfless eco-romanticism, but an interaction of making agents.

Dorothy's imagination ripples with intimate understanding of William's tendencies. She doesn't write (as we so often hear) under his shadow, but in dynamics of difference. *A Winter's Ramble in Grasmere's Vale*, composed in 1805 about her first days in Grasmere, late 1799, marks its way by marking and reversing William's paces of imagination.[12] His greetings to Grasmere vibrate with epic, individual purpose, or by the same measure of investment, darken with ominous signs. The positive steps are epitomized by that "glad preamble," its verse full of self-import:

> What dwelling shall receive me, in what Vale
> Shall be my harbour? Underneath what grove
> Shall I take up my home, and what sweet stream
> Shall with its murmurs lull me to rest?
> The earth is all before me. . . .   (1805 *Prelude* 1.11–15)

The pair at the end of *Paradise Lost*—"The World was all before them, where to choose / Thir place of rest, and Providence thir guide" (12.646–47)—is converted to a masculine singular, claiming special blessings, nurture, vocation, success, "my course," a "gift that consecrates my joy" (32, 40). The poet of *Home at Grasmere* voices a colonizing imagination that could give Keats's conquistador Cortez, staring at the Pacific, a run for his bounty: "The unappropriated[13] bliss hath found / An owner & that owner I am he / . . . exalted with the thought / Of my possessions" (MS B: 4ʳ–5ʳ; 85–90). Even writing of a "happy band" (39ʳ; 874), this poet marks self-constituting difference:

> Possessions have I wholly, solely mine
> Something within which yet is shar'd by none
> Not even the nearest to me & most dear   (B: 41ʳ; 897–99)

If Home at Grasmere is mythologized as "true community the noblest Frame / Of many into one incorporate" (B: 36ʳ; 819–20), the poetry equates "one" with *I*.

William's claims are always glancing at the "jarring world" this Frame would hold at bay, registering counter-portents (the dead or fled Swan-pair), or sensing a Lakeworld of uncertain sympathy with its designation as "~~this favourite Spot of ours~~" (B: 37ʳ; 836–38)—a claim crossed out after written:[14]

> The naked trees
> The icy brooks as on we passed appear'd
> To question us whence come ye to what end
> They seem'd to say what would ye said the shower,
> Wild Wanderers, whither thro' my dark domain
> The Sunbeam said be happy   (B: 10ʳ-11ʳ; 229–34)

The force of *appear'd* is its suspense between greeting and illusion, and in the illusion, its tonal uncertainty: invitation or challenge? Across the home-course, William's poetry will wander into tales of homes in disarray, frame its confident rhetoric in negative denials, and erupt into a late confession of unhomely "wild appetites and blind desires / Motions of savage instinct" (42ʳ; 913–14), lures to terrors and conflicts for which Nature's ministry may be inadequate.

Dorothy, the partner in this *we* and *our*, takes her *Ramble* elsewhere. In a retrospect, she tells of alienation become familiarity, marking then departing from William's winter-poetics:

> A Stranger, Grasmere, in thy vale,
> All faces then to me unknown . . .   (1–2)

The strange figure is herself rather than Grasmere, rendered in a past tense that bespeaks present familiarity. It is an accomplishment she records as her own, independent of William's moods of mind and its epic measures: "I left my sole companion-friend / To wander out alone" (3–4). William wanders seeking confirmations, trying to skirt, not always successfully, sensations of paths lost, obscured, bewilder'd, engulph'd. That "glad preamble" is set to "brace myself to some determined aim" (124). No surprise that the closing paragraphs of this Introduction declare (even provisionally), "The road lies plain before me" (668).

Dorothy writes in ballad meters, to capture ambling without agenda:

> Lured by a little winding path,
> Quickly I left the public road,

A smooth and tempting path it was,
By sheep and shepherds trod.   (5–8)

When the poet of *Michael* invites the readers to leave "the public way" (1),
he holds insider's authority about markers which such readers might
"pass by, / Might see and notice not" (15–16). Dorothy ventures on a locally marked path. She will evoke the language of Miltonic error—"Lured,"
"winding," "tempting"—to pastoralize error away, winking at William's
markers.

The most sustained retracing of William's poetics concentrates on an
arresting object:

Eastward, towards the lofty hills,
That pathway led me on
Until I reach'd a stately Rock
With velvet moss o'ergrown.

With russet oak, and tufts of fern
Its life was richly garlanded;
Its sides adorned with eglantine
Bedropped with hips of glossy red.   (9–16)

For Homans, this is a critical figure of Dorothy's plight as poet: it shows
"the adverse psychic effects" of "encountering a feminized or maternal
nature" already written by William (50), the "gorgeous and domineering"
Rock blocking her "spiritual and physical progress," halting her voice and
self-recognition—all those *Its* retreating from William's she-nature (53).
Homans has *Nutting* in mind; but more visible, and visibly different, is
"the spot" in *The Thorn:*

A beauteous heap, a hill of moss,

·   ·   ·   ·   ·   ·   ·   ·   ·   ·   ·   ·

All lovely colours there you see
All colours that were ever seen
And mossy network too is there,
As if by hand of lady fair,
The work had woven been,
And cups, the darlings of the eye
So deep is their vermilion dye.

Ah me! what lovely tints are there!
Of olive-green and scarlet bright . . .   (*1798* 36–46)

The *Ramble* is a counter-story to the traumatized *Thorn*-encounter. Dorothy refuses *she* in refusal of superstition, evoking William's text to negate it. In her figure there is, moreover, an ally of female authority, Charlotte Smith's *Apostrophe to An Old Tree:* [15]

WHERE thy broad branches brave the bitter North,
Like rugged, indigent, unheeded, worth,
Lo! Vegetation's guardian hands emboss
Each giant limb with fronds of studded moss,
That clothes the bark in many a fringed fold
Begemm'd with scarlet shields, and cups of gold,
Which, to the wildest winds their webbs oppose,
And mock the arrowy sleet, or weltering snows.   (1–8)

Stephen Parrish cites these lines as a source for Wordsworth's old Thorn (*Art* 107) but Smith's tree is temperamentally different: untraumatized and ungendered, brave and resilient.

It is to this temper that Dorothy's course appeals:

Beneath that Rock my course I stayed,
And, looking to its summit high,
"Thou wear'st," said I, "a splendid garb,
Here winter keeps his revelry."   (21–23)

Not bleak and turbulent, Dorothy's winter refuses grief that "summer days were gone": "No more I'll grieve; for Winter here / Hath pleasure gardens of his own" (26–28). This is not sentimentality (she crossed out *sigh* in favor of *grieve*); it is determination against *ubi sunt*. That Winter is masculine marks no she-subordination; it a welcome foil to the male "companion" left behind. And so her *Ramble* refigures the "icy brooks" of his *Home at Grasmere:*

—Beside that gay and lovely Rock
There came with merry voice
A foaming Streamlet glancing by;
It seemed to say "Rejoice!"   (33–36)

This Streamlet's voice is social, and the poet responds with her rhyme, closing her *Ramble* in a chime of her *choice* with the positive illusion of welcome in the *voice* that seems to say *Rejoice:*

My youthful wishes all fulfill'd,
Wishes matured by thoughtful choice,
I stood an Inmate of this vale,
How <u>could</u> I but rejoice?   (37–40)

"Stranger" has become "Inmate," a word wrested from William's index of alienation: an infant may be "inmate of this *active* universe" (*1805 Pre-lude* 2.266), and the poet of *Home at Grasmere* can hope that the new "Inmates are not unworthy of their home" (B: 38ʳ; 858) in joining all the "inmates . . . Of Winter's household" (13ʳ; 283–84); but he also writes of a servant girl as "an Inmate" of a home where she suffers sexual preda-tion (23ʳ, 503). The sense of *prisoner,* though not yet a dictionary-synonym for *inmate,* is already doing this work in such phases of imagi-nation, memorably in the Great Ode, where female nature's "Foster-child" is "her Inmate man," sentenced to "Forget the glories he hath known, / And that imperial palace whence he came."[16] Dorothy writes *Inmate* in the key of "familiar resident / one of the family or company / Indweller, inhabit-ant" (*OED*), no longer the bearer of the *Ramble*'s initial rhymes, *un-known/alone.*

   A social sense of inmates amid winter adversity prompts a poem that Lady Beaumont and the Lambs enjoyed, *Address to a Child, During a boisterous Winter evening.* This *During* was more than half a trial of imagination for its poet. Dorothy's *Address* may have been prompted by weather on her birthday, Christmas 1805.[17] In February 1805, her be-loved brother, Captain John Wordsworth, had perished in a horrific ship-wreck off the coast of England, and no storm thence was free of this nightmare. She writes to Lady Beaumont about this, awaiting Coleridge en route from Malta. It had been a while since he had left, with "no fur-ther tidings":

   The weather is dreadful for a sea voyage. Oh my dear Friend, what
   a fearful thing a windy night is now at our house! I am too often
   haunted with dreadful images of Shipwrecks and the Sea when I
   am in bed and hear a stormy wind, and now that we are thinking so

much about Coleridge it is worse than ever. . . . wind rain and snow are driving down the vale, and the chimney every now and then roars as if it were going to come down upon us. I am very anxious that this boisterous day should be followed by a gentle one.   (*EY* 663)

In the grip of anxiety, Dorothy writes a jingle for the boy in her care (Johnny, her brother's namesake), a jaunty verse that plays with the storm as a boisterous boy—as if a pendant to William's light-hearted fancy, "A whirl-blast from behind the hill" (1800 *Lyrical Ballads*):

> He will suddenly stop in a cunning nook,
> And ring a sharp 'larum;—but if you should look,
> There's nothing to see but a cushion of snow
> Round as a pillow, and whiter than milk,
> And softer than if it were covered with silk.
> Sometimes he'll hide in the cave of a rock,
> Then whistle as shrill as the buzzard cock;
> —Yet seek him,—and what shall you find in the place?
> Nothing but silence and empty space;
> Save, in a corner, a heap of dry leaves,
> That he's left, for a bed, to beggars or thieves!   (stanza 2)

> Hark! over the roof he makes a pause,
> And growls as if he would fix his claws
> Right in the slates, and with a huge rattle
> Drive them down, like men in a battle:
> —But let him range round; he does us no harm,
> We build up the fire, we're snug and warm;
> Untouched by his breath see the candle shines bright,
> And burns with a clear and steady light;
> Books have we to read,—but that half-stifled knell,
> Alas! 'tis the sound of the eight o'clock bell.
> —Come now we'll to bed! and when we are there
> He may work his own will, and what shall we care?
> He may knock at the door,—we'll not let him in;
> May drive at the windows,—we'll laugh at his din;
> Let him seek his own home wherever it be;
> Here's a cozie warm house for Edward and me.   (stanza 4)

Her presence writes no haunted or visionary *I*, but *we* safe at home, amused by the commotion outside. Instead of a private sublime terror, she uses imagination for sociable ends, indicting poetry to allay fears and to give her nephew a sense of sport amid fearful assaults.

Nature is a variable gender for Dorothy. William's is, too—severely, mysteriously female, or benignly maternal, sublimely masculine, but always self-directed: what does this mean for my security, my self-understanding, my vocation? Dorothy's varieties—inscrutable schemer, generous creator, jolly fellow, rambunctious boy—tend to social turns:

> 'Twas nature built this hall of ours;
> She shap'd the bank; she framed the bowers
> That close it all around;
> From her we hold our precious right,
> And here, thro' love-long day and night,
> She rules with modest sway.   (*Holiday* 11–16; Knight's text)

Nature's agency in human life creates society: *ours* and *we*, amid obligations and tributes.

Dorothy Wordsworth's Shadow-Narrative

Dorothy Wordsworth's most sustained story of life in the Lakes, *A Narrative concerning George and Sarah Green* (1808), at once celebrates and darkens this confidence. It recounts events related to a winter catastrophe visited on the poorest inmates of Grasmere. On Saturday 19 March 1808 the eponyms, husband and wife, hiked over the fells from their home at Easedale Tarn to the village of Langdale to sell butter, enjoy a farm-sale, and visit Sarah's daughter who was "in service" there (124). On the way back, they were "bewildered by a mist" (125) and fell to their deaths. Six children at home, infant to age eleven, waited. On Monday, the oldest, a daughter, sent to a neighbor to borrow a cloak so she could search; a general alarm went out, a team was assembled, and the bodies were found two days later. The community quickly organized to care for the orphans, and a subscription was undertaken for their happy placement; two children in service stayed with their families—one of these, the Wordsworths, accepted "our Sally" (*MY* 1: 201). Dorothy Wordsworth and Mary Wordsworth served on the "Committee of six of the neighbouring Ladies" charged with managing it all (132).

At William's request, Dorothy wrote the *Narrative* as a record of the community's endeavor. This is William's headnote (C 5):

> The following Narrative was drawn up by Dorothy Wordsworth at the request of her Brother, William Wordsworth: he entreated that she would give a <u>minute detail</u> of all the particulars which had come within her notice; thinking that end for which the account was written would be thereby better answered, viz. that of leaving behind a record of human sympathies, and moral sentiments, either as they were called forth or brought to remembrance, by a distressful event, which took place in the course of the month of March, 1808, at Grasmere in the County of Westmorland.
>
> WM. WORDSWORTH
Town End, Grasmere
May 11th, 1808

The sympathies and sentiments matter not as Dorothy Wordworth's, but as social action. The only other place her name appears is the scribal signature at the end (143). When she uses the first person, it represents a plural: "I am happy to tell you . . . our united efforts have been even more successful than we had dared to hope" (132). On the title page no "Author" appears:

> A NARRATIVE CONCERNING GEORGE AND SARAH
> GREEN OF THE PARISH OF GRASMERE ADDRESSED
> TO A FRIEND   (124)

Across the previous weeks Dorothy had been busy writing elements of the narrative, first to William, then to friends and potential subscribers.[18] She deftly opens *A Narrative* with a "You" figured as a community familiar, addressed for friendly sympathy:

> You remember a single Cottage at the foot of Blentern Gill:—it is the only dwelling on the western Side of the upper reaches of the Vale of Easedale, and close under the mountain; a little stream runs over rocks and stones beside the garden wall, after tumbling down the crags above. I am sure you recollect the spot: if not, you remember George and Sarah Green who dwelt there.   (124)

This *I* is not a privileged insider, like the hieratic poet of *Michael* inter-preting a heap of stones; Dorothy names markers for a trusted memory, assisted by that mode of "minute detail." The key is Dr. Johnson's bio-graphical method: to "lead the thoughts into domestick privacies, and display the minute details of daily life" (*Rambler* 60; 2: 211). William had already written to MP Richard Sharp to solicit his assistance in the ap-peal, enclosing his "brief account of [the] most melancholy event" with a postscript that "my Sister will write a minute narrative." He himself has "not entered into particulars, because I feared to persons of less feeling, or taking less interest in the country than you do, it might be tedious" (though he offers to read Dorothy's *Narrative* to him, should the occa-sion arise, "to throw much light upon the state of the moral feelings of the inhabitants of these Vales"). Across the nineteenth century the mode of minute particulars would be identified more closely with domestic fe-male chronicling—a skill set Dorothy has well in hand.[19]

Yet even as Dorothy's authority draws on this communal charge (and a brother's booster), her narrative, both in large contours and in minute par-ticulars, taps a psychic substratum of perils—in nature, of dependency, and the fragility of connections. One urgency rustles in her not wanting *A Narrative* published. To warm encouragers, she answers that she would spare the orphans being "brought forward to notice as Individuals"; but this neighbors a confession about herself in the notice: "I should detest the idea of setting myself up as an Author."[20] More than the decorum of female modesty is at work. It is not "Author" she detests; it is the idea of herself in this identity, a public text. Though puckishly, Charles Lamb may have struck a nerve when he told (and bolded to) William that having intro-duced this "Female Friend" to his readers, "**Expect a formal criticism on the Poems of your female friend** and she must expect it" (*L* 3: 141).

What might a reader of "Dorothy Wordsworth" (orphan at age six, sent far from her brothers and native home) see and notice—notice, crit-ically, even against her design? One caution is the mother whose name appears in the title. It is across visibly contrary vectors that Dorothy brings Sarah Green forward to notice:

> the awful event checks all disposition to harsh comments; perhaps
> formerly it might be said, and with truth, the Woman had better been
> at home; but who shall assert that this same spirit which led her to

come among her Neighbours as an equal, seeking like them society
and pleasure, that this spirit did not assist greatly in preserving her in
chearful independance of mind through the many hardships and pri-
vations of extreme poverty? Her Children, though very ragged, were
always cleanly, and are as pure and innocent, and in every respect as
promising Children as any I ever saw. (127)

Dorothy hints some gender-judgment in a displaced sermonizing about
"the Woman" and her proper place: "With her many cares and fears for
her helpless Family, she must at that time have mingled some bitter self-
reproaches for her boldness in venturing over the Mountains" (141). Yet
she also proposes that the family was held together by Sarah's cheer.

That Dorothy is thinking about female social agency is marked by the
unmixed antitypes. On one end is young Jane Green, the angel in the
house who "was as a Mother to her Brothers and Sisters when they were
fatherless and motherless. . . . nursed the Baby, and, without confusion
or trouble provided for the other Children . . . conducted other matters
with perfect regularity, had milked the cow at night and morning, wound
up the clock, and taken care that the fire should not go out" (134), and set
out to search for her parents (125).[21] The antithesis is Mrs. N----, a
committee-Lady "galled" that "the whole concern had not been entrusted
to her guidance," full of "cabals and heart-burnings" (133), ever "sullen
and dissatisfied" (136–37). Any "true interest in the Children's well-
doing" dims before this self-importance (ibid.), which Dorothy outs to
readers of the *Narrative*. What particularly irks her is the presumption
of authority: this Lady "had before (without any authority) herself (though
only recently come into the Country and having no connection with Grasmere) engaged to place all the Children with an old Woman in indigent
circumstances, who was totally incapable of the charge" (133).[22] Now, in
the way that Mrs. Elton's efforts (in Austen's *Emma*) to arrange a good
situation as governess for Jane Fairfax might seem not the worst impulse (Austen marks her as egotistical busybody), keeping the children
together and helping the Woman to provide for their care might not be
a horrible idea. The real grief would be having to send some orphans out
of Grasmere, to alien families grabbing Parish payment for boarders
they may maltreat and exploit for labor, thence to apprenticeships
scarcely distinguishable from slavery (131). Dorothy homes in on the

grab for authority over the orphans' social narrative. The "great advantage [of] giving us authority," she tells her friend Jane, is the containment of this "very selfconceited and very meddling" woman (11 May 1808; *MY* 1: 235).

The community is Dorothy's *loco parentis*. "From the moment we heard that their Parents were lost we anxiously framed plans for raising a sum of money for the purpose of assisting the Parish in placing them with respectable Families; and to give them a little School-learning" (132). About the orphans, *A Narrative* is also always about Grasmere, as context, as history, and as self-identification. "It is, when any unusual event happens, affecting to listen to the fireside talk in our Cottages; you then find how faithfully the inner histories of Families, their lesser and greater cares, their peculiar habits, and ways of life are recorded in the breasts of their Fellow-inhabitants of the Vale." The archival *record* (in the oldest sense, to get by *heart*, to take to *heart*) is the communal heart, the talk in "our" homes, from generation to generation, focused on inner histories. Such records render a more faithful chronicle than any public documentary of "those, who have moved in higher stations and had numerous Friends in the busy world . . . even when their doings and sufferings have been watched for the express purpose of recording them in written narratives" (128). Dorothy's care for the communal production and transmission contrasts the registers of William's "rural history" as an archive of "Distresses and disasters, tragic facts" that matter chiefly, traumatically, extravagantly, to the impressions on his mind (1799 *Prelude* 1.279–84). She will set herself up as author in a language of community, and in a community of language.

The location of family history in this language inflects her citation, with a slight but telling alteration, of a passage from William's as yet unpublished story of another family:

I may say with the Pedlar in the "Recluse"

> "I feel
> The story linger in my heart," my memory
> Clings to this poor Woman and her Family,

and I fear that I have spun out my narrative to a tedious length. I cannot give <u>you</u> the same feelings that <u>I</u> have of them as neighbours and fellow-inhabitants of this Vale; therefore what is in my mind a full and living picture will be to you but a feeble sketch.   (142–43)

The Pedlar is speaking about his last visit with a mother deranged and hopeless after several hardships and domestic disintegrations. William himself would not be "tedious" in relating the Greens' story (*MY* 1: 211), nor does he give any such demur to his Pedlar, no pause about feeble expressive power, or of inability to convey his heart to other hearts:

> It would have grieved
> Your very heart {soul} to see her. Sir, I feel
> The story linger in my heart. I fear
> 'Tis long & tedious, but my spirit clings
> To that poor woman so familiarly
> Do I perceive her manner, & her look
> And presence, & so deeply do I feel
> Her goodness that not seldom in my walks
> A momentary trance comes over me
> And to myself I seem to muse on one
> By sorrow laid asleep or borne away . . .   (MS D: 52ᵛ; 361–71)

For all the familiar clinging, William also frames a narrator able to spin a fantasy that lets him walk away, safe in conscience that he had left this poor woman "With the best hope & comfort I could give," and perplexed only that she, thanking him "for my will," seemed unable to thank him for "my hope" (53ʳ; 389–92). From De Quincey on, readers have reacted to the contradiction between the Pedlar's protests of heart and his motions of retreat, even abandonment.[23]

Dorothy's hesitation of kinship with this Pedlar ("I may say") is the reflex of the multiple material involvements of Grasmere: the search-team, the women's committee, and a community's care—all a chronicle of contrast to the serial, self-preserving departures of that Pedlar, aptly renamed "The Wanderer" by *The Excursion* (1814). Her text rewords his sigh, "my spirit clings / To that poor woman," into "My memory / Clings to this poor Woman and her Family," shifting the distancing *that* into a present *this*, substituting *memory* (a faculty not ready to consign all to spirit alone), and adding the Family that always focused Sarah Green's identity, energy, many cares and fears.[24] For the Pedlar, family lingers only in remnants that "steal upon the meditative mind"; while he speaks of "a bond / Of brotherhood . . . broken" at Margaret's death—she never failed to give a "daughter's welcome . . . I loved her / As my own child" (47^r-47^v; D: 81–85, 95–96)—he's a notably absent father. His narrative intent is to discipline grief, banish sorrow, and counsel his auditor (the reader's surrogate) in such "purposes of wisdom": "enough to sorrow have you given . . . / Be wise & chearful" (55^r; 508–10). All "the uneasy thoughts which filled my mind" (55^v; 519) are pressed into this instruction:

> what we feel of sorrow & despair
> From ruin & from change, & all the grief
> That passing shows of being leave behind,
> Appeared an idle dream that could not live.   (D: 55^v; 520–23)

The Author-auditor is allowed to succumb to "a brother's love" and "the impotence of grief" (D: 499–500) so that he can be bucked into better wisdom. MS B shows Wordsworth trying out various drafts of the dosage to get it just right: "The trouble . . . sent into my thought / Was sweet, I lookd and looked again, & to myself / I seemed a better and wiser man" (43^v); "for the tale which you have told I think / I am a better and a wiser man" (45^r). In stanzas William "effused" on the Greens in April, prior to Dorothy's *Narrative*, he translates "that Pair's unhappy end" into the wise consolation of philosophy, above and beyond the work of any social agency:[25]

> Our peace is of the immortal Soul,
> Our anguish is of clay;
> Such bounty is in Heaven, so pass
> The bitterest pangs away.

The valedictions against mourning are multiple:

> Three days did teach the Mother's Babe
> Forgetfully to rest
> In reconcilement how serene!
> Upon another's breast
>
> The trouble that the elder Brood
> I know not that it stay'd
> So long—they seiz'd their joy, and they
> Have sung, and danc'd, and play'd.

The pair are now united "in bond of love, in bond of God, / Which may not be untied!"—the final words. William's stanzas are as much about this signature metaphysics as about the Greens.

Dorothy, who copied this effusion for Coleridge and for Lady Beaumont, works out a different purpose of wisdom in her *Narrative,* urging her readers to "take part" in her prayer for the orphans "that the awful end of their Parents may hereafter be remembered by them in such a manner as to implant in their hearts a reverence and sorrow for them which may purify their thoughts and make them wiser and better" (143) —not closing off sorrow but sharing it as a family. The community is a crucial support. At the funeral, "Many tears were shed by persons who had known little of the Deceased; and all the people who were gathered together appeared to be united in one general feeling of sympathy for the helpless condition of the Orphans" (130). The narrative's figural ideal is this united feeling: "how closely the bonds of family connection are held together in these retired vallies" (133); "the Family were bound together by the same cares and exertions," sharing one "uncommonly feeling heart" (138–39). With such heart, in the family and the community, the orphans' dispersal is no diaspora. Not only do bonds hold but the vale turns into an extended family (one girl was accepted by descendants of George Green's first wife, not blood relatives). The catastrophe shifts the family to other ground, as if it had been just an incident in the schemes of nature: the "Poor Woman" is "at rest," and "all her Children have taken to their new homes, and are chearful and happy" (141), with advantages of education that "their parents' poverty would have kept them out of the way of attaining" (143). Of their fall, Dorothy comes near to saying *felix culpa.* Against the genre that William designated to Coleridge, "the tragedy" (*MY* 1: 221), she inclines to "Romance" (137), not in delusion but as a creditable sociology.

Yet what is deflected for the Greens plays beyond this sociology, bringing forward shades of dark psychology in Dorothy herself. When, at the outset, she marks a reference to "the spot" that claimed the pair, her writing overdrives the project of familiarizing into vectors of personal anxiety about separation, helpless wandering, and near annihilation:

> the spot . . . was at the top of Blea Crag above Easedale Tarn, that
> very spot where I myself had sate down six years ago, unable to see a

yard before me, or to go a step further over the Crags. I had left W. at Stickell Tarn. A mist came on after I had parted with him, and I wandered long, not knowing whither. When at last the mist cleared away I found myself at the edge of the Precipice, and trembled at the Gulph below, which appeared immeasurable. (125)

Meant to corroborate the Greens' peril, the recollection of her "own dreadful situation" in 1802—the year of William's accelerating courtship, marriage, and farewell to his French lover and their daughter—verges toward autobiography: W. leaving her to gothic destitution and helpless wandering, rendered in his lexicon of sublime terrors: mists, precipices, and immeasurable gulphs.

The Greens' fall could have been hers. Though her mist clears and she is happily able by evening to find her way home (125), the fall not taken is never far off her psychic map. It haunts an alternative history of social survival, one that amounts to death by another name:

> There is, at least, this consolation, that the Father and Mother have been preserved by their untimely end from that dependance which they dreaded. . . . and perhaps, after the Land had been sold, the happy chearfulness of George and Sarah Green might have forsaken them, and their latter days have been tedious and melancholy.

This is the narrative's last sentence (143), and for the Greens, "the poorest People in the Vale," the dreaded consequence was imminent: "They must very soon have parted with their Land if they had lived," by force of their very attachment to it: the "morsel of Land, now deeply mortgaged, had been in the possession of the Family for many generations, and they were loth to part with it: consequently they had never assistance from the Parish" (126), which would have meant the liquidation of all property. Dorothy's metaphor, *morsel*, encodes the horrible consequence, property having to be consumed: "they had sold their Horse; and were in the habit of carrying any trifles they could spare out of the house or stable to barter for potatoes or oat-meal. . . . They used to sell a few peats in the summer, which they dug out of their own hearts' heart, their Land" (127)—a pained depletion of the "salutary passion" in their "love of their few fields and their ancient home" (138).

While Dorothy proffers the "consolation" of the family having been spared worse and worst, her adhesion to this negative figures a condensation and displacement of her own psychic material. "How we are squandered abroad!" she laments to Jane Pollard after her brothers return to school and John sets sail for Barbadoes (27 January 1788); she utters the phrase again about her brothers in January 1790.[26] As her brothers move into the world, she worries of being "destitute of the means of supporting myself" (26 June 1791; *EY* 54). She is haunted by the orphan-diaspora of her early life, which prefigures the Green orphans', much less happily. She writes to Jane about a long-delayed bliss of a reunion with William and Kitt:

> We have been endeared to each other by early misfortune. We in the same moment lost a father, a mother, a home, we have been equally deprived of our patrimony. . . . These afflictions have all contributed to unite us close by the Bonds of affection notwithstanding we have been compelled to spend our youth far asunder. "We drag at each remove a lengthening Chain" this Idea strikes me very forcibly. Neither absence nor Distance nor Time can ever break the Chain that links me to my Brothers.   (16 February 1798; *EY* 88)

"But why do I talk to you thus?" she adds, then stays to answer from "the inmost Recesses of my Heart" (88). The quotation (which Radcliffe sounded in *The Mysteries of Udolpho*[27]) is from traveler-Goldsmith's assurance to his brother:

> Where'er I roam, whatever realms to see,
> My heart untravell'd fondly turns to thee;
> Still to my brother turns, with ceaseless pain,
> And drags at each remove a lengthening chain.
>
>   (*The Traveller* 7–10)

The other poetry that Dorothy's letter keynotes is related to this brother's turn. It is the conclusion of William's *An Evening Walk*, addressed in code to her (*A Young Lady of the Lakes, of the North of England*). The poet's hope "decks . . . a distant scene, / (For dark and broad the gulph of time between) / Gilding that cottage with her fondest ray" (1793; 397–99), the home he and Dorothy hope to share. To Jane she sighs, "perhaps your less gloomy Imagination and your anxiety to see your Friend placed in that happy Habitation might make you overlook the dark and broad

Gulph between" (*EY* 89). By *overlook* she means *look past* (even *glance over*); but to Dorothy's look, the topography is so forbidding as to seem impassible, broadened by her elision of William's "of time," and so more ponderous than mere temporal delay.

The frequency and minute detail with which Dorothy writes such recesses of the heart suggest a stream not far beneath the surface of consciousness, ready to fertilize some other ground—say, the *Narrative* of the Greens. An adopter of two of the orphans looms as a dark phantom of what she keeps trying to appease. Mrs. Dawson had been prey to melancholy

> since the sudden Death of a Son, twenty years of age, who was not only the pride of his Father's House, but of the whole Vale. She has other Children, but they are scattered abroad, except one Daughter, who is only occasionally with her, so that she has of late spent many hours of the day in solitude. (135)

Imprinted on the biblical curse of "scattered abroad" is Dorothy's kin-epithet. The bereft mother is her dark dream, the son a ghost of brother John, and the scattered children, the scattering of her childhood again. "Too soon these blessed days shall fly / And Brothers shall from Sisters part," she writes of a band of children fresh from "three days' mirth and revelry" on a holiday; when she fair-copied this text, she changed the second indicative *shall* to an unappeasable *must* (*CP* 176, 182).

The "Day of my Felicity," she told Jane in 1793, will be "the Day in which I am once more to find a Home under the same Roof with my Brother" (16 June 1793; *EY* 93). Yet even as this "idea of a home" abides in her heart (2–3 Sept. 1795; *EY* 146), also there is knowledge of William's recent return from France, leaving behind his lover and their infant daughter.[28] And then there's the common fate for a sister resident with a brother who marries: to be un-homed.[29] All this pressures the stiffly formal letter Dorothy writes to attorney-brother Richard, on the cusp of William's impending marriage (10 June 1802). Though she is confident of "the affection of my Brothers and their regard for my happiness" and knows she "shall continue to live with my Brother William," she would not strain affection with dependency: William, "having nothing to spare nor being likely to have, at least for many years, I am obliged (I need not say how much he regrets this necessity) to set him aside, and I will consider myself as boarding through my whole life with an indifferent person," she assures Richard (*EY* 359), resigning the status of family-inmate to become mere lodger. She asks him to arrange an annuity sufficient for her "to exercise my better feelings in relieving the necessities of others," and insists it is "absolutely necessary, to give it any effect," that it be Green-proof:

> independent of accidents of death or any other sort that may befal you or any of my Brothers, its principal object being to make me tranquil in my mind with respect to my future life. . . . I should be very loth to be oppressive to you, or any of my Brothers, or to draw upon you for more than you could spare without straitening yourselves.
>
> (359)

William's continuing love for her is at stake in these economies.

The bleak conclusion of Dorothy's *Narrative* is a late tremor of these concerns, scarcely stabilized by her postscripts. One, an "account of the stock of provisions in the House," indexes "all the things that were wanting even to the ordinary supply of a very poor house." What is there is dispersed in the sale of the "household goods"—all the family markers and affections scattered into commodity (144). The very end of Dorothy's manuscript (144) scatters dire textual fragments. Having recounted the sale, she recalls an affecting story of Sarah's Langdale-daughter, who, on learning of her missing parents, was ready to take off at sunset to search: "In her distraction she thought that she should surely find them." This report calls to mind old Mary Watson, frantic to join the search party for "her Son . . . drowned in the Lake six years ago." Dorothy's memory clings to this poor woman, too: "I never shall forget the agony of her face." Then later, in pencil, she adds a "tragical" sequel: "The end of Mary Watson herself," twinning the tragedy in *Michael* of a father heartbroken by a wastrel son:

> She was murdered a few years ago in her own cottage by a poor Maniac, her own Son, with whom she had lived fearlessly though everyone in the vale had had apprehensions for her—the Estate at her death fell to a Grandson. He had been sent to Liverpool to learn a trade, came home a dashing fellow, spent all his property—took to dishonest practices, and is now under sentence of transportation.
>
> (C 32)

The vale united in care takes the form of dread and apprehensions, with a fireside tale that issues sentences of dire aggression, default, disintegration.[30]

Dorothy's interactions with William's imagination lead her to quarrel with herself after all. *A Narrative*—the closest she ever came to setting herself up as "Author"—opens into a logic of narrative, of what story to tell, of what story narrative authority can, or can't help, bring forward. The abjection that Dorothy Wordsworth felt from identity as Author or Poet is due in part to the proximity of William and in part to cultural obstacles. But it also arises from her own vivid imagination, which, like his, is prone to ponder the fragility of its deepest devotions and the vulnerability of its most cherished ideals.

From the intimate world of Grasmere Lakes and Dorothy's hesitation about putting herself forward to notice as "Author," *Romantic Interactions* turns to the wide great world, where, just four years after the tragedy that claimed the Greens, another poet's instant celebrity would erupt into the raging spirit of the age—or *Byronism,* as everyone would come to call it.

III

A Public Attraction

CHAPTER SEVEN

Gazing on "Byron"

Separation and Fascination

An Intense Curiosity

"One may gaze on it for ever, and contemplate an exhaustless subject—all that the capacious imagination has produced, and is producing—the populous, endless world of fancy." Thus Barry Cornwall's "Chapter on Portraits" romances a portrait of Sir Walter Scott featured in the 1829 *Literary Souvenir.*[1] While the referent of the ever-productive, capacious imagination is this admired image, Cornwall's sentence double-plays to release a lively supplement: the gazer's productive imagination. "Let the reader look . . ." begins his next paragraph, its dynamic already clear: portrait as arresting text; gazer as arrested reader. Cornwall casts his gaze in continuity with the portraitist's scrutiny:

> We can scarcely imagine a thing much more pleasant indeed to an artist than to be brought face to face with some famous person, and permitted to examine and scrutinize his features, with that careful and intense curiosity, that seems necessary to the perfecting a likeness.
>
> (353–54)

Such an intensely curious gazer had been Scott himself back in 1816, on another face of fame:

> A countenance, exquisitely modeled to the expression of feeling and passion, and exhibiting the remarkable contrast of very dark hair and eye-brows, with light and expressive eyes, presented to the physiognomist the most interesting subject for the exercise of his art. The predominating expression was that of deep and habitual thought, which gave way to the most rapid play of features when he engaged in interesting discussion; so that a brother poet compared them to the sculpture of a beautiful alabaster vase, only seen to perfection when

lighted up from within. . . . but those who had an opportunity of studying his features for a length of time, and upon various occasions, both of rest and emotion, will agree with us that their proper language was that of melancholy. . . . It was impossible to behold this interesting countenance, expressive of a dejection belonging neither to the rank, the age, nor the success of this young nobleman, without feeling an indefinable curiosity to ascertain whether it had a deeper cause than habit or constitutional temperament.

(Quarterly Review 16: 176–77)

This is Lord Byron, Hamlet-styled: melancholy, noble, the observed of all observers. If the portrait of Scott provokes contemplation of the worlds ever burgeoning in his imagination, Byron draws attention to the allure of Byron himself—undefinable, tantalizing, pulsing with fascination.

Images and imaginations of Byron liberated (exhaustlessly, it seems) male as well as female swoons, the romance as durable a century and a half on in Mario Praz's ekphrasis as it was for the Regency *Quarterly* crowd. Writing in the sober 1950s, Praz feints a triangulated gaze, using "women" to front what is transparently an enchanted male-inclusive *We:*

> that fatal profile, the pronounced chin, the curving lips, the eyelids slightly lowered over the proud gaze of the eyes, the elegantly disarranged hair, and the Apollo-like neck rising from the open shirt. We still see Byron as he was seen by the women who were his contemporaries,—who some more and some less—dreamed of him.[2]

Byron was a dreamboat for everyone: as Praz's first gushing adjective concedes, to die for. Broadcasting his verbal appreciation sans signature in the *Quarterly*, Scott implied the gaze of all—or confirmed it. It was in a dreamy suspension of disbelief that another brother poet, Coleridge, rhapsodized to a friend in April 1816 (a month after his first and only view):

> If you had seen Lord Byron, you could scarcely disbelieve him—so beautiful a countenance I scarcely ever saw—his teeth so many stationary smiles—his eyes the open portals of the sun—things of light, and for light—and his forehead so ample, and yet so flexible, passing from marble smoothness into a hundred wreathes and lines and dimples correspondent to the feelings and sentiments he is uttering.

(*L* 4: 641)

He had it bad. Scott and Coleridge were part of a national crush. It blushed in female idolators, in the rapt circuit of brother poets, and she-poets enthralled by this dark and dazzling celebrity. But not always, not forever.

I conclude *Romantic Interactions* with "Byron"—not so much the historical referent as the multiple, various, conflicted radiations into a hot zone of interaction, both with the imaginary "Byron" and within a community for whom this "Byron" operates as a potent language for gender investments. After 1816 the investment would get a political edge from another Byron, Lady Byron. The sudden, mysterious breakup of Lord and Lady, soon a scandal branded "The Separation," shaded and sharpened portraits of Lord Byron, verbal and pictorial, across angles of vision that rendered judgment, tendered defense, made excuse, plea-bargained. In this agency were women, sometimes dreamy about Byron, sometimes wry about Byronism. First and foremost was Anne Isabella Milbanke (by late 1815, Lady Byron). In the whirl was her cousin (Byron's former handful of a lover) Caro Lamb; her friend (and erstwhile Byronist) Joanna Baillie; and in years to come, Felicia Hemans, Elizabeth Barrett, M. J. Jewsbury, L.E.L., then Lady Blessington, Caroline Norton, Emily Brontë, and with high transatlantic controversy, Harriet Beecher Stowe. Famous and fascinating, Byron gave ears to rapture, spawned antitypes and parodies, and wound up, paradoxically, writing the book on author as neither sole proprietor nor absolute monarch of what happens under his name.

The Separation

If a decent respect to the opinions of mankind requires that they should declare the causes which impel them to a Separation, the Byrons said nothing directly and everything indirectly. Lady Byron's "mysterious silence," declared Moore in his *Life of Byron*, had the effect of putting the portrait-pencil into the public hand, along with a palette of "dark hints and vague insinuations, of which the fancy" was "left to fill up the outline" (*BW* 3: 215–16). Knowledge dark and vague activated reading, activated writing, activated portraiture. Not for nothing does Leslie Marchand call his biography *Byron: A Portrait*. "When we think of Byron," says Praz, "the first thing that comes before our eyes is a physical presence, a profile" (147).[3] The template was pretty much in place in Thomas

Moore's biography. The "sketch" of "the personal appearance of Lord Byron" in its closing pages, Moore concedes, can be only belated, because "so frequently described, both by pen and pencil" (*BW* 6: 253). He'll give it a go, anyway, with assists from Coleridge and Scott:

> Of his face, the beauty may be pronounced to have been of the highest order, as combining at once regularity of features with the most varied and interesting expression . . . . as the passing thought within darkened or shone through them.
>
> His eyes, though of a light grey, were capable of all extremes of expression, from the most joyous hilarity to the deepest sadness, from the very sunshine of benevolence to the most concentrated scorn or rage . . . But it was in the mouth and chin that the great beauty as well as expression of his fine countenance lay.　　　　(*BW* 6: 253)

At this verge Moore summons cover from anonymous female testimony to say that "the excessive beauty of his lips escaped every painter and sculptor" (254). The female voice saves Moore from too much for manly decorum (even as he lets her say what all would endorse): Byron is more than himself; he is poetry embodied, the very avatar of poetic deity, Apollo Belvedere:

> you forgot the man, the Lord Byron, in the picture of beauty presented you, and gazed with intense curiosity . . . as if to satisfy yourself, that thus looked the god of poetry, the god of the Vatican.
>
> 　　　　　　　　　　　　　　　　　　　　(*BW* 6: 253)

Such looking appealed across genders: as J. J. Winckelmann's famous ekphrasis of this sculpture made achingly, vibrantly clear, the Apollo Belvedere focused homoerotic rapture (classically licensed) as much as anything else.

Portraiture became the master-trope for Byron not only by such associations but also by force of Byron's talent for affecting a portrait in propria persona:

> His features are well formed—his upper lip is drawn towards the nose with an expression of impatient disgust. His eye is restlessly thoughtful.
>
> He talks much, and I heard some of his conversation, which is very able, and sounds like the true sentiments of the Speaker.

So noted Miss Milbanke of the celebrity of 1812 (Elwin 106), as if she were giving the outline of George Harlow's profile drawing of haughty Byron blended into Richard Westall's dreamy, Hamlet-moody profile. It's one thing to read the form of features for true sentiment—that's by the book, as Scott demonstrates with his curiosity about depths beneath habit. But it's shrewd to guess, as canny Miss Milbanke does, that Byron's sentiments are a performance. Reviewing Moore's *Life of Byron* in January 1831, the *Quarterly* indexed the lifetime of artful synonymy: even when (especially when) Byron "seems most frank and simple," this is his skill in "producing what is called an effect"—with the fatal work now known to be have been tragically self-inflicted: this production is "fatally capable, not only of disguising, but of controlling and perverting" a true self.[4]

Miss Milbanke was still puzzling this out as her first impression:

> His mouth continually betrays the acrimony of his spirit. I should judge him sincere and independent—<u>Sincere</u> at least in society as far as he can be, whilst dissimulating the violence of his scorn.
>
> (Elwin 105)

The guarded sincerity that dissimulates scorn, violence, acrimony is nicely conveyed by the double play of *betrays:* is the spirit revealed by or contradicted by the public face?

Focusing this sort of curious attention, Byron was generating a dynamic of reading that would be named, even in his lifetime, "Byronism." Scott's occasion in the *Quarterly* was the publication of *The Prisoner of Chillon, and Other Poems* and, soon after, *Childe Harold's Pilgrimage, Canto III* (Byron's return to his instant fame-maker after a four-year hiatus). Both volumes were inescapably, strategically imprinted with The Separation. The *Quarterly* volume is dated "October 1816" but its actual date of issue, 11 February 1817, rendered it an anniversary piece on the breakup. Everyone knew the calendar. In a match that seemed absurd to all, Lord Byron and heiress Miss Milbanke wed on 2 January 1815. Daughter Ada was born in December, and within a month, a little month, on 15 January 1816, Lady Byron packed her up and left for her parents' home. Early in February Lady Byron's father sent Byron a letter notifying him of her wish for a separation. Byron was stung; rumors and gossip bubbled and boiled; the press got involved in mid-April, and by the end

LORD BYRON.

"Lord Byron, Engraved for the *New Monthly Magazine* by Henry Meyer, from a Drawing by G. H. Harlow." *New Monthly Magazine and Universal Register,* facing the title for collected vol. 3 (January to June [July], 1815), after George Henry Harlow, 1814–1815. By kind permission of Princeton University Library.

The title page advertised in capital letters "EMBELLISHED WITH A POR-TRAIT OF LORD BYRON." Though the portrait is inscribed, "Published August 1815 by H. Colburn, Conduit Street," Colburn, who published the *New Monthly,* gave it this prepublication preview. The February issue had carried a notice of of the month, Byron sold his books at auction, signed a deed of separation, left London, and then England (and wife, daughter, and sister)—forever, it turned out.

The scandal hot-wired the publications of 1816. Even the poem that Byron had written in ventriloquy of Napoleon's departure from France in 1815 was reborn in his June 1816 *Poems* as a voice that begged audition as his own Farewell to England:

> Farewell to the Land, where the gloom of my Glory
> Arose and o'er shadow'd the earth with her name—
> She abandons me now—but the page of her story,
> The brightest or blackest, is fill'd with my fame.

As this half-gloating, gender competitive adieu may have predicted, Byron did not so much bid farewell to England as extend the page of his fame, at home and abroad. Murray caroled to Byron that his dinner for booksellers at the Albion Tavern had cleared 7,000 copies each of *Childe Harold III* and *The Prisoner &c* (13 December; *L* 181). Byron was into it for more that this profit: he was painting himself for sympathy, not stinting on an undertone of legal claim to little Ada.[5] *Childe Harold III* opens in flagrante lachrimae ("Is thy face like thy mother's, my fair child! / Sole daughter of my house and heart?") and closes in an aria of aspersions on her mother's devotion to further malefaction. In stanza cxvi Byron worked calculations on *Ada* (now, only this "name"): "To aid ~~watch~~ thy Mind's development . . ." (Burnett ed. 205). The next stanza, both in letter-code and direct reference, cast Lady Byron, née "A.I.M.," as the custodian of the child's "Hate":

Byron's marriage, and the July 1 issue opened its "Account of the Right Hon. Geo. Gordon, Lord Byron" (517–30): "It would be no small praise to the subject of this article, if at a period of life when the generality of our young men of fashion seem ambitious to signalize themselves only by the accomplishments of driving four-in-hand, winning or losing fortunes at the gaming-table, or debauching the wives of their most intimate friends, he had devoted his leisure to the cultivation of intellectual talents even if his performances had not been distinguished by an extraordinary excellence. Still more than must it redound to his honour that enjoying the advantages of rank and affluence, and without any of those motives which stimulate indigent genius to exertion, fame excepted, he has raised himself to the very first rank among the living poets of his nation" (527).

Yet though dull Hate as duty should be taught,
I know that thou wilt love me—though my name
Should be shut from thee, as a spell still fraught
With desolation—and a broken claim:—
Though the grave closed between us—'twere the same,
I know that thou wilt love me—though to drain
My blood from out thy being, were an aim
And an attainment—all would be in vain . . .   (cxvii)

Ringing the changes from *my name* to A.I.M.'s vampiric *aim* to drain his blood from a mutual though broken *claim*, Byron works his own spell.[6] The Canto's closing word is *me!* (cxviii), the manuscript signed and dated, just below: "Byron June 9th 1816.—" (Burnett ed. 211). "His allusions to me in 'Childe Harold' are cruel and cold," Lady Byron wrote to her friend Anne Bernard, with pained acuity about the design: "with such a semblance as to make <u>me</u> appear so, and to attract all sympathy to himself."[7]

The Prisoner hosted two more attractions of sympathy for the sad, sorry, tormented, betrayed, childlorn, and now ex-pat Lord: *Stanzas to——* and *The Dream*.[8] At the back of *Childe Harold III* Murray advertised "*Poems*, containing FARE THEE WELL . . . ," issued just weeks after Byron quit England, in affordable octavo. If most of the volume's contents had other occasions, just about all were now readable as Separation Poetry, by dint not only of the primer, *Fare thee well!* (advanced to title-notice) but also the first poem, *To——* ("When all around grew drear and dark"), an ode to its unnamed addressee, in grateful praise of constancy amid adversity.[9] Absence made the mart grow fonder. Byron had quit England, but the poetry could still be had, cherished as a public letter from abroad.

Tinged with this longing, Scott's notice had the force of a compensatory love-letter, a public display of affection in Lady Byron's default. So keyed up was he about this affect that Scott begged Murray's counsel. "I have begun and left off several times," he agonized to him in January. With all the jitter of an anxious suitor, he urged him (and advisor William Gifford) to look over his essay

> with full power to cancel it if you think any part of it has the least chance of hurting his feelings. . . . I should feel more grieved than at anything that ever befell me if there should have slipped from my pen anything capable of giving him pain. . . . I wish Mr. Gifford and you

would consider every word carefully. If you think the general tenor is likely to make any impression on him, if you think it like to hurt him either in his feelings or with the public in Gods name fling the sheets in the fire & let them be as <u>not written</u>. But if it appears I should wish him to get an early copy and that you would at the time say I am the author at your importunity. No one can honor Lord Byrons genius more than I do and no one had so great a wish to love him personally though personally we had not the means of becoming very intimate. In his family distress (deeply to be deprecated and in which probably he can yet be excused) I still looked to some moment of reflection when bad advisers . . . were distant from the side of one who is so much the child of feeling and emotion.   (10 January 1817)[10]

To be revealed to Byron as the partisan "author" of a story of genius vexed by domestic and public Childe abuse is Scott's happy hope. He means to stand by his man-child of passion.

Unsigned, Scott's essay gave a public pattern of true love: Who could deny compassion to this distressed soul? "Nothing short of taking Lord B. 'for better for worse' would, I think, cure Walter Scott," Lady Byron joked on learning the author, with a shrewd grasp of the amatory pledge (Mayne, *Lady Byron* 266). To secure the cure, Scott had "calculated to give an unfavourable impression of her to the world" as one "of a very cold & unforgiving nature" (said Baillie to Scott himself; 21 Feb.; *L* 362). Sure enough, Scott's rapture was vibrant proxy that "the world yet loves you" (Murray informed Byron on 20 March); it "produced a sensation . . . the more efficacious for from the good fortune of its having appeared in perhaps our very best Number—of which I have sold already almost 10,000 Copies" (*L* 214–15). It was *The Corsair* of the day, starring Byron as the latest Byronic hero.

Yet as Scott makes clear, the case had to be argued. The Separation was a crisis not just for Lord and Lady Byron, but also for Lord Byron and his public. Anti-Byronists, freshly outraged, competed with the defenses of college friends, brother poets, and Whig allies. Legions of adoring women wished that Byron had chosen *them* for the honor of an abusive marriage. Meanwhile, other women, some of them charter Byronists, found themselves troubled by the Lord and rather partial to the Lady. In the affective warfare, The Separation etched the inequalities (social, legal, cultural) from which all wives, even a Lady, suffered; women felt the pain of a palpably wronged wife. "Pray try to be a little more indignant at bad men who ill-treat their wives," Baillie entreated Scott back in April 1816, knowing his soft spot for a lord in distress.[11] "If you can do us no good, you might at least be angry with us and that would be some sympathy," she sighed, with an unintended recoil effect in *with us: angry on our behalf* into *angry at us* (*L* 351). Byronism wasn't just fantasy-land; it was a cultural report-card.

Of the volatile female stakes Elizabeth, Duchess of Devonshire is a barometer. A fan ever since *Hours of Idleness*, she was "astonished" by the news of the separation by reason of "incompatibility" (27 February 1816). On March 8 she wrote to her sister that while she could "pity" lady Byron, "I think that, had I married a profligate man, knowing that he was so, and that I had a child, and was not ill used by him, I would not part from him." The news cycles then changed her mind: "I pity her from my heart," she wrote to her son on 22 March.[12] But then *Childe Harold* came round again. "I hear from England that Lord Byron's third canto of Childe Harold is beautiful," she wrote her son from Rome in December; "Lady Bessborough is sending it to me, and I long for it, as, however odious his character, he is a great Poet."[13] In 1816 Susan Ferrier fell in love all over again with *Childe Harold III*, and read it directly into the Separation: "I maintain that there is but one crime a woman could never forgive in her husband and that is a *kicking*," she wrote to a Miss Clavering; "Did you ever read anything so exquisite as the new canto of 'Childe Harold'? It is enough to make a woman fly into the arms of a tiger; nothing but a kick could have hardened her heart against such genius," she added, with a little kick at Lady Byron (131).[14] "Don't look at him, he is dangerous to look at," Lady Liddel hissed to her daughter Maria, on encountering Byron on the roof of St. Peter's in Rome, the next spring.[15]

There was fallout for the rest of Byron's life, a flare-up in 1824 when his memoirs were destroyed within days of the news of his death, and a new flash in 1830 with Moore's *Life of Byron*, which indulged in a long brief for the inevitable domestic failings of genius. Partisan to Lady Byron, Baillie detoxed faster than other intoxicated women of the Regency. A couple of years after the Separation, she gleefully circulated a caricature of Byron, wrought from another woman's gaze upon the noble body in its Venetian mode:

Miss Montgomery saw L<u>d</u> Byron not very long ago at Venice and says, he has become very fat, his face being round as a cheese & his body somewhat of the form of a large china jar that we have our drawing room . . .

—she wrote in September 1818, to none other than Scott (*L* 382).[16] This Carolean cartoon of the roly-poly Lord in domestic decor is her lightest touch. Other images are etched in acid, limning a Dorian Gray avant la lettre. Fresh from Moore's *Life of Byron*, she ranted to Margaret Holford Hodson about the line of defense that held that since the Lord a-courtin' was "known" "to be what he proved to be afterwards & having married such a character," his Lady had no grounds for grievance and "ought to have submitted to her fate" (28 May 1830; *L* 617–18). By this point, too, Baillie had read both Leigh Hunt's ambivalent *Lord Byron* (1828) and the long appreciation of Moore's *Byron* splashed across *Blackwood's* February and March 1830 issues, concluding in a ten-page defense of Byron's misery in marriage, his pain over his wife's "inexplicable desertion," and his public martyrdom.

Blackwood's followed up in May in its serial *Noctes Ambrosianæ*, addressing "this Lord and Leddy Byron bizzness" to rebuke the Lady for a pamphlet she had issued to answer some of Moore's remarks.[17] To the *Noctes* fraternity, this was a grievous violation of "conjugal duties" to a "dead husband's reputation" (27: 825). While *Blackwood's* had not always liked the poet's way with women, here the knights closed ranks. Miss Milbanke may have flattered herself that she could reform Byron (they had read their Moore) but she had, after all, married "Byron":

NORTH: May I without harshness or indelicacy say, here among ourselves private, my dear James, in this our own family-circle, that by marrying Byron, she took upon her, with eyes wide open, and conscience clearly convinced, duties very different indeed from those of which, even in common cases, the presaging foresight shadows . . .

SHEPHERD: She did that, sir. By ma troth, she did that.

NORTH: Byron's character was a mystery then—as it is now—but its dark qualities were perhaps the most prominent—at least they were so to the public view, and in the public judgment. Miss Milbank knew that he was reckoned a rake and a roué; and although his genius wiped off, by impassioned eloquence in love-letters that were felt to be irresistible, or hid the worst stain of, that reproach, still Miss Milbank must have believed it a perilous thing to be the wife of Lord Byron. . . . she pledged her troth, and her faith, and her love, under probabilities of severe, disturbing perhaps fearful trials in the future, from which, during the few bright days of love, she must have felt that it would be her duty never, under any possible circumstances, to resile.   (823–24)

If the Lady had gotten in over her head, she was not innocent of the depths. Even Hunt, a bit more sympathetic, was still critical: while Byron "married for money" he "wooed with his genius; and the lady persuaded herself that she liked him, partly because he had a genius" and partly because she had a fantasy "that her love, and her sincerity, and her cleverness, would enable her to reform him" (*Lord Byron* 9–10). She, too, was cunning in her overthrow, the careful pilot of her proper woe.

To *Blackwood's*, the real problem was the Lady's venturing her own voice, her own story, her own authority, in a publication which refused to keep some things hidden:

NORTH: That Byron behaved badly—very badly to his wife, I believe . . . but I think Lady Byron ought not to have printed that Narrative. Death abrogates not the rights of a husband to his wife's silence, when speech is fatal—as in this case it seems to be—to his character as a man. Has she not flung suspicion over his bones interred,—that they are the bones of a—monster?   (27: 824)

The *Blackwood's* men enact the Byronism of casting the Lady as *femme fatale*, killing "Byron." The moral Clytemnestra of His Posthumous Lord (the Byron-scripted figure in *Lines, on Hearing that Lady Byron was Ill*) was the villainess.

But the gothic story cut both ways. Of Byron's bad behavior at the time, Hunt—taking a dark page from *The Corsair* or *Lara*—told readers of *The Examiner*, 21 April 1816,

the story is mixed up with all sorts of inconsistent and villainous accusations, some of them so monstrous, that even the first public propagators of the scandal professed the singular delicacy of being able only to hint at them.   (248)

This was Baillie's tack with Scott back in February 1816, against the grain of public "reports":

> it was generally said this was occasioned by his improper connection with a beautiful Actress of Drury Lane. It is not however believed, by those who have the best opportunity of knowing, that gallantries as they are called of any kind had any thing to do with it. Your kind & manly heart will be grieved when I tell you, from authority that cannot be doubted, that he had used her brutally, and that no excuse can be pleaded in his behalf but insanity . . . . When I say brutally I use the word that was made use of to me, not knowing any particulars.
>
> (26 February; *L* 346–47)

Impatient of the cant of manly "gallantries" (affairs), Baillie writes a gothic tale worthy of Radcliffe. "I had good cause to know that her motives for marrying him were of a very generous nature bordering on romantic," she continues, marking the bad bargain in the fog of romance:

> Her happiness now, at the age of 24 is wrecked for life. . . . According to the marriage settlements, the whole of Lady Byron's large fortune will go to him after her Mother's death, except three hundred a year which is her pin money.   (*L* 347)

After she read Scott's gush in the *Quarterly,* she elaborated the story, as if outlining a related genre, the latest cautionary marriage-plot novel from Charlotte Smith: "it is not easy for those nearly concerned, who see an excellent young creature with all her large fortune & fair prospects, fall a sacrifice to the deliberate, calculating selfishness of a man, who only feigned an attachment to her for his own worldly interest" (3 March 1817; *L* 365).[18] Into the Byronic ledger of latent seething passion she enters some new information:

> The firearms & daggers, kept at night on the table of Lord B's bed room, Lady B. herself made light of, and said that she never supposed they were intended against her tho' he once pointed a pistol at her with threats. I must not tell you the darkest part of L$^{\underline{d}}$ B's character, and if I did, you would most likely not believe it.   (*L* 366)

Not for nothing had her brother Dr. Matthew Baillie diagnosed Byron "mad" in January 1816.

If Scott was incredulous, Baillie's villain wasn't a stretch for another northern novelist, also of a gothic bent. Ellis Bell's Heathcliff, in the eyes of the *Examiner*, evoked Byron's Corsair: "Linked to one virtue and a thousand crimes." It shuddered at English proximity, "so near our own dwellings as the summit of a Lancashire or Yorkshire moor" (21). Heathcliff is a patent Byronic hero: darkly, savagely rebellious, a Satanic majesty fatal to Isabella Linton, soul-sister of naive Isabella (she was christened) Milbanke, and as besotted as any of the cautionary cases in Wollstonecraft's *Rights of Woman*.[19] Like all these lost causes, head-strong, heart-strong Isabella is complicit in her undoing, marrying (Heathcliff remarks, defensively, sarcastically) "under a delusion" of romantic portraiture,

> picturing in me a hero of romance, and expecting unlimited indulgences from my chivalrous devotion. I can hardly regard her in the light of a rational creature, so obstinately has she persisted in forming a fabulous notion of my character, and acting on the false impressions she cherished.   (*Wuthering Heights* 339)

Like Byron, this husband from hell has legal sanction: "I keep strictly within the limits of the law," he boasts; Isabella hasn't "the slightest right to claim a separation," and moreover would "thank nobody for dividing us" (340–41). His prototype, a titled Englishman and society darling, did not have to be this scrupulous about rights, and his wife became a belatedly adept reader of the grand drama. "He has been assuming the character of an injured & affectionate husband with great success to some," sighed Anne Isabella in the first weeks, knowing that his missives to her were being broadcast as part of "a long design" (Elwin 409).

Fare thee well!

The most notorious design in this un-shy trafficking was that *Fare thee well!*—some lines of poetry that Byron sent to his "Dearest Bell" in late March or early April (*BLJ* 5: 51–52), just after the draft Separation Agreement, before the finalization five weeks later. "I had a copy of Verses from his Lordship yesterday—very tender and so he talks of me to Every one," Bell wrote to her mother (Elwin 448). Intimacy notwithstanding, copies were legion. Byron showed his friend Moore the lines ("the tears, as he said, falling fast over the paper as he wrote"), then sent either this paper, blotted, or a fresh copy off to Murray,[20] who quickly shared it (Byron knew he would) with Gifford, Rogers, Canning, Frere, and many others, even Caroline Lamb. Byron then asked Murray to print it up, along with a nasty *Sketch* on Lady Byron's maid. Murray relished this last piece, cheering for the general male-clubbing. "It is tremendously exquisite," he wrote to Byron on 1 April; "the most astringent dose that was ever presented to female Character" (*L* 159). Byron's private label debuted a week later, on April 8, for distribution to fifty close friends. The network quickly went wide.

Old nemesis Henry Brougham poached a copy, dashing it over to the *Champion*'s editor John Scott, who featured the two poems in the 14 April Sunday paper, elaborated with attacks on Byron's character.[21] A feeding frenzy ensued, piracies erupted, and within days everyone from Wordsworth to Staël had weighed in.[22] Coleridge (who had received a Valentine's Day gift of £100 from Byron) tendered an unsigned essay (as with Scott, the affect of disinterested authority) titled "Lord Byron" for the next Thursday's *Courier* (18 April). Rapt by the exquisite "pathos and tenderness" of *Fare thee well!*, he couldn't believe that anything so "touching and affecting" could be the work of "more affectation of feeling than of reality; more hypocrisy than truth." He was willing to spin even *A Sketch from Private Life* as the helpless rancor of loving husband against the meddling "person against whom the sketch is directed."[23]

If one loved Byron, anything could be rationalized; and if one were his wife, it was inconceivable not to forgive him. This is Byron's "long design" with *Fare thee well*, its rhetoric tuned to coax the reader, any reader, into the affective position of addressee:

> All my faults—perchance thou knowest—
>> All my madness—none can know;
> All my hopes—where'er thou goest—
>> Wither—yet with *thee* they go.—
> Every feeling hath been shaken,
>> Pride—which not a world could bow—
> Bows to thee—   (1816 *Poems*, p. 23; lines 45–51)

In this valediction forbidding grievance, not only does a reader feel addressed by Byron, but by inhabiting Lady Byron's rhetorical assignment, feels a differentiating sympathy, at her expense. This is Separation Politics par excellence. Rushing *Fare thee well!* over to Scott, William Black-wood (Murray's Edinburgh agent) scarcely paused to report back to Murray, "One cannot read 'Fare Thee Well' without crying" (17 April 1816; Smiles 1: 365). Coleridge cited one "fair correspondent" (Staël) saying that "if her husband had bade her such a farewell, she could not have avoided running into his arms and being reconciled immediately—*Je n'aurois pu m'y tenir un instant"* (*Essays* 2: 427–29). It wasn't satire but accurate cultural chronicle when in 1825 "M.J.J." has an accomplished album-keeping Miss boast of having "wept over Lord Byron's descriptions of his own miseries" (*Phantasmagoria* 1: 94).

The whole world interacted. Shops filled with cartoons and caricatures; pamphlets volleyed parodies, gossip, poems cast in the voice of Lady Byron (in a range of tones), spuriously attributed to her or the Lord, and so forth. Piracies of "Domestic Pieces" were fleet and legion.[24] Cartoons embellished the goods. Among the flash was George Cruikshank's full color, acid *FARE THEE WELL* (Byron boating away, mistresses along, with one lass weeping on the shore; with the poem below) and another from his father, Isaac Cruickshank, *The Separation: a Sketch from the private life of Lord IRON.* "Byron" spun out of Byron's own management and any hope of recall:

> Fame assuredly brings in its train as many penalties as privileges; and were confirmation needed of so undisputed a fact, the life of Byron would most readily afford it. Let alone the circumstance that the privacy of a popular author is perpetually invaded, the sacred history of his domestic life profanely revealed, or, if this cannot be known, monstrous conjectures are palmed upon the credulous for undoubted truth; the very creations of his mind once released from his keeping by that magician, the Press, are beyond his recall, and may become like lesser Frankensteins or mischievous sprites, to tease and torment.

So wrote Camille Toulmin in 1847 in Lady Blessington's *Book of Beauty,* about Angolina, slandered in Byron's *Marino Faliero* (79), with Byron now enrolled in the female plight.

In 1816, however, it wasn't exactly the case that Byron was only invaded and profaned by alien agents, teased and tormented by his own renegade creations. He was also a creator and impresario. Before that *Quarterly* essay, Scott's first, dryer reaction was to measure the wheels of

Isaac Robert Cruikshank, *The Separation* (1816), one of the many cartoons to comment on the scandal. By kind courtesy of British Museum, London. © Trustees of the British Museum. George Cruikshank's *Fare Thee Well*, printed with the text of the poem, shows Byron leaving by boat, bidding "Fare thee well!" to a lorn lady on the shore, holding a babe, while his arm is around a buxom maid, with other doting women still on board the boat.

such production, which he tracked with a proto-Wildean regard of the Byronic Art of Life. *Fare thee well* was a "very sweet dirge indeed," but it was "a strange thirst of public fame that seeks such a road to it." And so he coined some brilliant verbs of Byronic self-production: "Lord Byron . . . has Childe Harolded himself, and out-lawed himself, into too great a resemblance with the pictures of his imagination."[25] The June *Eclectic* reviewed *Fare thee well!* as if it were the latest offering from Drury Lane, praising the actor's "skill" in "displaying the semblance of passion." Verses put before "the public eye" bespoke *"sentiment"* instead of "feeling," crafted "productions of the *affecting* kind" (596–97). "Lord Byron," said the *Critical Review* in November about *Childe Harold III*, shamelessly made the public

> a party to the unfortunate disputes between himself and his most amiable wife, by the studious publication of painful particulars that would otherwise have remained in the seclusion of a domestic circle. At least, this is unjust, if it be not cruel: Lord Byron avails himself of his popularity to make his own representations of the facts, and of the impressions which those facts have made upon him; while his unhappy lady, both unable and unwilling to retaliate, bears all the odium his statements are calculated to draw down upon her.
>
> (4: 497)

Not playing Byron's game, and taking the lady's part, the *Critical* outlined Byron's characterology and narratology: "he is to be regarded as a man driven from his home by the unforgiving hard-heartedness of a wife, and she as a woman undeserving of the love of so beautiful a poet, and so noble a gentleman" (497). Finding Byron's designs against the "unfortunate" Lady distasteful, the *Portfolio* opened its notice of *Childe Harold III* limning an unholy triple alliance of prurient public, Byronic narcissism, and bookseller opportunism:

> Indeed, it is the real romance of that person's life, immeasurably more than the fabled one of his pen, which the public expects to find in his pages, and which not so much engages its sympathy, as piques it curiosity, and feeds thought and conversation. The Noble Poet, in the mean time, is content with—it should be said he is ambitious of— this species of distinction; the booksellers, printers, and stationers, all

profit by the traffic to which the exhibition gives rise; and thus every
part is a gainer in this remarkable phenomenon of the time . . .

(23 November 1816, p. 73)

Call it synergy, call it complicity, this exhibition (the real romance of life)
was public drama, starring Byron as Noble Poet, the character profiting
"at the expense of . . . his character" (73).

The *Critical Review* saw it all as profitable fame-work: "he knows he
is touching upon a matter that has unusually excited public curiosity:
what he wrote, therefore, was sure of being read." To those who "thought
that the lines were most delightfully pathetic, and wondered how a man,
who shewed he had so little heart, could evince so much feeling," the *Critical* gave a rave to the "skill" at hand: "to fabricate neatly-turned phraseology" and to "introduce to advantage all the common-places of affection"
is a production of "much more talent than tenderness."[26] Looking back in
1821, John Scott summed up the phenomenon as a grand publicity stunt
of "theatrical woe," produced without a spasm of sincerity:

> Seared in his heart, and lone, and blighted—
> More than this, *I scarce can die:—*

> thus concludes Lord Byron's Farewell, on the occasion of his leaving
> England, and we have had good reason since to admire the strength
> of the vivacious principle in his breast. His subsequent productions
> have seemed to intimate that dying was as far from his own thoughts,
> as his death is far from the wishes of book-sellers and book-readers.

("Living Authors"; *London Magazine* p. 52)

Decades later, a less sour satirist of "Byronism," Walter Edgar McCann,
joked that "the ill-fated marriage, the scandal, 'the British public in one
of its periodical fits of morality,' and the banishment" were no tragedy,
but "a plea for Byron to grow more Byronic than ever."[27]

If from 1816 Byron's "textual seductions and manipulations" of his
public become the principal subject of his fictions,[28] oppositional readings quickly follow. In his retrospect from 1830, Moore's best spin was to
blame Lady Byron for mistaking, or even taking advantage of, Byron's
Byronism, by literalizing the self-evident theatrics:

> there is hardly any crime so dark or desperate of which, in the excite-
> ment of thus acting upon the imaginations of others, he would not

have hinted that he had been guilty; and it has sometimes occurred to me that the occult cause of his lady's separation from him, round which herself and her legal adviser have thrown such formidable mystery, may have been nothing more, after all, than some imposture of this kind, some dimly hinted confession of undefined horrors, which, though intended by the relater but to mystify and surprise, the hearer so little understood him as to take in sober seriousness.   (*BW* 6: 242)

Moore's Byron is an actor caught up in typecasting, and in thrall to a public panting for the typology of which Lady Byron was at first too credulous, and then later, a calculating exploiter.

About the public theater of 1816, however, she was not all that mystified; she was pretty smart about Byron's way of acting upon all imaginations—"the whole system":

> He is the absolute monarch of words, and uses them, as Bonaparte did lives, for conquest, without more regard to their intrinsic value, considering them only as ciphers, which must derive all their import from the situation in which he places them, and the ends to which he adapts them, with such consummate skill.

So she wrote to a friend as the Separation-poems were being broadcast, with a prescient sense of postmodern theory.[29] This way with words was sensed by other skeptics. Proposing "Literary Fraud," the *Portfolio* deconstructed the affect of sincerity: *Stanzas to——* (in the *Prisoner & c*) "are not genuine," but "are artfully enough contrived to appear so" (128). To answer such charges in 1832, Moore hastened to a long footnote to *Fare thee well!*, insisting on the genuineness of Byron's tears, swelled with "tender recollection" and with no designs on "the public eye." (It was only a friend's "injudicious zeal" for a copy that tore the verses from his desk.)[30] But fresh in public memory was Leigh Hunt's dissent in *Lord Byron* (1828): Byron's very artfulness ("he said it so well") overplayed; the skill of the verses gave the lie to "genuine passion." He "sat down to *imagine* what a husband might say, who had really loved his wife," but the real love (said Hunt) was "love of publicity" (191) and love of self: "his poetical power of assuming an imaginary position, and taking pity on himself in the shape of another man" (11). Conceding that he "thought differently on this business at the time" (i.e., in his essay "Distressing Circumstance" for an 1816 *Examiner*), Hunt performed a public correction, his evidence being the deft calculation of the verses that had "set so many tender-hearted white handkerchiefs in motion": "He had no love for the object of it, or he would never have written upon her in so different a style afterwards" (11)—not only in the poems of 1816, but in styling the wife from hell called Donna Inez in *Don Juan I* a few years later.

"Byron" & Byron

Lockhart, *Blackwood's* unsigned reviewer of this first installment of *Don Juan* (1819), found himself defending Lady Byron's honor in this round of Separation-warfare: thinly coded Donna Inez is a "cold-blooded mockery . . . brutally, fiendishly, inexpiably mean" (5: 514). That the indictment ran for paragraphs suggests that more than Lady Byron was at stake. In Lockhart's heart of hearts, she stood for all who loved and were deceived by Byron, the injured reviewer-*we* sounding personal:

> Every high thought that ever kindled in our breasts by the muse of Byron—every pure and lofty feeling that ever responded from within us to the sweep of his majestic inspirations—every remembered moment of admiration and enthusiasm is up in arms against him. . . . The consciousness of the insulting deceit which has been practiced upon us, mingles with the nobler pain arising from the contemplation of perverted and degraded genius—to make us wish that no such being as Byron ever had existed. It is indeed a sad and an humiliating thing to know, that in the same year there proceeded from the same pen two productions, in all things so different, as the Fourth Canto of Childe Harold and this loathsome Don Juan.   (5: 514–15)

It was a bad breakup, not only for Lockhart but the spirit of the age.[31] It scarcely mattered if Lady Byron herself, still a bit Byronic in 1819, rather enjoyed *Don Juan*. Though she saw Byron clearly availing himself of "the prejudices" he had generated to "give a plausible colouring to his accusations," she liked the skill: "the quizzing in one or two passages was so good as to make me smile at myself—therefore others are heartily welcome to laugh."[32] Love-scarred Lockhart only fumed, unable to smile.

Byron had been coloring his case in several modes, including the romance pathos that was his first purchase on fame. In that Separation-poem *The Dream*, he mystifies his marriage as a helpless trance, rendered in alienated third-person abstraction, in elegy for lost youth:

> I saw him stand
> Before an Altar—with a gentle bride;
> Her face was fair, but was not that which made
> The Starlight of his Boyhood;—
>
> .   .   .
>
> And he stood calm and quiet, and he spoke
> The fitting vows, but heard not his own words,
> And all things reel'd around him; . . .   (VI; *Prisoner & c*)

Intimating an insane dissociation of sensibility and second-best love, Byron ironizes the fitting vows. His friend Kinnaird got the design, and capitalized on the performance for fun and perhaps erotic profit with the skeptics: "Kinnaird has had the cruelty [to] read Ladies into Hysterics by it," Murray reported gleefully to Byron 13 December 1816, with a note about the incipient Byronism: "I hope he had not the wickedness to take any naughty advantage of his art" (*L* 180).

If it was recognized as "art" in this circle, others felt and broadcast a poignant confession. Moore's *Life* presented the relevant stanza as a "historically" valid document.[33] Baillie, for one, was beside herself in outrage at the first offing of this faux history: "he says, he pronounced his marriage vows scarcely knowing what he said, his mind fitted with another object," she seethed, in "bitterest . . . indignation," to Scott (3 March 1817; *L* 365–66). Yet the spin was working. Even crusty Gifford crumbled: "never since my intimacy with Mr Gifford," Murray wrote to Byron, "did I see him so heartily pleased or give one fiftieth part of his commendation with one thousandth part of the warmth. . . . he speaks in extacy of the Dream" (12 September 1816; *L* 173)—as if one of the Ladies seduced and hystericized by Kinnaird's theatrics.

Scott plays his part with a supplement to *The Dream* in the opening pages of his *Quarterly* article, introducing a restless, idealistic adventurer gaining excuse for false-fitting vows under cover of ravishing, romantic genius:

> the objects of his admiration lose their attraction and value as soon
> as they are grasped by the adventurer's hand, and all that remains is
> regret for the time lost in the chase, and astonishment at the halluci-

nation under the influence of which it was undertaken. The disproportion between hope and possession which is felt by all men [is]
doubled to those whom nature has endowed with the power of gilding a distant prospect by the rays of imagination. These reflexions,
though trite and obvious, are in a manner forced from us by the poetry of Lord Byron, by the sentiments of weariness of life and enmity
with the world which they so frequently express—and by the singular
analogy which such sentiments hold with incidents of his life so recently before the public. (16: 174)

The romance of Byron was bigger than any domestic affair. Detach Byronism from the local material and translate it into the passions of metaphysical mind, and a world of men, too, could swoon into dark and thrilling, potent and perilous seduction.

"Byron" prevailed by flattering a male reader's sympathy as modern
metaphysics. Writing without signature for *Blackwood's* on *Childe Harold IV* (with a preface once more wringing the marriage wreck),[34] John
Wilson sighed the spirit of the age:

> It would be worse than idle to endeavour to shadow out the linea-
> ments of that Mind, which, exhibiting itself in dark and perturbed
> grandeur, has established a stronger and wider sway over the pas-
> sions of men, than any other poetical Intellect of modern times.
>
> (3 [May 1818], 216)

These opening lines quickly shade into a testimony in resonant first-
person plurals:

> We feel as if there were a kind of absurdity in criticising the power
> that hurries us along with it like whirlwind. When standing within
> the magic circle, and in the immediate presence of the magician, we
> think not upon his art itself, but yield ourselves up to its wonder-
> working influence. We have no wish to speculate on the causes which
> awoke and stirred up all the profoundest feelings and energies of our
> souls,—the deep pathos, the stormy passion, has been enjoyed or
> suffered,—and, in the exaltation or prostration of our nature, we own
> the power of the poet to be divine,—and, with a satisfied and unques-
> tioning delight, deliver ourselves up to his gentle fascination, or his
> irresistible dominion.
>
> (3: 216)

As "that Mind" works poetic seduction, men of "Intellect"—privately but in solidarity—deliver themselves to the thrill that women are happy to eroticize. The feeling in the poetry of the "continual presence" of the poet himself in "self-representation or self-reference" constitutes the "real excellence," its "power, sovereign and despotical," said a clearly enthralled Wilson (216). Byron was, as the Lady said, the absolute monarch of words:

> "The wondrous Childe" passes before our eyes, and before our hearts, and before our souls. And all love, and pity, and condemn, and turn away in aversion, and return with sympathy; and "thoughts that do lie too deep for tears" alike agitate the young and the old,—the guilty and the sinless,—the pious and the profane,—when they think on the features of his troubled countenance. (216)

In this star of Byron, a figuring as the Christ child may be risked against blasphemy.[35] Even Wordsworth's Great Ode is recruited to help the man and poet that Wordsworth despised.

Jeffrey, who had no patience with Wordsworthian thoughts, and was exasperated by this Ode, was stirred to sublimity by *The Corsair:*

> He has delineated, with unequalled force and fidelity, the workings of those deep and powerful emotions which alternately enchant and agonize the minds that are exposed to their inroads. . . . It is by this spell, chiefly, we think, that he has fixed the admiration of the public. . . . he alone has been able to *command* the sympathy, even of reluctant readers, by the natural magic of his moral sublimity, and the terrors and attractions of those overpowering feelings, the depths and heights of which he seems to have so successfully explored.
> (*Edinburgh Review* 23 [April 1814], 198–99)

In the lexicon of *force and fidelity, command, moral sympathy, overpowering feelings, depths and heights,* Jeffrey renders a Burkean sublime, a manly aesthetic distinct from female hysterics, and an analytic distinct from common spellbinding. While this gender-differential enabled a safe homosocial sympathy, the strain on cool analytics, and its potentially communicative disease, was caught by Jane Austen, for one.

In *Persuasion* (which she was writing between summer 1815 and summer 1816), she has Captain Benwick, mourning the death of his fiancée, confess to Anne Elliot the solace he finds in the wild despairs of Byron's lovelorn Giaour, "all the impassioned descriptions of hopeless agony":

> he repeated with such tremulous feeling, the various lines which imaged a broken heart, or a mind destroyed by wretchedness, and looked so entirely as if he meant to be understood, that she ventured to hope he did not always read only poetry, and to say, that she thought it was the misfortune of poetry to be seldom safely enjoyed by those who enjoyed it completely; and that the strong feelings which alone could estimate it truly were the very feelings which ought to taste it but sparingly. (I.11)

In Austen's register, Byronism shifts from affect to unsparing pathology. Austen finished *Persuasion* just after Byron left England. In a memoir rushed into print the year Byron left the world altogether (1824), Sir Egerton Brydges repeats the tremulous feeling, even as he tries to discipline the taste, admitting "a magic in impressions powerfully represented, even though they are themselves not such as we approve" (15).

The issue for Brydges is not a poetry which gives voice to individual wretchedness, but a life that attracts by force of its own romance of wretchedness: "we are often seized with an irresistible impulse to gaze curiously and intently on that which fills us with horror while we gaze" (28). The rapture is as addictive as any love-potion, and the drama is part of the punch: upon "the yielding, overwhelmed, and astonished reader," "the spell is pronounced, . . . the reader listens, trembles, admires, dreads, condemns . . . prays for liberation—yet admires again!" (231). And so it goes. In 1831, with a generation's and perhaps a gender's distance, M. J. Jewsbury could render a droll report of the glamour in all its paradoxes and mystifying power:

> Lord Byron was sceptical, selfish, dissipated, and eccentric, and was believed to have taken higher degrees in evil than he really had; but he wrote impassioned and brilliant poetry that revolutionized the public taste, spell-bound the public heart; and though much of this poetry contained scepticism, selfishness, profligacy, and eccentricity, yet, by some strange anomaly, grave and good people, after protesting against these elements, spoke of and quoted the remainder with enthusiasm,—nay, very often felt an enthusiasm for the man.
>
> (*Athenæum* 194, 16 July 1831, p. 456)

The syntactic pivots (*but, though, yet, after, nay*) deftly chart the deft contradictions of Byron's Byronism and the dynamic conflicts of its attractions.

Decades later, Stowe, as bitter as Lockhart about her own youthful seduction, avenges herself by putting the charmer into the lineage of "les Femmes Fatales" that a sobered-up, better-informed, disengaged woman (now) knows how to analyze:

> There have been women able to lead their leashes of blinded adorers; to make them swear that black was white, or white black, at their word; to smile away their senses, or weep away their reason. No matter what these sirens may say, no matter what they may do, though caught in a thousand transparent lies, and doing a thousand deeds which would have ruined others, still men madly rave after them in life, and tear their hair over their graves. Such an enchanter in man's shape was Lord Byron. (*Lady Byron* 84)

The Byron-vamp plays double: satirizing the groupies, Stowe also skewers Byron as femme fatale vamping in a man's shape. But the venom is transparently the antidote to enchantment.

Byron by Parody

Byronism was the confabulation of such paradoxes, and its star was Byron himself, with a train of those lifetime eponyms: *Byronic, Byronian, Byronism, Byromania*. As the fascination becomes the subject, the readings of its dynamics sharpen and, as the various circulations of *Fare thee well!* make clear, the theatrics of Byronism plunge deeper into parody. As early as 1814 Byron himself intuited this potential, and tried to preempt it by affecting boredom with the serial "pictures" stamped out in "the gloomy vanity of 'drawing from self'"—so he sighed in his preface to *The Corsair* (ix). Yet he was complicit:

> He was so sensible of the striking effect of a good exterior, that he always took care to display himself to the best advantage. He never failed to appear remarkable. (Iley 2: 340)

In the circuit of model and image, the original falls to multiple productions: Melancholy Byron, Aloof Aristocrat Byron, Dandy Byron, Alba-

Lord Byron, from the frontispiece in *My Recollections of Lord Byron*
by Countess Guiccioli (London: Richard Bentley, 1869). This engraving by R. Whitechurch is one of many based on the dramatic "cloak"
portrait by Thomas Phillips, 1814.

nian Byron. These images in turn supplied frontispieces for the volumes,
intimating both Byron and his heroes. In perfect synergy, Byron used the
royalties to pay for one of the most famous, Thomas Phillips's Lordship
in Albanian drag. By the time American painter William West found
Byron in Italy in June 1822, to render what was not intended to be but
would become the famed "last portrait" of the famous Lord, the model
was nearly exhausted by his idols of imitation: "portraits . . . though a

William Finden, engraving of Byron in Albanian costume, with lightning bolts added, 1841, after Thomas Phillips's portrait, 1813. Finden's engraving was summoned by John Murray for the frontispiece for *Childe Harold's Pilgrimage* (London, 1841), the source of this image. Though Phillips's portrait was a sensation when it was exhibited at the Royal Academy in 1814, it disappeared from the public view until the publication of this engraving.

little varied in the drapery and attitude, . . . all copied from the same original," snarked Jeffrey in 1822; "nothing but corsairs and misanthropes," *New Monthly* chimed in, in 1826.[36]

Such ceaseless production from Byron Central Casting may have confirmed the glamour, but Byron himself was not always doing the casting.[37] Immortal Byron was also a genre, and a pattern for mere mortals. Shifting the glamour from agent to effect, the formulaic stylizing set the persona into a riot of impersonations. A world of young men took to the fashion. In 1825, *Westminster Review*, derogating the cult of "poetess," gave a feminizing, and effeminizing, spin to the Byronic patent "poet." On the occasion of reviewing L.E.L's *The Improvisatrice*, it proposed that any entrepreneur could "engage to manufacture a poet out of any young person, particularly a female, by supplying her with a dictionary of love phrases similes, &c., with as little exertion of intellect, as is employed in manufacturing a stocking in the loom" (3: 539). Not genius of mind, just style and affect, were the requirements. Reviewing Moore's *Byron* in 1831, Thomas Babington Macaulay wryly etched the franchise among a "large class of young persons." Scanning the "unbounded" "popularity of Lord Byron," he read the effects in mass manufacture, conveying theatrical Byronism into the mechanics of farce:

> They bought pictures of him; they treasured up the smallest relics of him; they learned his poems by heart, and did their best to write like him, and to look like him. Many of them practised at the glass, in the hope of catching the curl of the upper lip, and the scowl of the brow, which appear in some of his portraits. A few discarded their neckcloths, in imitation of their great leader. For some years the Minerva press sent forth no novel without a mysterious, unhappy, Lara-like peer. The number of hopeful under graduates and medical students who became things of dark imaginings,—on whom the freshness of the heart ceased to fall like dew,—whose passions had consumed themselves to dust, and to whom the relief of tears was denied, passes all calculation. This was not the worst. . . . From the poetry of Lord Byron they drew a system of ethics, compounded of misanthropy and voluptuousness; a system in which the two great commandments were, to hate your neighbour, and to love your neighbour's wife.
>
> (*Edinburgh Review* 53: 571–72)

This was the assembly kit. In 1845 George Gilfillan reviewed Byronism gone wild:

> Byron's success in getting public attention to his personal woes, has produced two bad consequences: it has taught many to counterfeit sadness, and it has produced a false sentiment in the public mind. "How care-worn and wretched that man looks!" "Oh, no wonder, he's a man of genius; preserve me from his midnights!" (379)

Gilfillan was writing in complaint and protest about the moral license given by the cult of genius, but his sentences were just a heartbeat from spoof.

Walter McCann's satire, twenty years on, rendered a meta-discourse of this mimetic operation, confirming Gilfillan's diagnosis of the fandemic, and amplifying Macaulay's into high absurdity: "A visit to the fashionable circles of an evening would invariably disclose at least a half-dozen young noblemen wrapped in the solitude of their own absurdity, seated all alone in some dismal corner, gloomy and misanthropic" (779). Magic in one is silliness in six, a chorus of Byrons by the book:

> In all the universities the fever raged with such violence that its symptoms came to be at once recognized. It always broke out in open shirt collars and flaring neckties. There were more Lara-like young medical students and corsair-like lawyers than one would care to count. Their rooms were adorned with pictures and busts of their idol, their shelves with his works, and their private portfolios with imitations of his verses. . . . A man whose intended had been really cruel enough to jilt him, was looked upon as singularly fortunate. . . . There was also an immense deal of voyaging done to Italy and to Greece. (779)

An epiphenomenon of the romance of the Byronic hero, the stylizing turned magic to mimicry, aura to automaton—a prehistory to Walter Benjamin's fearful insight that "the work of art reproduced becomes the work of art designed for reproducibility" (224). Back in the nineteenth century, the reproduction tilted to farce: "The consequences were, of course, very bad," sighed McCann; "The only consolation was, that the cases were not isolated. Nearly everyone's story was alike" (779–80). A panorama of spectatorial aesthetics—swoons and sighs, fantasies and gossip—at once proved and parodied Byronic charisma. It was Byronism with a vengeance. "The whole of your misanthropy . . . is humbug," one John Bull protested in an open *Letter to the Right Hon. Lord Byron* (1821); "you thought it would be a fine, interesting thing for a handsome young Lord to depict himself as a dark-souled, melancholy, morbid being, and you have done so, it must be admitted, with exceeding cleverness." This national voice (a more self-possessed Lockhart, actually) concocts a cartoon of success, set in an Austenian gabfest, where the aloof Lord—formerly mad, bad, and dangerous to know—gets bandied about as a pop-confection, conjured and conjugated, dissected, inventoried, and assayed:

> every boarding-school in the empire still contains many devout believers in the amazing misery of the black-haired, high-browed, blue-eyed, bare-throated, Lord Byron. How melancholy you look in the prints! Oh! yes, this is the true cast of face. Now, tell me, Mrs. Goddard, now tell me, Miss Price, now tell me, dear Harriet Smith, and dear, dear Mrs. Elton, do tell me, is not this just the very look, that one would have fancied for Childe Harold? Oh! what eyes and eyebrows!—Oh! what a chin!   (*Letter* 80)

A perfect extrapolation of his Lordship's self-styling as *Homme Fatal*, this chatty blazon is murderously funny.[38] John Bull's infinitives imply a perpetual reproduction:

> To quarrel with your wife over night, and communicate all your quarrel to the public the next morning, in a sentimental copy of verses! To affect utter broken-heartedness, and yet be snatching the happy occasion to make another good bargain with Mr. John Murray! To solicit the compassion of your private friends for a most lugubrious calamity, and to solicit the consolation of the public, in the shape of five shillings sterling per *head* . . . To pretend dismay and despair, and get up *for the nonce* a dear pamphlet!—O, my Lord . . .   (*Letter* 108)

Even Byron joined the game. However, it was played, he could only win: "I have just read 'John Bull's letter,'" he wrote to Murray from Ravenna; "it is diabolically <u>well</u> written—& full of fun and ferocity.—I must forgive the dog whoever he is." Tendering several guesses, he urged Murray to "find him out" (*BLJ* 8: 145).[39]

The aura of the misanthropic melancholy exile, trailing clouds of scandal, precipitates into a female fantasy competition of compassion for a trophy-husband:

> well, after all, who knows what may have happened. One can never
> know the truth of such stories. Perhaps her *Ladyship* was in the
> wrong after all.—I am sure if I had married such a man, I would have
> borne with all his little eccentricities—a man so evidently unhappy.—
> Poor Lord Byron! who can say how much he may have been to be pit-
> ied? I am sure I would; I bear with all Mr. E.'s eccentricities, and I am
> sure any woman of real sense would have done so to Lord Byron's:
> poor Lord Byron!—well, say what they will, I shall always pity him.
>
> (*Letter* 80–81)

So Austen's Augusta Hawkins Elton might say, tiring of her "Mr. E.," and primed for an upgrade and new adventure with a Lord.

"He could only be laughed at by a woman, and they worshipped instead," wrote Virginia Woolf in her diary; "I haven't yet come to Lady Byron," she adds, "but I suppose, instead of laughing, she merely disapproved. And so he became Byronic" (3). But it was actually Lady-Byron-to-be who coined the term *The Byromania*, to title a heroic-couplet satire she dashed off in 1812 on first beholding the celebrity spectacle:

> Woman! how truly called "a harmless thing!"
> So meekly smarting with the venom'd sting.
> Forgiving saints!—ye bow before the rod,
> And kiss the ground on which your censor trod. . . .
> Reforming Byron with his magic sway
> Compels all hearts to love him and obey—
> Commands our wounded vanity to sleep,
> Bids us forget the <u>Truths</u> that cut so deep,
> Inspires a generous candour to the mind
> That makes us to our friend's oppression kind.
> Amusing Patroness of passing whim
> Which calls the <u>weaker</u> sex to worship <u>him</u>,
> See Caro, smiling sighing, o'er his face
> In hopes to imitate each strange grimace
> And mar the silliness which looks so fair

By bringing signs of wilder Passion there.
Is Human nature to be cast anew,
And modelled to your Idol's Image true?
Then grant me, Jove, to wear some other shape,
And be an anything—except an Ape!!
A.I.M. 1812

Although Ethel Mayne thinks this a feeble satire (*Lady Byron* 44), A.I.M. has a pretty sharp aim on the dynamic of mania: reception miming its mesmerizing subject. Tapping that novel-soaked fantasy of rake reform, she sets the grammar of "Reforming Byron with his magic sway" to play double, deftly relaying the she-fantasy of reforming Byron into a reverse sway: Byron's deforming of the weaker sex into multiple abject parodies, aping groupies. In such multiplication, the idol who "compels all hearts to love him and obey" spells a caution to any fantasy of wedding vows. "Yesterday I went to a <u>morning</u> party at lady Caroline Lamb's" ("Caro," above), A.I.M. wrote in her diary after meeting Byron, in March 1812, just weeks after the flash debut of *Childe Harold.* Her pun tweaks at the farce in which this "object at present of universal attention" proves fugitive, a bid to mourning: "Lady C. has of course seized on him, [more fun: *C./seized*], notwithstanding the reluctance he manifests to be shackled by her." With her own verses, she beat Byron to the sequel: "What a shining situation she will have in his next satire!" (Elwin 106).

Yet even as the glamour is anatomized and demystified, it fascinates and enchants. "I made no offering at the shrine of Childe Harold," she closes her first entry, only to concede with cautious curiosity, "though I shall not refuse the acquaintance if it comes my way" (Elwin 106). It did, with an eye on her fortune. In October, the genius of the shrine made an offering to her, of marriage, through an intermediary, his friend and Miss Milbanke's aunt Lady Melbourne. Miss Milbanke refused. But Lady Melbourne, panting for the connection to Byron, wrote a faux-Austenian letter to her resistant niece later that month:

He desires me to say, how much obli^d he is to you for the candour,
& fairness, with which you have told him your Sentiments,—that
although unfavourable to his hopes, or more properly to his Wishes,
for hopes he declares he had not, your conduct on this occasion as
encreased the high opinion he had before entertain'd of your abilities,
& excellent qualities & encreases the regret he feels at your decision,

as well as his admiration for your character. . . . He says to me, "I cannot sufficiently thank you for the trouble you have taken on my Account. . . . I never will renew a Subject which I am convinced would be hateful to her, & no condescension or indulgence from her, will ever lead me to suppose that I can be more to her than the most common Acquaintance to whom she shows civility when she meets them in society. (Elwin 156)

The next January, *Pride and Prejudice,* with its Byron-like hero and its skeptical A.I.M.-like heroine was out, and by spring 1813 Miss Milbanke had fallen for Mr. Darcy: "I really think it the most probable fiction I have ever read," she wrote to her mother; "the interest is very strong, especially for Mr. Darcy" (Elwin 159). Did Byron guess this, too?[40]

Miss Bennet spurns a proposal from proud Mr. Darcy; then, gradually revising first impressions, less certain of dark rumors, and captivated by his portrait at Pemberley ("she stood before the canvas on which he was represented, and fixed his eyes upon herself" [III.1]), she knows she will accept, should he ask again. So Miss Milbanke did in September 1814. Austen's Byronism, by the force of probability, returned its credit to A.I.M.'s interest in the prototype, despite her satirical armature. Probability was the prime redeemer of novels as moral literature.[41] But probability is not prediction. Mistaking one for the other, A.I.M. fell for the idea of Reforming Byron, not guessing that he was not altogether disappointed by her initial rejection, feeling (he admitted to Lady Melbourne) that they both had escaped "a *cold collation,* & I prefer hot suppers" (*BLJ* 2: 246).

The Last and Lasting Byron

As A.I.M.'s fall shows, parodies competed with Childe Harold straight. When William West arrived at Byron's villa in Montenero in June 1822, he was as besotted with hot Byronism as Scott was back in 1816, in quaking awe (so he is quoted in *New Monthly Magazine,* 1826):

My reverence for Lord Byron's genius made me almost afraid to encounter him; I expected to see a person somewhat thin and swarthy, with a high forehead and black curly hair—a stern countenance and lofty and reserved manners,—perhaps a black mantle and a diamond-hilted dagger . . . the haughty misanthrope whose character had always appeared so enveloped in gloom and mystery.   (244–45)

Primed for a star turn, he was taken aback by a plump body and quotidian personality. No less prepossessed by a Byronic imaginary, no less unsettled was Lady Blessington's first impression:

> Genoa, April 1st, 1823. Saw Lord Byron for the first time. The impression of the first few minutes disappointed me, as I had, both from the portraits and descriptions given, conceived a different idea of him. I had fancied him taller, with a more dignified and commanding air; and I looked in vain for the hero-looking sort of person with whom I had so long identified him in imagination.   (*Conversations* 5)

"I want a hero," she might have said. She, too, weighs the difference from the portraits:

> His manners are as unlike my preconceived notions of them as is his appearance. I had expected to find him a dignified, cold, reserved, and haughty person, resembling those mysterious personages he so loves to paint in his works, and with whom he has been so often identified by the good-natured world: but nothing can be more different.   (7)

Byron reveled in the tease. "I am sure, that if ten individuals undertook the task of describing Byron," Blessington conjectured, "no two, of the ten, would agree . . . or convey any portrait that resembled the other"; "Byron, changing every day, and fond of misleading those whom he suspects might be inclined to paint him, will always appear different from the hand of each limner" (72). Byron holds his sway, has his way, by leading the train.

West enters this field with a figure of the misleader. Staging the body in romantic cloaks, he limned the affable affect of the aristocrat who had charmed him through the long hours of sitting, with a couple of gleams of the old romance. Though still styled, Byron's gaze is now at his beholder, inviting interaction. But was this Byron off stage? or Byron's latest staging—a monster masked by aristocratic grace? "I left him," said West, "with an impression that he possessed an excellent heart, which had been misconstrued on all hands from little else than a reckless levity

Lord Byron, by William Edward West (1822). © Scottish National Gallery of Modern Art. This is the famous "Last Portrait."

of manners, which he took a whimsical pride in opposing to those of other people" (248).[42]

Byron's excellent heart led him to Greece, where he died in the Missolonghi swamps twenty months later, 19 April 1824. The news reached London friends (Hobhouse and Kinnaird) on the morning of 14 May. The Times carried a glowing eulogy on the 15th. Then a second death. On the 17th Hobhouse, Moore, other friends, and a representative from Lady Byron gathered in Murray's rooms at Albemarle Street, and after heated argument, fed Byron's *Memoranda* of 1819–1822 (the basis of a biography) to the fireplace. Byron had given Moore the manuscript to sell to Murray, and both could have retired on the profits. But having ventured a peek, Murray found it "abominable," "horrid & disgusting." Reading more, Gifford confirmed that its publication "would render Lord Byron's name eternally infamous." Moore vehemently protested, but Murray, with an eye to his existing copyrights, decided to martyr venture capital to "Lord Byron's honour & fame."[43] Yet in this suttee, Byron's mysteries acquired a new life, bruited in the papers (the *Times* reported it on 19 May) and leaving in the smoke and ashes a scandal about scandal—of secrets conspiratorially suppressed.[44] What survived, paradoxically (with Moore's memory and a prudent judgment) was an option on a "Life of Byron." For this, the burning of the *Memoranda* turned out to have been a memorable launch, the best advertisement ever.

With Moore's *Byron* in the wings, Alaric Watts, savvy editor of the *Literary Souvenir,* bet that West's last "Portrait of Lord Byron" (which he had engraved by Francis Engleheart) would gleam as "one of the most attractive features" of the 1827 annual (viii).[45] West's portrait had been a sensation in Paris: "The French have caught the contagion of Byronism," Moore wrote to Byron in 1821 (*BLJ* 8: 114). Yet as late as May 1826 West's *Byron* was not widely known in London. Watts's pitch was a boast of authenticity, a "correct likeness" instead of all those theatrical postures: "what we have long wanted, is a resemblance of him at a period when his variable character had undergone its utmost change" (*Souvenir* ix)— when, in effect, Byron had tired of "affectation[s] of singularity" to compose himself true.[46] From gallery to souvenir, this last portrait would capitalize on elegiac affection, harnessed to the mobility of art as commerce, no longer the treasure of elite households and galleries.

But the problem with West's *Byron* was that it was, and was not, "Byron": there was no gaze averted in disdain or visionary preoccupation; no rhapsody of curly hair, dark eyes, exquisitely exposed throat. It didn't look "Byronic"; it didn't even look "poetic" (no props of quill, paper, books, and bust of Shakespeare nearby).[47] The dapper Victorian-accoutered "Poet," patterned on Phillips, was more probable. Even worse than West's *Byron* was Engelheart's engraving of it. Fat and flaccid, Byron's body hides within a diva-robe big enough for a bedspread. Charles Turner's engraving of West was no help either. Can Childe Harold have become this?

One of many derivatives of Thomas Phillips's "cloak" portrait, 1814, this was engraved by William H. Ward & Co. for the frontispiece in *The Works of Lord Byron, Letters 1804–1813*, ed. W. E. Henley (New York: Macmillan, 1897). Phillips's portrait is patterned on Charles Mayne Young portraying Hamlet, in the portrait by G. H. Harlowe from 1809.

"The Last Portrait of Lord Byron," *Literary Souvenir* (1827), facing p. 33, engraved by F. Engleheart, after William West's portrait of 1822. It was featured as the occasion for, and the motive for, L.E.L.'s *Stanzas, Written beneath the Portrait of Lord Byron, painted by Mr. West.*

Byron at Pisa, engraved by Charles Turner, after William West's
Byron, 1822; published by Colnaghi Galleries, London, 5 No-
vember 1826. By kind permission and courtesy of Nottingham
City Museums and Galleries, Newstead Abbey.

Watts tried to prevent that murmur by calling upon "the most gratifying testimony . . . to its authenticity" from Friends of Byron, among them Leigh Hunt and John Cam Hobhouse, "competent authority on the subject" (ix). But it wasn't a lock. Some years on, Watts's son tried, gamely, to brush up the iconography of the family investment:

> The poet is seated against a dark sky background, enveloped in a
> cloak which, thrown over the shoulder, he is drawing round with his
> right hand. The collar of the shirt, thrown well back, displays the
> neck in half-profile; the face looking full over the left shoulder. It is,
> whether as regards composition or resemblance, a powerful work.
>
> (*Life* 1: 251–52)

Nice try. But even Byron's own stylized languor affects a slight boredom with the "utmost change" (Watts got this right). And there was that body, a Byron who might not get a callback for the part of the Byronic hero. Admitting the "dissimilarity to his former self," even Moore was amused at the sideburns and longer hair that Byron had cultivated to counter a catty report that he "had a 'faccia di musico'"—an aging castrato, not only un-Byronic but unmanned (like the "Musico" in *Don Juan* destined for a seraglio post). That was back in 1819. It was a superannuated form that West confronted in 1822, flummoxed by a "person inclining to fat, and, apparently, effeminate." Though there was "a considerable deal of the dandy in his appearance," the sum was less continuous with lady-killer Childe Harold than the old-boy version of the foppish college-boy that so dismayed Isaac D'Israeli: a "fantastic and effeminate thing," "all rings and curls," his "shirt collar . . . all thrown over from his neck."[48]

West worked with all this resistance, rendering a Byron wearily iconic, half ironic, so carefully careless of regard as to defeat idolizing—yet for all the camping, not entirely self-possessed: the Byronic "hidden" self in 1822 is the adipose body under the theatrical garb, the utmost sum of a certain kind of living.[49] Byron himself was chagrined about the blubber, which cape, whiskers, and longer hair could not quite romanticize. On 10 June 1823, the best he could tell his cousin Lady Hardy (who didn't like the portrait) was that the fault was not West's:

> for I was <u>then</u> —what it appears—but since that time—and indeed
> since you saw me— —I am very much reduced—partly by uncertain

health in the winter and partly by the rigorous abstinence necessary to preserve it— —But it is so far better—that it makes me more like what I used to be ten years ago—in part at least. (*BLJ* 10: 98)

Imagining himself a bit ridiculous in this Lady's gaze ("No! I am not Prince Hamlet"), Byron pleads plans for a rehab of crash-dieting, to re-fashion a self "more like what I used to be ten years ago—in part at least." Ten years ago was 1813, when Byron was the celebrity of *Childe Harold*, not yet plighted to A.I.M., the world all before him.

West got it right when he said that Byron's posings in 1822 seemed a wistful attempt to assume "a countenance which did not belong to him, as though he were thinking of a frontispiece for Childe Harold" (245). It was Vegas Elvis trying to conjure Memphis Elvis. Byron might have been thinking not just of his Regency avatar, but also recalling the cabinet of miniatures of his "most intimate Schoolfellows" that he had commissioned just before the Childe Harold Grand Tour: "it will be a kind of satisfaction to retrace in these images of the living the idea of our former selves, and to contemplate in the resemblances of the dead, all that remains of judgment, feeling, and a host of passions" (*BLJ* 1: 197–98). Composing and posing himself for West, Byron inhabits the idea of a former self, but not without a reflexive elegy for a resemblance as good as "dead."

It would not be the intimate schoolfellows, however, but women in the business of poetry, in intimate imagination with the Byron that flashed in and as Childe Harold, who would retrace the idea into multiple living ideas. Writing about Byron, or like Byron, became an interaction, in the glint and glow of his celebrity, by which women aspiring to fame could show their credentials and, in the venture, discover a lively authority.

CHAPTER EIGHT

Byron and the Muse of Female Poetry

She-musing on Byron

If, in John Wilson's musing, Byron's power was to create the reader who "feels, for a moment, that the voice which reaches the inmost recesses of his heart" is addressing this heart alone (*Edinburgh Review* 30: 90), Byron's paradoxical coup was to create this intimacy in massive plurals: male and female, aristocrat, swell, and clerk. All turned out to have an "inner Byron." If men wrote to each other about the spell of Byron, women wanted to write to Byron himself, thanking him for recreating them—and then creating him, in reciprocity, as the object of their penetrating understanding, speaking his language and reading themselves as its object.

Hot from a session with his poetry, Sarah Agnes Bamber wrote to confess (or boast) that "an impulse grateful as irresistible impels me to acknowledge your Pen has called for the most exquisite feelings I have ever experienced." (A meeting in propria persona would seem merely belated.) A letter from MH (not, alas, Wordsworth's M. H.) swooned to *Childe Harold* as seduction itself, a reading-date that left her feeling "animated by a new soul, alive to wholly novel sensations and activated by feelings till then unknown."[1] Fresh from a summer 1812 romance with *Childe Harold,* Anna of Kensington Palace greets Byron as her soulmate, speaking to her from his poetry. In response, she offers herself as the reader of his heart:

> My Lord, Tho I have not the honor of being personally known to you, . . . I have been indebted to your muse, for soothing & interesting some of my Saddest hours, I have wept over Child Harold's griefs & sympathized in his wrongs. I would have rejoiced when he rejoiced but there seems no joy for him in this World. Often have I wandered in these gardens with your poem for my Companion & "with thee, conversing have forgot all time."[2]

Her affective reading of Byron's romance answers Byron's penetrating reading of her: "With thee conversing I forget all time," says Eve to her partner in Paradise (*PL* IV.639).

Anna is eager to produce herself in a current of communication to rival the circuit of male professional evaluation, testifying to Byron's genius not from educated taste and discernment, but from a feeling of deep sympathy with Byron as a pained kin-author:

> I have hung in rapt attention over every Line of Child Harold, I am not a Critic but an inexperienced young Woman, but the language of genius & of nature must be felt & never makes its appeal in Vain to my heart. & who can read those lines unmov'd, those beautiful lines to Thyrza particularly, who! without feeling the tenderest compassion for their unhappy author & indignation against those wicked people who (as I have heard) have by their treacheries & injuries, thrown as misanthropic gloom, over so noble & so great a Mind, a Mind which I am sure, was form'd by nature to be the delight & comfort of private & Social Life, as much as it ever shines conspicuous in the World of Talent. I have often remarkd with pleasure occasional, (tho, evidently sought to be supprest) traits of tenderness & warm affection, bursting thro, the gloom, which too generally pervades your poem. . . . I do most deeply enter into your feelings, peculiarly so perhaps because I have felt the same {cause} in some respects, to despair.

Where some women (as we'll soon see) imagined themselves as the referent of Thyrza, Anna tenders an identification with the poet. She implies herself not only as the partner of his heart in this pulse, but also as a potential cure in the prospect of "the delight & comfort of private & Social Life" that she is sure Byron deserves. To pave the way, she returns some poetry of her own (lines mourning the death of a close friend) with a commentary that replays the last, sad stanza of *Childe Harold's Pilgrimage II* (xcviii) with an intimizing revision about the woe of old age in survival of all whom one has loved, oneself left "alone on earth":

> These lines, are part of some compos'd at a time . . . when I so much wanted consolation, I experienced the most cruel indifference to my griefs from one who, I had a right to expect, should have wiped away my tears or wept with me—

"before the Chastner humbly let me bow"
"our hearth divided and our hopes destroyed."

The loss and alienation sighed in Byron's line, "Before the Chastener humbly let me bow, / O'er hearts divided and o'er hopes destroy'd," she shifts into a communicated misery: *our* in the intimacy of a shared *hearth* and the *heart* it holds, literally, imaginatively, and in the new rhyme, in implied answer to *alone on earth.* Maybe a misremembering, but for someone as keenly tuned to poetic language as Anna, her text has the look of purposeful revision.

If one's reading of *Childe Harold* reaches the end of Byron's page, the sequel is to take up its phrases as the stimulus to adventures in correspondence. Here is another writer to Byron, dwelling on that last stanza:

> You are unhappy—a being feared and mistrusted, even by those
> whom the fashion of the hour leads to flatter you—you are 'alone on
> earth'—There needs no more to excite a deep interest for you—.
>
> (anon., quoted in Throsby 117)

The existential solitary, she hints, has a cure at hand. Young Elizabeth Barrett fantasized eloping as "Lord Byron's PAGE," or in an upgrade, as his lover.[3]

A variant of this partnering romance is to apprehend oneself coded in Byron's poetry as the referent of his passion. Henrietta d'Ussières hoped that the mention in *Childe Harold* of "A sister whom he lov'd, but saw her not / Before his weary pilgrimage begun" (I.x) was "applicable" to her.[4] Swooning to the poems *To Thyrza* (in the 1812 *Childe Harold*), and certain of their coding, a recently widowed Lady Falkland replied quickly in key, on June 12, laying claim to Byron as her destiny: "Surely I cannot be mistaken—Byron, my adored Byron, come to me—I shall feel each hour an age until you are pressed to a Heart, warm—ardent as your own." When, two weeks on, he hadn't come, she refreshed her case with an appeal to textual evidence: "Tell me my Byron—if those mournful, tender effusions of your Heart & mind, to that Thyrza . . . were not intended to myself?"[5] The Lady not only interpreted intention, but in the identifactory romance upped the ante to an exclusive claim of refashioned Byronism: "I will most joyfully receive your hand—but remember I must be loved exclusively—your <u>Heart must</u> be <u>all my own</u>."[6] When Byron did not

return assurances the next day, she wrote again on 13 July, gamely interpreting his silence as noble reticence, and demonstrating her ardor as
perfect reader, with no trafficking in intentional fallacy:

> I have again read your Romaunt—& feel more than ever convinced
> that . . . I may trace myself. . . . it is not a loveless Heart I offer you—
> but one whose every throb beats responsive with your own—come to
> me therefore my Life my own my own.

In the absence of dialogue, the Lady supplies dialectical reading, filling
Byron's silence with her active imagination.

Reading to interpret, interpreting to respond, she writes her own romance to marry to his.[7] Though Byron had met the lady and had been
kind to her after her husband, a cherished friend, was killed in a drunken
duel, he had no memory of her, asking his agent John Hanson (many
months later) to return the letters from this "foolish woman I never saw
who fancies I want to marry her" to a kinsman of hers, "for she plagues
my soul out with her d----d letters" (*BLJ* 3: 17). The Lady would not be
discouraged: "Why, my adored boy, don't you return my affection . . . ?";
"Pray do tell me, George" (Marchand, *Biography* 347). Her presumption
of intimacy, cooing a name not used even by Byron's closest friends and
lovers, is no less astonishing than the spell of his poetry against actual
disclaimers and contempt.

The sensations excited by Byron's pen in the first wave of *Childe Har-
old* were an inspiration for the female pen, but so, too, were the later
Cantos and editions, with conflicting pressures on the female pen. The
Separation fissured first sympathies, put more risk into the fidelity to
Byron, or put identifications under stress or cast them into slant of irony.
By 1821, writing for *London Magazine,* John Scott could theorize the
dilemma. Byron speaks "to the poetic sympathies" in terms that provoke
"interest" for some "evident connection with real and private circumstances" in his life, but it is a fatal interest insofar as "what is striking in
the poetry is made a set-off against what is objectionable in morals" (3:
51). Yet what was a set-off for John Scott's morals was the very thing for
other readers, a thrilling seduction from moral measures.

Just months into the summer of 1816 (in advance of Byron's Separation spin in *Childe Harold III*), Mary Shelley was writing its stars, in two
peculiar forms, into the imaginary societies of *Frankenstein*. One is little

William Frankenstein's "favourite," "Louisa Biron": "a pretty little girl" who outshines the "one or two little *wives*" that this "little darling" boy "has already" acquired (I.v; 45)—a light joke about an alternative fate for Lady Byron, had she the wit to be a favourite rather than a wife.[8] The other is a fiftyish Byronic professor, "short, but remarkably erect" (II.ii; 29), wielding a vigorously phallic discourse on scientific conquest. Were Byron to live so long, and turn from poetry to science, or the poetry of science, this sketch of M. Waldman seems a fair enough guess, in its romance of conquest. The "modern masters" of natural philosophy, he lectures to a rapt young Victor Frankenstein, "penetrate into the recesses of nature, and shew how she works in her hiding places . . . They have acquired new and almost unlimited powers" (I.ii; 29). And thence a dire creation, pitiful, fascinating, and fatal.

The First Female Byron

Turn the recesses of Byronic penetration into the female heart, and Byron is the modern master. But turn Byron himself into such a recess to penetrate and women may become the scientists: scientists of Byronism. With another Byron-imprint in *Frankenstein* Shelley renders a gothic jest at Shelleyan-Frankenstein's fashioning of his ideal, the best-laid plans of passionate Byronism gone awry: "His limbs were in proportion," Frankenstein sighs in the memory, as if in a romance of men imagining a capacity to remedy Byron's one physical defect. Aside from this, Frankenstein seems to have been consulting a Regency portrait, or Scott's rapt ekphrasis, for guidance: "I had selected his features as beautiful. Beautiful! . . . his hair was of a lustrous black, and flowing; his teeth of a pearly whiteness" (I.iv; p. 37).

If Frankenstein's Creature betrayed its Byronic patterning with a sad deformity that amounts to a death sentence, the actual Byron's death launched a post-mortem industry. In about ten weeks another "Byron" was born into print, heralded on the front page of the *Literary Gazette*, 3 July 1824, by its savvy editor William Jerdan (writing unsigned, as the voice of news itself). For all those mourning "the light of Childe Harolde's flame extinguished," the reader is promised, L.E.L.'s *Improvisatrice* has re-lit the torch with "transcendant beauties of thought, expression, imagery and fervent genius, with the blaze of which they are surrounded and illuminated" (417). Byron had become a brand-name for fresh vending.

This blaze reborn is not quite by the book of Byronic ravishment, however. L.E.L.'s title poem, a tragic love-romance, has been reorganizing the trademarks for female imagination. Byronism burns not only in a performing she-artist (the Improvisatrice) but also, with a strangely feminizing sympathy, in the young man who gazes upon her. L.E.L. stages his initial gaze on the familiar pattern—the passionate lady's captivation by the idol that fired the brains, and pens, of all those Regency she-readers, transfixed and transformed by *Childe Harold* in the flesh:

> There are some moments in our fate
> That stamp the colour of our days;
> As, till then, life had not been felt,—
> And mine was sealed in the slight gaze
> Which fixed my eye, and fired my brain,
> And bowed my heart beneath the chain.   (416–21; pp. 28–29)

This is Byronic enthrallment mad and bad, by the fateful power of a slight gaze. Yet L.E.L. soon complicates the gender formation, not only by casting the heroine's enthrallment in the language of tormented Childe Harold, but also by feminizing her male-gazer. As his noble gaze fixes her eye and transfixes her heart, he reciprocates with an "almost female softness":

> 'Twas a dark and flashing eye,
> Shadows, too, that tenderly,
> With almost female softness, came
> O'er its mingled gloom and flame.
> His cheek was pale; or toil, or care,
> Or midnight study, had been there,
> Making its young colours dull,
> Yet leaving it most beautiful.
> Raven curls their shadow threw,
> Like the twilight's darkening hue,
> O'er the pure and mountain snow
> Of his high and haughty brow:
> Lighted by a smile, whose spell
> Words are powerless to tell.

Such a lip! oh, poured from thence
Lava floods of eloquence
Would come with fiery energy,
Like those words that cannot die.   (422–39; pp. 29–30)

Prefigured as a female dream—"Pale, dark-eyed, beautiful, and young,/ Such as he had shone o'er my slumbers" (50–54; p. 4)—this dreamboat ripples across gender codes. First, in a complement to the Childe-Harolding of the lady, there is his alliance with Burton's feminized melancholy men, unmanned by too much midnight study. Then (on the Italian site), there is a glance in Landon's poetry of his twinship with midnight Desdemona, her skin white as "snow" (*Othello* 5.2.4–5). Readers might even glimpse in this dark-eyed, raven-haired, melancholy beauty of a lord an ekphrasis of the portrait of L.E.L. herself, by H. W. Pickersgill, on display at the Royal Academy, as *The Improvisatrice* filled and emptied nearby bookstores.

At the moment of the gazers' meeting, L.E.L. lets a phrasal confusion suggest the gender confusion. As Lorenzo claims the Improvisatrice's heart with that old Byronic magic—"that low and honey tone,/ Making woman's heart his own;/ . . ./ Treasures for her heart to keep" (442–43, 447; p. 30)—L.E.L.'s syntax, in a shimmer of grammatical confusion, solicits a suggestion that he is making his own heart over as hers. In this exchange of hearts, the Byronic she-artist can claim, or fantasize claiming, her admirer "As if soul-centred in my song" (454; p. 31)—yet another syntactic double-play that blurs the agent and object of possession. Managing all these grammars is poet Landon, staging love at first burn to thrill readers of both sexes.

He spoke not when the others spoke,
    His heart was all too full for praise;
But his dark eyes kept fixed on mine,
    Which sank beneath their burning gaze.
Mine sank but yet I felt the thrill
Of that look burning on me still.   (456–61; p. 31)

Even as Lorenzo's dark eyes work their power on her, Landon's poetry of these eyes captivates her reader. With her pen on the pulse of burning Byronism, L.E.L. hyperbolizes and gender-radiates it for all.

Letitia Landon by Henry William Pickersgill, 1825. This portrait, in a
pose of Byronic self-possession, was painted in the dawn of Landon's fame.
Reproduced by kind permission of Michael Landon and Broadview Press.

At the end of the tale, both lovers have become Byronic martyrs: the she-minstrel has died of Byronic grief (Lorenzo has been long plighted to another), and he, soon a widower from this poignantly bad plight and the missed chance with the soulmate Improvisatrice, has become a melancholy Byronic recluse:

> His brow, as sculpture beautiful,
>   Was wan as Grief's corroded page,
> He had no words, he had no smiles,
>   No hopes: his sole employ to brood
> Silently over his sick heart
>   In sorrow and in solitude.
> I saw the hall where, day by day,
> He mused his weary life away.   (1539–46; p. 103)

He is a funereal artifact, a death-bound Desdemona arrested into a lifeless spectacle of Grief, fixed in a gallery, fixated on another artifact, a portrait of his dead "Minstrel-Love."

This portrait, meanwhile, is animated with all the fire of heart and soul lost to him. It wins the Byronic sweepstakes of aesthetic power:

> One picture brightest of all there!
> Oh ! never did the painter's dream
>   Shape thing so gloriously fair!
> It was a face! the summer day
>   Is not more radiant in its light!
> Dark flashing eyes, like the deep stars
>   Lighting the azure brow of night;
> A blush like sunrise o'er the rose;
>   A cloud of raven hair, whose shade
> Was sweet as evening's, and whose curls
>   Clustered beneath a laurel braid.
> She leant upon a harp: one hand
>   Wandered, like snow, amid the chords;
> The lips were opening with such life,
>   You almost heard the silvery words.
> She looked a form of light and life,
>   All soul, all passion, and all fire . . .   (1551–68; pp. 103–4)

The illusion conveyed, "You almost heard the silvery words," is resonant of this animation; resonant, too, the present-event echo of imagined audition of *words* almost *heard*. While Landon's summary, "She looked a form of light and life," refers to the image, its syntax lets the portrait seem alive with active looking. Reprising the first encounter, Landon makes the portrait vibrate with all the power, even the very elements, of Lorenzo's first-glance magic: the initial allure of his dark flashing eyes and raven curls (420, 430; p. 29) are now the allure of the portrait; his burning gaze (459; p. 31) is now its emanation. Landon's narrative arc transfers Byronic passion, with the female of "all soul, all passion, and all fire" seeming, without willing, to have drained the Byronic male for this effect.[9] In the aura is the breath of male raptures over Byron: Coleridge (with Scott's endorsement in the 1816 *Quarterly*) comparing Byron's face to "a beautiful alabaster vase, only seen to perfection when lighted up from within" (16: 177).

Landon's authorial self-fashioning through Byronism as living and then dying portraiture made *The Improvisatrice* a sensation, commanding six editions in its first year and securing L.E.L.'s twinned claim to the eponym and to the title of "The Female Byron." It was no stretch for another commercially entrepreneurial editor, Alaric Watts, to turn to her to hype the engraving of West's problematic "Byron" scheduled for the 1827 *Literary Souvenir*. L.E.L. was already famed for her "poetical sketches" in *The Literary Gazette*—a series of responses to paintings (or their engravings) that staged affective aesthetics, a little theater of popular "appreciation." The annual's full title, *The Literary Souvenir; or, Cabinet of Poetry and Romance*, intimated a space for this, and more: private thrills, meditation, or fancy. L.E.L.'s *Stanzas, Written beneath the Portrait of Lord Byron, painted by Mr. West* greets Byron not in an illusion of presence, but as a patently mediated subject, by West, by her gaze, and for a reader's fantasy. Her opening lines seem issued by an inspired Improvisatrice:

> 'Tis with strange feelings that I gaze
> Upon this brow of thine,
> Magnificent as if the mind
> Herself had carved her shrine.   (1–4)

Tuned to the devoted female readership of the annuals, L.E.L. sets "strange" as latent agency for female gazing, again reversing that array of male gaze / female object, and bolstering the female agency with the hypothesis of Byron's she-mind as a she-Pygmalion, carving his brow (its *thine* is rhymed to and claimed for *her shrine*). The implicit ally is her pen, and its production is a penetrating explication of a misunderstood text—continuous with all those Regency-era mash-notes, but more self-possessed:

> At the first glance, that eye is proud,
>   But, if I read aright,
> A fountain of sweet tears lies hid
>   Beneath its flashing light
> Tenderness, like a gushing rill
> Subdued, represt, but flowing still.   (7–12)

The glance is L.E.L.'s reading his eye, scanning its pride for what "lies hid / Beneath": pain, sweetness, tenderness. Proposing herself as its best reader, L.E.L. deftly recovers "Beneath the portrait of Byron painted by Mr. West" a Byron pulsing "Beneath" the dazzle, subdued, repressed, but a heart to love. This deep Byron, which L.E.L.'s lines tease out, is the Childe-Harold Byron discernible beneath the superannuated West-Byron, the poet whose signature is nothing if not the aura of hidden depths—that self famously given, in the poetry of *Childe Harold,* to "feel / What I can ne'er express, yet can not all conceal" (*IV* clxviii).

Yet for all this capable interpretation, L.E.L.'s romance of reading is also staging, without quite stage-managing, the durable question of Byronism: has she conjured the old Byronic allure from West's rather more inscrutable Byron? or is the still flowing current of Byron's magic, from beyond the grave, making a reader who imagines she is making Byron?

> What should it be, that thus their faith can bind?
> The power of Thought—the magic of the Mind!
> Link'd with success, assumed and kept with skill,
> That moulds another's weakness to its will.

This exemplary colloquy on charisma, from *The Corsair* (1.181–84), glosses the power of Byronic heroic allure as a text: features, lines, prompts for definition, and provocations for close inquiry in the allure of reading aright, against common measures.

His features' deepening lines and varying hue
At times attracted, yet perplex'd the view,
As if within that murkiness of mind
Work'd feelings fearful, yet undefined;
Such might it be—that none could truly tell—
Too close enquiry his stern glance would quell.   (1.209–14)

The Corsair stages a verbal portrait in a textual relay of penetration and frustration, the difference between *reveals* and *conceals* blurred by the effect of performance in both events:

. . . his forehead high and pale
The sable curls in wild profusion veil;
And oft perforce his rising lip reveals
The haughtier thought it curbs, but scarce conceals.
Though smooth his voice, and calm his general mien,
Still seems there something he would not have seen.   (1.203–8)

Translation to the dynamics of Byronism was no stretch for Scott back in the Regency. "Those who have looked on Byron will recognise some likeness," he said of this portrait in verse (*Quarterly* 16: 184). The double grammar of "something he would not have seen" (would not have others see; would not have seen in himself, but others might see) is *the* Byronic question. It is this indeterminacy that spurs the drama of L.E.L.'s reading—not just by the Byron-script of passions shimmering beneath the work of skill, but by her own determination to read beneath the layers of years, back to the Regency idol not yet become the Separation scandal. L.E.L. penetrates, as she says, by reading *in* and *in*, to the *inmost* (43–47).

She is after bigger game than this, however. In advance of Moore's *Byron*, that vade mecum "eagerly seized upon as a sort of authority upon the Art of Being Byronic," she is working this Art for a sensation in the literary culture of the 1820s and 1830s: the Byronic heroine, variously exotic, transgressive, fatal, cross-dressed, begat by L.E.L., with precocious stamp, then by Jewsbury (*The Enthusiast*'s Julia), by Sand (herself and Lélia in 1833), and by Hemans everywhere, less under this title than in a romance with the dramatis personae and language of Byron's poetry, from as far back as the Regency.[10] L.E.L.'s performances set high the stakes. "Have we not a Byron in Miss Landon?" exclaimed Victorian anthologist Fredric Rowton in 1848 (viii), scarcely staying to answer before dubbing her "the female Byron," "the Byron of our poetesses" (424–25). It was all that Jerdan had promised.

The epithet was earned not only by Landon's poetry (urbane, skeptical, passionate, with jaded wit and more than a few tales of treacherous love) but also by a female-Byron life which, ever since she started living on her own in London, stirred rumors, gossip, and slanders about romantic liaisons. Rowton rehearses the twinship: "both acquired worldwide fame in youth; both were shamefully maligned and misrepresented; both became gloomy and misanthropical under falsehoods asserted of them; both died young, and abroad" (424).[11] As L.E.L. reads Byronic torment into West's half-serene, half-sardonic portrait, she is also performing as one who knows how to read this way, because she feels, has felt, his pain on her pulses:

> The mind can win eternity
>   With its immortal name,
> But all too often happiness
>   Is the price of fame:
> For not a barbed shaft can fly
> But aim to strike the mark on high.   (61–66)

This *aim* may even hint at Lady Byron (née A.I.M.), the barb of Byron's fame. Yet as L.E.L. herself could testify, it is the professional female poet whom fame taxes most: in a favorite cultural fable, female fame is a purchase against female happiness.

This is ever Hemans's story, rehearsed again in a Byron-toned poem in the same *Literary Souvenir* that housed West's *Byron* and L.E.L.'s *Stanzas*. Under the title *Corinna at the Capitol*, Hemans sets this famous she-poet's dazzling performance in this Roman site, linking the scene (in a footnote) to a line in *Childe Harold IV* lamenting the fall of she-Rome from "the trebly hundred triumphs" of her ancient glory. Hemans's Corinna is Byronic in celebrity, but fated (like the referent, Staël's diva Corinne) for a gendered fall. If Byronic genius disdains domesticity, she-genius, in Hemans's measures, cannot but forsake it.[12]

L.E.L.'s *Stanzas* re-argue the case: the unhappiness of fame is not the penalty of "woman," but of sheer being in the world, suffering its petty rivalries and local contempts. L.E.L.'s "Byron" is a liberal text for female genius to read of and sigh of her heroic tortures:

That lip is curled with sneering smile,—
    Alas! what doth it prove?—
Not in the warfare of the world
    Are lessons taught of love.
So much is there hard to be borne,
The heart must either break or scorn.   (13–18)

By the time the verse gets to this *heart* and its fated double courses, it's all generic, with mere variations of case:

And differently the poison works
    On every differing mind,
Some grow false as the false they blamed,
    And thus 'tis with mankind:
But there are some whose loftier mood
Grows maddened on such things to brood.
The young warm heart whose faith and love
    Were all too prompt at first,
What must it feel when these are turned
    To darkness and distrust?
Wormwood to know that heart has been
Dupe of the false, prey of the mean.   (19–30)

Tracing Shakespeare and Byronized Shakespeare (Hamlet, Othello, Leontes), L.E.L. reads out the genealogy of the Byron hero, to which she annexes her own poetic persona: "the Mind, that broods o'er guilty woes,/ Is like a Scorpion girt by fire" (*The Giaour*); "wrung with the wounds which kill not, but ne'er heal"; "life's enchanted cup but sparkles near the brim./ . . . The dregs were wormwood" (*Childe Harold III* vii-ix), and so forth. It may be that such "Byronic tags and phrases" play as "second-order signs" of an already famed "poetical discourse of personal disillusionment" (McGann and Reiss 23). But L.E.L. is not so much signing on, as showing her skill in reading the system. It is the inmost soul of the categorical "poet" that Landon-the-Byronic-poet reads unchanged in, and beneath, the disarming visage of West's *Byron:*

I read it in thy gifted page,
   In every noble thought,
Each lofty feeling, and sweet song
   With tenderness deep fraught;
For there thine inmost soul was shown,—
Their truth, their beauty, were thine own.   (43–48)

If L.E.L. ends by returning to Byron his own living myth, martyr to liberty, it is by a detour into her living myth of the heart-tormented poet, assigning it to female poetics and persona. Her reading *I* chimes with the enpaged *thy*, a marriage of poet to poet.

Marrying Byron

The uncanny syntax of Rowton's epithets—"a Byron in Miss Landon," "the female Byron," "the Byron of our poetesses"—names a feminized Byron as well as a Byronized Landon, a union of poetries, and a marriage on the pages of poetry. Marriage to Byronic poetics was teenager Elizabeth Barrett's pledge in her *Stanzas on the Death of Lord Byron*, rendered in homage in the Spenserian stanzas that carried Byron to fame in *Childe Harold*. The "widow'd brow" of Hellas (10) figures her own bereavement, and it is consoled with a textual partnering. Her *Stanzas* bears an epigraph from the end of *Childe Harold IV*, in which Byron's voice, "I am not now / That which I have been" (clxxxv), is now her elegiac motto. When Barrett promises, "my soul shall find / A language in these tears!" (28–29), it is clear that the language is Byron's—in the stanza, its glancing allusions, and direct quotations. "The 'dark blue depths' he sang of" (30) marry the meters of her own song. Byron gave the heart a language.

Under such power, material facts hardly mattered.[13] Such triumph of Poet over husband, of glamour over action, struck M. J. Jewsbury as the half-dangerous, half-comic mystification. Here she is writing (sans signature for the 1832 *Athenæum*) a sentence that could have been at home in Wollstonecraft's *Vindication of the Rights of Woman:*

> Lord Byron's remark, that he would leap into a river after a woman, but not hand her out of her carriage, is on a par with the chivalric system that led knights to do battle in honour of her fair eyes, but not to make her comfortable in daily life.[14]

At the far end of the Separation scandal's public run, Harriet Beecher Stowe, a rhapsodic Byronist in her youth (she was born in 1811), refreshed the social text of Jewsbury's satire, and virtually waged Wollstonecraft's *Vindication of the Rights of Woman* anew in her mirror-titled *Lady Byron Vindicated* (1870).[15] Harriet Martineau certainly caught the spirit, using her obituary notice of Lady Byron as a polemical occasion, a case in point of social prejudice against a "well educated" woman:

> Mr. Moore and Lord Byron could have known but little of the education of girls at the opening of the century, and must have been bad judges of the minds and manners of sensible women, if they were sincere in their representations of Miss Milbank, as a "blue," as a "mathematical prude," and so forth.[16]

Brainy women could see the forces of male judgment against Lady Byron's strengths.

As Stowe's language of vindication suggests, the issue was bigger than Lady Byron: it was a mystique in which women collaborated—among them, poets inspired by Byronic figures and language, tales and tropes. One might regret Byron, yet remain Byronic. Take Hemans. "I am glad to find that you were struck with 'the calm & dignified character of truth' in Lady Byron's 'remarks,'" Baillie purred to her about the pamphlet issued in refutation of Moore (July 1830; *L* 1195), relieved (she said to Margaret Holford Hodson) to find "that a great proportion of the respectable part of the public are on her side, and for the romantic Misses & fawning Wives, she must contrive to be satisfied without their approbation, or even under their unsparing censure" (28 May 1830; *L* 618). Hemans would seem primed not only for approbation but for sympathy with Lady Byron: just two years after Byron quit England for Italy, never more to see his wife, Captain Hemans followed suit. But her reactions to Lord Byron, riven beyond ambivalence, are a primer of the female-Byronist dilemma.

Not given to Jewsbury's dry distance, "Mrs. Hemans" was a consummate Byronist. In public displays of affection, she echoed his poetry in hers, often featuring it in her epigraphs. She modeled her heroines after his heroes and heroines, emulated his forms and genres, memorized his poetry and read it to her young sons. She loved everything, even what prudish reviews hadn't: *Beppo, Don Juan, Sardanapalus.*[17] "One of her favourite ornaments" was a brooch with a lock of Byron's hair. She half-imagined herself as his domestic haven. "After having heard those beautiful stanzas addressed to his sister by Lord Byron . . . read aloud twice in manuscript," reports her friend Henry Chorley, "she repeated them to us, and even wrote them down with a surprising accuracy," dwelling on a couplet: "There are yet two things in my destiny, / A world to roam o'er, and a home with thee" (*Memorials* 2: 21–22). This verse is from an epistle, "My Sister—my sweet Sister," that Byron wrote in summer 1816 and sent to Augusta and to publisher Murray, in a double-track of public and private receptions. He would not have minded Murray's circulation of it (if *Fare thee well!* is precedent, he'd have expected as much); but he wouldn't print it without the sister's consent, and she demurred.[18] When it finally appeared in Moore's *Byron* (1830), the *Quarterly* offered its readers nine of its sixteen stanzas with a gushing prologue: "in the whole body of his poetry," there is not "anything more mournfully and desolately beautiful" (44: 202–3). Hemans read herself into the romance, too.

Yet for all its mournful beauty, or on this very throb, "My Sister" was calculated Separation-Poetry: writing to the "sweet Sister," Byron was aiming at the sour Wife, the praise of the one's unconditional sympathy indexing the other's cold rejection. Taking this spin, it was not with Mrs. Byron that Mrs. Hemans identified, but with the soulmate sister. Surviving the rumors, she was wild to read Moore's *Byron* ("her anxiety to see the memoirs was extreme," said Chorley). But the revelations were too much to manage: "her disappointment at the extracts" in the periodicals (Chorley reports) was "so great as to prevent her reading the work when published." It wasn't just the domestic mystery, nor the "strange mixture of cruel mockery and better feeling, which breathe through so many of his letters" that dismayed her; it was (well before Stowe outed the sexual liaison with the sweet sister), Byron's "exceeding the widest limits within which one so passionate and so disdainful of law and usage might err and be forgiven." Though she was ready to play the part at which Lady Byron failed, the loving forgiver, she could not. She read no Moore that day, and put away her treasure-brooch (*Memorials* 2: 22–23).[19]

Yet if, as a woman, Hemans might sense the wrongs of Lady Byron, in poetic faith, she couldn't separate from Lord Byron. She kept true to her textual marriage, dispatching Moore's *Byron* to another universe and advertising, in poem after poem, her faith that there was a poet, if not a man, that a woman poet and her readers could still love.[20] Breaking up is hard to do. Hemans could even mine Byron's self-pitying defense of his marital doom in the poem that outraged her admired Baillie, *The Dream*, for an epigraph for her own "Land of Dreams":

> And dreams, in their development, have breath,
> And tears and tortures, and the touch of joy;
> They leave a weight upon our waking thoughts,
> They make us what we were not—what they will,
> And shake us with the vision that's gone by.

Signed "F. H.," her poem appeared in the December 1828 *Blackwood's* (24: 783–84), just months after its review of Hunt's disenchanted *Lord Byron*. She published it again in her *Songs of the Affections* (1830), as if an antidote to the infection of Moore's *Life*. The plurals *our, we, us* are the liberal markers by which F. H. compounds her subjectivity, her inmost tears and tortures, with Byron's, not only by the enchantment of his language but also by a participation in his noble éclat. Back in 1826 Hemans had exclaimed to Jewsbury about the "power" that Byron "condenses into single lines," citing a phrase from *The Dream*: "curdling a long life into one hour" (Chorley 1: 174–5)—itself about condensation of Byron: "a thought, / A slumbering thought, is capable of years, / And curdles a long life into one hour" (24–26).

Chosen Ears

It is this kind of condensation, in the intimacy of poetic sympathy, that John Wilson paraphrased as Byron's power. L.E.L. anatomizes the demographic in an elegy of 1836 titled simply *Byron:*

> All nature owned its bitter spell,
> And answered to the tone;
> For in the sorrow of the strain
> Each heart recalled its own.   (9–12)

This is not "nature" but a textual romance multiplied across a world of beating hearts. Another Wilson, famous, flagrant courtesan Harriette Wilson, always ready to flirt with Byron, wrote to him from Paris to purr, "Don Juan kept me up the whole of last night." It was as if the poem were a surrogate lover: she could not list the beauties that "struck and de-lighted" her "because that would be at the expense of another night's rest" (*Memoirs* 2: 643). Such thrill is the durable testimony of Camille Toul-min's rapture (in 1847) over *Childe Harold* in *Heath's Book of Beauty:* it was "the first which aroused the feeling of poetry in [all] hearts,—that power which is an additional sense, a blessing and delight . . . which, un-like all other senses, vibrates only to pleasure" (87).[21] The Byron of all hearts is the vibratorium of writing, reading, and writing.

Harriette Wilson's first meeting with Byron, at a masquerade in 1814, amounts to a Pygmalion event, a portrait come to life in a spectral space between imagination and memory:

> I found myself in the still quiet room I have before described. It was entirely deserted, save by one solitary individual. He was habited in a dark brown flowing robe . . . His head was uncovered, and presented a fine model for the painter's art. He was unmasked, and his bright penetrating eyes seemed earnestly fixed . . . His whole countenance so bright, severe, and beautiful, that I should have been afraid to have loved him. (2: 616)

No less than Scott in 1816–17, Wilson, banking on the public love for Byron freshly fueled by his death, brings him back to life in 1825 through the retro-allure of his famous Regency portraits. She even proposes that she has come upon Byron inhabiting the paradox of sincerely performing for himself, a theatrical character that he was running through a rehearsal, "a mere masquerade-attitude for effect, practised in an empty room" (2: 616).

The revenant sites included Byron-haunts, especially if there was a portrait to romance. L.E.L. deepens her recovery of pre-scandal Byron with what looks like two chapters of an intended Byron-series in *Fisher's Drawing Room Scrap-Book*, the annual she edited: *Lines Suggested on Visiting Newstead Abbey* (1839) and *The Portrait of Lord Byron at New-stead Abbey* (1840).[22] But the poignancy and mystery, for readers of *Fish-er's*, is L.E.L.'s own ghost-status by the time of publication—she had died, in exotically mysterious circumstances, in October 1838, at Cape Coast Castle, in Africa. With the allure of this posthumous mystery, Landon's titles install Byron in that favorite nineteenth-century tourist genre, "Homes and Haunts," where, in Byron's case, "haunts" involves not just his favorite places, but places that might be haunted by him, or haunted in ways that can enchant others.[23] *Lines* mentions the name *Byron* only in paratext, a long title-footnote about the site, with the verse conveying "Byron" in the codes of poetry and genius, a heart of uncommonly keen feeling, a genius of uncommon torments. The genre is the code itself, from the opening question, "What makes the poet?" to the final stanza, a "fable and . . . moral" of "Genius": "Of all the trees that down their shadows cast, / Choose you a wreath from any but the laurel" (54–56). Of the fourteen quatrains, only the one just prior turns to Byron per se:

> Vainly did he resist—half mirth—half rage,
> The weight with which the world on genius presses;
> What bitter truths are flung upon his page,
> Truth which the lip denies—the heart confesses.   (49–52)

Even this *he* is not so much Byron, as a generic drug, half poison / half elixir, for poetic genius—including "the female Byron." Byron is the occasion for, the legitimizer of, this mythology.

The romance of Landon's *The Portrait of Lord Byron at Newstead Abbey* (1840) is both its turn, and return, to the pre-Separation idol that is Westall's *Byron*, and the idyll of Newstead, which those 1839 *Lines* recommended as rehabilitated, its house no longer "neglected," its furnishings no longer "alienated" (*Fisher's* 1839, p. 44 n.). And thus the portrait at the Abbey is primed to host the ghost of Young Byron, or the fantasy of oneself as such: the whole scene is "in the most perfect state of repair, and, independent of the interest it derives from having once belonged to, perhaps, the first of English poets, it possesses very considerable claim to admiration, as a splendid and beautiful private residence." An admirer might even fantasize proprietary residence, inflected (L.E.L.'s statement of independent interest aside) with the "interest" of its famous resident. For it was at this site that Young Byron first felt his calling:

> Young Byron stood forth alone, unannounced by either praise or promise,—the representative of an ancient house, whose name, long lost in the gloomy solitudes of Newstead, seemed to have just awakened from the sleep of half a century in his person.

So Moore gives Byron's "very first introduction of himself to the public" as poet, half a decade before the éclat of *Childe Harold* (*BW* 2: 134), a figure at once mysteriously unoriginated and bearing, by mystique of name, clouds of gloomy glory from England's romantic past.

L.E.L.'s *Portrait . . . at Newstead* takes the romance into 1813, the year that Westall rendered his profile of the pensive dreamer, the thrillingly beautiful lord at the launch of his world-dazzling career.[24] Posing to Westall, "the novelty of reputation transported [Byron] to an affectation of singularity in appearance," said *New Monthly* in 1826 (mindful of the prelapsarian moment), "long ere the troubles of a life, perhaps not altogether embittered by himself, had blanched a hair of his head, nor added a line to his countenance" (242).

Westall's Byron is a theatrical Prince Hamlet, the observed of all observers, staging himself in casual, cool preoccupation.[25] Had Childe Harold sat to Westall, this would be it. Westall had just finished illustrating the seventh edition of *Childe Harold I-II* for Murray (*BLJ* 3: 33–34), and Murray, deciding that this "Byron" was liberal enough for both Lord and Childe, had it engraved for the preface. It was the picture to fall in love with.[26] "I contemplate [it] at times with calm delight, and at times with rapture," said one of Byron's first memoirists:

> It is the picture of emanating genius, of Byron's genius. . . . I have seen him in the very position represented. . . . It brings him completely to my mind. I have been in the habit of contemplating it with great affection, though sometimes mixed with a sorrow for those opinions on which I found it impossible to accord with him, and for those acts which incurred the disapprobation of the good and the wise; but never did I look upon it with such sorrow as on the day I heard that he was no more.   (Dallas 287–89)

Loving Westall's Byron in retrospect is loving a genius more precious in view of impending detractions and disapprobations, all pointed toward that final, historical "no more."

L.E.L. is keyed to all these images, and chiefly to Moore's long awaited *Life of Byron*, another framing of "portraiture" (*BW* 6: 244). It was a short step in May 1830 for "Christopher North" (John Wilson's pseudonym), in *Noctes Ambrosianæ XLIX*, to take up the trope of Moore's *Life* as a "portrait" and play it out: "The original sat to him often, and in many lights" (*Blackwood's* 27: 829). Even what can't be lit gets drawn into the aura. Christopher North used the lexicon both to vindicate Moore and

George Gordon, Lord Byron (at the age of 25), painted by Richard Westall in 1813, captures the celebrity icon in the first year of his international fame, following the overnight sensation of *Childe Harold's Pilgrimmage. A Romaunt* (1812). © National Portrait Gallery, London.

(once again) to assail Lady Byron's pamphlet as anti-portraiture, a piece of treachery that "astounded the whole world—opened their eyes, but to dazzle and blind them" (829). Her radiation was Lady Byronism, not Lord Byronism, with reciprocal negative effect.

The Lady was despised for disrupting Byronism in an allied, visible way, refusing a bid to the assembly of "all the Byron Beauties" (North's phrasing).[27] By the time L.E.L. was rendering her *Portrait,* the men curating Byron's fame had thought to gather his conquests into just this trophy case. Here is Stowe's acid representation of this clubby project:

> The Memoir being out, it was proposed that there should be a complete annotation of Byron's works gotten up, and adorned, for the further glorification of his memory, with portraits of the various women whom he had delighted to honor.
>
> Murray applied to Lady Byron for her portrait, and was met with a cold, decided negative.   *(Lady Byron Vindicated* 121–22)

Lady Byron's "negative" was not only self-indicting but it proved a casting call for others. L.E.L. would seem a prime candidate for the gallery, and the main conduit of an extension to "all of Britain's Beauties."

L.E.L.'s honor is not to join the Beauties, however. It is to read Byron back into the aloof, melancholy, cool youth that was Westall's *Byron.* But with a difference. If Westall's *Byron* fixed the archetype of the Byronic-Romantic Poet, the "Byron" facing away from L.E.L.'s *Portrait* in the 1840 *Drawing Room Scrap-Book* is a flat engraving, a cartoon instead of a flashback. Byron imprints the page as accomplished artifact, cabineted in display books, everywhere in copies and reproductions, the Regency aura a mere guess.[28] From this engraving L.E.L. sets out to raise the dead, as a public service: her first person is now *we* instead of the *Souvenir*'s "I."[29] Her poem has two acts. An epigraph of three stanzas on Westall's "Byronic" Byron reads the enthralling picture of 1813 into the fatal future:

> It is the face of youth—and yet not young;
>   The purple lights, the ready smiles have vanished;
> The shadows by the weary forehead flung,
>   The gayer influences of life have banished.

'Tis sad, and fixed—yet we can fancy gleams
  Of feverish spirits, suddenly awaking.
Flinging aside doubts, fancies, fears, and dreams,
  Like some red fire on startled midnight breaking.
'Tis an uncertain thing—a mind so framed,
  Glorious the birthright which its powers inherit,
Mingling the loved—the feared—the praised—the blamed—
  The constant struggle of the clay and spirit.   (1–12)

L.E.L.'s ekphrasis, advertised on the title-page of the *Scrap-Book* in the genre of "Poetical Illustration," renders a poetical "Byron" prematurely seasoned into alluring antitheses: young, not young; shadows and lights; fire at midnight; spirit contending with clay—the very code of the Byronic hero.

The pure form is to be recovered at the fount, and so (once again) off to Newstead Abbey, a shrine for all poets, to thrill to the shade of "the youthful poet!" (22):

His name is on the haunted shade,
  His name is on the air;
We walk the forest's twilight glade,
  And only he is there.
The ivy wandering o'er the wall,
  The fountain falling musical,
Proclaim him everywhere,
The heart is full of him, and flings
Itself on all surrounding things.   (13–21)

With this heart-*flings* cast back to Byron's face ("shadows . . . flung"; "gleams / Of feverish spirits, . . . / Flinging aside doubts"), L.E.L. draws a verb from the famous, Separation-saturated opening of *Childe Harold III*: "I am as a weed, / Flung from the rock, on Ocean's foam, to sail / Where'er the surge may sweep, the tempest's breath prevail"—so Byron passions as he leaves Albion's lessening shores, hoping that his song may "fling / Forgetfulness around" (iii). "What bitter truths are flung upon his page," L.E.L. had said in her *Lines* of 1839 (51).

If the tacit fable is her page, too, she plays this suggestion in the 1840

George Gordon, Lord Byron, steel engraving by Henry Robinson, 1840, after Westall's image of 1813, to accompany L.E.L.'s *The Portrait of Lord Byron at Newstead Abbey* in *Fisher's Drawing Room Scrap-Book* (London: Fisher, Son & Co., 1841), opposite p. 11. The interest was heightened by the fact that L.E.L. had died in October 1831, under mysterious circumstances, in Cape Coast Colony, Africa, where she had relocated with her new husband, a colonial administrator—and so the occasion was a posthumous romance of L.E.L. as well as her subject.

Portrait poem, which shimmers into self-portraiture. Looking at Westall's *Byron* and knowing what is to come, L.E.L. speaks with an intimacy that bears her "poetic" credit:

> So framed is such a mind, it works
>   With dangerous thoughts and things;
> Beneath, the fiery lava lurks,
>   But on the surface springs
> A prodigality of bloom,
> A thousand hues that might illume
>   Even an angel's wings!
> Thrice beautiful the outward show,
> Still the volcano is below.   (58–66)

This lurking *lava*, by phonic and lettered repetition, haunts the "*lavish* wealth that lies / Close to the surface" (43–44). With diagnostic savvy, L.E.L. writes, "It is the curse of such a mind / That it can never rest" (67–68). It takes one lava of imagination to know another:

> And this then is love's ending! It is like
> The history of some fair southern clime.
> Hot fires are in the bosom of the earth,
> At length the subterranean element
> Breaks from its secret dwelling-place, and lays
> All waste before it; the red lava stream
> Sweeps like the pestilence.

So wrote L.E.L. of herself in 1827, in *Love's Last Lesson* (73–82; pp. 302–3), shaping her opening line to channel *Manfred:* "Teach it me, if you can,—forgetfulness!"

Signing on to Byron

L.E.L. doesn't just channel Byronic lava but produces its pulse and flow for female veins. She couldn't have known his address to Caro's heart as "a little volcano! that pours *lava* through your veins" (April 1812; *BLJ* 2: 170), nor his calling his own poetry "the lava of the imagination whose eruption prevents an earth-quake" (to Miss Milbanke, 20 November 1813, hoping to re-spark a so-far unavailing proposal of marriage; *BLJ* 3:

179). But she (and everyone) knew the Giaour's passion, "like the lava flood / That boils in Ætna's breast of flame" (1101–2)—knew it at least, or again, from Moore's 1830 apologia for Byron's failure at marriage: "the utter unreasonableness of . . . expecting to find the materials of order and happiness in a bosom constantly heaving forth from its depth such 'lava floods'" (giving L.E.L. fresh credit in her figures). Moore went on to beg "full allowance" for "the great martyr of genius himself, whom so many other causes, beside that restless fire within him, concurred to unsettle in mind."[30] Byron could have ghost-written it, maybe did. It was Jeffrey's "Byron" in late 1816:

> In Lord Byron . . . we have a perpetual stream of thick-coming fancies . . . which seem called into existence by the sudden flash of those glowing thoughts and overwhelming emotions, that struggle for expression through the whole flow of his poetry.
>
> (*Edinburgh Review* 27: 278)

The casual *we* soon becomes an insistent plural: this volcano is not just in Byron but is Byron in the body public: "A great living poet is like . . . a volcano in the heart of our land. . . . he darkens and inflames our atmosphere with perpetual explosions of fiery torrent" (27: 280).

Byron was so worn by the trope in 1823 that he could only relay its exhaustion, distancing himself further with a female bearer: Lady Adeline Amundeville. World-weary, the Lady hints of latent Byronic reserves, a passion that might be kindled if only it could find a spark:

> . . . Adeline was not indifferent, for
>   (*Now* for a common place!) beneath the snow,
> As a Volcano holds the lava more
>   Within—*et cetera*. Shall I go on?—No!
> I hate to hunt down a tired metaphor:
>   So let the often used volcano go.
> Poor thing. How frequently by me and others
> It hath been stirred up till its smoke quite smothers.
>
> I'll have another figure in a trice. . . .   (*Don Juan* XIII.36–37)

Byron signals his jadedness by rhyming *lava more* with *metaphor* (and even, *go on ?—No!* with *(vol)cano go*. L.E.L. wakes up the metaphor as a repression in the weariness of social belles such as Lady Adeline, and fires it for a female purchase on the existential passions, or original Byronism.

For posthumous readers, Byron was as undead as dead, the lava of genius pouring forth anew with each memoir, and weirdly self-resurrected by a belated series of first publications. One was Medwin's *Conversations* (1824), which exhumed Byron to retail a nightmare death-in-life:

> I need not tell you of the obloquy and opprobrium that were cast upon my name when our separation was made public. . . . All my former friends, even my cousin George Byron, who had been brought up with me, and whom I loved as a brother, took my wife's part. . . . I was looked upon as the worst of husbands, the most abandoned and wicked of men, and my wife as a suffering angel. . . . I was abused in the public prints, made the common talk of private companies, hissed as I went to the House of Lords, insulted in the streets, afraid to go to the theatre. . . . The Examiner was the only paper that dared say a word in my defence, and Lady Jersey the only person in the fashionable world that did not look upon me as a monster. *(MCB 48)*

Was this pained memory, or Byron's talented talk? "The case was the reverse," protested Lady Byron anyway; "The Press was with Lord Byron almost without exception. Why was 'the Separation made public'? [My father] had asked for 'a private and amicable' arrangement—" (annotation; *MCB* 49). Even Hobhouse, writing in the *Westminster Review* January 1825, confirmed her view of "The Press," adding that "Lord Byron was never hissed as he went to the House of Lords nor insulted in the streets" (25–26). Byron was spinning Byronism, linking it to Mary Shelley's now famous tale of a creature helplessly despised "as a monster."

Conceived in Byron's villa in the year of the Separation (1816), *Frankenstein* must have read like half-biography to Byron. Here he is once again, but for the first time, in 1833:

> The man who is exiled by a faction has the consolation of thinking that he is a martyr; he is upheld by hope and the dignity of his cause, real or imaginary: he who withdraws from the pressure of debt may indulge in the thought that time and prudence will retrieve his circumstances: he who is condemned by the law, has a term to his banishment, or a dream of its abbreviation; or, it may be the knowledge

or the belief of some injustice of the law, or of its administration in his own particular; but he who is outlawed by general opinion, without the intervention of hostile politics, illegal judgment or embarrassed circumstances, whether he be innocent or guilty, must undergo all the bitterness of exile, without hope, without pride, without alleviation. This case was mine. Upon what ground the public founded their opinion, I am not aware; but it was general, and it was decisive. Of me or of mine they knew little, except that I had written what is called poetry, was a nobleman, had married, became a father, and was involved in differences with my wife and her relatives, no one knew why, because the persons complaining refused to state their grievances.   (*Some Observations; BW* 15: 65–66)

Framed in 1821 for publication, this is a calculation of absences and negations—no cause, no knowledge, no statements, all climaxing in exile. Goethe wryly remarked (in October 1816) that the Separation-drama "was so poetical in its circumstances . . . that if Byron had invented it, he could hardly have found a more fortunate subject for his genius."[31] The latest rehearsal had a fresh thrill for the Byron-lorn in 1833.

From the grave, Byron writes himself once again as Byronic hero, hounded like Frankenstein's Creature into exile, from exile to self-execution:

The press was active and scurrilous; and such was the rage of the day, that the unfortunate publication of two copies of verses, rather complimentary than otherwise to the subjects of both, was tortured into a species of crime, or constructive petty treason. I was accused of every monstrous vice by public rumour and private rancour: my name, which had been a knightly or a noble one since my fathers helped to conquer the kingdom for William the Norman, was tainted. I felt that, if what was whispered, and muttered, and murmured, was true, I was unfit for England; if false, England was unfit for me. I withdrew: but this was not enough. In other countries, in Switzerland, in the shadow of the Alps, and by the blue depth of the lakes, I was pursued and breathed upon by the same blight. I crossed the mountains, but it was the same; so I went a little farther, and settled myself by the waves of the Adriatic, like the stag, who betakes him to the waters.   (*ibid., BW* 15: 66–67)

One of those published verses was by his design, and not "complimentary" to its subject, Lady Byron's maid. Despite his noble name, it was noble nastiness to a servant—"unmanly," said the *Eclectic*.[32] Even Byron's friends regretted it, torturing their excuses. Does Byron's amnesia deserve amnesty? The *Quarterly* turned a spoof when it reprinted the passage (more fully) from Moore's *Byron*, with a headline: "The Exile of Ravenna thus sums up his own case" (44: 210).

Herself subject to public rumor and private rancor in the rage of the day, L.E.L. cut the Lord some slack and fanned the myth: "a mind so framed" (*The Portrait* 9). Her Byrons are ultimately a love affair with her intimate knowledge of this framed figure, her designated muse:

> The deep enchantment we have felt,
> When every thought and feeling dwelt
> Beneath his spirit's thrall. (126–27)

Embodying the romance of this persona, Lady Blessington grew Byronic, summoning his eyes and voice for an enchanted essay, "Thoughts on Lord Byron," in *The Keepsake for 1839:*

> Often have I stood on the spot, where Byron reclined when drinking in inspiration at the Coliseum, and mentally repeated the lines—
>
> > "Amidst this wreck, where thou has made a shrine
> > And temple more divinely desolate,
> > Among thy mightier offerings here are mine,
> > Ruins of years—though few, yet full of fate—"

As she gives the rest of this stanza, *Childe Harold IV* cxxxi, the first-person "mentally" becomes her own ("Thoughts" 182–83). The pose of Byron that accompanies her thoughts is a feminine seductress, odalisque in pose. It is meant to suggest Byron's stagey absorption by the grandeur before him but its contours invite almost any viewer, absorbed by Byron thus absorbed, to imagine herself in this figure. It wasn't just that Byron gave self-pity a cast of grandeur and heroic doom that women could inhabit, but that Byron could be claimed as a soul-sister in this sublimity. The call to sympathetic projection extends back to the original ruin of years, the Separation: "Well can I picture him to myself," said Lady Blessington (183), rushing irate from a circle, where the impertinence of some individual, assuming the garb of prudery, had insulted him by a marked avoidance, or a supercilious recognition; impertinences, which though contemptible, were sure to produce pain and irritation to his too susceptible feelings. Can it then be wondered at, that under such inflictions, the finest aspirations of his genius were mingled with bitterness.

Blessington's is yet another identifactory romance: "I picture him to myself rushing irate from a circle" tests a grammar that has them both involved. She writes like one who's been there.

Lady Caroline Lamb's version of identification was to write a *New Canto* for *Don Juan,* a masquerade that she managed to publish on the heels of Byron's first installment. Camping Byronic style, fashion, and attitude, she opens in a parodic ventriloquy of his studied weariness:

> I'm sick of fame—I'm gorged with it, so full
> I almost could regret the happier hour
> When northern oracles proclaimed me dull ...   (1–3)

Now refusing the equation of enchantment to thraldom, Lamb ironizes the agency. Tuning her verse to his famous way with rhymes, she mimes his vanity:

> And now, ye coward sinners (I'm a bold one,
> Scorning all here, not caring for hereafter,
> A radical, a stubborn, and an old one),
> Behold! each riding on a burning rafter,
> The devils (in my arms I long to fold one)
> Splitting their blue and brazen sides with laughter,
> Play at snapdraggon in their merry fits,
> O'er some conventicle for hypocrites.   (XIV)

She does Byronic devilry by his numbers, easily miming his contempt for the mere hypocrites of the creed, his parade as the star pupil of what Southey only belatedly called "the Satanic school" (*W* 10: 206). She even trumps him by getting a little closer than he had in *Don Juan* I–II to homosexual signifying (courting a devil's embrace), and tweaks the sighs

Byron Contemplating the Coliseum, *Keepsake* 1839, facing p. 180, to accompany an article by Countess Blessington. By kind permission of Princeton University Library. The pose is both rapt and performative, inviting any reader to partner himself or herself with Byron in this Byronic contemplation.

of middle-age at the end of Byron's first canto, by teasing a rhyme of *old one* out of the boasting *bold one* and then, in Byronic style, recovering with a flaunting *Behold!* Lamb-Byron does not just imitate or parody but deftly ghosts Byron's voice, Byron's confessions, Byron's bravado.[33] In a relay of celebrity rivalry, she closes with "Byron" vowing to "keep my name in capitals, like Kean" (the Byron of the London stage).

What would Byron have made of all these female claims? "The more the merrier," he said in his last year of his life in portraits, and of the desire that confirms glamour:

> One will represent me as a sort of sublime misanthrope, with moments of kind feeling. This, *par example,* is my favourite *rôle.* Another will portray me as a modern Don Juan; and a third . . . will, it is to be hoped, if only for opposition sake, represent me as an *amiable,* ill-used gentleman "more sinned against than sinning." Now, if I know myself, I should say, that I have no character at all. . . . I am so changeable, being every thing by turns and nothing long.
>
> (Blessington, *BCB* 220)

Byron turns Humean metaphysician, inserting himself, along with a jocular purchase on Lear's tragedy, into that "theatre" of mind, "where several perceptions successively make their appearance; pass, re-pass, glide away, and mingle in an infinite variety of postures and situations" (*Treatise* I.IV.vi)—a Cleopatra of modern epistemology, or a Byron of modern celebrity in print culture, where the theater is the public mind.

In this circuitry, magazines not only chased celebrities but also promoted them, turning writers into stars of the season. By the time he was writing *Don Juan XI* the annuals had entered the relay. Although Byron was not in England, he was in its orbits of publication, as text and as reader. *Canto XI* returns Juan to an England fashioned from Byron's Regency "Years of Fame," layered into the celebrity press of 1823:

> At great assemblies or in parties small,
> He saw ten thousand living authors pass,
>   That being about their average numeral;
> Also eighty "greatest living poets,"
> As every paltry magazine can show *its.*   (XI.54)

Paving the way with the wicked rhyming of "poets" and "show *its*," Byron gives *pass* a double-shift, across present procession and imminent passage into oblivion. Even for a sole holder, the title seems plural in the perpetual flux, as the kin rhyme of *poet* and *show it* in the next stanza proposes, the difference of case scarcely mattering in the halls of fame:

> In twice five years the "greatest living poet,"
>   Like to the champion in the fisty ring,
> Is called on to support his claim, or show it,
>   Although 'tis an imaginary thing.   (XI. 55)

An annual can flash in the ring with a champion gambit: a famous living poet writing about a famous dead poet, waiting in the wings for resurrection, to feed a public craving.

Don Juan had all along made a spectacle of Byronic turns. In *Canto XIII*, the company at Norman Abbey includes "young bard Rackrhyme, who had newly / Come out and glimmered as a six-weeks' star" (84), twin to the season's *debutantes* who are brought "out" to the marriage market (XII.31). Byron's racked rhyme in *XIII*.84, by linking that young bard's *newly* linked to *truly* ("When invited elsewhere, truly . . .") reprises the signature of this now famous poem's famous hero, introduced by *new one, true one*, then *Juan*—and so writes the hero and the poem named for him into the temporal flux. Juan emerges as a game of variable seasonal desires, with Byron happy to cast women as the prime designers:

> with women he was what
>   They pleased to make or take him for, and their
> Imagination's quite enough for that;
>   So that the outline's tolerably fair,
> They fill the canvas up—and "verbum sat."   (XV.16)

Byron's Latin, keynoting the old adage ("A word is sufficient"), plays across languages into the modern era of portraiture, with "sat" shifting into the predicate of "verbum." The wit turns Juan into an object for female designing (he sat for their canvases), his flesh made word, a text for their reading and rendering.

By 1823 (when he was writing the last two completed cantos of *Don Juan*), Byron was reviewing the first stage of his fame, staging it at Norman Abbey in Regency England for an otherworldly young woman who may or may not fall for the figure. This is Aurora Raby, a coolly detached lass, "nothing dazzled by the meteor / Because she did not pin her faith on feature" (56).[34] Aurora evokes A.I.M. *redivivus* and unknowable—especially in comparison to the Auroras translated by Lady Blessington and Stowe. Blessington's "Aurora Raby" in *Heath's Book of Beauty for 1847* is transparently Miss Milbanke succeeding in her fantasy of reform: "We believe that Aurora was designed to be not only the conqueror, but the retainer, of the wayward heart of the libertine Don Juan" (23), she proposes, converting the boyish parody back to the traditional rake that modeled Regency Byron. When Stowe met Lady Byron, she read her as an Aurora seemingly destined for and invested with this mission:

> When I was introduced to her, I felt in a moment the words of her husband:—
>
> "There was awe in the homage that she drew;
> Her spirit seemed as seated on a throne."
>
> Calm, self-poised, and thoughtful, she seemed to me rather to resemble an interested spectator of the world's affairs, than an actor involved in its trials.   (*Lady Byron* 206)

In Aurora, Blessington reads a reformist Annabella, while Stowe imagines Aurora as the Lord's late flowering respect for the Lady he had worked to defame.[35] The stanza that Stowe quotes, *Don Juan XV: 47*, carries the sentence forward into a figure of Byronic self-alienation: "on a throne / Apart from the surrounding world." Stowe doesn't name Aurora except by the implication of this quotation, but the kinship of Lady Byron to this figure is clear enough.

Reading Stowe, Lady Caroline Norton (herself husband-scarred, scandal ridden, deemed Byronic by her readers),[36] discerned the latest coded representation of unconfessed respect:

> Byron seems at one time to have been really attracted by the spiritual, unworldly nature of his future wife; the exquisite sketch of Aurora Raby, in "Don Juan," represents her as she appeared to him when he first met her in fashionable society, and in it he bears testimony to the charm of her thoughtful, serious, and yet girlish nature, so different from the common type.   (*True Story* 184)

As Stowe's gloss proposes in the same key, Annabella redone as Aurora is Byronism cool, an extracted strain of "the pure and the impure in his poetry" that "often run side by side without mixing" (397):

> What can more perfectly express moral ideality of the highest kind
> than the exquisite descriptions of Aurora Raby,—pure and high in
> thought and language, occurring as they do, in a work full of the most
> utter vileness? (398)

Reading Aurora, Stowe, Norton, and Blessington re-imagine a Lord worthy of his Lady, as if to redeem him at last, succeeding in the fantasy at which she spectacularly failed.

Writing against Byron is nothing if not Byronic, however. The stanza in *Don Juan XV* that Stowe raids precedes Byron's own stage-setting along the sight-line of A.I.M. back when, as an interested spectator of the world's affairs, she was inspired to coin that word *Byromania:*

> His fame too,—for he had that kind of fame
>   Which sometimes plays the deuce with womankind,
> A heterogeneous mass of glorious blame,
>   Half virtues and whole vices being combined;
> Faults which attract because they are not tame;
>   Follies trick'd out so brightly that they blind:—
> These seals upon her wax made no impression,
> Such was her coldness or her self-possession. (XV.57)

However we adjudicate this motive *or*, it pivots a she-resistance to the famous impresser, or in A.I.M.'s terms, a refusal to be the ape of fame. In the next canto, when Aurora's eye is caught, and turns its gaze on Juan, the effect is even worse, because the indications are inscrutable:

>   he caught Aurora's eye on his
>   And something like a smile upon her cheek.
> Now this he really rather took amiss:
>   In those who rarely smile, their smiles bespeak
> A strong external motive, and in this
>   Smile of Aurora's there was nought to pique
> Or hope, or love, with any of the wiles
> Which some pretend to trace in ladies' smiles.

'Twas a mere quiet smile of contemplation,
    Indicative of some surprise and pity;
And Juan grew carnation with vexation . . .   (XVI.92–93)

Juan "took amiss" not in the old Byronic way of seduction (took a miss); he is unsettled by his inability to refer to the usual tracings, even along lines of self-delusion. If Juan is the magnetic celebrity of these late cantos, his author will rehearse the phenomenon through a female resistance to interaction—at least in the eye of this one potent, but unreadable, review of "The Byromania." It is a relay of Romantic Interactions that is still with us, of authorial self-discovery that finds its definition in lines of resistance to the very enchantments of celebrity.

Introduction

1. Theologian, philosopher, historical writer, artist, speculative scientist, and admired engraver, Isaac Taylor was the brother of poets Jane and Ann Taylor.

2. In the next decade, another poet would use *interaction* to describe the foundational formation of "moral" sense, in a dynamic at once interpersonal, social, and spiritual: "All the instinctive moral powers /.../... howe'er they grew, / From inner impulse— outer force, / Or interaction of the two" (Alfred Domett, *A Dream of Two Lives* 2.5.145–49).

3. Because of Mary Shelley's agency in the initial publication, I use her edition (*Essays & c*, 1840); except for an accidental or two, this text is identical to modern editions.

4. The punning on *determined* (resolved upon; destined) is famous in the lines Shakespeare writes for Richard III's greeting to the audience: "I am determined to prove a villain" (1.1.30)—amplified for the Romantic age by Edmund Kean's signature, celebrated performance in this role.

5. Explicating this narrative in the first chapter of *A Literature of Their Own* (1977), "The Female Tradition," Showalter comments that "the development of this tradition is similar to the development of any literary subculture": a "minority group finds its direction of self-expression relative to the dominant society" (11).

6. Franklin, "Juan's Sea Changes" 63.

7. Mellor, "The Female Poet and the Poetess" 261–62, 265–66.

8. Mellor, *Romanticism and Gender* (1993) and *Mothers of the Nation: Women's Political Writing in England, 1780–1830* (2000); Behrendt, *British Women Poets and the Romantic Writing Community* (2009).

Chapter One: Charlotte Smith's Emigrants *and the Politics of Allusion*

1. John Guillory (siding with Pierre Bourdieu) reads canonicity as this framework, a cultural capital accessible to the literate class. Adela Pinch argues otherwise: Smith's attraction to quotation displays "a relationship to poetic language

and literary tradition" that need not spell subjection to "patriarchal literary tradition" and a subjectivity "always already written" (60–63); rather, Smith shows how reading may activate feeling and supply a language for its expression. In both views, however, the author (or poet) is a creation of, rather than a critical agent within (or against), a system of language.

2. For the events of 1792, see Greer 31; about ten thousand of the *réfractairs* banished on the order of 26 August 1792 emigrated to England (28). For Saint-Just, see Soboul 89; for Smith, see *L* 60–62.

3. *London Review* 24 (July 1793), 42.

4. Curran comments on Smith's mythic self-mirroring in the exiles' sudden fall "from opulence to penury" ("The 'I' Altered" 201–02).

5. See Betty Bennett, *British War Poetry, 1793–1815*.

6. "I have not courage to put my name," More said to Horace Walpole (the Earl of Orford), "for fear I should be thought pert and political" (April 1793; Roberts 1: 421). Her occasion was Dupont's "monstrous" indictment of the "tyranny" of the Church, wildly applauded by the French Assembly.

7. Norma Clarke's remark about women writers in the male culture of the periodicals of the 1830s is relevant: one "way for a woman to survive was to join in the chorus of anti-female, anti-woman-writer abuse. This was a literary device: a stage female was brought into being rather like the stage villain of melodrama. Women who resorted to the stage female could wrap a cloak of masculinity around themselves and achieve respectability" (29).

8. On 4 July, Smith asked her publisher for copies of *Desmond* for her family (*L* 46). The French Assembly took emergency measures when war with the Austro-Hungarian Empire broke out in April: *réfractairs* were deported, the king's guard disbanded, and the *fédérés* called to Paris. Louis's veto provoked the invasion of the Tuileries and the end of the monarchy in August.

9. Vol. 3, Letter V (42). "Geraldine Verney subsists under a feudal oppression almost as dire and certainly as degrading to her humanity as could be found anywhere in pre-revolutionary France" (Curran, ed., xiii). As one more "reply" to Burke's *Reflections*, *Desmond* is transparent, not only in the republican polemic but also in fictional detailing. Like *Reflections*, it is epistolary; the name of Desmond's mentor and Painite interlocutor, Erasmus Bethel, shares, as if in rebuke, the initials of Edmund Burke. On the politics, see Diana Bowstead, and Mellor, *Mothers* 106–21, which pays fine attention to the retro-gender ideologies that linger in male-republican politics.

10. On Smith and Dodsley (the younger brother who inherited the firm of R. and J. Dodsley), see Sarah Zimmerman 57.

11. For Smith in France in early September 1791, see J. Labbe, "Gentility" 91. *Desmond* reflects "the terms and even the time-frame" of Williams's summer-

1790 *Letters from France,* as Curran points out in his edition (x). At a celebration at Paris's Hôtel d'Angleterre on 14 November 1792, British enthusiasts named "Mrs. Smith and Mrs. H. M. Williams" in a toast to those "Women of Great Britain" who have "distinguished themselves by their writings in favour of the French revolution" (Alger 326).

12. *Analytical Review* XIII (August 1792), 428.

13. "I am sensible also (to use another quotation) that ——'Adversity—— / Tho' like a toad ugly and venomous, / Wears yet a precious jewel in its head,'" v–vi (quoting *As You Like It* 2.1.12–14). For Hamlet, see 1.4.15–1 and 3.1.71–72 (slightly rearranged). It was with this last voice rhymed into her own that Smith began her "Dedication: To My Children" in her first novel, *Emmeline* (1778): "O'erwhelm'd with sorrow—and sustaining long / 'The proud man's contumely, the oppressor's wrong,' / Languid despondency, and vain regret, / Must my exhausted spirit struggle yet?" Although her husband forced her publishers to suppress the verse in the second edition, she had her revenge in the sixth edition of *Elegiac Sonnets* (1792), in which she lodged *Verses Intended to have Been Prefixed to the Novel of Emmeline, but then Suppressed* (86–87), with no further suppression.

14. In vol. 2, Letter X, Desmond asks "whether such extreme poverty and wretchedness did not shew the necessity of some alteration in the government where they existed?" (122) and defends Paine's *Rights of Man.* In vol. 3, Letter XVII, he writes against Burke, cheering "a people who have no object than to obtain, for themselves, that liberty which is the undoubted birth-right of all mankind" (207) and cheering the British sympathizers who cite "Locke, and Milton, and Bacon, and (what is better than all) common sense" to remind us "that government is not for the benefit of the governors, but the governed" (210). Such views "shocked and offended" Smith's aristocratic friends, says Hilbish (149). Though her source is problematic (a memoir by Smith's sister, published in 1834 under the aegis of Tory Sir Walter Scott), the point is not negligible. *Anti-Jacobin* saw in *The Young Philosopher* "political opinions and sentiments" that were "unconstitutional" and "dangerous," and cautioned Smith that "the best of our female novelists interferes not with church nor state. There are no politics in Evelina or Cecilia" (2/1 [1798]: 189–90; citing Burney's novels). "Politics are certainly out of place in a novel," lectured Mrs. Elwood in 1843, refreshing the report that Smith lost "valuable friends" for her violation (60). As late as 1903, a Tory aristocrat could see even in Smith's disdain of "the legitimate sonnet" a case of "Romantic lawlessness" and could find "irresponsible treason" in her "Rights of Man" voice, in wonder that she "was not prosecuted for sedition" (St. Cyres 687, 691)—a fate that many did suffer in the Pitt ministry's regime.

15. See vol. 1, Letter XIV. For the historical document, see Appendix B in Curran's edition.

16. "Being very justly of the opinion, that the great events which are passing in the world are no less interesting to women than to men, and that in her solicitude to discharge the domestic duties, a woman ought not to forget that, in common with her father and husband, her brothers and sons, she is a citizen; Mrs. Smith introduces . . . conversations of the principles and occurrences of the French Revolution" (406). The reviewer is William Enfield, leading Dissenter and man of letters (Forster, Raven, and Bending, *The English Novel 1790–1829* 1: 575).

17. Stanton has a slightly different, modernized transcription, and (disputing the Princeton record) says the addressee is Thomas Cadell Sr. (*Collected Letters* 54–55), who did publish *The Emigrants* (at 826 lines, about two-thirds the projection in this letter). He and Thomas Cadell Jr. (with William Davies) published all the lifetime editions, from the 5th on, of *Elegiac Sonnets &c.* G. G. J. and J. Robinson, known for its liberal political list, published *Desmond*, which quickly went into a second edition; but in the increasingly reactionary political climate of the 1790s no more editions were possible, and the firm, fined in November 1793 for selling Paine's *Rights of Man*, published nothing further by Smith.

18. The epithet is St. Cyres' (688). *Elegiac Sonnets* debuted in 1784, went into an immediate second edition, and a sixth by 1792; the three pre-*Desmond* novels appeared in rapid succession in 1788, 1789, and 1791. All this work, and more, made Smith's arguably the first female literary career in the English-speaking world (Curran, "Charlotte Smith and British Romanticism" 68).

19. Burney, with a French husband and friends, was suspect. Even Tory More, as she reported to Walpole on 14 September 1793, had been accused "of opposing God's vengeance against popery, by my wickedly wishing that the French priests should not be starved, when it was God's will that they should" (Roberts 1: 428). Her appeal "brought upon the author a torrent of abuse" in the form of another Protestant pamphlet (More, *Works* [1833] 2: 380).

20. In *The Banished Man* a landlord nervous about sheltering some emigrants worries about one being "a spy for the Jackybins" (4: 82).

21. For the social incidence, see Weiner 54–69; and Greer 28–29, chap. 4, and table 1 (112). Across the 1790s the emigrants to England amounted to less than 1% of the population (Greer 20); twenty to twenty-five thousand arrived in 1792.

22. See, e.g., *British Critic* 1 (August 1793), 405; *Critical Review* ns2/9 (1794), 299.

23. To Burke's dismay at the revolt "against a mild and lawful monarch" (56), Paine countered that the object was not the king but "the despotic principles of the government" (17); moreover, a "casual discontinuance of the *practice* of despotism is not a discontinuance of its *principles*" (284). Even after the execution of Louis XVI and other "horrors," Williams held to principle: "PRINCIPLES are

never to be abandoned, however unsuccessful may be the attempt to carry them in *practice*," she wrote from Paris, March 1793 (270).

24. Claudia Johnson (iii) identifies the unsigned author as Burke. Reports filled the front of the *Times*, 14 September 1792 (2–3); for further accounts, see Simon Schama 633–34.

25. Along with advocating relief of "the pressing distresses of the poor emigrant priests," More hoped to enlighten "religious people, both in the church and among the different sects, whose fondness for French politics entirely blinds them to the horrors of French impiety" (to Walpole, April 1793; Roberts 1: 421). Over ten thousand French—mostly artisans, shopkeepers, and aristocrats (e.g. Talleyrand, Chateaubriand, Louis Phillipe)—emigrated to the United States (Greer 92).

26. In 1792, More published a caustic satire on Painite principles in a Burkish pamphlet, *Village Politics*. "From liberty, equality, and the rights of man, good Lord, deliver *us!*" she wrote to Walpole, January 1793, as Louis XVI was being tried for treason (Roberts 1: 419).

27. Their ground opinion is this: "we think she is mistaken in the estimate of their merits, when she represents them as actuated entirely by religious principle. . . . The slightest observation will shew how intimately their emoluments and their power were connected with the political system they adhered to, and having once chosen their party, it was not in their power to avoid being involved in the ruin which overwhelmed it" (*Critical Review* 2s 10 [March 1794]: 319–20).

28. *Collected Letters* 105; Smith gives the second phrase to her surrogate Mrs. Denzil, in *The Banished Man* (which she was writing at the same time), with similar sarcasm about the British legal establishment: very little "compels me to stay in 'This land, that from her pushes all the rest!'" (II.XI; p. 218). I was not able to trace the quotation; advice welcome.

29. End-noted information (faintly signaled in the poem text) is far more textually attenuated than same-page footnotes (as reset by editors: Curran, *The Poems of Charlotte Smith;* Wu, *Romantic Women Poets;* Mellor and Matlak, *British Literature;* Labbe, *The Works of Charlotte Smith*).

30. In the Church, the gap between rich and poor was extreme, the wealthiest bishops enjoying an annual income of 50,000 livres and poor vicars getting by on 300 (Schama 349–50). The higher ecclesiastical ranks were filled with the younger sons of aristocracy; in 1789 all the bishops were nobles. The Third Estate comprised 96% of the population (Soboul 9, 15–16).

31. For the toxicity of "rights of man" language, see, e.g., *Church and King*, a song (tuned to *Rule Britannia*) published in *Gentleman's Magazine*, March 1793: "The *Wrongs*, miscall'd the *Rights*, of Men" (1.28; Bennett 71). Smith uses the phrasing in Thomson's play in a back-note to *To the Shade of Burns,* the sonnet honoring this champion of freedom and liberty (a "noble Spirit" shining amid

"labouring Poverty"): he is "a Poet 'of nature's own creation'" (vol. 2: 102). She arrays Volume II to give its political poems an affiliated force: *To the Shade of Burns, The Sea View, The Dead Beggar, The Female Exile* (23–32). To say "Death vindicates the insulted Rights of Man" within "a short time of the execution of Louis XVI" seemed to Viscount St. Cyres grounds for being "prosecuted for sedition" (691).

32. *Paradise Lost* 2.628; among the "forms terrible to view" that Virgil places "in the jaws of hell" are "horrid Hydra," "Gorgons," and "vain chimaera" (Dryden, *Aeneid* 6.286–99).

33. In the studies of women and Milton by Joseph Wittreich and by Gilbert and Gubar, this Milton-infused simile, strangely, receives no comment.

34. Editors Baird and Ryskamp note similar language in two later "As when" similes in Young's *Night Thoughts* (9.1–8 and 513–25, both troping the poet as vexed traveler); *The Poems of William Cowper* 2: 362.

35. In dedicating *The Emigrants* to Cowper, Smith declares her affection for *The Task* and credits her blank verse (itself a trope of "liberty") to inspiration by Cowper and Milton (vi).

36. "From 1761 to 1801, 2,428,721 acres were enclosed through 1,479 parliamentary acts," with increasing momentum in the last years (MacLean 14–21).

37. The preface to *Desmond* scoffs at "the idea of our having a *natural* enemy in the French nation; and that they are still more *naturally* our foes, because they have dared to be freemen" (5). To Burke, Wollstonecraft retorts, "Did the pangs you felt for insulted nobility, the anguish that rent your heart when the gorgeous robes were torn off the idol human weakness had set up, deserve to be compared with the long-drawn sigh of melancholy reflection, when . . . the sick wretch, who can no longer earn the sour bread of unremitting labour, steals to a ditch to bid the world a long good night" (*A Vindication of the Rights of Men* 152–53). Burke "pities the plumage, but forgets the dying bird," Paine famously summed it up in *The Rights of Man*: "Not one glance of compassion, not one commiserating reflection . . . has he bestowed on those who lingered out the most wretched of lives, a life without hope, in the most miserable of prisons" (24).

38. This theme was a pro-war favorite, as Bennett's anthology shows: e.g., "Heroes bleed in Glory's cause, / . . . They bleed to save the guiltless maid, / To guard the tender orphan's head / From insult and dismay" (121).

39. Bennett reports that the poetry of 1793 to 1815 featured "the war widow" (52), but her copious selections proceed from 1794, as do those in Mary Favret's penetrating study of how the war widow's vulnerability undermines the gender division of men at war and women at home (545).

40. Steven Behrendt (*British Women Poets* 86) treats Spence's essay. Women were barred from attending debates in the House of Commons after 1778. "Politics

belong to the men, and to hear a woman talk with virulence of one party or the other, is as unbecoming as to hear one of us declaim against the particular cut of a pair of ruffles," advised a man writing for *Lady's Magazine* in 1784 (205; cited by Linda Colley 249, 404 n. 22); female activism had to be patriotic (ibid. 259–63).

41. See E. P. Thompson 112–14. In a note, Spence reports that the *Morning Chronicle* rejected her piece, a fate shared by Capel Lofft's attempts to interest "a respectable Bookseller" in a similarly themed paper (129 n.).

42. As the hope of new liberty was betrayed by violence, the Revolution became a contradictory symbol for women, argues Anne Mellor ("English Women Writers and the French Revolution" 255); women began to urge "evolutionary reform" over bloody revolution (*Mothers* 87). One of women's first group identifications was as victims of men (Barker-Benfield xviii)—a discourse to which Smith contributed in recounting in preface after preface and serial coded fictions her ordeal with her husband and the trustees of her children's estate.

43. Also involved was a national pride of affection for their king, vulnerable in the crisis of 1788–89, when it seemed the prince might be appointed regent. See John Barrell, "Sad Stories" 78–79, citing John Brewer's "The Monstrous Tragi-Comic Scene: British Reactions to the French Revolution," in *The Shadow of the Guillotine: Britain and the French Revolution* (London: British Museum, 1989).

44. Bennett, *British War Poetry* 69–89.

45. Burns, *L* 2: 281–82 (quoting William Roscoe). Especially in France, the queen was despised, subject to erotic, pornographic, lesbian imagery, and hints of maternal incest (Lynn Hunt, esp. 113; Schama 221–26). One engraving depicts her as a bare-breasted harpy, clutching *The Rights of Man* in her claws (Schama 226). Blake incinerated Burke's idolatry: "The Queen of France just touchd this Globe / And the Pestilence darted from her robe" (notebooks, *P&P* 500). Yet as desexualized doomed widow and mother she won sympathy, even from republicans. Women were moved to view the war "as a cause in which their own welfare and status were peculiarly involved" (Colley 256). Thus, Spence writes: "permit me to entreat, (in the name of every Woman who would tremble for the property, the Happiness, or the Life of her Husband and Children) that you will not rashly draw the sword, and expose our Land to the Scourge of War" (89). As the king's trial loomed, Smith hoped that her friend Barlow might agree with her that the king and his family might be exiled with a settlement, "so long as they do not disturb the peace of the Republic" (3 November 1792; *L* 49).

46. The redaction seamlessly patches 2.104–16, 127–36, 145–69, with the epithet of Bernois (France's Henry IV, founder of the Bourbon dynasty) at 116 alertly emended from "darling of . . ." to "father of his people" (*Universal* 93: 147–48).

47. See Colley 240.

48. Gender notwithstanding, Thomas Weiskel reads Collins's Vengeance as "defiantly phallic" (113). Roger Lonsdale's edition (419 n.) supplies a male genealogy: Horace (*Odes* 1.2.2–3), Milton (*Paradise Lost* 2.173–74), Dryden (*Aeneid* 6.800–801), and Pope (*Odyssey* 24.623).

49. Virgil, *Aeneid* 2.730 ff.; Dryden's translation, p. 61. Although Smith knew Virgil's Latin (quoting from it in *Montalbert*), Dryden's was the popular translation. Thanks to Ron Levao for noting this allusion and assessing its force.

50. Taking a cue from the singular attention to these linked portraits in the *Analytical*'s review of *The Emigrants* (after a brief paragraph of praise, it printed 254–324), Smith refashioned 254–312 for the 1797 *Elegiac Sonnets* (2: 78–81) under the title *Fragment, Descriptive of the Miseries of War; from a Poem called "The Emigrants," Printed in 1793*. She replaced 281–91 ("yet, in Death itself" to the predators lured by the scent of blood) with three rows of asterisks, and stopped before the twelve lines indicting "savage war" (which the *Analytical* included in its excerpt). Reading *The Emigrants* itself, Ann Radcliffe turned Smith's scenario into a faintly political allusion, summoning the feudal chief's horror at discovering the ruins at his castle and his murdered family to render an obscure gloss on M. St. Aubert's mysterious agony, as if he were one bent, "in hopeless sorrow, over the ashes of the dead, shewn 'by the blunted light / That the dim moon through painted casements lends" 2.300–301; in *The Mysteries of Udolpho* I.VII (p. 190).

51. On 8 June 1791 she asked publisher Davies to send her Williams's *Farewell, for Two Years, to England. A Poem* (published the same year); *L* 34.

52. In contrast to her unmarked allusions to Collins and Virgil, Smith writes notes to identify "Gray" and "Milton, Sonnet 22d" (*Emigrants* p. 68). Borne by the knowledge that he has overplied his eyes in "libertyes defence, my noble task," blind Milton steers "Right onward"—a heroic phrase that he repeats for Christ's rout of the rebel angels: "Hee on his impious Foes right onward drove" (*PL* 6.831).

53. In autumn 1797, both *London Review* and *Scots* published this poem.

54. *British Critic* (1: 404–5) and *London Review* (24: 43–45) praised the portraits of the exile mother (Book I) and dauphin (Book II), and *Monthly Review* (months later) admired Smith's rendering of "those particulars in the case of the emigrants, which have excited sympathy in the minds of the humane of all parties," and the "lines descriptive of the present pitiable state" of the dauphin (ns 12: 375).

55. The countess's sister is the Duchess of Devonshire, and her daughter is Lady Caroline (later Lamb), for a hot season the lover of Lord Byron.

56. Volume II had about 250 subscribers, featuring aristocracy, Dr. Burney, poets Bowles and Cowper, The Late Dr. Fordyce, and William Hayley (Blake's and Smith's patron). It is apt to this resetting that sensibility is the only mode in which Hilbish can even comment on *The Emigrants*, which she deems Smith's

"most inferior" poem: weakened by its "bit of philosophy" (281, i.e., her "inter-est . . . for the politically oppressed" [151]) but praiseworthy in advocating "En-gland's respect for these exiles, both on the basis of their birth and their honor that has impelled them to resign their country for conscience's sake and to seek in England an asylum" (281).

57. Adriana Craciun (145–46) indexes the literature after 1793 flowing with sympathy for the emigrants (and praise of British "Liberty"): Maria Julia Young's poem *Adelaide and Antonine: or The Emigrants* (1793); *The Emigrant in London, A Drama in Five Acts, By an Emigrant* (1795: "Oh England, how truly doth thou deserve the double title of parent and asylum of the unfortunate"); *Journal of a French Emigrant, fourteen years old* (1795); Mme. de Genlis's *The Young Exiles; or Correspondence of Some Juvenile Emigrants* (1799); Mrs. Pilkington's *New Tales of the Castle; or, The Noble Emigrants, a Story of Modern Times* (1800). Grenby notes that the emigrant plot "became a staple of gothic anti-Jacobin fiction" and senti-mental children's tales, e.g., Lucy Peacock's *The Little Emigrant* (1799).

58. See also Grenby's introduction to *The Banished Man*, xxx–xxxiii.

59. Crowe was the public orator of Oxford; the sixty-six lines appeared with-out signature in *European Magazine, and London Review* 27 (June 1795): 418–19; Coleridge put lines 1–40 in the *Watchman* no. 5 (2 April 1796): 144–45 (Pat-ton, ed., *The Watchman* 179–80). With her sonneteer's eye, Smith quotes fourteen lines (14–28; half of the first and last) but miscopies "(tho' child of peace)" as "the" (2: 114).

60. Smith told her publishers Cadell and Davies that she devised the *Frag-ment* from "a part . . . much applauded," proposing that it "would rather promote than injure the sale of the copies" of *The Emigrants* they still had "on hand" (*L* 269–70).

Chapter Two: Mary Wollstonecraft Re:Reading the Poets

1. A series of *Monthly* essays opened with "Question"; see, e.g., 2 July 1796, p. 453. Wollstonecraft's authorship may have been known in some circles in April 1797; it was declared in January 1798 by Godwin when he published the letter, slightly revised, in *Posthumous Works of the Author of a Vindication of the Rights of Woman* (4: 159–75; cp. Preface in vol. 3). For Wordsworth's reading of the *Monthly*, including this issue, see Duncan Wu, *Wordsworth's Reading 1770–1799*, 101–3. The descriptions of nature in Wollstonecraft's *Letters Written During a Short Residence in Sweden, Norway, and Denmark* (1796) may also have influ-enced Wordsworth (Holmes, ed., 26–43).

2. See *Mary*, chapter XVIII for Milton and Young in this use (1: 107–9); Young again in ch. XXII (1: 132); and Charlotte Smith's despairing sonnet "To

Hope!" in ch. XXIII (1: 141). Smith's popular *Elegiac Sonnets* was in a fourth edition by 1786.

3. The play was first published in 1728; I quote from the 1795 performance text, most proximate to Wollstonecraft's writing of *The Wrongs of Woman*.

4. "Is she not more than painting can express, / Or youthful poets fancy when they love?" (*Fair Penitent* 3.1.255–56).

5. Mary Poovey views the "narrator—and by implication Mary Wollstonecraft"—as caught in "the very delusion it is the object of the novel to criticize" (98). I find Wollstonecraft's management of poetic quotation tuned more to what Mitzi Myers sees in her reviewer mode: a "resistant model of reading" that, by countering the disposition of female readers "toward submersion in the events of the text," serves "a broader cultural analysis of female submission" (89).

6. The first quotation is from *Rights of Woman* 150; the reiteration is in Wollstonecraft's unsigned article on Elizabeth Inchbald's *A Simple Story* (published in 1791) in the *Analytical Review* (10: 102). If (as Myers observes) the literary criticism in Wollstonecraft's reviews "is never purely aesthetic but always socially implicated" (88), it is also the case that the social criticism in *Rights of Woman* is always aesthetically explicated.

7. And so Godwin italicizes the word in his republication of W. Q.'s letter (*Post. W*: 161).

8. For my fuller discussion of Wollstonecraft's pressure on Rousseauvian "nature," see *Borderlines* 4–6. The text she quotes and critiques in *A Vindication of the Rights of Woman* is William Kenrick's nearly immediate translation, *Emilius and Sophie: or, A New System of Education* (1762).

9. Though Wollstonecraft does not cite Blake's *Songs of Innocence* (1789), she knew him, and he was the illustrator for her *Original Stories from Real Life* (1788). Blake's *Songs* presents a kin critique of innocence as a sometimes fatally vulnerable ignorance.

10. Mary Poovey sees Wollstonecraft as cowed by Milton into indirect attacks by allusions and italics (72–73), but *A Vindication of the Rights of Woman* launches more than a few direct attacks, often with pointed allusion.

11. Thus Sandra Gilbert describes one mode of female Milton readings (*Madwoman* 204).

12. In *The Marriage of Heaven and Hell* (1790), the Blakean "voice of the Devil" arraigns the "Errors" of "All Bibles": "Energy" gets "calld Evil" and "Reason, calld Good" (plate 4); "The history of this is written in Paradise Lost" (plate 5). The Blakean Devil contends, "The reason Milton wrote in fetters when / he wrote of Angels & God, and at liberty when of / Devils & Hell, is because he was a true Poet and / of the Devils party without knowing it" (plate 6).

13. For the male investment, see *PL* 4.442–43; 8.554, 574.

14. Dr. Gregory is also revisited. His *Comparative View of the State and Faculties of Mankind* (1765) supplied the first of the "Select Desultory Thoughts: Addressed to Females" that prefaces the *Reader* (this unit a sort of Wollstonecraft-commonplace book): "As the two sexes have very different parts to act in life, nature has marked their characters very differently, in a way that best qualifies them to fulfil their respective duties in society" (5); he has several entries in this section. In *Rights of Woman* (where fictions of *act, nature,* and *character* matter), Wollstonecraft says it is precisely because Dr. Gregory has much good advice for "the most respectable" of women that she will pause at "arguments that so speciously support opinions" of "the most baneful effect on the morals and manners of the female world" (215); "The remarks relative to behaviour, though many of them very sensible, I entirely disapprove of, because it appears to me to be beginning, as it were, at the wrong end" (217).

15. Hazlitt is more in line with retro-Gregory than even Aikin, who demurs in her preface: "The politic father will not then leave as a 'legacy' to his daughters the injunction to conceal their wit, their learning, and even their good sense, in deference to the 'natural malignity' with which most men regard every woman of a sound understanding and cultivated mind" (*Epistles* vi)—referring to remarks on which Wollstonecraft had animadverted (*RW* 222–23; Gregory, *Legacy* 31–32).

16. In *Feminist Milton* Joseph Wittreich argues that Milton "calculated" such "contradictions" to thwart regard of him as a unified voice of orthodoxy, and to rupture any equation of his views with those of a speaker, such as Adam or even the epic narrator. Yet to propose, as he does, that Wollstonecraft reads Milton as "an advocate for women, not their adversary" (41–42) is to elide both her discourse of animadversion and her highly audible sarcasm. Hailing her comments on Milton's "pleasing picture" of the Edenic pair, Wittreich elides the sarcasm here, too (42).

17. This verse, too, More tried to claim for *Cœlebs in Search of a Wife,* patching an epigraph for Book II from 383–84 and 389–91. For an incisive analysis of Milton's contradiction, see Ronald Levao, especially 96 and n. 26. In *Rights of Men* Wollstonecraft summoned Adam's voice for a bitter critique of feudal class hierarchy: "Among unequals there can be no society" (72).

18. Wittreich cites Wray to give an instance of Milton's uses in "defense" of women (54), but it is a dubious case. To the proposal that Adam may not speak for Milton, Wray retorts, "if the Author had right Sentiments of Woman in general, he might more emphatically aggravate an ill Character, by Comparison of an ill to an innocent and vertuous one, than by general Calumnies without Exception" (4).

19. Milton's theology gets satirized on the score of slavery, too: the "owners of

negro ships, never smell on their money the blood by which it has been gained, but sleep quietly in their beds, terming such occupations *lawful callings;* yet the lightning marks not their roofs, to thunder conviction on them, 'and to justify the ways of God to man'" (*LSR* 260).

20. For a sampler of the repeated scorn, see *RW* 67, 132, 158, 264, 392, 437.

21. This contempt can even overdrive Wollstonecraft's reading: "What are the cold, or feverish caresses of appetite, but sin embracing death, compared with the modest overflowings of a pure heart and exalted imagination?" she writes (446) on behalf of rational love, but with a weird refraction of the most misogynist passage in *Paradise Lost* (2.746–814): scarcely "embracing," Sin is raped by her father Satan, then by their son Death, then eternally by his issue, hellhounds that forever gnaw at her womb. Poovey suggests Wollstonecraft's fear that female desire may justify misogyny (76); conceptually and textually, Sin precontaminates unfallen Eve.

22. This couplet appears on the title-page obverse of William Thompson's (and Anna Wheeler's) *Appeal of One Half the Human Race, Women, Against the Pretensions of the Other Half, Men, To Retain Them in Political, and Thence in Civil And Domestic Slavery* (1825), a tract intent to raise "from the dust that neglected banner which a woman's hand nearly thirty years ago unfolded boldly, in face of the prejudices of thousands of years" (vii).

23. For Dryden's triplet poetics, see the brilliant essay by Christopher Ricks.

24. The young lady's "commonplace" book is parodied in the opening chapter of Austen's *Northanger Abbey* (drafted in the 1790s) in the poetic extracts that shape Catherine Morland's expectations and self-regard.

25. Shakespeare is frequently a choral voice in Wollstonecraft's work, as the ample indexing in Todd and Butler's *Works*, Macdonald and Scherf's superb edition of the *Vindications*, and Todd's *Collected Letters* makes clear.

26. While I appreciate Tilottama Rajan's important work on the historical production of social psychology, I find the *Reader* not necessarily pointing women to the domestic sphere via an "instructional form" that assumes "universal truths, without raising the question of their representation" (171). Wollstonecraft knows the social text but also knows that literary texts can play to their readers with indeterminate interest and effect.

27. Maria's "Hamlet" is deftly discussed by Claudia Johnson (*Equivocal Beings* 62). Hamlet's alienated melancholy and skepticism imprint *Rights of Men* 87, and Wollstonecraft's letters (*CL* 72, 103, 156), especially to Imlay (*LSR* 332, 241; cf. *CL* 238, 284, 307—all quoting the soliloquies).

28. This political refraction emerges from gothic frames. For Mary, "a small taper made the darkness visible" of a shipboard hell (*Mary* ch. XIX; 118), and she is soon voicing gothic Macbeth's final despairing soliloquy (119). In *Rights of*

Men, darkness is Catholicism at the advent of the Reformation: "this faint dawn of liberty only made the subsiding darkness more visible" (18).

29. It mattered to Wollstonecraft that Milton's esteem in the tradition of liberal politics had just been refreshed by the publication in 1791, in inexpensive octavo, of *The Ready and Easy Way to Establish a Free Commonwealth* (the first free-standing edition since 1659 and 1660)—one of the many answers to Burke's *Reflections*.

30. Mary Shelley, by contrast, restores Pope's gender in Lord Lodore's regard of Lady Lodore's "usual feminine infirmities—'The love of pleasure, and the love of sway'; and destitute of that tact and tenderness of nature which should teach her where to yield and how to reign" (ch. IX, 105–6; cp. Pope, *Of the Characters of Women* 210).

31. She returns to the same lines in Letter IV, with a comparative sociology, to propose that the blame of stray-producing "stars" is better understood as the fate of an "idle" female "mind" in a healthy body (*LSR* 37–38).

32. Turning the cynic's reduction of what women are good for to taunt her own readers, Wollstonecraft might have been heartened by Coleridge's remark in 1813 that it may be "a high compliment to Women" that Shakespeare has put "all the sarcasm on them . . . in the mouth of villains, like Iago" (*Lectures* 1: 553).

33. Wollstonecraft's *seraglio* twins Hamlet's *nunnery*. Even anti-Wollstonecraftian More could cite the same lines from *Hamlet* in her *Strictures on . . . Female Education*, to convey her disgust at the "code of artificial manners" in popular authorities on "female instruction" (66).

34. Hamlet's satire imprints Mary Hays's Wollstonecraft-influenced *Appeal to the Men of Great Britain in Behalf of Women* (1798) in the chapter "What Women Are": if women "cannot say with honest Hamlet, that they 'know not what seem is,'" this "inconsistency and uncertainty of character" reflect "defects . . . of education rather than of nature" (67–68).

35. Godwin did reciprocate, not only in person but in a textual afterlife of coded homage to Wollstonecraft. In *Fleetwood* (1805) Fleetwood and Mary read together, and "in such discussions we intermix 'Grateful digressions . . .'" (1832 ed., 245). In his last novel, *Deloraine*, Godwin transfers the erotics to a father-daughter reading (the daughter double-mirroring Mary Shelley and Mary Wollstonecraft), as if to stabilize male/paternal authority: "with our graver studies and more serious disquisitions we would intermix 'grateful digressions, and solve high dispute' with sportive interruption, and affectionate caresses, such as might best beseem father and daughter" (153). For a fine discussion of this dynamic of reading (though with a telling mistake about these caresses as "conjugal"), see Julie Carlson, *England's First Family of Writers* 56–61.

36. 5 August; *CL* 316; Godwin put this letter in *Posthumous Works* as Letter LXI.

37. *A Midsummer Night's Dream* 2.1.166 ff. Private letters to Imlay summon the passions of still other Shakespearean heroes: Lear's misery and anger, and Macbeth's anxiety (*CL* 304, 313, 241).

38. Goethe's novel (1774) was translated in 1779 as *The Sorrows of Werter: A German Story*. More, for one, castigated Godwin's epithet as evidence of Wollstonecraft's "*German*" ideas, in particular, "a direct vindication of adultery" in "The Wrongs of Woman" transparently influenced by Goethe and by August von Kotzebue's *The Stranger* (1790). The English translation of this popular work led to a success on the London stage in the 1790s (*Strictures* 44–45).

39. For *Elegiac Sonnets* (1786) Smith wrote three sonnets in the persona of Werter, with two more in the fifth edition (1789). The first remarks on Werter by Wollstonecraft, from the January 1789 *Analytical Review*, are about a verse translation she thought too "smooth" for Goethe's "ungoverned sensibility": the "energy and beauty of language" give "such reality to his misery, that we are affected by his sorrows, even while we lament the wanderings of his distempered mind" (III, 73). But reviewing a fantasy sequel to *Werter* the next year, Wollstonecraft sees Goethe authorizing "a sickly veil of artificial sentiment," one "as contrary to nature as virtue" (*AR* VI [April 1790]: 468). And another such fantasy supplement prompted her to satirize: "It has lately been the fashion to celebrate the Sorrows of Werter, and poetical ladies . . . are all so partial to the man, who *could* die for love" (*AR* VII [July 1790]: 299–300). This satire of poetical ladies may deflect anxiety about how even a rationally principled woman might succumb not just to partiality but to an identificatory romance of suicidal Werterian passion.

40. The occasion of the article (December 1788) is a treatise by the abolitionist and Princeton University president Samuel Stanhope Smith, *An Essay on the Causes of the Variety of Complexion and Figure in the Human Species*, refuting Kames's view of original diversity by arguing for the effects of circumstances. Wollstonecraft is moved to speculate that "under ground" the various social superstructures abide "like passions" and "similarity of minds," and that it only "capricious national prejudices" that exploit the "dissimilitude of forms" (*AR* 2: 431–35)—an analogy for the critique of gender prejudices that propels *Rights of Woman*. Here, too, "the Mosaical account" is indicted as a "vague conjecture" that can only produce "a distrust of revelation" (*AR* II: 432).

41. In the 1802 Preface to *Lyrical Ballads*, Wordsworth advocates a poetry of man and nature enlivened by passion, "naturally . . . alive with metaphors and figures" (xxvi). The force of Wordsworth's poetry, said S. T. Coleridge in a retrospect of twenty years, was to awaken "attention from the lethargy of custom" and

direct it "to the loveliness and the wonders of the world before us," otherwise lost in a film of familiarity (*BL* 2: 7, ch. 14).

42. Between *Rights of Woman* and W. Q.'s letter fell Wollstonecraft's mad affair with Imlay, which Godwin aired along with her private letters to him. The unreined passions of her imagination (she tells Imlay) have sapped the vitality of "sentiment, arising from the same delicacy of perception (or taste) as renders [the mind] alive to the beauties of nature, poetry, &c" (3 July 1795; *CL* 309–10). In her last letter to him she laments his vulnerability to sexual "sensations" (March 1796; *CL* 339).

43. Her brother John Aikin also wrote for Joseph Johnson's *Analytical Review*, and later in the 1790s he edited the liberal *Monthly Magazine*.

44. Literary "pleasure" is "a fresh support to virtue" by making "*visible* the wisdom of the Supreme Being," Wollstonecraft argued in 1788 (*AR* II: 439). Thus she praises Barbauld in other reviews, *AR* I (1788), III (1789), XII (1792) and in *The Female Reader* (Preface ix), which includes Barbauld's prose, as well as three of her poems: "The Mouse's Petition," "An Address to the Deity," and "On a Lady's Writing"—this last, a trio of neoclassical couplets about "writing" as character: "And the same graces o'er her pen preside, / That form her manners and her footsteps guide."

45. Wollstonecraft's distress reflects Barbauld's own division between social desire and social possibility. In *The Female Speaker* (1811) Barbauld presents the first view of Adam and Eve (4.288–311, p. 234, including "For contemplation hee . . . ," etc.). Like More, Barbauld means to mentor young women for "the happiest destination": the fulfillment of "domestic cares and duties" (Preface iv). Toward this destination, she selects her Shakespeare: Portia's wifely concern for Brutus's sleepless torments; Imogen's loving fidelity; Rosalind (as Ganymede) tutoring Orlando in true love; Cordelia's enduring love for her mad, deposed, deranged father Lear (also Ferdinand's faithful service to Miranda).

Chapter Three: The Poets' "Wollstonecraft"

1. See, e.g., the smug pseudoscience of Ferdinand Lundberg and Marynia Farnham, *The Modern Woman: The Lost Sex* (New York: Harper & Row, 1947) 144–45 and 159–63, excerpted in Carol Poston's groundbreaking edition of *A Vindication of the Rights of Woman* 273–76.

2. This is from a review of Claire Tomalin's *Mary Wollstonecraft*, 6 September 1974. Levine's cartoon (*New York Review of Books* 19/7; rpt. Poston 222) was commissioned to complement V. S. Pritchard's condescending review of Eleanor Flexner's biography of Wollstonecraft. Despite a few stabs at understanding, Pritchard calls Wollstonecraft "sad," "domineering," "unstable," "angry," "frail,"

with "ruthless highmindedness," "bossy," "reckless," "unscrupulous," "egotistical," and "really self-absorbed."

3. For the manuscript circulation, see Caroline Franklin, *Mary Wollstonecraft* 107; the poem was first published in the 1825 *Works* (1: 195–97). To Edgeworth, the "champion for the rights of women" advanced only a "vain contention for superiority" (*Letters for Literary Ladies* 45–46), on track to Lundberg and Farnham, who see in "the ideology of feminism" only a desire "to turn on men and injure them . . . to deprive the male of his power, to castrate him" (in Poston ed., 274–75).

4. Anne Mellor sees Barbauld tacking between social justice (Wollstonecraft) and separate spheres (More) by urging women to wield their traditional capital ("angel pureness," etc.) to influence "moral development, mutual sexual appreciation, tolerance, and love"—to "take seriously their ethical responsibilities and emotional capacities to exercise an ethic of care to prevent conflict and violence at home and abroad" (in Claudia Johnson, ed., "Mary Wollstonecraft's *A Vindication*" 153–54). For more on the tricky tone of Barbauld's protest, see editors McCarthy and Kraft, in Barbauld, *Selected Poetry* 130.

5. I'm indebted to Franklin's *Mary Wollstonecraft* for alerting me to this poem (83). I supply line numbers, in addition to Colls's page-numbers.

6. Claudia Johnson reads *unsex'd* as antithetical to "the sex"—i.e., *oversexed, ungovernable* (*Equivocal* 9)—and surveys Wollstonecraft figures in late eighteenth and early nineteenth century novels (195).

7. For a sharp, informed account of the gothic labyrinth as a master-trope in reactionary polemics, see Fred Botting, *Gothic* 80–90.

8. Mathias, *Shade* 47–48. The nearly full-page footnotes parade across pp. 44 to 53.

9. Editors Pamela Clemit and Gina Walker identify "C. K." as C. Kirkpatrick Sharpe (192).

10. For this reception, involving Wollstonecraft's home-court, the *Analytical Review* (vol. 8; 1790), the conservative *Critical Review* (vol. 70; 1790), the *English Review* (vol. 17; 1791), and the *Gentleman's Magazine* (vol. 16/1; 1791), see my *Borderlines* 11–12, and Macdonald and Scherf, eds. 10–11, 417–29.

11. W. Clark Durant's edition of Godwin's *Memoirs* (1927) gives the final 1837 text (xxx–xxxi). Lynda Pratt's edition has the 1797 text and the variants across 1808, 1815, 1823, 1837 (5: 36).

12. Southey published his poem before he met Wollstonecraft (sometime before February 1797): "of all the literary characters the one I most admire," he wrote to his brother Thomas after meeting her; "she is a first rate woman—sensible of her own worth, but altogether without arrogance or affectation" (28 April 1797; Letter #213, in Pratt, ed., *Collected Letters, Part One*).

13. Wollstonecraft's reputation was a long way from rehabilitation; even William Thompson felt, in the introduction to *Appeal*, that he had to indicate some unspecified "narrow views" (vii).

14. Coleridge quotes Edward Gibbon's *The History of the Decline and Fall of the Roman Empire* (6. vols., 1776–1788, 1: 233) [*The Watchman*, ed. Patton, 90 n. 3]).

15. For the internal quotation, Lloyd cites Godwin's last editorial note to *Wrongs* (*Post. W* 2: 166), reprising a sentence in Wollstonecraft's Preface (*Post. W*, vol. 1). *Wrongs of Woman* was published in the first two volumes of *Posthumous Works*. Godwin's "Conclusion by the Editor" is in vol. 2 (158–67). The quotation used by Lloyd can be found on 2: 166. Wollstonecraft's Preface to *Wrongs* appears across five unnumbered pages at the front of *Posthumous Works*, vol. 1. The sentence to which I refer is on the second of these unnumbered pages.

16. Cp. *CL*, 5 August 1795, 316.

17. The voice of Mary, "O why was I born with a different Face" (*Mary* 21), gave Emily Sunstein her main title for *A Different Face: The Life of Mary Wollstonecraft* (1975).

18. In the first edition only; this phrasing was removed in the second edition.

Chapter Four: Lyrical Ballads *and the Pregnant Words of Men's Passions*

1. 18 March 1818; *Nb* 3: 4397. Cp. Lecture 13, *Lectures* 2: 218.

2. Thus Derek Attridge, at the end of a long footnote to "The Project of Wordsworth's Preface" (50 n. 5), explains why he follows Wordsworth and Western discourse in referring to "Nature" as feminine and "the poet" as masculine. His postscript, "much could be said about the role of gender in the determination of an appropriate poetic language," is the logic of my chapter.

3. Steele, *The Tatler* 181 (June 6, 1710) 3: 352—the sole instance of *unmanly* in volume 3.

4. To call common people "real men," Laura Mandell notes, had force in a culture that was "in the process of feminizing the lower classes" (56). Francis Jeffrey's review of the 1800 *Lyrical Ballads* blandly objected that the emotion of "an enlightened and refined character, is not only expressed in a different language, but is in itself a different emotion from the love, or grief, or anger of a clown, a tradesman, or a market-wench"; *Edinburgh Review* 1 (1802), 66.

5. Quotations of the *Preface* will be to 1800 (I: v–xlvi), unless otherwise indicated.

6. Mellor, "Teaching" 145 (cp. Margaret Homans, *Women Writers* 18–28 *et passim*); Ross, "Romantic Quest" 28, 38, 49, and "Naturalizing Gender" 392; Richardson 21–22. James Heffernan (232) notes that even in the sympathy of many of

the *Lyrical Ballads* with women's plights, none "endorses or envisions a levelling of genders," let alone approaches Mary Hays's *Appeal to the Men of Great Britain in Behalf of Women* (1798), which indicts the "passions and prejudices" of men for the social and political degradation of "the whole [female] sex" (31–32).

7. Her first pages set her "war . . . for the *rights of men*" against the "impassioned" lady-pleasing flourishes of Burke's rhetoric (1–6), and *Rights of Woman* opens in "masculine" contempt for such (and all) "delicacy of sentiment," "pretty feminine phrases," and "exquisite sensibility" (6–7).

8. I'm grateful for Karen Swann's brilliant attention to Wordsworth's anxieties about an effeminized/feminized literary marketplace (though she sees *Lyrical Ballads* redounding "to the advantage of a masculine, Romantic poetic identity"; "Martha's Name" 61); to Adela Pinch's adroit *Strange Fits of Passion;* to Alan Bewell's fine study of Wordsworth and hysteria; and to Frances Ferguson's subtle attention to poetic figure in various male and female formations.

9. For the issue of gender in both these works, see Barker-Benfield 139–48.

10. Part I, Section I, Chapter I, "Of Sympathy." In the politics of the 1790s, "sensibility" was routinely claimed as an ethical principle for political allegiance, whether to a royal family, or its suffering subjects. See Claudia Johnson, *Equivocal Beings* xxii; and Esther Schor, *Bearing the Dead.*

11. It arrived in their household in April 1798 (Pinion 31), probably with Godwin's greeting.

12. Ch. XV; 2: 101–42.

13. From his 1817 volume Coleridge quotes lines 47–59, which I abridge a bit.

14. MSV 11^r (Parrish, ed. 271; cf. Reading Text 1.451–53).

15. Hazlitt, "Coleridge," *Spirit of the Age* 66.

16. Milton's sonnets were admired, but secondary to *Paradise Lost.* Shakespeare's were neglected, or worse—famously, for Wordsworth's generation, by George Steevens's Advertisement to his and Dr. Johnson's *Plays of William Shakspeare* (1793): "We have not reprinted the Sonnets . . . because the strongest act of Parliament that could be framed would fail to compel readers into their service" (vii). Coleridge cited both Charlotte Smith and Bowles as models for his composition of sonnets ("Introduction to the Sonnets," *Poems* 1797, p. 71).

17. Following his brief for Bürger, William Taylor put a paper in the July 1796 *Monthly Magazine* describing poets (versus versifiers) "as men inspired by the power of imagination and pouring forth the strong language of fancy and feeling": "in the rude state of nature, before the art of versification was known, men felt strong passions, and expressed them strongly. Their language would be bold and figurative; it would be vehement and abrupt" (2: 454).

18. Editors Owen and Smyser propose the influence on Wordsworth's prefaces (*PrW* 1: 114).

19. For a sample census, see Butler and Green, eds. 383.

20. The fear "remains disturbingly present, unexorcised by . . . self-disparagement" (Glen 48).

21. Barbara Johnson's canny deconstruction notes the punning collation of the project described in the Preface and the psychic experience named in this ballad (91). But where she sets the poetics of formal containment (metrical fitting) against the passion of the psychic fit, I see Wordsworth identifying poetic form as a force of reproduction.

22. *EY* 238, a letter of 14 or 21 December 1798; this draft begins with the second stanza of 1800.

23. Good and Cooper, 4: 131. A fortuitous link to *Lyrical Ballads* appears on the next page, where the story of "Mr Hackman and Miss Rae" is cited as a case in point (132)—i.e., "Martha Ray," the name in *The Thorn*. Swann ("Martha's Name") gives a great account of Hackman's murder of her (1779) and the circulation of this scandal in British letters (72–76).

24. *On the Principles of Method*, Essay IV, in *The Friend* 1818 (Rooke, ed., 1: 448–49).

25. Where Stephen Parrish reads the poem as an address to Emma (*Art* 208, 212), I read an apostrophe to personified "Love," with "Emma" and "pretty Barbara" as nominal instances.

26. *The Female Vagrant* is his "first history of an individual mind," remarks Paul Sheats (87).

27. Coleridge, *Essays* 3: 290; editor David Erdman is certain that Coleridge wrote this note.

28. DCMS 20 8^v–9^r; editors Butler and Green date Dorothy Wordsworth's copy of "Lines related to *Complaint of a forsaken Indian Woman*" between 14 September 1798 and 22 December 1800, the last entry of this journal-book, after which "Lines" appear (xxiv; for "Lines," see 287–88). Considering the textual situation and Dorothy's domestic distress, I think she transcribed the "Lines" between 14 May and 22 December 1800 (in the Grasmere journal written during the first months of William's courtship): "to die / Is all that now is left for me. / If I could smother up my heart, / My life would then at once depart" (15–18). On my namings in these chapters: resisting the condescending sexism in the differential "Wordsworth" and "Dorothy," I name the domestic figures by forenames and only the public poet "Wordsworth."

29. For Wordsworth's interest in *Zoonomia*, which he borrowed from bookseller Joseph Cottle (*EY* 199, 214–15), see James Averill 153–59, 166–68; for the

refraction of Darwin's reports into humanitarian lessons, see Mary Jacobus, *Tradition* 234–37; Brett and Jones, eds. 283.

30. In a letter of 30 November 1795, detailing household pleasures and comforts at Racedown in Dorset (enabled by a bequest of £900 from Raisley Calvert), Dorothy W. remarks, "The peasants are miserably poor; their cottages are shapeless structures (I may almost say) of wood and clay—indeed they are not at all beyond what might be expected in savage life" (*EY* 162).

31. For the involution of hysteria and witchcraft in Western social history, see Ilza Veith's chapter 4, and Marc Micale, "Hysteria and Historiography" 234–37. Veith's is the foundational study of hysteria. Alan Bewell argues that "historically, hysteria played a major role in the demystification of witchcraft," by allowing demonic possession to be understood as one of its symptoms (364). It also gave Wordsworth the grammar for his consideration of how language and mind interact (360)—set, in quarantined extremes, as female spectacle for a male poet.

32. See Pinch's *Strange Fits* for a great discussion of this dynamic of infection.

33. I'm quoting Patrocinio Schweickart (41), who draws, in turn, on Lévi-Strauss's discussion, in *Elementary Structures of Kinship*, of women as objects of exchange in male social systems.

34. For the anxiety among men of letters about the feminized, mass market appeal of erotic gothic romance, including *Christabel*, see Swann's incisive "Wandering Mother"; in a companion essay, "The Debate on the Character of *Christabel*," she shows how the language of the reviews repeats the poem's "tactical gendering" (545).

35. Thomas Allsop, ed. (1836) 2: 228—a remark included in the selections featured in the notice of *Letters &c* in *The Court Journal* (1835), 824. "The instinct to stand guard over its boundaries, to assert its distinctness, Coleridge considered the first indication of a masculine mind, and one supremely obvious in Wordsworth's," said John Jones in his iconically (Keatsian) titled *The Egotistical Sublime* (1954; p. 29).

36. The title page of his treatise identifies him as Physician to his Majesty, President of the Royal Society of Physicians, and Professor of Medicine in the University of Edinburgh.

37. For Lear's hysteria in relation to patriarchy, see Coppélia Kahn.

38. The *Morning Post* (24 December 1799); *Essays*, ed. Erdman, 1: 43–44.

39. Partition 1, subsection 3 (*Terror and Affrights, Causes of Melancholy*) Mem. 2, Subs. 4, *Symptomes of Women's Melancholy* (1: 302–3). Swann reads this passage in relation to *Christabel*, which was intended for *Lyrical Ballads* ("Wandering Mother" 535).

40. For my explication of these poetics, see *The Questioning Presence* 53–60.

41. There is a common root for *hysteros* (the latter) and *hystera* (womb) in the Sanskrit *úttaras,* but the *Greek-English Lexicon* doesn't say why the womb is so called (2: 1905–6). Froma Zeitlin suggested to me that *hystera* may draw on *hysteros* to name the second, or later, sex. John Belton noted to me that one meaning of *hysteron,* "afterbirth," proposes that the "later" delivery may have been thought to be the womb itself (*hystera*); a new one was supposed to grow back; see also Richard Rand (52). Coleridge derides "the fallacy of Hysteron Proteron" (written in Greek letters) in the "preposterous" logic of faith: it's not that evidence produces faith, but that faith produces evidence (*Statesman's Manual* Appendix E, xxxviii). *OED* credits him for coining the verb *hystero-proterize* (ms. note in his copy of Southey's *Life of Wesley*), playing on the standard Puttenham-*Poesie* example, "putting the cart before the horse": "We must explain the force of the horse by the motion of the cart-wheels, and hystero-proterize with a vengeance!"

42. I build on Parrish's brilliant reading of *The Thorn* (taking a cue from the first paragraph of Wordsworth's Note, I: 211) as a case-study of "superstition," in which "Martha Ray" exists only in "the narrator's imagination": in a howling storm, he ran to mountain spot where he saw a gnarled thorn-stump overgrown with lichen and red moss; he later heard a legend (Martha Ray: pregnant, jilted, infanticidal, agonized in remorse) then retrojects it, to "turn the tree into a woman, the brightly-colored moss into her scarlet cloak, and the creaking of the branches into her plaintive cry" (100–105). An analogue to and a radical extension of this deconstruction is Jonathan Culler's explication of "the Nietzschean deconstruction of causality"—one that shifts *The Thorn* from a case of superstition, into *the* case of narrative and discourse; see esp. 86–88.

43. "Placed in intolerable circumstances of stress, and expected to react with unnatural 'courage,'" Showalter argues, thousands of soldiers showed symptoms of hysteria; the language of "shell shock" was valuable for its "power to provide a masculine-sounding substitute for the effeminate associations of 'hysteria' and to disguise the troubling parallels between male war neurosis" and "female nervous disorders" (*Female Malady* 171–72).

44. For this lineage, see Susan Stewart, "Lyric Possession," esp. 41–43.

45. Closing quotation for XIX was added in 1802 (I: 47). Closing quotation to *The Mad Mother* was not added until 1805 (I: 142). Perhaps an accident in both cases, the lapses acquire the look of symptom in the poetics of contagious passion.

46. Southey remarked in one of the first reviews, "he who personates tiresome loquacity becomes tiresome himself" (200).

47. *Literary Remains* 3: 333. *OED* gives Coleridge's usage as the earliest.

48. Editors de Selincourt and Darbishire find the use of the name "strange"

(*PW* 2: 514); Brett and Jones find it "completely inexplicable" (290). Parrish thinks it is just a chance "association" brought to mind by the grandson (105–6). Swann ("Martha's Name") brilliantly explicates Wordsworth's purchase, noting the circulation of the scandal among English men of letters—and beyond that, a literary culture that thrived on tales of infanticidal mothers.

49. *Tradition* 241; Jacobus cites John Langhorne's *The Country Justice* (1774–77), *The Cruel Mother* (in David Herd's 1776 *Ancient and Modern Scottish Songs*), Richard Merry's *Pains of Memory* (1796), Taylor's version of Bürger's *The Lass of Fair Wone* (*Monthly Magazine*, April 1796). In 1800 Wordsworth copied some stanzas of *The Cruel Mother* into a commonplace book: "And there she's lean'd her back to a thorn / Oh! and alas—a day, . . . And there she has her baby born. . . . She has honked a grave ayont the sun . . . And there she has buried the sweet babe in" (DCMS 26; *PW* 2: 513–14). For the links, see W. J. B. Owen, "The Thorn"; for the magazine culture, Robert Mayo.

50. Citing sheer expression, Coleridge won't call Deborah "Poet" or even "a poet": "Nature is the Poet here" (*Lectures* 1: 69); her song is just an "effusion of a woman highly elevated by triumph, by the natural hatred of oppressors"; its language issues from "passion," "victory," and "circumstances" (2: 494; cp. 1: 310). Reading the epoch of Deborah against 1790s England, Swann gives a sharp analysis to Wordsworth's interest in the Song as a work of female power that effects "the consolidation and liberation of a public voice" ("Martha's Name" 79).

51. Geoffrey Hartman is the godfather of all discussion of Wordsworthian "inscribing, naming, and writing" as "types of a commemorative and inherently elegiac act" (223).

52. Wordsworth told his publishers that he wanted the unit "immediately" before *Michael* (18 December 1800; *EY* 307). Although the 1802 and 1805 *Ballads* did not preserve the sequence, the *Naming* unit held, enhanced in the *Poems* of 1815, and placed there just after *Poems founded on the Affections* and just before *Poems of the Fancy*, suggesting affiliation with both.

53. This is the only such internal "Advertisement." In volume I, *The Idiot Boy* and *The Rime of the Ancient Mariner* have title-page distinction; in volume II, *The Brothers, Ruth, The Old Cumberland Beggar*, and *Michael*.

54. To Susan Eilenberg these acts of "literary appropriation" involve no irony, except against a namer's false consciousness. It's all "Adam's prerogative, taking dominion over the earth by means of nomination," in namings that are "bold and unembarrassed, though circumscribed"— in sum, exercises of "social power," an "audacity" of colonizing, imperializing language ("The Poetry of Property," *Strange Power* 60–86). With less of a hard edge, Heather Glen reads ironized acts of "proprietorship" and self-assertion that fail to assimilate the otherness of a "world indifferent to human purposes" and "fundamentally alien" (303–38).

55. Coleridge, the "Friend" in the trio, records the chagrin in a notebook: "Poor fellow at a distance idle? In this haytime when wages are so high? Come near— thin, pale, can scarce speak—or throw out his fishing rod" (*Nb* 1: 761). *Poor* at first designates class (and so a culpable idleness), and then Coleridge's stunned pity.

56. For the variants, see Butler and Green, eds. 249. David Simpson sees the place-naming repeating in a finer tone the presumptive man-naming (*Irony* 72–76). Michael Friedman (191–92) and Glen (310–17) see the named "admonishment" (82) eliding class privilege, while Eilenberg discerns a rupture: "Seeing in the man a reflection of their own idleness exaggerated to blameworthy proportions, the company treats him as something which they are at liberty to condemn" (82), but not without a residue of social and even existential anxiety. My sense of indeterminate ironies respects Wordsworth's acute regard of the material economy of rural labor. When in January 1801 he sent the 1800 *Lyrical Ballads* to Charles James Fox (former Whig leader in Parliament), it was with a letter commenting on the "calamitous effect" of "the encreasing disproportion between the price of labour and that of the necessaries of life" (*EY* 313).

57. For Wordsworth, the lakeside incident was a chapter in autobiography: "the fact occurred strictly as recorded" (FN 19). The first draft of *The Prelude* drives toward the declaration, "O Nature! Thou hast fed / My lofty speculations, and in thee / For this uneasy heart of ours I find / A never-failing principle of joy" (*RV* 11ᵛ–12ʳ; Parrish, ed. 210–12; cf. Reading Text 2.492–95).

58. DCMS 25 (83ᵛ); Butler and Green, eds. 243.

59. Wordsworth's sister-in-law to be, Joanna Hutchinson did not spend her "early youth" in "cities" and was not as "distant" from the family as this opening paragraph relates (1–17).

60. Sonia Hofkosh (109) alerted me to this fragment on "Ravishment."

61. The contemporaneous comment appears in DCMS 33; see Butler and Green, eds. 398.

62. *BL* 2: 104. Coleridge quotes *To Joanna* 51–65 and in a footnote collates Drayton's lines (155–64; using *The Works of the British Poets*, ed. Robert Anderson, 13 vols., 1792–95; 3: 538):

> Which COPLAND scarce had spoke, but quickly every hill
> Upon her verge that stands, the neighbouring vallies fill;
> HELVILLON from his height, it through the mountains threw.
> From whom as soon again, the sound DUNBALRASE drew,
> From whose stone-trophied head, it on the WENDROSS went,
> Which, tow'rds the sea again, resounded it to DENT.
> That BROADWATER, therewith within her banks astound,
> In sailing to the sea told it to EGREMOUND,

Whose buildings, walks and streets, with echoes loud and long
Did mightily commend old COPLAND for her song!

63. That is, Dr. William Dodd. For this episode as Coleridge's imitation of Joanna in a "subversion of the sublime," see Reeve Parker, "Finishing off 'Michael'" 64.

Chapter 5. William's Sister

1. "William Wordsworth" 339; cp. de Selincourt, *Dorothy Wordsworth* 1. De Quincey implicates himself, less severely: "can a man forget . . . his intellectual superiority? I could not perhaps have loved, with perfect love, any woman whom I have felt to be my own equal intellectually; but then I never thought of her in that light, or under that relation" (341). All references in this chapter to De Quincey's remarks on the Wordsworths are from this essay, in *Literary Reminiscences*.

2. Keats's canny term for this "poetical Character"; letter to Richard Woodhouse, 27 October 1818 (*John Keats* 214).

3. For Romantic tropes of female as "alter-ego of the male poet," see the groundwork of Irene Taylor and Gina Luria (120); Wordsworth epitomizes how "the muses of Romantic poetry" crystallize in the "sister image or mirror image of the poet," his "imaginative extension of himself" (115). See also Alan Richardson, on the poet's appropriation of female feeling ("Romanticism and the Colonization of the Feminine"); Marlon Ross on William Wordsworth as bearer of the tradition that "reasserts and solidifies the priority of male needs and desires" by exploiting "the socio-historical experience of woman's subordinate position," transforming it "into a natural and essential place (a transcendent idea)" to be "objectified" and "contained" by male desire ("Naturalizing" 391); cp. *Contours* 4–5.

4. Secretarial work was also needlework: "still at work at the Pedlar, altering & refitting. . . . William left me at work altering some passages of the Pedlar"; "I worked hard, got the backs pasted the writing finished, & all quite trim"; "worked a little at Wm's waistcoat"; "I stitched up the Pedlar" (13, 14, 23 February, 7 March 1802; *GJ* 67–68, 71, 75).

5. For John Barrell this oscillation expresses conflict between a female "subject who (it is imagined) remains undifferentiated from nature" and a male speaking subject "imagined to have achieved an identity fully differentiated from it" (141); "Dorothy" is figured simultaneously to "recapitulate and historicise the transition Wordsworth has already made," and to remain an unaltered "present . . . guarantee" of "the language of the sense" ("The Uses of Dorothy" 162).

6. The 1834 text of *Selections from the Poems of William Wordsworth, Esq. chiefly for the Use of Schools and Young Persons* (ed. Joseph Hine, first published 1831) adds compatible capitals in line 71 ("Wherever Nature led") and line 90

("For I have learned / To look on Nature . . ."); see Butler and Green 373. Words-worth cared enough about the signifying to fret, "What is the reason that our modern Compositors are so unwilling to employ Capital Letters?" (*LY* 4: 644).

7. With debts to David Ferry and Richard Onorato, I explicate this dynamic of negative assertion in *The Questioning Presence* 60–70.

8. This is the first line of *The Mad Mother* (p. 141 in 1798, and then more proximate to *Lines* in 1800 (1: 145), separated from it only by *The Rime of the Ancient Mariner*. Marjorie Levinson remarks that the epithet *wild* locates the Sister on "the boundary of the familiar" gesturing to "the unimaginable relations outside it" (*Wordsworth's Great Period Poems* 49).

9. Ferry's gendering indulges italicized generalization: "*All* men are like this in their relation to nonhuman nature, since *even* this innocent young child is a lib-ertine and destroyer . . . the boy's behavior was inevitable. It was the behavior of mankind" (25). Bloom softens the judgment: the nutter is "only a boy," of "almost radical" innocence; the poet's "displacement of responsibility" onto a "gentle Maiden" is a "touching" gesture (*Visionary* 129–30). Ross gives sharp attention to the gender-generosities of the exculpatory readings, "Naturalizing" 393–94.

10. Mellor, "Teaching"; Homans, *Women Writers* 54; cp. Ross, "Naturalizing" 393–95. *Tintern Abbey* and *Nutting* are often read as pendants. As Homans puts the case, a sister or sororal maiden is brought out "to receive the brother's wishes, to confirm for him his hope that what he has gained in the course of the poem will find a habitation in [her] consciousness" (*Bearing* 120).

11. Cooke 140–41; see also Rachel Crawford: the hazels are "clearly virile," "upright yet virginal" (as if a contradiction) (202, 204); and Gregory Jones: "The tumescent hazels and their tempting nuts are almost comical in their obscene maleness" (225). (Jones's condescension to other critics entails conspicuously under-researched claims about the critical literature; and I was sorry to see that Crawford got dates and a lot of transcription details wrong).

12. Crawford cites a religious tradition of virginity as "a trope for a power and independence (from the cycles of reproduction) that is more accurately mascu-line than feminine," and notes, with credit to Marina Warner's work on the cult of Virgin Mary, that Saint Jerome was willing to say that a vestal virgin "will cease to be a woman, and will be called a man" (208 and n. 16).

13. Referring to Spenser's knights, Milton refuses praise to any "virtue, unex-ercised and unbreathed, that never sallies out and sees her adversary" (*Areo-pagitica* 728).

14. For variants and manuscript history, see Butler and Green.

15. The signature phrase is from the 1802 Preface (1: xxviii). Ferry has a fine ear for this manly information, "practiced and knowledgeable in the 'wise re-straint' that enhances pleasures, 'voluptuous' and expert in it": the scene reflects

"the habitual luxuriousness of all his tastes. He held back from taking his pleasure, not from any sense of decency or qualms of conscience or respect for the virtue of the glade, but entirely to make his later pleasure more delightful" (23).

16. Whether the pained boy is father to the moral man, or the moral man in retrospect fathers a pained boy, posed a serious crux: the poet of MS 15 and the draft in the letter to Coleridge hesitates at confounding not just "present feelings" with past feelings, but also his "present being with the past" (*EY* 242; MS15 66^r: 89; Butler and Green 554–55).

17. From his initial stylizing as a "Figure quaint," Frances Ferguson comments, the boy enters the bower "not as a creature of nature but as an artful character stepping from the pages of romance narrative, so that a dichotomy between art and nature tonally prefigures the account of the boy's violation of nature" (72–73). The poet's loaded prefiguration may be compared to Mary Russell Mitford's "Nutting," a sketch in her popular collection, *Our Village*, which invites the reader along on a day of "sally[ing] forth" for hazel-nutting, a gleeful "sport," with exuberant pleasure, for adults and children of both sexes, in the "plunder," and no moralizing at all.

18. B&G 218–19nn, and 304 for MSS 15, 16, 24; letter to Coleridge, December 1798 (*EY* 241).

19. The "flat conventionality" is at odds with the vibrant recollection, remarks Heather Glen: the guilt-based morality fails to "engage the self's deepest energies" (275). To David Perkins, the coda is a "mistake" (184). Bloom proposes a knowing displacement, the poet "adjuring a gentle Maiden" to "restore the spirit he has driven away" (*Visionary* 130). Others describe a dramatic design, with varying degrees of irony against the poet-speaker. The final lines, "quite inadequate, in tone and feeling, to the rest of the poem," Ferry argues, reflect a speaker who seems "to have missed the point or to have got only part of it, and so to have oversimplified" (24–25). Parrish designates *Nutting* "a dramatic poem," a "contest that rages within the poet's sensibilities" (*Art* 29), and Levinson follows suit: "a dramatically located and rhetorically controlled utterance upon which we eavesdrop—a dramatic monologue scenario" (*Romantic Fragment Poem* 65).

20. See Stephen Greenblatt, *Renaissance Self-Fashioning* 157–92.

21. December 1798, *EY* 238; 241–42; in his edition Parrish notes that the text in *EY* scrambles the sequence of the letter-ms., putting Dorothy's remark (p. 240) away from the verse it introduces (*Prelude 1798–1799*, 131). On the fragment poetics that coordinate the published coda and the initial dash, see Levinson, *Romantic Fragment Poem* 62–63.

22. B&G 544–47. My transcription, tracking the probable order of composition, omits a few minor cancellations and overwritings, and also varies slightly

from their reading text (302) and transcription. I've mostly elided repeated phrases.

23. B&G 305 n. Douglass Thomson treats the quotations from *As You Like It* (289–91), but not the social discipline of female "gentleness," nor the contradiction posed by the logic of Orlando's plea to the argument advanced in the Preface to *Lyrical Ballads:* "low and rustic life," far more than urbane inland breeding, nurtures human compassion and sympathy.

24. Commenting on the Duke's lesson in "gentleness," Greenblatt notes not only the instructor's authority as "the pinnacle of the play's social order," but also the engagement of the entire world of the play "in articulating cultural codes of behavior" ("Culture" 228).

25. On the coordination with orthodoxies on female education, see Ross, "Naturalizing" 392–400, and Mary Jacobus's supplement in *Romanticism, Writing* 250–51.

26. William's letter to Dorothy, appropriately, survives only in her transcription for her closest female friend, Jane Pollard, to whom she has just said, in another letter, "I am very sure that Love will never bind me closer to any human Being than Friendship binds me to you my earliest female Friend, and to William my earliest and my dearest Male Friend" (16 June 1793; *EY* 96).

27. *GJ* 1802: 20–21 February (70–71); 6–7 March (75); 4 May (94).

28. Parrish, ed. 232–33; cp. Reading Text, 1799 *Prelude,* First Part: 57–66.

29. For Wordsworth's association of Fancy with feminine and "inferior" capacities, see Julie Ellison's essay. Fancy is "mother Fancy" in a sonnet in the 1807 *Poems, in Two Volumes.*

30. Fadem, "Dorothy Wordsworth" 17, 24, 26, 28.

31. Kathleen Jones (30). Jones also notes the contrary effect of another gift, the Wollstonecraft-reviled Dr. Gregory's *A Father's Legacy to His Daughters.*

32. I quote Fadem 17. For the debts to her journals, see the foundational essays by Frederick Pottle, William Heath, Rachael Brownstein, and especially Thomas Frosch on William's writer's block. Assessments vary. Heath regards the sister-marked poetry as inferior to that issuing from the poet's solitary broodings (120–21), while Donald Reiman counts the 1802 poems that derive "imaginative force" from his association with her as among his best ("Poetry" 194, 200).

33. The length and detail of this record (*GJ* 9–10), as well as its atypically delayed entry (she met the beggars on 27 May), suggest to Frosch that William was taken by Dorothy's anecdote and asked her to write up a "useful" account (622). Frosh reads no anxious influence, however: he sees William acknowledging external influence by honoring "nature"—even though Frosch recognizes, without theorizing, his "writing from Dorothy's viewpoint" and in her place (629).

34. *Sequel to the Foregoing: composed many years after* 11, 24 (first published in *The Poetical Works of William Wordsworth*, London 1827).

35. Dictated in the early 1840s, Isabella Fenwick's notes entered the reception history in the 1850s. Most were first published in Christopher Wordsworth's *Memoirs* (2. vols.; London: Edward Moxon, 1850), then as notes in the 7-vol. edition of Wordsworth (London: Edward Moxon, 1857), then entire in vol. 3 of Alexander Grosart's arrangement in his 3-vol. edition of Wordsworth's prose (London: Edward Moxon 1876).

36. This is the fourth in "Sonnets Dedicated to Liberty" in 1807 *Poems*. For the subtitle date, see Curtis, ed., *Poems in Two Volumes* 157. Four decades on, William gives credit: "In the cottage of Town-End, one afternoon, in 1801, my Sister read to me the Sonnets of Milton." But the pattern of predating suggests an end-run around her agency: "I had long been well acquainted with them, but I was particularly struck on that occasion with the dignified simplicity and majestic harmony that runs through most of them. . . . I took fire, if I may be allowed to say so, and produced three sonnets the same afternoon, the first I ever wrote, except an irregular one at School. Of these three the only one I distinctly remember is '*I grieved for Buonaparte* &c'" (FN 19).

37. For William's subscription to *Elegiac Sonnets*, see Bishop C. Hunt Jr. 90.

38. Dorothy records the morning on Westminster Bridge: "Saturday morning at ½ past 5 or 6, the 31st of July [1802] . . . It was a beautiful morning. The City, St pauls, with the River & a multitude of little Boats, made a most beautiful sight as we crossed Westminster Bridge. The houses were not overhung by their cloud of smoke & they were spread out endlessly, yet the sun shone so brightly with such a pure light that there was even something like the purity of one of nature's own grand Spectacles." Of Calais: "We walked by the sea-shore almost every evening with Annette & Caroline or Wm & I alone . . . seeing far off in the west the Coast of England . . . the Evening star & the glory of the sky. . . . Now came in view as the Evening star sank down & the colours of the west faded away the two lights of England, lighted up by the Englishmen in our Country, to warn vessels of rocks or sands"—the sight prompting William's *Fair Star of Evening*. And, finally, of the occasion of "It is a beauteous Evening": "the day had been very hot, & William & I walked alone together [i.e., *sans Annette*] upon the pier— the sea was gloomy. . . . Near us the waves roared & broke . . . on the calm hot night. . . . Caroline was delighted" (*GJ* 123–25).

39. For the sonnets of August 1802 informed by William's "thoughts on marriage, paternity, and England," see Judith Page. The poet's imagining that his girl lies "in Abraham's bosom all the year" poses "a substitute father for the father Wordsworth knows he will never be" (198). That "Abraham's bosom" is the place

of rest after death projects a radical transfer of paternal care from the world in which he has any responsibility (200).

40. My slightly tidier rendition of the image and transcription in B&G 500–501; cp. 276–77.

41. "Composed on the road between Nether Stowey & Alfoxden, extempore," Wm recalled; "I distinctly recollect the very moment when I was struck, as described 'He looks up at the clouds &c'" (FN 13). De Selincourt thus decides that Dorothy's journal is "indebted" to William's "'extempore' poem" (*PW* 2: 503), but I agree with Beth Darlington that paraphrase is "most improbable": "She does so nowhere else in her journals or letters, and it was . . . very largely for his sake that she kept records at all"; the likely explanation, as with the daffodils and Leech Gatherer, is that he referred to her description (426). See also James Averill 93. Jack Stillinger's edition notes only that Dorothy "provides a similar description" (500); but in *Multiple Authorship* he designates her "one of the most interesting and important cases of source becoming part author": "she gave him recollections, words, phrases, and images as well" (72).

42. For Heath the "finest" and "most significant" poetry is independent of Dorothy and "far beyond" her range in its "subjects, mood, and comprehensiveness of vision" (121).

43. The tribute to Mary Wordsworth is in DCMS 153, p. 26, noted in FN xiv and xx. John Jones notes that in his two iconic poems of solitude—*Resolution and Independence* and *I wandered lonely as a cloud*—Wordsworth "conceals the truth, in defiance of his own principle of fidelity to fact, that he was not alone" (31–32); both poems are cited by Stillinger in *Multiple Authorship* (72).

Chapter Six: Dorothy's Conversation with William

1. Woolf (1932) 202, admiring how Dorothy Wordsworth, "taking only the simplest facts, so orders them that the whole scene comes before us, heightened and composed." The journals have been admired for vivid description, social animation and sympathy, a chronicle of Lakeland life, and a mode of female autobiography; see, variously, Elizabeth Hardwick, John Nabholz, Rachel Brownstein, Robert Con Davis, Margaret Homans, Kurt Heinzelman, Pamela Woof.

2. DCMS 122, Record ID (p. 1). This record also shows some rather obscure Brothers of the Lyre, certainly less noteworthy in the day than, say, Hemans and Sigourney: William Hamilton, Robert Pearce Gillies, James Hamilton, Henry Laid, Revd. Charles Townsend, William Whewell, William Rowan Hamilton, as well as other men who are relatives, or not known best for poetry.

3. Wordsworth's remarks on presenting his sister's poems appear near the

end of the Preface to *Poems* 1815 (xli). Lamb's comment is in a letter to him, 16 April 1815 (3: 141).

4. So Mary Wordsworth reports to Dora and William in 1837 (*Letters* 181).

5. For the title variants, see *CP* 185. For the first gloss, see Homans, *Women Writers* 42. The key generic affiliation is the "Irregular Ode," no disclaimer but a claim to inspiration inapt to regular form. Like titles are applied by female and aspiring poets in the eighteenth century and early decades of the nineteenth: John Smith, *The Precaution, In Irregular Stanzas* (1713); Lady Anna Riggs Miller, *Novelty: An Irregular Essay* in comic verse (1778); Samuel Jackson Pratt, several poems, serious to comic, named *Irregular Verse* (1785); Anne Batten Cristall, *Thelmon and Carmel: An Irregular Poem* (1795); Mrs. Rowson, *The Birth of Genius, An Irregular Poem* (1804); Helen Maria Williams, *Part of an Irregular Fragment* (1823), Charles Dibdin, *The Wreath of Love; an Allegory, in Four Cantos of Irregular Verse* (1825); Henry Kirke White, *The Eve of Death, Irregular* (1830); Henrietta Prescott, *A Poem in Irregular Verse* (1839), and Dorothy again, in *Irregular Stanzas / Holiday at Gwerndovennant*, (1826), and *Loving and Liking: Irregular Verses, Addressed to a Child* (c. 1832). Even so, the term carries an inflection of excuse: "Let us hear what vagaries fancy has been playing in your mind," M. St. Aubert encourages his daughter in Radcliffe's *Udolpho*—to which young Emily replies of her poem, "the lines go in sort of a tripping measure, which I thought might suit the subject well enough, but I fear they are too irregular" (ch. 1; 1:42–43).

6. To amend the force of these mothers of the mind, Dorothy is a generous mother to young Julia's poetic efforts (see *LY* 2: 332, 349, 424).

7. Fadem 78. De Selincourt set the terms in *Dorothy Wordsworth* 388, echoed by Fadem, Hardwick, Brownstein, and early Woof. Fadem proffers the chivalry that by "inflating Dorothy's stature" as a writer, "we in fact do her a disservice" (17). Hardwick deems the poems "not good" by standards of meter, "formal constructions," and "generalizing power" (94; cp. Brownstein 51)—as if these standards were absolute. Woof endorses Dorothy's "correct" sense of her deficiencies (101). Only Levin notes relative standards (61), commenting that Dorothy's "jumbled" modes anticipate the celebrated experimentalism of some later male writers (98). As recently as 1985, the Modern Language Association's massive *English Romantic Poets: A Review of Research and Criticism* could manage no entry on Dorothy Wordsworth's poetry (nor on any female poet, for that matter).

8. For an anatomy of this disablement, see Homans on the "masculine tradition" that "depends on and reinforces the masculine orientation of language and of the poet" and entails "woman's association with nature and her exclusion from a traditional identification of the speaking subject as male" (*Women Writers* 12, *et passim* on the Wordsworths); Ross, *Contours* 3–6; and Woof: "Dorothy pro-

gressively absorbed rather than challenged Wordsworth's critical stance" (97). For Dorothy Wordsworth's oppositional mode, see Levin on her "suspension of male romanticism as well as the suspension of its literary forms" (8); Homans's next study sees in the journals a refusal of William's "apocalyptic tendencies" in favor of "the literal meaning inherent in appearances over symbolism that requires absent signification" (*Bearing the Word* 59); Mellor's chapter on Dorothy Wordsworth, in *Romanticism and Gender,* focuses on her devotion to physical over metaphysical life.

9. Likely composed late 1820s (*CP* 188). With the title *Floating Island,* Wordsworth placed it in the Miscellaneous Poems of *Poems, Chiefly of Early and Late Years* (1842) 231–32, signed here (as if to please Lamb, too late) D. W., identified in a headnote as "Author of the Address to Wind, & c."

10. This phenomenon was known in the Lakes; see William Wordsworth, "A Guide through the District of the Lakes" (*PrW* 2: 184).

11. *Recollections of a Tour Made in Scotland* (1803), de Selincourt ed. 1: 286.

12. The text in her commonplace book (1826–32), *A Winter's Ramble in Grasmere's Vale,* is a light revision of the last ten stanzas of *Grasmere—A Fragment,* a twenty-two-stanza poem written ca. 1805. Knight cites an 1805 ms. (8: 259), Catherine Clarkson's copy of this and four more poems Dorothy wrote out in her *Recollections of . . . Scotland,* three from this early decade. I derive the *Ramble* stanzas from the commonplace book variants of *Grasmere* in *CP* 169–70.

13. This remarkable adjective is quite rare in prior English poetry, used only by Blair, in *The Grave,* to gloat over death claiming the "long-demurring *Maid*" of "lonely unappropriated Sweets" (p. 28; 521–22). The usual instances of *unappropriated* in eighteenth-century writing are in description of a material or monetary resource unused, waiting for appropriation. The poets are in tune.

14. John Jones observes that while *Home at Grasmere* figures a "scene of solitude-in-relationship sustained through sympathy," the idealism is "restrictedly Paradisal, seeking Grasmere too exclusively for retreat and shelter" (133–34). William never published this poem.

15. *Elegiac Sonnets & c,* 1797, 2: 50; republished in *The Annual Register for 1797,* p. 199.

16. For the senses of *estrangement* and *alienation* in William's lexicon of *inmate,* see NED (1901): "not originally or properly belonging to the place where he dwells; a foreigner, stranger" (5: 307).

17. Dated "1806" in 1815 *Poems,* my text here; it is in "Poems Referring to the Period of Childhood" credited: *By a female Friend of the Author.* For Lamb, see *Letters* 3: 141.

18. I use the version that the Clarksons read (in Levin's Longman edition), both for intrinsic interest and its availability. Hilary Clark's edition, based on de

Selincourt's transcription of the copy dedicated or inscribed to Joanna Hutchinson, is cited for text specific to it, by chapter and page. Dorothy's correspondents across March, April, and May begin with William (and implicitly De Quincey, with whom he was staying), then Catherine Clarkson, Lady Beaumont, and Jane (Pollard) Marshall. William in turn wrote to MP Richard Sharp, Rev. Francis Wrangham, Basil Montagu, Lady Holland, Coleridge, Scott, and Samuel Rogers. See *MY* 1: 200–250.

19. William's letter, 13 April 1808; *MY* 1: 210–11. Boswell quotes Dr. Johnson on this mode at the outset of *Life of Johnson* (1: 5); Dorothy read it in 1800 (*GJ* 19). Austen gives an echo in Mr. Knightley's satiric remarks to Emma (1815): "Your friend Harriet will make a much longer history when you see her.—She will give you all the minute particulars, which only a woman's language can make interesting.—In our large communications we deal only in the great" (326). In 1842 M. A. Stodart consolidated the mode for "Female Writers": women's "mental faculties" consist in "closeness of observation and the power of entering into minute details" (21).

20. The lengthy explanation of concern for the young orphans and of aversion to putting herself forward is in a letter to Catherine Clarkson, 9 December 1810 (*MY* 1: 453–54). The *Narrative* had considerable circulation however; De Quincey had the impression that it was read by the royal family ("Recollections of Grasmere," 1839; *Reminiscences* 2: 61). Jane Austen's retreat from notice as "author" may have similar lines of reticence. Though she was pleased by "the applause which from time to time reached her ears from those who were competent to discriminate" (reports her brother Henry in a carefully crafted posthumous "Biographical Notice"), "so much did she shrink from notoriety, that no accumulation of fame would have induced her, had she lived, to affix her name to any productions of her pen. In the bosom of her own family she talked of them freely. . . . But in public she turned away from any allusion to the character of an authoress" (1: 6).

21. To Lady Beaumont, Dorothy describes Jane as "she who filled the Mother's place in the house" (20 April 1808; *MY* 1: 224). De Quincey cuts Sarah some slack in social sympathy, but blames the mist-chaos on her ("Recollections" 85–86), and waxes rhapsodic on Jane's "fortitude," "lodged in so frail a tenement as the person of a little girl, not much, if anything, above nine years old," facing "sudden mysterious abandonment—of uncertain peril" and rising to "the perfect energies of womanhood" (62).

22. Levin remarks that although the Norths had been resident at Rydal Mount since 1803, Dorothy still regards her as a newcomer (Longman edition, 133 n.).

23. Wordsworth even thought *heart* not the right register, and at MS D: 362 (52ᵛ) penciled in *soul* (Butler ed. 311), the reading he kept for *Excursion, Book I*

(1814) 812. De Quincey satirizes the material narrative, impatient that the Wanderer could not part with a guinea to help Margaret out, or undertake some practical measures to find the fugitive husband; "On Wordsworth's Poetry," *Tait's Edinburgh Magazine*, September 1845, p. 548.

24. Though de Selincourt clucks that Dorothy Wordsworth has "misquoted" (*George & Sarah Green* 86; endorsed by Clark 29, 50; Homans 59), I think it's a motivated rewording. As serial fair-copier of *The Ruined Cottage* Dorothy knew the text intimately.

25. My text is *MY* 1: 219–20. The full title William gave Coleridge is "Elegiac Stanzas composed in the Churchyard of Grasmere, Westmorland, a few days after the Interment there of a Man and his Wife, Inhabitants of the Vale, who were lost upon the neighbouring Mountains, on the night of the nineteenth of March last." He never published his "effused" verses, though he would permit Coleridge to recite, circulate, or publish them "to any profit for the poor Orphans." De Quincey put an abridgement in "Recollections of Grasmere" (*Tait's*, vol. 6, September 1839, p. 573; *Recollections* 2: 74–75).

26. *EY* 16, 25. With Antonio's ventures "squandered abroad," Shylock gloats that "his means are in supposition" (*Merchant of Venice* 1.3.21). The first phrase haunts Dorothy; Levin sees in the continuing chronicle in *Grasmere Journal* of "people affected by the economic pressures of the time, dislocated from the land" a reflection of Dorothy's deepest anxieties about her own abjection (*Dorothy Wordsworth & Romanticism* 36; and see the fuller discussion, 36–49).

27. Applied to M. St. Aubert, in fresh grief at the loss of his wife (vol. 1, ch. III, p. 72).

28. That Annette Vallon adopted the name "Madame Williams," Kathleen Jones comments, suggests that she regarded herself as William's wife, expecting him to return to France to legalize the union and be responsible for their daughter (38).

29. Richard Matlak proposes that William felt burdened by Dorothy in 1800, her maintenance "a ball and chain to his freedom," keeping him from joining Coleridge in the high life at Ratzburg (57). Wollstonecraft's "Observations on the State of Degradation to which Woman is Reduced by Various Causes" (the title of ch. IV in *RW*) cites the abjection of the erstwhile "mistress" of a now married brother's home and family; she is "viewed with averted looks as an intruder, an unnecessary burden on the benevolence of the master of the house, and his new partner" (140; this is the singular instance of the word *intruder* in *Rights of Woman*). Dorothy records in her journal (knowing William will read it) a graveyard saunter with newlyweds William and Mary, during which they encounter a stone "erected to the memory of an unfortunate woman": "the verses engraved upon it expressed that she had been neglected by her Relations" (October 1802; *GJ* 127).

30. To Homans, all these postscripts enact a "corrective" to the romance paradigm and the "saccharine ending" of the *Narrative* proper (*Women Writers* 59–60); I read as a stark eruption of currents already in the narrative, and in the mind of its author, from its first pages. As my conversations indicate, Homans's and Levin's work on Dorothy Wordsworth has been foundational to my own.

Chapter Seven: Gazing On "Byron"

1. C. R. Leslie's engraving of the portrait faces *LS*, p. 193.

2. For Praz's remark (147), I thank Robert Beevers (1). Richard Holmes, though pretending to self-possessed analytical discourse, gives a sense of its covering for a Praz-affect: "beautiful, brooding, and damned. Byron's image—the dark, curly locks, the mocking aristocratic eyes, the voluptuous mouth, the chin with its famous dimple, and the implicit radiation of sexual danger—became famous throughout Britain" and "launched an international style. The dark clothes, the white open-necked shirt exposing the masculine throat, the aggressive display of disarray and devilry, these were the symbols of the Romantic poetic type: the Fallen Angel in rebellion" (34).

3. A recent anthology, with gorgeous color plates and a wealth of black-and-white illustrations, edited by Christine Kenyon Jones, offers sharp, historically informed essays on the styles, imagery, iconography and cultural circulation of Byron in portraiture.

4. *Quarterly Review* 44: 169. The dialectic of "Byronic masquerade," argues Jerome McGann, makes it is difficult to distinguish "figure from ground because the presumptive ground, 'the real Lord Byron,' becomes a figural form in the poetry" ("Anonymous Lyric" 106).

5. Even the most extraordinarily errant fathers could exercise this presumptive claim.

6. I thank Jack Cragwall's sharp eyes. Byron first thought to close *Canto the Third* with the heroic self-sufficiency of cxii: "I stood and stand alone,—remembered or forgot." Just below, he wrote, "End of Canto third." Then he post-scripted the two "I have not loved the world" stanzas (cxiii–cxiv), and four more on his daughter. See T. A. J. Burnett's edition (202–5).

7. Signed A. Byron, the letter is printed by Stowe 53, and 466–67.

8. *The Dream* implies the wedding day as an unwilling trance and presage of doom; *Stanzas to---* cherish a "woman" (half-sister and lover Augusta) who, despite the sex, "didst not forsake" the "slander'd" poet—a coded antitype to the wife: "Though trusted, thou dist not disclaim me, / Though parted, it was not to fly, / Though watchful, 'twas not to defame me, / Nor, mute, that the world might belie" (IV). In a later issue of the first edition of *Childe Harold III* Murray adver-

tised first among "The Following Works in the Press: '*The Prisoner of Chillon, a Fable; The Dream: Darkness: The Incantation, & c*'" (81)—an opportune insertion of the well-received *Dream* (the next longest poem), which appeared in the title of Scott's article (16: 172), where it is quoted lavishly (182, 205). My thanks to Doucet Fischer for conversation about these editions.

9. "Given to me (& I believe composed by Ld B. Friday April 12th 1816," Murray wrote on his ms. (*Letters of John Murray* 162 n. 2). Although Augusta wasn't named here either, even as "sister," the *Eclectic* easily tagged "his Lordship's sister" before printing the whole (598–99; the only poem so featured). In candor rivaling Caro's gossip (Murray had shown her the stanzas), Byron let the poetry tweak the rumors: "when the cloud upon us came." In the train of Separation-coding were *Bright be the place of thy soul* (an elegiac blessing), *When we two parted* (a poem of bitter grief, dated "1808" [p. 15] but transferable), two poems titled *Stanzas for Music*, both audible as effusions for Lady Byron, then *Fare thee well!*, and four poems on Napoleon's defeat, voicing the loyalty of his troops and then the exile's own Farewell (to France)—all superimposed by June 1816 on his Lordship's Farewell to England, in retrojected epic prototyping. A prefacing "Advertisement" unwound a long sentence of careful calculation and stimulation, pretending apology for redundant publication: "As some of the Verses in this Collection were evidently not intended for general circulation, they would not have appeared in this authentic form, had they not been already dispersed through the medium of the public press, to an extent that must take away the regret which, under other circumstances, the reader might perhaps experience in finding them included amongst the acknowledged publications of the Noble Author" (5). Byron planned the volume and corrected proof. Priced at two shillings, the run of 1,056 sold out, with an immediate second issue, and a second edition by year's end.

10. Scott, *L* 4: 365. Gifford edited the *Quarterly*. Murray sent the review to Byron on 7 February and identified Scott to him on the 18th (*L* 195–96). Byron listed Scott's "An Alabaster Vase lighted up within," in a census of "various comparisons" he had seen of himself (15 October 1821; *BLJ* 9: 11), and he replied to Scott's valentine in kind, sighing of a "notion of addressing you a hundred times in my head—and always in my heart" and attributing delay to "the same principle of tremulous anxiety with which one sometimes makes love to a beautiful woman of our own degree with whom one is ~~in love~~ enamoured in good earnest." Scott's chivalry redeemed the wife's default: "you went out of your way in 1817—to do me a service when it required not merely kindness—but courage to do so;—to have been seconded by you in such a manner would have been a proud memorial at any time [a "second" is a trusted representative in a duel of honor, usually charged with determining the site, checking the weapons, and monitoring fair play]—but

at such a time—when 'all the World and his Wife' (or rather <u>mine</u>) as the proverb goes—were trying to trample upon me was something still higher to my Self esteem" (12 January 1822; *BLJ* 9: 85). Byron often sounds the phrase he quotes from Swift's *Third Conversation*, in which gossip wends from a philandering lord and his suspicious wife to a gathering attended by "all the World, and his Wife" (193); as elsewhere he superimposes sequential topics. For a sharp account of the Byron-Scott romance, see Sonia Hofkosh, 44–49.

11. If Byron "has acted very wrong in some respects," Scott told Murray, "he has been no worse than half the men of his rank in London who have done the same" (22 Jan. 1817; Smiles 1: 377).

12. Vere Foster, *The Two Duchesses* 412–14. The son, Augustus Foster (himself a hopeful suitor of Miss Milbanke; 362) thought the Byrons, a clear mismatch, were a fit fate for each other: "she <u>would</u> marry a poet and <u>reform</u> a rake. As to him, he has at length proved himself the true Childe Harold" (to his mother, 23 March; 414)—pretty much Scott's view at the time.

13. 16 November, to Augustus Foster (Foster 424–25). "Lady Byron's fate is the most melancholy I ever heard, and he must be mad or a Caligula," the Duchess wrote from Rome on 22 March 1816; "Caro will have told you some of the stories. It is too shocking, and her life seems to have been endangered whilst with him from his cruelty, and now by her sufferings" (413–14). By 1816 Byron was a sore point at Devonshire House, not only by force of Caro (Lady Bessborough's niece) but also for skipping out of a half year's rent owed to the Duchess on the lease on Piccadilly Terrace (Marchand, *Byron, a Biography* 2: 718).

14. For this reference I thank Andrew Elfenbein (60), who notes that reading Byron was "an escape into a realm of transgressive sexuality, love with a glamorous aristocrat who seemed to cry out for female companionship" (63). For more women's reactions to Byron, see also his dissertation, *Byron, Byronism, and the Victorians* (Yale University 1992).

15. Quoted in Ralph Milbanke, *Astarte* 17. Lady Liddell, a friend of the Milbankes, was "horror-struck" at this sudden encounter, in May 1817, with the man she had never before met.

16. Cp. the report of Newton Hanson (son of John Hanson, Byron's business agent) on Venetian Byron, November 1818: "pale, bloated, and sallow. He had grown very fat, his shoulders broad and round, and the knuckles of his hands were lost in fat" (ms. in *Letters*, ed. Prothero 4: 267n).

17. The pamphlet, dated 19 February 1830, was issued by Lady Byron within weeks of Moore's *Life of Byron* vol. 1, to refute aspersions against her parents. Baillie helped distribute it; among its recipients were Margaret Holford Hodson and Felicia Hemans. Alert to its interest and wanting to appear gentlemanly,

Murray and Moore printed it in *BW* (6: 275–80). Stowe gives it full in *Lady Byron* 106–12.

18. And thus the *Anti-Jacobin Review and Magazine* (reviewing *The Young Philosopher*) objected to a transparent Benjamin Smith in the screw-up husbands populating several of Charlotte Smith's novels: "whatever her husband's foibles or faults might be, it was her *duty* not to blazen them abroad, but to conceal them, as far as possible, from the eyes of the world" (2/1 [1798], 4).

19. Heathcliff's abuse constitutes female experience, comments Elaine Showalter; only a woman would create this kind of hero (*A Literature* 139–43). And Brontë may still be enchanted (argue Gilbert and Gubar), underestimating "both the ferocity of the Byronic hero and the powerlessness of all women, even 'ladies' in her society," in legalized thrall (*Madwoman* 288).

20. Citing remarks (in Byron's pre–marriage era letters, July 1813–February 1814) on the conflict of feeling and writing, Andrew Nicholson floats the possibility that Byron, "so overwhelmed by emotion that he himself could not get the lines down on paper to his own satisfaction," dictated to Augusta, who fair-copied (in *Manuscripts: Lord Byron*, XII, p. 83). For Moore's report, see *BW* 10: vi (the "M.S. . . . blotted all over with the marks of tears").

21. "Lord Byron's Poem's on His Own Domestic Circumstances" was the headline. Brougham was the *Edinburgh's* sarcastic reviewer of *Hours of Idleness*, not editor Francis Jeffrey, as Byron supposed when he retaliated with *English Bards, and Scotch Reviewers*, which scored a few hits on Brougham anyway (1809; 1811, 4th ed., 518–19). Now Lady Byron's legal advisor, Brougham was dishing dirt about Byron throughout the spring of 1816. Byron still did not know he was the Edinburgh reviewer; when he learned so from abroad, he promised a duel if he returned to England. See also McGann's notes (*BPW* 3: 494); "circumstances of publication" (80–89); and "Byron and 'The Truth in Masquerade'" which assesses the accumulating contexts, from coterie circulation and private printing, to press piracies, to Murray's 1816 editions.

22. Reprints flourished, among them *The Morning Chronicle's* on the 16th, defending Byron and attacking the *Champion*. Leigh Hunt put *Fare thee well!* and stanza 2 of *A Sketch* (on the vulnerability of a pure youthful mind to gossip) in the 21 April *Examiner*, at the end of "Distressing Circumstance in High Life," a lengthy article pitying Byron's distress and attacking his enemies.

23. David Erdman attributes this essay on the basis of style and some internal evidence (*Essays* 2: 427). In the relay of brotherly love, Byron added as a facing-page epigraph for the text he authorized for the 1816 *Poems* (June), lines from Coleridge's *Christabel* ("Alas! they had been friends in Youth; / But whispering tongues can poison truth," etc.; p. 30 [408–13; 419–26]). With Byron's

advocacy, *Christabel* had just appeared, in May, in a small volume published by Murray.

24. See Samuel Chew (ch. 3, with antipathy to Lady Byron). Sherwood, Neely & Jones led the surge with *Fare Thee Well!* and *A Sketch*. Bensley and Son of Fleet Street and E. Cox and Son of the Borough issued both under a main title, *Poems on his Domestic Circumstances* (1816), the thirty pages of poems prefaced by eleven pages of gossip, news reports, and correspondence between Ralph Noel (Lady Byron's father) and the editor of the *Morning Chronicle*. R. Edwards of Fleet Street, using the same main title, added a frontispiece copied from an engraving of Richard Westall's dreamy profile portrait (1813), inscribed "'Lord Byron'/Fac Simile/'Sweet as his native song'" (Peach 41). By 1817 William Hone (also of Fleet Street) was into the twenty-third edition of *Poems on Domestic Circumstances*. The scandal imprinted editorial titles, from Thomas Moore's "Domestic Pieces—1816" (1830s; *BW* 10: vi and 181–210) to E. H. Coleridge's 1904 *Poems of the Separation* (lxviii and 376–79).

25. 16 May 1816 (Lockhart, *Scott* 5: 128, 127). Writing on 18 April to the *Champion*'s editor John Scott, Wordsworth, in a high anti-Whig mood on several subjects, called Byron "insane" and the verses "doggerel," proposing that the best antidote would be a refusal to give the credit of "high genius" to self-infatuated "charm" and "wickedness" (*MY* 2: 304–5).

26. December 1816, 577–78, reviewing *The Prisoner of Chillon & c.* "It would be a piece of idle affectation," said Jeffrey in the *Edinburgh Review* the same month, to consider *Fare thee well!*, etc. "as mere effusions of fancy, or to pretend ignorance of the subjects to which they relate" (27: 292).

27. McCann 778; the (by now famous) quotation on the British public is from Thomas Babington Macaulay's essay on Moore's *Life of Byron* (1830), *Edinburgh Review* 53 (June 1831), 547.

28. McGann, "Hero" 148. For Byron's dread of being read by others, particularly women, as a peril to "the powers of self-creation" that seem not just a "masculine inheritance" but to "inhere in the masculine body itself," see Hofkosh (38). For the successes and distresses of Byron's effort to manage "Byron," see Ghislaine McDayter, "Conjuring Byron." For an account of Byron's more capable agency, see Jerome Christensen, who argues that a "collaborative invention of a gifted poet, a canny publisher, eager reviewers, and rapt readers" exploited "the need for a hegemonic metaphor that would resolve conflicts embedded in questions of national, sexual, and social identity that were as yet unspeakable" (xx); Elfenbein's contemporaneous, deft analysis in *Byron and the Victorians*, ch. 2: "The Creation of Byronism"; and Tom Mole's recent *Byron's Romantic Celebrity: Industrial Culture and the Hermeneutic of Intimacy*.

29. Lady Anne Barnard's transcription of Lady Byron's letter to her, pub-

lished by Stowe 51 and 455. McGann reads a talented syntactic equivocation in "Fare thee well! and if for ever, / Still for ever, fare *thee well:* / Even though unforgiving, never / 'Gainst thee shall my heart rebel": the sequence poses "Lady Byron's" as the 'unforgiving' heart, but the grammar tells us that heart is Byron's own" ("Truth" 13). In addition, I think Byron hints that his head (with advice) may rebel, deciding to exercise legal claim to Ada, a possibility that preyed on Lady Byron (Elwin 337). McGann takes the script for Zarina in *Sardanapalus* Act 4 to be a "semi-private code" of reproach to Lady Byron, her cold intransigence an implied contrast to Zarina's benevolence to her errant (Byronic) husband ("Hero" 142–47).

30. Note on *Fare thee well!*, *BW* 10: 185–186; see also *Life* (1830) 1: 476. Byron sets the question out for public notice again in Donna Julia's artful letter of farewell to Don Juan at the end of Canto I (1819). Julia protests that she writes in haste (192), but not so hastily that she can't make a "copy of her Letter" (191), which the narrator has (Juan's copy is soon torn up for a cannabalism lottery, in Canto II); nor was she so rushed that this copy could not be "written upon gilt-edged paper / With a neat little crow-quill, slight and new" (198). This is not to discredit Julia's heartache (she's more Byronic hero in this anguish than ever-boyish Juan); it is to note that in this kind of Byronism, performance and pathos inhabit the same media.

31. Alaric Watts, Sr.—"no more enthusiastic devotee and partizan than this young man" in the Childe-Harold decade (Watts 1: 112)—is a case in point in his son's retrospect on the way *Don Juan* "greatly revolted" public "sentiment": "The great mass of the reading public had, up to that time, sided with 'my lord' in his differences with 'my lady'" (110), deeming "an inability on the part of the lady, not absolutely culpable, but unfortunate, to comprehend and make allowance for the venial aberrations of the poetic temperament"; *Don Juan* disclosed "a new and startling aspect . . . a side of this magnificent human being . . . wholly out of harmony with the impressions of . . . the noble vein of sentiment displayed in his writing" and chiming, too audibly, with "recent rumours" (111). Like Lockhart, this public "had a sort of feeling, perhaps, that it had rather been taken in," and was not in a forgiving vein (112).

32. Mayne, *Lady Byron* 283. Though unsigned, *Don Juan I-II* was transparently Byron's. His protests to Murray about extratextual reference are either disingenuous or precociously postmodern: "if, in a poem by no means ascertained to be my production, there appears a disagreeable, casuistical, and by no means respectable female pedant, it is set down for my wife. Is there any resemblance? If there be, it is in those who make it: I can see none" (*Some Observations, BW* 15: 64); Byron first wrote "by no means very moral female pedant" (*Prose* 93 n.).

33. "Life, 1815"; *BW* 3: 140. And so it is enlisted, with a raft of Separation

poetry, by the compiler of *The True Story* as documentary evidence in refutation of Stowe (60–83).

34. Byron dated the dedicatory letter to Hobhouse "January 2, 1818" and referred within to this "anniversary of the most unfortunate day of my past existence" (iii, v; *BPW* 2: 120–21).

35. The phrase is from (the only prior use I could locate) Sir John Stradling's *Divine Poemes, In Several Classes. Written to his most Excellent Maiestie, Charles* (1625), *The first Classis:* "O wondrous Childe, great God, the Prince of peace, / Mayne subiect of all holy prophecies" (stanza 182). The review of *Childe Harold IV* in the *New Monthly Magazine*, Sept. 1818, also uses the phrase: "the soul of the 'wondrous Childe,' seems to have been tempered and chastened even by its own fire" (10: 156). "Wondrous Child" is, of course, a common epithet for young Jesus.

36. Jeffrey, *Edinburgh* 36: 420; West, *New Monthly* 16 (1826), 243. For the theatricality of Byron in his portraits, see Suzanne Hyman; for Byron's staging a look for his portraits, see Christine Jones. For the royalty-financing, see Holmes 34.

37. The word *glamour* entered English, via Scotland, around 1800, denoting a wizard's spell, then an embodied enchantment, then (the modern sense) the auratic affect. In Byron's life and legend, remarks James Soderholm, all these senses overlap (*Fantasy* 4–5). Thus also the portraits: the general public, notes Robert Beevers, never saw the originals, just reproductions flourishing in a lack of copyright and the new technology of steel-plate engraving (4, 20, 70).

38. Elfenbein proposes that male-authored parodies such as this lampoon female admiration so as to imply the refinement of male appreciations (*Byron and the Victorians* 66–67).

39. Lockhart was determined to prevent discovery; he had recently married Scott's daughter.

40. Both Lord Byron and his wife-to-be owned *Pride and Prejudice* (Murray, *Letters* 512).

41. In an omnibus essay on Austen for the *Quarterly Review* (1821), Richard Whately praised "probability" as the vehicle of "moral lessons . . . not forced upon the reader" but springing "incidentally from the circumstances." With this "unpretending" moral work, Austen redeems the "prejudice" that has "stigmatized the whole class" (24: 356–57, 360).

42. Byronism erupted anyway, West's visit to Montenero capped with dramatic violence, as the political feuds of Teresa's family, the Gambas, invaded the casa. Count Gamba was bloodied, and everyone, including West, took up pistols; a few days later, the Gambas were expelled from Tuscany, and the whole menage had to pack up and move out.

43. For Murray's reaction, see William Johnstone Hope's letter to Lady Byron's solicitor, G. B. Wharton (Doris Langley Moore, *Late Lord Byron* 21–22). Gifford's reaction and its influence on Murray are taken from Hobhouse's diary, quoted in Marchand, *Biography* 1249.

44. On board were Moore, Murray, Hobhouse, Kinnaird, Augusta Leigh, Lady Byron, Wilmot Horton, Samuel Rogers, Henry Luttrell, and others. When the London press (*Times, Observer, John Bull*) picked up the news, there was "much public excitement" (Smiles 1: 444). The public guessed a scandal: "it must be taken for granted that the Memoirs were throughout utterly unfit for publication in any shape; and that Mr. Moore and Lord Byron's other friends did not expurgate them only because they were incapable of expurgation," said the *New Monthly* (22: 84). Stowe believed that the motive for burning was not the incest of Byron and Augusta, a rumor ever since the Separation, but the slanders against Lady Byron, in offense to gentlemanly codes of conduct (72–73). Louis Crompton suggests fears that Byron's "passion for communicativeness and his love of veiled confessions" coursed through homoerotic-codes, in which Moore was not literate but some of Byron's enemies were (339; see also 126–29).

45. Watts had been editor of the *New Monthly,* an association that ended when he published Polidori's *Vampyre* as Byron's, falling for the fraud on the expectation of profit. Still, he was amused by the Byronic Vampyrics, writing in campy horror to his close friend, Miss Priscilla Wiffen, in June 1820 ("Dearest Zillah," whom he would marry a year later), "I really begin to suspect Lord Byron to be an absolute power of evil incarnate. He has sent home for publication some compositions absolutely blasphemous. He and Shelley are 'magnificent monsters'" (Watts, 1: 106).

46. Watts is quoting nearly verbatim from an essay on this portrait in the *New Monthly:* "What we have wanted of Lord Byron is a resemblance of him at a period when his variable character had gone its utmost length towards being fixed" (16: 243).

47. The portrait was never popular, scarcely used for covers or frontispieces. David Piper gives it a bit of space (138), but only to say that it is bland, tidy, vacuous and, of course, adipose.

48. West, in the *New Monthly* XVI (1826), 245; Moore, *Life of Byron* (1832 *BW* 4: 204); D'Israeli, in Cline 142. Thanks to Gillen Wood for the reference to Moore and "musico" (see *Don Juan* 4.86, describing one of the enslaved of the opera company).

49. For a chorus of testimony on this appearance, see John Clubbe 23–24. Clubbe's essay gives an impressively detailed account of West and the portrait.

Chapter Eight: Byron and the Muse of Female Poetry

1. On Byron as an enchantment, a language of the heart, for alienated girls and women, see Corin Throsby 115. These two quotations are given by Fiona MacCarthy 162.

2. My excerpts of this letter, dated 3 September 1812, in the John Murray Archive, National Library of Scotland (Acc 120664 folder 105), are from a transcription courtesy of Peter Cochran.

3. Barrett, *Letters* 2: 7, and *Brownings' Correspondence* (1: 361).

4. Paston and Quennell 127; this lass also hit on Napoleon, as he paraded near Lausanne on a return from his victorious Italian campaign in 1798.

5. The three elegiac, heartbroken Thyrza poems were screens for Byron's grief over the recent death of his beloved Cambridge choirboy John Edleston; they are on pp. 232–40, part of a train of love-elegies. I quote Lady Falkland's mash-notes, here and below, from Marchand, "Come to me" (22–23); see also Marchand, *Biography* (1: 346–47); Paston and Quennell 15–22.

6. For the female reader fantasizing "that she alone could truly understand the poet and redeem and reform him through her love," see Simon Bainbridge's essay (21).

7. Throsby goes so far as to recruit twentieth-century reader-response theory, proposing that the Byronic text, appearing at once transparent and secret, activates a reader's imagination (117, with reference to Wolfgang Iser's foundational essay, "The Reading Process").

8. Little Louisa may also be modeled on Byron's "bastard" daughter, whom Byron may have surnamed from Mary Shelley's jest: just after *Frankenstein* was published (1 January 1818), Byron told Kinnaird that he would "acknowledge" her by "giving her the name of *Biron* (to distinguish her from little Legitimacy)" (13 January; *BLJ* 6: 7).

9. Although Angela Leighton reads this finale as a woman's conversion into "sexual or artistic property for the man," lifeless, "fixed, unchanging, and thus fit for domestic use" (61–62), I see it depleted of male proprietary force both by the vibrancy of the portrait, and by the lassitude of the lover, who seems fixed, and fixated, in a tomblike domicile.

10. The "Art of Being Byronic" is McCann's satiric phrase of 1868 on the young man's mania (799). Hemans's Byronic heroines star in *The Widow of Crescentius, The Vespers of Palermo, The Bride of the Greek Isle,* and *The Indian City.* For the allure of Byron to female poets, see Angela Leighton, *Writing Against the Heart.*

11. Some rumors were on target. Cynthia Lawford has uncovered Landon's sustained, child-issuing affair with a married William Jerdan. Like Byron, she

died just after completing her thirty-sixth year, in a foreign land, in circumstances so mysterious as to seem to have been a chapter of her poetic tales, or Byron's.

12. For my fuller discussion of Hemans and female fame, see *Borderlines* 68–77.

13. The very phrase, "the dark blue depths" she sang of, was not Byron's song: it was, ironically, despised Southey's, at the opening of *Thalaba the Destroyer* (1801): "In full-orbed glory, yonder moon divine / Rolls through the dark blue depths." Southey's phrase caught Shelley's eye, as he launched *To a Balloon, laden with Knowledge*: "Bright ball of flame that thro the gloom of even / Silently takest thine ethereal way / And with surpassing glory dimm'st each ray / Twinkling amid the dark blue depths of Heaven" (1–4)—published posthumously, way too late for Barrett's notice.

14. "On Modern Female Cultivation" (28 January 1832), p. 66. I attribute Jewsbury's authorship from the placement of the essay below a signed poem, and its tonal and thematic congruence with other signed writings. See also Norma Clarke, 229–30 n. 40, and Dennis Low.

15. One of the orchestrated tirades against Stowe's initial magazine publications (the *Atlantic* in the United States and *Macmillan's* in England) slotted it with that species of vanity prompting "those continual efforts, which we hear of ladies taking this or that position usually occupied by men; hence too those 'Woman's Rights Conventions,' and other manifestations of contempt for man in a country the most indulgent in the world, towards the ladies, and where an immense number of married men are simply slaves to their wives" (J.M., *The True Story*, Introduction 8)—a pointed trope for the abolitionist author of *Uncle Tom's Cabin*.

16. Daily News, 24 May 1860; *Biographical Sketches* 283. Mayne says that Martineau had heard from servants of Byron's cruelty to his wife on their honeymoon (*Life of Lady Byron* 161)—an account that rival biographer Elwin is eager to dismiss as "the partisanship of a militant feminist" (250), the adjective he is also happy to give to the Lady herself, as if proof of partisanship: "Annabella's militant prudence" is the phrase that opens the penultimate paragraph of his biography (470).

17. For her addiction, see my "Hemans and the Romance of Byron" and the index of my *Felicia Hemans*. She would not have been aware of Byron's ridicule (as bluestocking, Christian moralizer, stilted and apostrophic poet) in the letters to Murray published in Moore's *Byron*. She didn't read Moore beyond review-excerpts, none with comments on her. Moore replaced her name with asterisks in the nastiest letter (28 September 1820), and the nastiest of all (12 August 1820) was first published by Marchand.

18. Hemans may have had the verses from Murray, or from her friends in the

Quarterly circle, Heber and Milman. For Augusta's demur, see Byron to Murray, 28 August and 5 October 1816 (*BLJ* 5: 90–1, 110). The verses first appeared in Moore's *Byron* (1830) 2: 38–41.

19. Volume I of Moore's *Byron* appeared January 1830; in February and March, *Blackwood's* (Hemans was a frequent contributor and steady reader) carried John Wilson's unsigned fifty-four-page notice, full of excerpts, climaxing in several pages mostly sympathetic to Byron on the failed marriage (27: 443–54). Hemans may also have read notices in the *Athenæum* (25 December 1830; 1 and 8 January 1831), and in the *Quarterly* (January 1831), which took a dim view of Moore's defense: "It is sufficiently obvious that Lord Byron did not solicit Miss Milbanke's hand under the influence of anything which could deserve the name of love . . . he had espoused a lady of large expectations" (44: 196–97). Hemans read here that Moore had "too faithfully portrayed" the "basely profligate course of sensual indulgence" in Byron's life abroad, a "mass of pollution" documented in "whole realms of letters, filled with minute, graphic, exulting records" of "licentious adventures" (44: 204–6).

20. Contrast her anxiety about having an epigraph from Shelley for a poem forthcoming in *Blackwood's:* she asked William Blackwood to remove Shelley's name (14 February 1828; Wolfson, *Hemans* 495–96), but it had already gone to press. The Byron-saturated, best-selling *Records of Woman* had new editions across the 1830s, and Hemans featured Byron-epigraphs in *Songs of the Affections* (1830): *The Spirit's Return* and *Parting Words* (both *Manfred*), *The Image in the Heart* ("And thou art dead"), *The Fountain of Oblivion* (a phase from a letter in Moore's *Life*), *The Magic Glass*, *The Minster*, *The Beings of the Mind* (all *Childe Harold IV*), *The Storm Painter in His Dungeon* and *The Song of Night* (*Childe Harold III*), *The Sleeper* (*Don Juan II*). Byron supplies more epigraphs for her than any other poet, including her favorites, Wordsworth, Scott, and Baillie.

21. Toulmin (later known as essayist and novelist Mrs. Newton Crosland) was born the year that *Childe Harold's Pilgrimage* debuted (1812).

22. The line below the last title, *Inscribed to Lord Byron's Sister, Mrs. George Leigh*, even puts the "sweet Sister" issues into a respectable married name.

23. "I penetrated the recesses of the mystic grove . . . one of the favorite haunts of the late Lord Byron," writes Washington Irving of a visit to Newstead Abbey (155–56); while "every sight and sound . . . seemed calculated to summon up recollections of poor Lord Byron" (159), Irving is haunted by Byron's affections, alternately fantasizing a missed marriage with a childhood sweetheart of the region, or conjuring a pure fraternal romance: "I searched the grove for some time, before I found the tree on which Lord Byron had left his frail memorial. It was an elm of peculiar form, having two trunks, which sprang from the same root, and, after growing side by side, mingled their branches together. He had selected

it, doubtless, as emblematical of his sister and himself. The names of BYRON and AUGUSTA were still visible. They had been deeply cut in the bark, but the natural growth of the tree was gradually rendering them illegible, and a few years hence, strangers will seek in vain for this record of fraternal affection" (157).

24. Kinnaird sat for his portrait with Byronic props, including Westall's 1813 *Byron*, a bust of Napoleon, and *Parisina*. See Marchand, *Biography*, facing 990; and in color, MacCarthy, facing 83.

25. The iconic "gaze diverted from the spectator, aloof and self-proposed for admiration," Piper writes analytically (133). With affective elaborations of his own, Holmes mimes the viewer's swoon: "Byron's eyes were raised apocalyptically to heaven, his hair quiffed and tinted, his brow blanched, his throat swollen with passion, and even his decorative collar-pin altered from a gentleman's cameo to a large, glassy lover's keepsake" (34).

26. Byron supported Westall's turn to Charles Turner for a mezzotint of the portrait the same year (fig. 11). Though Westall hated another attempt, by Thomas Blood, Byron didn't mind having this printed either (Peach 44). Turner's *Byron* spawned international progeny, including Henry Robinson's in the 1840 *Drawing Room Scrap-Book* (fig. 14). Westall's *Byron* was matched in 1814 by Thomas Phillips's dark-cloak *Byron*, exhibited at the Royal Academy and promiscuously engraved (Peach 57; see, e.g., fig. 6), one engraving, in turn, serving as a model for Phillips's famous Albanian *Byron* (1814; cf. fig. 7). Another engraving, by John Agar (1814; see Beevers 35), provided the pattern for a lush Victorian Byron by Alonzo Chappel, in Duyckinck's *Portrait Gallery*.

27. The phrase "all the Byron beauties," with assurances of Lady Byron's desire "to contribute anything in her power to the real monument of Byron's genius," is conveyed in the September 1832 *Noctes Ambrosianæ LXII* (*Blackwood's* 32: 412). By 1832 Alfred Howard's *The Beauties of Byron* was out. The project cited in *Noctes* is most likely W. Brockedon's *Finden's Illustrations of the Life and Works of Lord Byron, with Original and Selected Information on the Subjects of the Engravings*, organized by William Finden and Edward Finden (London: Murray, 1833–34). Volume 1 (1833) featured an engraving of W. J. Newton's miniature of Annabella, with a five-page piece of "information" on the courtship, marriage, and separation. In 1836 the Findens issued a supplement, in Continental flair: *Les Dames de Byron; or, Portraits of the Principle Female Characters in Lord Byron's Poems, Engraved from Original Paintings by Eminent Artists*.

28. There were several Westall offspring. For *European Magazine* January 1814 Blood distilled a profile without the fist and the neckwear-jewel, where it faced a memoir written merely to prop the portrait and puff the forthcoming *Corsair* (4). James Heath engraved an image for *Lady's Magazine*, April 1815; an anonymous reverse image supplied the frontispiece for a pirated *Poems on his*

Domestic Circumstances (London: R. Edwards, 1816). The Royal Academy displayed another version in April 1825, the anniversary of Byron's death. See Peach 41–42.

29. While memoirs of Byron were legion by the mid-1830s, the *Scrapbook* garnered interest from the recent scandal-tinged death of L.E.L. in Cape Coast Castle, Africa.

30. *Life* "1816"; 1830 1: 471–72; then in *BW 3*: 220.

31. Mayne, *Byron* 253; Mayne seconds Goethe on the serendipity (*Lady Byron* 199).

32. This was A *Sketch from Private Life* ("Born in the garret, in the kitchen bred, / Promoted thence to deck her mistress' head; / . . . Rais'd from the toilet to the table,—where / Her wondering betters wait behind her chair"), attacking Lady Byron's one-time governess, then her maid and then nurse during her pregnancy and childbirth (while Byron was carousing with an actress). Byron overstates Mary Anne Clermont's agency in all this. Although he was as misinformed about her culpability as he claimed the "reasonable world" was about him, he was pleased enough with his verses to put them in the three-volume edition of 1819 (Murray) and in collections thereafter. See *Eclectic* 2d series 5 (June 1816), 596.

33. For sharp discussions of Lamb's cheeky impersonations and performances as Byron, see Peter Graham 119–24, and Duncan Wu, "Appropriating Byron."

34. On Juan as Regency-Byron, see Soderholm 161–62; McGann, "The Book of Byron" 287. On Regency Annabella transparent in Aurora, see Stowe and Norton (*True Story* 184). On Aurora's resistance to Juan's glamour, see Peter Manning's canny *Byron and his Fictions* 251.

35. Caroline Franklin notes the Aurora-modeling of angelic Eva in *Uncle Tom's Cabin*, this lass introduced with another Aurora stanza (*DJ* 15.43); *Byron and Women Novelists* 33–34.

36. Caroline Norton's view of Annabella was not disinterested, but most likely inflected by Lord Melbourne, Annabella's cousin and unhappy husband (then widower) of Byron's lover for a season, Caroline Lamb. The scandal that consumed Caroline Norton was her affair, years later with Lord Melbourne, while she was married—and so she had a sense of Byronic passion as well. Thus said Henry Nelson Coleridge of Caroline Norton's Byron-mirroring collection, *The Dream, and other Poems* (1840): "This lady is the Byron of our modern poetesses. She has very much of that intense personal passion" (*Quarterly Review* 66 [1840], 376). This sentence was subsequently used in Colburn's advertisements for the volume.

WORKS CITED

Abbreviations

attr.: attributed by   /e: edition (e.g., 2/e: 2d edition)
rev.: revised   s: series (e.g., 2s: second series; ns: new series)
tr.: translator   P/UP Press/University Press
v(s).: volume(s)   [?]   [informed, speculative attribution]
&c.: & (other works/publishing partners/other publishers or booksellers)

Aikin, Lucy. *Epistles on Women, Exemplifying Their Character and Condition in Various Ages and Nations. With Miscellaneous Poems.* London: J. Johnson, 1810.

Alger, John Goldworth. *Paris in 1789-94.* London: George Allen, 1902.

[Allsop, Thomas]. *Letters, Conversations, and Recollections of Samuel Taylor Coleridge.* 2 vs. London: E. Moxon, 1836.

Analytical Review, or history of literature, domestic and foreign 8 (1790): 416; on Wollstonecraft, *Vindication of the Rights of Men.*

———. 17 (September 1793) 91–93; on Charlotte Smith, *The Emigrants.*

———. 20 (1794) 254–55; on Charlotte Smith, *The Banished Man.*

Annual Register, or General Repository of History, Politics, and Literature, for the Year 1797. London: G. G. and J. Robinson, 1798.

Anti-Jacobin Review and Magazine, or, Monthly Political and Literary Censor 2/1 (August 1798): 187–90; on Charlotte Smith, *The Young Philosopher.*

———. 9 (April–August 1801): 515–20. C. K. "The Vision of Liberty. Written in the Manner of Spencer."

———. 50 (July 1816): 632–36; on Coleridge, *Christabel & c.*

Athenæum, Journal of English and Foreign Literature, Science, and the Fine Arts 165 (25 December 1830): 801–4; 166 (1 January 1831): 1–6; and 167 (8 January 1831): 22–24; on Thomas Moore's *Letters and Journals of Lord Byron, with Notices of His Life.*

Attridge, Derek. *Peculiar Language: Literature as Difference.* Ithaca: Cornell UP, 1988.

Augustan Review 3 (July 1816): 14–24; on Coleridge's *Christabel & c.*

Austen, Henry. "Biographical Notice of the Author." *Northanger Abbey and Per-suasion: by the Author of Pride and Prejudice, Mansfield-Park, &c. With a Biographical Notice of the Author.* 4 vols. London: John Murray, 1818. 1: 3–8.

[Austen, Jane]. *Emma.* 1816. Ed. Francis Ferguson. Longman, 2006.

——. *Northanger Abbey.* London: John Murray, 1818.

——. *Persuasion.* 1818. Ed. William Galperin. New York: Longman, 2007.

——. *Pride and Prejudice.* 1813. Ed. Claudia L. Johnson and Susan J. Wolfson. New York: Longman, 2003.

Averill, James H. *Wordsworth and the Poetry of Human Suffering.* Ithaca: Cornell UP, 1980.

Baillie, Joanna. *The Collected Letters of Joanna Baillie.* Ed. Judith Bayley Slagle. 2 vs. London: Associated UPs, 1999.

Bainbridge, Simon. "Lord Ruthven's Power: Polidori's 'The Vampyre,' Doubles and the Byronic Imagination." *Byron Journal* 34/1 (2006): 21–34.

Barbauld, Anna Letitia. *Poems.* 1773; "new edition," London: Joseph Johnson, 1792.

——. *The Female Speaker; or, Miscellaneous Pieces, in Prose and Verse, Selected from the Best Writers, and Adapted to the Use of Young Women.* 1811; 2/e., London: (various booksellers), 1816.

——. *Selected Poetry and Prose.* Ed. William McCarthy and Elizabeth Kraft. Peterborough, Ontario: Broadview P, 2002.

——. *The Works of Anna Lætitia Barbauld, with a Memoir.* Ed. Lucy Aikin. 2 vs. London: Longman, 1825.

Barker-Benfield, G. J. *The Culture of Sensibility: Sex and Society in Eighteenth-Century Britain.* Chicago: U Chicago P, 1992.

Barrell, John. "The Uses of Dorothy." *Poetry, Language, Politics.* Manchester UP, 1988. 137–67.

——. "Sad Stories: Louis XVI, George III, and the Language of Sentiment." *Refiguring Revolutions: Aesthetics and Politics from the English Revolution to the Romantic Revolution.* Ed. Kevin Sharpe and Steven N. Zwicker. Berkeley and Los Angeles: U California P, 1998. 75–98.

Barrett, Elizabeth. *The Brownings' Correspondence.* Ed. Philip Kelley and Ronald Hudson. 10 vs. Winfield, KS: Wedgestone P, 1984–1992.

——. *The Complete Poetical Works of Elizabeth Barrett Browning.* Ed. Harriet Waters Preston. Boston: Houghton Mifflin, 1900.

——. *The Letters of Elizabeth Barrett Browning to Mary Russell Mitford, 1836–1854.* Ed. Meredith B. Raymond and Mary Rose Sullivan. 3 vs. Winfield, KS: Wedgestone P, 1983.

[——]. "Stanzas on the Death of Lord Byron." *Globe and Traveller* (June 1825);

v. 1, *The Complete Works of Elizabeth Barrett Browning*. Ed. Charlotte Porter and Helen A. Clarke. 3 vs. New York: Thomas Y. Crowell, 1900.

Barthes, Roland. *A Lover's Discourse: Fragments*. 1977. Tr. Richard Howard. New York: Hill and Wang, 1978.

Beevers, Robert. *The Byronic Image: The Poet Portrayed*. Oxford, UK: Olivia P, 2005.

Behrendt, Stephen C. "British Women Poets and the Reverberations of Radicalism in the 1790s." *Romanticism, Radicalism, and the Press*. Detroit: Wayne State UP, 1997. 83–102.

———. *British Women Poets and the Romantic Writing Community*. Baltimore: Johns Hopkins UP, 2009.

Benjamin, Walter. "The Work of Art in the Age of Mechanical Reproduction." 1936. Tr. Harry Zohn, 1968. *Illuminations*. Ed. Hannah Arendt. New York: Schocken, 1985. 217–51.

Bennett, Betty T. *British War Poetry in the Age of Romanticism: 1793–1815*. New York: Garland, 1976.

Bentley, Richard. *Milton's "Paradise Lost."* London: Tonson &c., 1732.

Bewell, Alan J. "A 'Word Scarce Said': Hysteria and Witchcraft in Wordsworth's 'Experimental' Poetry of 1797–1798." *ELH* 53 (1986): 357–90.

Blackwood's Edinburgh Magazine 3 (May 1818): 216–224 and *217–218. "Fourth Canto of Childe Harold." [John Wilson; attr. John Murray, letter to Byron 22 September 1818, *L* 261].

——— 5 (August 1819): 512–18. "Remarks on *Don Juan*." [Lockhart, attr. Nicholson, *Byron's Prose* 360]

——— 27 (February/March 1830): 389–420, 421–54; on Moore's *Byron*. [John Wilson, attr. *Blackwood's* May 1830, p. 828].

——— 27 (May 1830): 803–32. *Noctes Ambrosianæ XLIX*.

——— 32 (September 1832): 381–412. *Noctes Ambrosianæ LXII*.

Blair, Robert. *The Grave. A Poem*. London, M. Cooper, 1743.

Blake, William. *The Complete Poetry & Prose of William Blake*. Ed. David V. Erdman. 1965; New York: Anchor/Doubleday, 1982.

———. *Visions of the Daughters of Albion*. 1793. *The Early Illuminated Books*. Princeton: Princeton UP, 1993.

Blessington, Marguerite, Lady. "Aurora Raby." *Heath's Book of Beauty for 1847*. Ed. Countess of Blessington. London: Longman &c., 1847. 23.

———. *Lady Blessington's* Conversations of Lord Byron. 1834; ed. Ernest J. Lovell Jr. Princeton: Princeton UP, 1969.

———. "Thoughts on Lord Byron." *The Keepsake for 1839*. 180–83.

Bloom, Harold. *The Anxiety of Influence: A Theory of Poetry*. New York: Oxford UP, 1973.

————. *The Visionary Company: A Reading of English Romantic Poetry.* 1961; Ithaca: Cornell UP, 1971.

Boswell, James. *The Life of Dr. Samuel Johnson, LLD.* 2 vs. London: Henry Baldwin, 1791.

Botting, Fred. *Gothic.* London and New York: Routledge, 1996.

Bowstead, Diana. "Charlotte Smith's *Desmond:* The Epistolary Novel as Ideological Argument." *Fetter'd or Free? British Women Novelists, 1670–1815.* Ed. Mary Anne Schofield and Cecilia Macheski. Athens: Ohio UP, 1986. 237–63.

Brett, R. L., and A. R. Jones, eds. *Wordsworth & Coleridge: Lyrical Ballads, The text of the 1798 edition with the additional 1800 poems and the Prefaces.* 1965. London: Methuen, 1971.

British Critic 1 (August 1793): 403–6; on Charlotte Smith, *The Emigrants.*

————. 4 (December 1794): 621–23; on Smith, *The Banished Man.*

British Lady's Magazine 4 (October 1816): 248–51; on Coleridge, *Christabel & c.*

Brockedon, W. *Finden's Illustrations of the Life and Works of Lord Byron, with Original and Selected Information on the Subjects of the Engravings.* London: John Murray, 1833–34.

[Brontë, Emily] Ellis Bell. *Wuthering Heights, A Novel.* London: Thomas Cautley Newby, 1847.

Brownstein, Rachel Mayer. "The Private Life: Dorothy Wordsworth's Journals." *Modern Language Quarterly* 34 (1973): 48–63.

Brydges, Sir [Samuel] Egerton. *Letters on the Character and Poetical Genius of Lord Byron.* London: Longman &c., 1824.

Bull, John. [John Gibson Lockhart]. *Letter to the Right Hon. Lord Byron* (London: William Wright, 1821). *John Bull's Letter to Lord Byron.* Ed. Alan Lang Strout. Norman: U Oklahoma P, 1947.

Burke, Edmund. *A Philosophical Enquiry into the Origin of our Ideas of the Sublime and Beautiful.* London: R. and J. Dodsley, 1757.

————. *Reflections on the Revolution in France.* 1790. 2/e. London: J. Dodsley, 1790.

[————]. "Case of the Suffering Clergy of France, Refugees in the British Dominions." London Times, 18 September 1792. 3.

Burnett, T. A. J., ed. See Byron, George Gordon, Lord.

B[urne]y, Dr. [Charles]. *Monthly Review* 2s 29 (June 1799): 202–10; on *Lyrical Ballads.*

[Burney, Frances]. *Brief Reflections relative to the Emigrant French Clergy: earnestly submitted to the humane Consideration of the Ladies of Great Britain.* By the Author of *Evelina* and *Cecilia.* London: Thomas Cadell, [November] 1793.

Burns, Robert. *The Letters of Robert Burns.* Ed. J. De Lancey Ferguson. 2 vs. Oxford: Oxford UP, 1931.

[Burton, Robert.] *The Anatomy of Melancholy, What it is, with all the kinds, causes, symptoms, prognostics, and several cures of it. In Three Partitions, with their several Sections, Members, and Subsections, Philosophically, Medically, Historically Opened and Cut Up.* By Democritus Junior. 2 vs. London: Vernor, Hood & c, 1800.

Butler, James, and Karen Green, eds. LYRICAL BALLADS *and Other Poems, 1797–1800, by William Wordsworth.* Ithaca: Cornell UP, 1992.

Byron, A. I. Noel [Anne Isabella, Lady Noel Byron]. *Remarks Occasioned by Mr. Moore's Notices of Lord Byron's Life.* London: private printing, [1830]. Rpt. *Remarks on Mr. Moore's Life of Lord Byron,* By Lady Byron. Byron, *Works* (1832), 6: 275–80.

Byron, George Gordon, Lord. *Byron's Letters and Journals.* Ed. Leslie A. Marchand. 12 vs. Cambridge: Harvard UP, 1973–82.

——. *Childe Harold's Pilgrimage, A Romaunt.* 3/e London: John Murray, 1812.

——. *Childe Harold's Pilgrimage, Canto the Fourth.* London: John Murray, 1818.

——. *Childe Harold's Pilgrimage, Canto the Third.* London: John Murray, 1816.

——. *Childe Harold's Pilgrimage, Canto III, A Facsimile of the Autograph Fair Copy.* Ed. T. A. J. Burnett. New York: Garland P, 1988.

——. *Complete Miscellaneous Prose.* Ed. Andrew Nicholson. Oxford: Clarendon P, 1991.

——. *Conversations.* See Blessington, Lovell, Medwin.

——. *The Complete Poetical Works.* Ed. Jerome J. McGann. 7 vs. Oxford: Clarendon, 1980–93.

——. *The Corsair, A Tale.* 3/e. London: John Murray, 1814.

——. *Don Juan. Complete Poetical Works,* v. 5.

——. *English Bards and Scotch Reviewers. A Satire.* 4/e. London: James Cawthorn, 1811.

——. *Poems.* 1/e, 2d issue. London: John Murray, 1816.

——. *The Prisoner of Chillon, and Other Poems.* London: John Murray, 1816.

——. "Some Observations upon an Article in *Blackwood's Edinburgh Magazine.*" *W* [1833] 15: 55–98.

——. *The Works of Lord Byron: With His Letters and Journals, and His Life.* By Thomas Moore, Esq. 17 vs. London: John Murray, 1832–34.

——. *The Works of Lord Byron: Poetry.* Ed. Ernest Hartley Coleridge. 7 vs. London: John Murray, 1898–1904.

Carlson, Julie A. *England's First Family of Writers: Mary Wollstonecraft, William Godwin, Mary Shelley.* Baltimore: Johns Hopkins UP, 2007.

The Champion, 14 April 1816. News on the separation of Lord and Lady Byron.

Chew, Samuel. *Byron in England: His Fame and After-Fame.* London: John Murray, 1924.

Chodorow, Nancy. "Family Structure and Feminine Personality." *Women, Culture and Society.* Ed. M. Z. Rosaldo and L. Lamphere. Stanford: Stanford UP, 1974.

Chorley, Henry F[othergill]. *Memorials of Mrs. Hemans, with Illustrations of her Literary Character from her Private Correspondence.* 2 vs. London: Saunders and Otley, 1836.

Christensen, Jerome. *Lord Byron's Strength: Romantic Writing and Commercial Society.* Baltimore: Johns Hopkins UP, 1993.

Clarke, Norma. *Ambitious Heights: Writing, Friendship, Love—The Jewsbury Sisters, Felicia Hemans, and Jane Welsh Carlyle.* New York: Routledge, 1990.

Clemit, Pamela, and Gina Luria Walker, eds. *Memoirs of the Author of A Vindication of the Rights of Woman.* Petersborough, Ontario: Broadview P, 2001.

Cline, C. L. "Unpublished Notes on the Romantic Poets by Isaac D'Israeli." *Studies in English* 21 (1941): 138–46.

Clubbe, John. "The West Portrait of Byron." *Byron Journal* 8 (1980): 22–30.

Cobb, Richard. Review of Claire Tomalin, *The Life and Death of Mary Wollstonecraft. TLS,* 6 September 1974, 941–44.

Coleridge, Ernest Hartley, ed. *The Works of Lord Byron: Poetry.* 7 vs. London: John Murray, 1898–1904.

Coleridge, H. N. "Modern English Poetesses." *Quarterly Review* 46 (January–June 1840): 374–418.

Coleridge, Samuel Taylor. *Aids to Reflection, in the Formation of a Manly Character on the Several Grounds of Prudence, Morality, and Religion.* London: Taylor and Hessey, 1825.

——. *Biographia Literaria, Or Biographical Sketches of My Literary Life and Opinions.* 1817; ed. James Engell and W. Jackson Bate. 2 vs. Princeton: Princeton UP, 1983.

——. *Collected Letters of Samuel Taylor Coleridge.* Ed. Earl Leslie Griggs. 6 vs. Oxford: Clarendon, 1956–71.

——. *Essays on His Times in* THE MORNING POST *and* THE COURIER. Ed. David V. Erdman. 3 vs. Princeton: Princeton UP, 1978.

——. "Lord Byron." *Courier,* 18 April 1816; in *Essays* 2: 427–29; attr. Erdman.

——. ["my Ghost-Theory"], in *The Landing-Place, Essay III. The Friend: A Series of Essays in Three Volumes, to Aid in the Formation of Fixed Principles in*

Politics, Morals, and Religion, with Literary Amusements Interspersed (London: Rest Fenner, 1818) 1: 244–50.

———. *On the Principles of Method.* In *The Friend* (1818). Ed. Barbara E. Rooke. 2 vs. Princeton: Princeton UP 1969. 1: 448–57.

———. "Historical Sketch of the Manners and Religion of the ancient Germans . . ." *The Watchman,* no. III (17 March 1796); Patton, ed. 89–92.

———. *Lectures, 1808–1819, On Literature.* Ed. R. A. Foakes. 2 vs. Princeton: Princeton UP, 1987.

———. *Literary Remains of Samuel Taylor Coleridge.* Ed. Henry Nelson Coleridge. v. 3. London: William Pickering, 1838.

———. *The Notebooks of Samuel Taylor Coleridge.* Ed. Kathleen Coburn. 3 vs.; vs. 1 and 2, New York: Bollingen/Pantheon, 1957, 1961; v. 3, Princeton: Princeton UP / Bollingen, 1973.

———. "On the Slave Trade," *The Watchman* No. IV, Friday, March 25, 1796. Patton, ed. 130–40.

———. *Poems.* 2/e. Bristol: J. Cottle / London: Messrs. Robinsons, 1797.

———. Prospectus for *The Watchman.* Bristol, 1976.

———. "Reflections on Entering into Active life, *A Poem which affects Not To Be* POETRY." *Monthly Magazine* 2 (October 1796): 712.

———. *The Statesman's Manual, or the Bible the Best Guide to Political Skill and Foresight: A Lay Sermon Addressed to the Higher Classes of Society.* London: Gale and Fenner &c., 1816.

———. *The Watchman.* Ed. Lewis Patton. Princeton: Princeton UP, 1970.

Colley, Linda. *Britons: Forging the Nation 1707–1837.* New Haven: Yale UP 1992.

Collins, William. *Odes on Several Descriptive and Allegoric Subjects.* London: A. Millar, 1747.

Colls, John Henry. *A Poetic Epistle Addressed to Miss Wollstonecraft. Occasioned by Reading Her Celebrated* Essay on the Rights of Woman, *and her* Historical and Moral View of the French Revolution. London: Vernor and Hood / G. and T. Wilkie, 1795.

Cooke, Michael G. *Acts of Inclusion.* New Haven: Yale UP, 1979.

Cornwall, Barry [Bryan Waller Procter]. "A Chapter on Portraits." *The Literary Souvenir, or, Cabinet of Poetry and Romance.* Ed. Alaric A. Watts. London: Longman & c, 1829. 347–55.

Cottle, Joseph. *Reminiscences of Samuel Taylor Coleridge and Robert Southey.* London, 1847; New York: Wiley and Putnam, 1848.

Courier, 18 April 1816, "Lord Byron." Coleridge, *Essays* 2: 427–29.

Cowper, William. *The Poems of William Cowper.* Ed. John D. Baird and Charles Ryskamp. 3 vs. Oxford: Clarendon P, 1995.

———. *The Task, A Poem in Six Books*. London: J. Johnson, 1785.

Cox, Jeffrey N. *Poetry and Politics in the Cockney School: Keats, Shelley, Hunt and their Circle*. Cambridge: Cambridge UP, 1998.

Craciun, Adriana. *British Women Writers and the French Revolution: Citizens of the World*. New York: Palgrave Macmillan, 2005.

Crawford, Rachel. "The Structure of the Sororal in Wordsworth's 'Nutting.'" *Studies in Romanticism* 31 (1992): 197–211.

Critical Review 70 (1790): 694; on Wollstonecraft, *Rights of Men*.

Critical Review; or annals of literature; extended and improved by a society of gentlemen. 2s 4 (April 1792): 389–98; and 5 (June 1792): 132–41; on Wollstonecraft, *Vindication of the Rights of Woman*.

——— 2s 6 (September 1792): 99–105; on Charlotte Smith, *Desmond*.

——— 2s 9 (October 1794): 299–302; on Charlotte Smith, *Emigrants*.

——— 2s 10 (March 1794): 318–21; on Frances Burney, *Brief Reflections*.

——— 2s 24 (October 1798): 197–204; Aristarchus [Robert Southey], on *Lyrical Ballads*.

——— 5s 4 (November 1816): 495–506; on Byron's *Childe Harold III*. (December 1816): 567–81; on Byron's *Prisoner of Chillon & c.*

Crompton, Louis. *Byron and Greek Love: Homophobia in 19th-Century England*. Berkeley and Los Angeles: U California P, 1985.

Crowe, William. *Verses Intended to Have Been Spoken in the Theatre to the Duke of Portland, at His Installation as Chancellor of the University of Oxford, in the Year 1793*. See Coleridge, *The Watchman*.

Culler, Jonathan. *On Deconstruction: Theory and Criticism after Structuralism*. Ithaca: Cornell UP, 1982.

Curran, Stuart. "Charlotte Smith and British Romanticism." *South Central Review* 11.2 (1994): 66–78.

———. "The 'I' Altered." 1988; *Romanticism and Feminism*. Mellor, ed. 185–207.

———. *Poetic Form and British Romanticism*. New York: Oxford UP, 1986.

———, ed. *Desmond. The Works of Charlotte Smith*. London: Pickering Chatto, 2005.

———, ed. *The Poems of Charlotte Smith*. New York: Oxford UP, 1993.

Curtis, Jared. *The Fenwick Notes of William Wordsworth*. London: Bristol Classics, 1992.

Dallas, Robert Charles. *Recollections of the Life of Lord Byron, from the Year 1808 to the End of 1814*. London: Charles Knight, 1824.

Darlington, Beth. "Two Early Texts: *A Night Piece* and *The Discharged Soldier*." *Bicentenary Wordsworth Studies in Memory of John Alban Finch*. Ed. Jonathan Wordsworth with Beth Darlington. Ithaca: Cornell UP, 1970. 425–48.

Darwin, Erasmus. *Zoonomia; or the Laws of Organic Life.* London: J. Johnson, v. 1, 1794; v. 2, 1796.

Davis, Robert Con. "The Structure of the Picturesque: Dorothy Wordsworth's *Journals.*" *The Wordsworth Circle* 9 (1978): 45–49.

De Quincey, Thomas. "On Wordsworth's Poetry," *Tait's Edinburgh Magazine,* September 1845. 545–54.

[———]. "Recollections of Grasmere," *Tait's Edinburgh Magazine* (September 1839) 569–81; *Literary Reminiscences; from the Autobiography of an English Opium-Eater.* 2 vs. Boston: Ticknor, Reed, and Fields, 1852. Chapter XV (2: 61–101).

[———]. "Theory of Greek Tragedy." *Blackwood's Magazine* 47 (February 1840): 145–53. Author identified by *Letters to a Young Man, and Other Papers.* Boston: Ticknor, Reed, and Fields, 1854.

———. "William Wordsworth." *Tait's Edinburgh Magazine* (January, February, April, 1839) 1–12, 90–103, 246–54; *Literary Reminiscences; from the Autobiography of the English Opium-Eater.* 2 vs. Boston: Ticknor, Reed, and Fields, 1851. 1: X–XII (255–366).

de Selincourt, Ernest. *Dorothy Wordsworth: A Biography.* Oxford: Clarendon P, 1933.

———, ed. *George & Sarah Green, A Narrative By Dorothy Wordsworth.* Oxford: Clarendon P, 1936.

———, and Helen Darbishire, eds. *The Poetical Works of William Wordsworth.* 5 vs. Oxford: Clarendon, 1956.

Domett, Alfred. *Ranolf and Amohia: A dream of two lives.* New ed., rev. London: Kegan Paul, Trench & Co. 1883.

Dryden, John. *Virgil's* Aeneid. 1693. New York: Airmont P, 1968.

———. *Palamon and Arcite; or The Knight's Tale. Fables, Ancient and Modern; Translated in Verse.* 1700; 5/e. London: J. and R. Tonson, 1745.

———. *The State of Innocence and Fall of Man.* 1677; *Comedies, Tragedies, and Operas.* 2 vs. London: Jacob Tonson, 1701. 1: 594–618.

Durant, W. Clark, ed. *Memoirs of Mary Wollstonecraft, Written by William Godwin.* 1927; New York: Haskell House, 1969.

Duykinck, Evert A. *A Portrait Gallery of Eminent Men and Women of Europe and America, with Biographies.* 2 vs. New York: Johnson, Wilson and Co., 1873. Portraits by Alonzo Chappel.

Dyer, G[eorge]. *Ode VII: On Liberty. Poems.* London: J. Johnson, 1792. 32–38.

Eclectic Review 2s 5 (June 1816): 595–99: "Lord Byron's *Poems.*" [Josiah Conder; attr. Reiman, ed., B II: 736].

Edgeworth, Maria. *Letters for Literary Ladies.* London: Joseph Johnson, 1795.

Eilenberg, Susan. "The Poetry of Property." *Strange Power of Speech: Wordsworth, Coleridge, and Literary Possession.* New York: Oxford UP, 1992.

Elfenbein, Andrew. *Byron and the Victorians.* Cambridge: Cambridge UP, 1995.

Eliot, George. "The Natural History of German Life." *Westminster Review* ns 10 (July 1856): 51–79.

Eliot, T. S. "Hysteria." *Prufrock and Other Observations* (1917). *The Complete Poems and Plays: 1909–1950.* New York: Harcourt, Brace & World, 1952.

——. "Tradition and the Individual Talent." 1917. *Selected Essays, 1917–1932.* New York: Harcourt, Brace, 1932. 3–11.

Ellis, Mrs. [Sarah Stickney]. *The Daughters of England: Their Position in Society, Characters, and Responsibilities.* 1842; New York: Appleton, 1843.

Ellison, Julie. "'Nice Arts' and 'Potent Energy': The Gendered Economy of Wordsworth's Fancy." *Centennial Review* 33 (1989): 441–67.

Elwin, Malcolm. *Lord Byron's Wife.* New York: Harcourt, 1962.

Elwood, Mrs. [Anne Katharine Curteis]. "Mrs. Charlotte Smith." *Memoirs of the Literary Ladies of England from the Commencement of the Last Century.* London: Henry Colburn, 1843; Philadelphia: G. B. Zieber, 1845. 55–61.

Emerson, Ralph Waldo. *Poetry and Imagination. Letters and Social Aims.* Boston: James R. Osgood and Co., 1876. 4–67.

English Review 17 (1791): 61; on Wollstonecraft, *Vindication of the Rights of Men.*

The English Romantic Poets; A Review of Research and Criticism. 4/e. Ed. Frank Jordan. New York: MLA, 1985.

European Magazine, and London Review 27 (June 1795): 418–19. "Verses Intended . . ." See Crowe, William.

——. 65/2 (January 1814): 2–4. "Memoir of the Right Hon. George Gordon Byron, Lord Byron of Rochdale." "[with a portrait.]"

——. 81 (January 1822): 58–70. On Byron, *Sardanapalus, The Two Foscari,* and *Cain.*

Evans, Robert O. "Hysteron Proteron." *Princeton Encyclopedia of Poetry and Poetics.* Ed. Alex Preminger and T. V. F. Brogan. Princeton: Princeton UP, 1993. 547.

Examiner 434 (21 April 1816): 247–50; and 435 (28 April 1816): 266. [Leigh Hunt], "Distressing Circumstance in High Life."

——. 8 January 1848: 21–22; on Ellis Bell, *Wuthering Heights.*

Fadem, Richard. "Dorothy Wordsworth: A View from 'Tintern Abbey.'" *Wordsworth Circle* 9 (1978): 17–32.

Favret, Mary A. "Coming Home: The Public Spaces of Romantic War." *Studies in Romanticism* 33 (1994): 539–48.

Ferguson, Frances. *Wordsworth: Language as Counter-Spirit.* New Haven: Yale UP, 1977.

Ferrier, Susan. *Memoirs and Correspondence of Susan Ferrier 1782–1854, based on her private correspondence in the possession of, and collected by, her grand-nephew John Ferrier.* Ed. John A. Doyle. London: John Murray, 1898.

Ferry, David. *The Limits of Mortality: An Essay on Wordsworth's Major Poems.* Middletown, CT: Wesleyan UP, 1959.

Finden, William, and Edward Finden. *Les Dames de Byron; or, Portraits of the Principle Female Characters in Lord Byron's Poems, Engraved from Original Paintings by Eminent Artists.* London: Charles Tilt, 1836.

Flynn, Elizabeth A., and Patrocinio P. Schweickart, eds. *Gender and Reading: Essays on Readers, Texts, and Contexts.* Baltimore: Johns Hopkins UP, 1986.

Fordyce, James. *Sermons to Young Women, in Two Volumes.* London: A. Millar and T. Cadell, J. Dodsley, J. Payne, 1766.

Forster, Antonia, and James Raven, with Stephen Bending, eds. (*1770–1779*). V. 1 of *The English Novel 1770–1829: A Biographical Survey of Prose Fiction Published in the British Isles.* Oxford: Oxford UP, 2000.

Foster, Vere, ed. *The Two Duchesses: Georgiana, Duchess of Devonshire; Elizabeth, Duchess of Devonshire. Family Correspondence of and Relating to . . .* London: Blackie & Son, 1898.

Franklin, Caroline. *Byron and Women Novelists.* U Nottingham: School of English Studies, 2001.

——. "Juan's Sea Changes." *"Don Juan," Theory and Practice.* Ed. Nigel Wood. Buckingham, England; and Philadelphia, Open UP, 1993. 56–89.

——. *Mary Wollstonecraft: A Literary Life.* New York: Palgrave Macmillan, 2004.

Friedman, Michael H. *The Making of a Tory Humanist: Wordsworth and the Idea of Community.* New York: Columbia UP, 1979.

Frosch, Thomas R. "Wordsworth's 'Beggars' and a Brief Instance of 'Writer's Block.'" *Studies in Romanticism* 21 (1982) 619–36.

Gentleman's Magazine and Historical Chronicle 61.1 (February 1791): 151–54; on Wollstonecraft, *A Vindication of the Rights of Men.*

Gilbert, Sandra M., and Susan Gubar. *The Madwoman in the Attic: The Woman Writer and the Nineteenth-Century Literary Imagination.* New Haven: Yale UP, 1979.

Gilfillan, George. "John Keats." *A Gallery of Literary Portraits.* London: Simpkin, Marshall / Edinburgh: William Tait, 1845. 372–85.

Gilligan, Carol. *In a Different Voice: Psychological Theory and Women's Development.* Cambridge: Harvard UP, 1982.

Gisborne, Thomas. *An Enquiry into the Duties of the Female Sex.* London: T. Cadell Jr. and W. Davies, 1796.

Glen, Heather. *Vision & Disenchantment: Blake's* SONGS *and* WORDSWORTH'S LYRICAL BALLADS. Cambridge: Cambridge UP, 1983.

Godwin, William. *Deloraine*. London: Richard Bentley, 1833.

——. *Fleetwood; or The New Man of Feeling*. 1805; London: Richard Bentley, 1832.

——. *Memoirs of the Author of A Vindication of the Rights of Woman*. London: J. Johnson and G. G. and J. Robinson, 1798; 2d "corrected" ed., J. Johnson, 1798. Citations are from 1st ed., unless otherwise noted.

——. Preface. *Letters and Miscellaneous Pieces*. Wollstonecraft, *Posthumous Works*, v. 3; unnumbered pages.

Goldsmith, Oliver. *The Traveller; or a Prospect of Society. A Poem*. London: J. Newbery, 1764.

Good, John Mason. *The Study of Medicine* (London, 1822, cited in *OED* 1971). 3/e. Augmented by Samuel Cooper. 5 vs. London: Thomas and George Underwood, 1829.

Graham, Peter W. DON JUAN *and Regency England*. Charlottesville: UP Virginia, 1990.

Gray, Thomas. *Ode on a Distant Prospect of Eton College*. London: R. Dodsley, 1747.

A Greek-English Lexicon. Compiled by Henry George Liddell and Robert Scott. Rev. and Augmented Throughout by Sir Henry Stuart Jones. 2 vs. Oxford: Clarendon P, 1968.

Greenblatt, Stephen. "Culture." *Critical Terms for Literary Study*. Ed. Frank Lentricchia and Thomas McLaughlin. Chicago: U Chicago P, 1995. 225–32.

——. *Renaissance Self-Fashioning: From More to Shakespeare*. Chicago: U Chicago P, 1980.

Greer, Donald. *The Incidence of the Emigration During the French Revolution*. Cambridge: Harvard UP, 1951.

Gregory, Dr. John. *A Father's Legacy to his Daughters*. New edition. London: W. Strahan, and T. Cadell / Edinburgh: J. Balfour, and W. Creech, 1774.

——. *A Comparative View of the State and Faculties of Man. With Those of the Animal World*. London: J. Dodsley, 1765.

Grenby, M. O. *The Anti-Jacobin Novel: British Conservatism and the French Revolution*. Cambridge: Cambridge UP, 2001.

——, ed. Charlotte Smith, *The Banished Man*. Smith, *Works*, v. 7.

Guillory, John. *Cultural Capital: The Problem of Literary Canon Formation*. Chicago: U Chicago P, 1993.

Hale, Sarah Josepha. "Caroline Norton." *Woman's Record; or, Sketches of all Distinguished Women from the creation to A. D. 1854: arranged in four eras: with selections from authoresses of each era*. New York: Harper & Bros, 1855. 761–62.

Hardwick, Elizabeth. "Amateurs: Dorothy Wordsworth and Jane Carlyle." *New York Review of Books* 19.9 (30 November 1972): 3–4.

Hardy, Thomas. *Tess of the D'Urbervilles*. London: James R. Osgood, &c., 1891.

Hartman, Geoffrey H. "Wordsworth, Inscriptions, and Romantic Nature Poetry." *Beyond Formalism: Literary Essays 1958-1970*. New Haven: Yale UP, 1970. 206-30.

——. *Wordsworth's Poetry, 1787-1814*. 1964; New Haven: Yale University Press, 1971, with "Retrospect 1971."

Hays, Mary. *Appeal to the Men of Great Britain in Behalf of Woman*. London: J. Johnson and J. Bell, 1798.

Hazlitt, William. "Coleridge." *The Spirit of The Age; or Contemporary Portraits*. 2/e. London: Colburn, 1825. 55-76.

——. "My First Acquaintance with Poets." *The Liberal* 2 (April 1823): 23-46.

[——]. "On Personal Character." Signed "T." Table Talk No. VIII. *London Magazine*, March 1821. 291-98.

——. "The Round Table." *The Examiner*, Sunday, 12 February 1815. 108.

Heath, William. *Wordsworth and Coleridge: A Study of Their Literary Relations in 1801-1802*. Oxford: Clarendon P, 1970.

Heffernan, James A. W. "Wordsworth's Leveling Muse in 1798." *1798: The Year of the "Lyrical Ballads."* Ed. Richard Cronin. New York: St. Martin's P, 1998. 231-53.

Heinzelman, Kurt. "The Cult of Domesticity: Dorothy and William Wordsworth at Grasmere." Mellor, ed. 52-78.

Hemans, Felicia. "Corinna at the Capitol." *Literary Souvenir, or, Cabinet of Poetry and Romance*. Ed. Alaric A. Watts. London: Longman &c., 1827. 189-91.

——. "The Land of Dreams." *Blackwood's Edinburgh Magazine* 24 (December 1828): 783-84; by "F. H."

——. *Selected Poems, Letters and Reception Materials*. Ed. Susan J. Wolfson. Princeton: Princeton UP, 2000.

Hilbish, Florence May Anna. *Charlotte Smith, Poet and Novelist (1749-1806)*. Philadelphia: University of Pennsylvania, 1941.

Hine, Dr. Joseph, ed. *Selections from the Poems of William Wordsworth, Esq. chiefly for the use of schools and young persons*. 1831; London: Edward Moxon, 1834.

[Hobhouse, John Cam]. "Dallas's *Recollections* and Medwin's *Conversations*." *Westminster Review* 3 (January 1825): 1-35.

Hofkosh, Sonia. "The Writer's Ravishment: Women and the Romantic Author— The Example of Byron." Mellor, ed. 93-114.

Holmes, Richard. "The Romantic Circle." *New York Review of Books* 44/6 (10 April 1997): 34-35.

——, ed. Wollstonecraft's *Letters Written During a Short Residence in Sweden, Norway, and Denmark*. Harmondsworth, UK: Penguin, 1987.

Homans, Margaret. *Bearing the Word: Language and Female Experience in Nineteenth-Century Women's Writing*. Chicago: U Chicago P, 1986.

———. *Women Writers and Poetic Identity: Dorothy Wordsworth, Emily Brontë, and Emily Dickinson*. Princeton: Princeton UP, 1980.

Hume, David. *A treatise of human nature: being an attempt to introduce the experimental method of reasoning into moral subjects*. 3 vs. London: John Noon, 1739–40.

Hunt, Bishop C., Jr. "Wordsworth and Charlotte Smith." *The Wordsworth Circle* 1 (1970); rpt. 35 (2004): 80–91.

Hunt, Leigh. *Lord Byron and Some of His Contemporaries; With Recollections of the Author's Life, and of His Visit to Italy*. 2/e. 2 vs. London: Henry Colburn, 1828. See also *Examiner*.

Hunt, Lynn. "The Many Bodies of Marie Antoinette: Political Pornography and the Problem of the Feminine in the French Revolution." *Eroticism and the Body Politic*. Ed. Lynn Hunt. Baltimore: Johns Hopkins UP, 1991. 108–30.

Hyman, Suzanne K. "Contemporary Portraits of Byron." *Lord Byron and His Contemporaries: Essays from the Sixth International Byron Seminar*. Ed. Charles E. Robinson. Newark: U Delaware P, 1982. 204–36.

[Iley, Matthew]. *The Life, Writings, Opinions, and Times of the Right Hon. George Gordon Noel Byron, Lord Byron*. "By an English Gentleman, in the Greek Military Service, and Comrade of His Lordship." 3 vs. London: Matthew Iley, 1825 (attr. Chew, Lovell).

[Irving, Washington]. *Abbotsford and Newstead Abbey*. London: John Murray, 1835.

Iser, Wolfgang. "The Reading Process: A Phenomenological Approach." *NLH* 3 (1972): 279–99.

Jacobus, Mary. *Romanticism, Writing, and Sexual Difference: Essays on* THE PRELUDE. Oxford: Clarendon P, 1989.

———. *Tradition and Experiment in Wordsworth's* Lyrical Ballads *(1798)*. Oxford: Clarendon P, 1976.

[Jeffrey, Francis]. *Edinburgh Review* 1 (October 1802) 63–83; on the "new poetry."

[———]. 12 (April 1808) 131–51; on Crabbe, 1807 *Poems*.

[———]. 23 (April 1814): 198–229; on Byron, *The Corsair* and *The Bride of Abydos*.

[———]. 27 (December 1816): 277–310; on Byron, *Childe Harold III* and *The Prisoner of Chillon*.

[———]. 36 (February 1822): 413–52. "Lord Byron's Tragedies."

Jehlen, Myra. "Archimedes and the Paradox of Feminist Criticism." *Signs* 6 (1981): 575–601.

[Jewsbury, Maria Jane] M. J. J. *Phantasmagoria; or Sketches of Life and Literature*. 2 vs. London: Hurst & Robinson/Edinburgh: Archibald Constable, 1825.

[———] M. J. J. "The Young Author." *Phantasmagoria* 1: 189–98. First pub. *Literary Souvenir* (1825), 85–93.

[———]. Contributions to *The Athenæum* 1830–31; identified in a file (Fryckstedt 470–73, 65–70); 1831 reviews also in the City University Contributor Record (www.soi.city.ac.uk). For 1832, I concur with Norma Clarke's guesses "on the basis of subject matter and style" (229–30 n. 40).

[?]. *Athenæum* 222 (28 January 1832): 65–66. "A Brief Historical Notice of the Position of Women in Society, Introductory to a Paper 'On Modern Female Cultivation.'" This essay follows a poem "By Miss Jewsbury" in the section of "Original Papers" (65).

Athenæum 191 (25 June 1831): 404–5; *Selections from the Poems of William Wordsworth, chiefly for the Use of Schools and Young Persons*.

Athenæum 194 (16 July 1831): 456–57; "Shelley's 'Wandering Jew.'"

Johnson, Barbara. "Strange Fits: Poe and Wordsworth on the Nature of Poetic Language." *A World of Difference*. Baltimore: Johns Hopkins UP, 1987. 89–99.

Johnson, Claudia L. *Equivocal Beings: Politics, Gender, and Sentimentality in the 1790s: Wollstonecraft, Radcliffe, Burney, Austen*. Chicago: U Chicago P, 1995.

———. Introduction, Hannah More's *Considerations* and Frances Burney's *Brief Reflections*. Augustan Reprint Society no. 262. Los Angeles: UCLA, William Andrews Clark Memorial Library, 1990. iii–xii.

———. *Jane Austen: Women, Politics, and the Novel*. Chicago: U Chicago P, 1988.

———, ed. *The Cambridge Companion to Mary Wollstonecraft*. Cambridge: Cambridge UP, 2002.

Johnson, Dr. Samuel. *The Rambler*, no. 60 (13 October 1750). *The Rambler*. 6 vs. London: J. Payne and J. Bouquet, 1752. 2: 207–15.

Jones, Christine Kenyon. "Fantasy and Transfiguration: Byron and His Portraits." *Byromania*. Ed. Frances Wilson. 109–36.

———, ed. *Byron: The Image of the Poet*. Newark: U Delaware P.

Jones, Gregory. "'Rude Intercourse': Uncensoring Wordsworth's 'Nutting.'" *Studies in Romanticism* 35 (1996): 213–43.

Jones, John. *The Egotistical Sublime: A History of Wordsworth's Imagination*. 1954; London: Chatto & Windus, 1964.

Jones, Kathleen. *A Passionate Sisterhood: Women of the Wordsworth Circle/The Sisters, Wives, and Daughters of the Lake Poets*. New York: St. Martins P, 2000.

Kahn, Coppélia. "The Absent Mother in *King Lear*." *Rewriting the Renaissance: The Discourses of Sexual Difference in Early Modern Europe*. Ed. Margaret W. Ferguson, Maureen Quilligan, and Nancy J. Vickers. Chicago: U Chicago P, 1986. 33–49.

Keats, John. *John Keats: A Longman Cultural Edition*. Ed. Susan J. Wolfson. New York: Pearson, 2007.

Knight, William, ed. *Poetical Works of William Wordsworth*. London: Macmillan, 1896. v. 8.

Knoepflmacher, U. C. "Genre and the Integration of Gender: From Wordsworth to George Eliot to Virginia Woolf." *Victorian Literature and Society*. Ed. James R. Kincaid and Albert J. Kuhn. Columbus: Ohio State UP, 1984. 94–118.

Labbe, Jacqueline. "Gentility in Distress: A New Letter by Charlotte Smith (1789–1806)." *The Wordsworth Circle* 35 (2004): 91–93.

——, ed. *The Works of Charlotte Smith*. V. 14. London: Pickering & Chatto, 2007.

[Lamb, Caroline]. *A New Canto*. London: William Wright, 1819.

Lamb, Charles. *The Letters of Charles and Mary Anne Lamb*. 3 vs. Ed. Edwin W. Marrs Jr. Ithaca: Cornell UP, 1975.

L.E.L. [Letitia Elizabeth Landon]. "Byron." *English Bijou Almanac for 1836*. London: Albert Schloss, 1835.

——. *The Improvisatrice; and Other Poems*. London: Hurst, Robinson / Edinburgh: Constable, 1824. 1–105.

——. "Lines Suggested on Visiting Newstead Abbey." *Fisher's Drawing Room Scrap-Book*. London: Fisher, Son, 1839. 44–45

——. "Love's Last Lesson." *The Golden Violet, with its Tales of Romance and Chivalry: and Other Poems*. London: Longman &c., 1827. 298–306.

——. "Stanzas. Written beneath the Portrait of Lord Byron, Painted by Mr. West." *Literary Souvenir, or, Cabinet of Poetry and Romance*. Ed. Alaric A. Watts. London: Longman &c., 1827. 33–36.

——. "The Portrait of Lord Byron at Newstead Abbey." *Fisher's Drawing Room Scrap-Book*. London: Fisher, Son, 1840. 11–14.

Langbaum, Robert. *The Poetry of Experience: The Dramatic Monologue in Modern Literary Tradition*. 1957; New York: Norton, 1971.

Lawford, Cynthia. "Diary." *London Review of Books* 22.18 (21 September 2000): 36–37.

Le Beau Monde, or, Literary and Fashionable Magazine 2 (October 1807) 138–42; on Wordsworth's *Poems, in Two Volumes*.

Le Breton, Anna Letitia. *Memoir of Mrs. Barbauld, including Letters and Notices of Her Family and Friends. By her Great Niece*. London: George Bell and Sons, 1874.

Leighton, Angela. *Victorian Women Poets: Writing Against the Heart.* Charlottesville: UP Virginia, 1992.

Lemprière, John. *A Classical Dictionary.* 8/e. London: T. Cadell and W. Davies, 1812.

Levao, Ronald. "'Among Unequals What Society': *Paradise Lost* and the Forms of Intimacy." *Modern Language Quarterly* 61.1 (2000): 79–108.

Levin, Susan M. *Dorothy Wordsworth & Romanticism.* New Brunswick: Rutgers UP, 1987; rev. Jefferson, NC, and London: Mc Farland & Co., 2009.

——. *Dorothy Wordsworth: A Longman Cultural Edition.* New York: Pearson/Longman, 2009.

Levine, David. Cartoon of Mary Wollstonecraft. *New York Review of Books* 19/7 (2 November 1972), to accompany V. S. Pritchett's essay, "The Strength of an Injured Spirit," on the occasion of *Mary Wollstonecraft,* by Eleanor Flexner (New York: Coward, McCann & Geoghegan, 1972).

Levinson, Marjorie. *The Romantic Fragment Poem: A Critique of a Form.* Chapel Hill: U of North Carolina P, 1986.

——. *Wordsworth's great period poems: Four essays.* Cambridge: Cambridge UP, 1986.

Literary Gazette 389 (3 July 1824): 417–20; on L.E.L., *The Improvisatrice &c.* [William Jerdan].

Literary Souvenir; or, Cabinet of Poetry and Romance. Ed. Alaric A. Watts. London: Longman &c., 1827.

Lloyd, Charles. *Lines to Mary Wollstonecraft Godwin. Blank Verse.* London: T. Bensley, 1798. 62–72.

Lockhart, John Gibson. *The Life of Sir Walter Scott (1837–39).* 10 vs. Edinburgh: T. and A. Constable, 1902.

London Review 22 (July 1792): 21–23; on Charlotte Smith, *Desmond.*

London Review (European Magazine) 24 (July 1793) 41–45; on Charlotte Smith, *The Emigrants.*

London Times 14 September 1792, 2–3: "news received yesterday from Paris"; reports on "subscriptions for the Clergy of France."

——. 18 September 1792, 3: "Case of the Suffering Clergy of France."

Lonsdale, Roger, ed. *The Poems of Gray, Collins, and Goldsmith.* New York: Longman, 1969.

Lovell, Ernest J. Jr., ed. *His Very Self and Voice: Collected Conversations of Lord Byron.* New York: Macmillan, 1954.

Low, Dennis. "Maria Jane Jewsbury." *The Literary Protégées of the Lake Poets.* Burlington, VT: Ashgate P, 2006.

Lowell, James Russell. "Wordsworth." *The Writings of James Russell Lowell.* 10 vs. Boston and New York: Houghton, Mifflin, 1894. 6: 354–415.

Macaulay, Thomas Babington. *Edinburgh Review* 53 (June 1831): 544–72; on Thomas Moore, *Life of Byron* (1830).

MacCarthy, Fiona. *Byron: Life and Legend.* New York: Farrar, Straus, Giroux, 2002.

Macdonald, Lorne, and Kathleen Scherf, eds. *Mary Wollstonecraft: The Vindications.* Peterborough, Ontario: Broadview P, 1997.

Mackenzie, Henry. *The Man of Feeling.* London: T. Cadell, 1771.

MacLean, Kenneth. *Agrarian Age: A Background for Wordsworth.* 1950; Hamden, CT: Archon, 1970.

Mandell, Laura. "Rehistoricizing Romantic Ideology: New Perspectives on Class and Gender Conflict, 1730–1800." *Blake: An Illustrated Quarterly* 27 (1993): 46–63.

Manning, Peter J. *Byron and His Fictions.* Detroit: Wayne State UP, 1978.

Marchand, Leslie A. *Byron: A Biography.* 3 vs. New York: Knopf, 1957.

———. *Byron: A Portrait.* Chicago: U Chicago P, 1970.

———. "'Come to me, my adored boy, George': Byron's Ordeal with Lady Falkland." *Byron Journal* 16 (1988): 21–28.

Martineau, Harriet. "Life and Character of Lady Noel Byron." *Daily News,* 24 May 1860; rpt. as "Lady Noel Byron." *Biographical Sketches.* New York: Leypoldt and Holt, 1869. 282–91.

Mathias, T. J. *The Pursuits of Literature. A Satirical Poem in Four Dialogues. With Notes.* 1796; 7/e, rev. London: T. Becket, 1798.

———. *The Shade of Alexander Pope on the Banks of the Thames, A Satirical Poem, With Notes,* by the Author of *The Pursuits of Literature.* London: T. Becket, 1799.

Matlak, Richard. "Wordsworth's Lucy Poems in Psychobiographical Context." *PMLA* 93 (1978): 46–65.

Mayne, Ethel Colburn. *Byron.* New York: Books for Libraries P, 1924.

———. *The Life and Letters of Anne Isabella, Lady Noel Byron.* London: Constable, 1929.

Mayo, Robert. "The Contemporaneity of the *Lyrical Ballads.*" *PMLA* 69 (1954): 486–522.

McCann, Walter Edgar. "Byronism." *The Galaxy* 5 (June 1868): 777–81.

McDayter, Ghislaine. "Conjuring Byron: Byromania, Literary Commodification and the Birth of Celebrity." Wilson, ed., *Byromania.* 43–62.

McGann, Jerome J. "The Book of Byron and the Book of a World." 1982–83; *The Beauty of Inflections: Literary Investigations in Historical Method and Theory.* Oxford: Clarendon P, 1988. 255–93.

———. *Byron and Romanticism.* Ed. James Soderholm. Cambridge: Cambridge UP, 2002.

———. "Byron and the Anonymous Lyric." 1992; Soderholm, ed. 93–112.

———. "Byron and 'The Truth in Masquerade.'" *Rereading Byron.* Ed. Alice Levine and Robert N. Keane. New York: Garland, 1993. 93–112.

———. "Hero With a Thousand Faces: The Rhetoric of Byronism." 1992; Soderholm, ed. 141–59.

———. "What difference do the circumstances of publication make to the interpretation of a literary work?" Soderholm, ed. 77–92.

———, ed. *Lord Byron.* See Byron.

———, and Daniel Riess, eds. *Letitia Elizabeth Landon: Selected Writings.* Peterborough, Ontario: Broadview P, 1997.

Medwin, Thomas. *Conversations of Lord Byron: Noted During a Residence with His Lordship at Pisa, in the Years 1821 and 1822.* London: Henry Colburn, 1824.

———. *Medwin's Conversations of Lord Byron.* Rev. 3/e, annotated by contemporaries. Ed. Ernest J. Lovell Jr. Princeton: Princeton UP, 1966.

Mellor, Anne K. "English Women Writers and the French Revolution." *Rebel Daughters: Women and the French Revolution.* Ed. Sara E. Melzer and Leslie W. Rabine. New York: Oxford UP, 1992. 255–72.

———. "The Female Poet and the Poetess: Two Traditions of British Women's Poetry, 1780–1830." *Studies in Romanticism* 36 (1997): 261–76.

———. "Mary Wollstonecraft's *A Vindication of the Rights of Woman* and the Women Writers of Her Day." Claudia L. Johnson, ed., *Cambridge Companion.* 141–59.

———. *Mothers of the Nation: Women's Political Writing in England, 1780–1830.* Bloomington: Indiana UP, 2000.

———. "Teaching Wordsworth and Women." *Approaches to Teaching Wordsworth's Poetry.* Ed. Spencer Hall with Jonathan Ramsey. New York: MLA, 1986. 142–46.

———, ed. *Romanticism and Feminism.* Bloomington: Indiana UP, 1988.

———, and Richard Matlak, eds. *British Literature, 1780–1830.* Fort Worth: Harcourt Brace, 1996.

Micale, Marc S. "Hysteria and Historiography: A Review of Past and Present Writings." *History of Science* 27 (September and December 1989): 223–61; 319–51.

Milbanke, Anne Isabella. *Byromania.* Mayne, *Life and Letters.*

Milbanke, Ralph, Earl of Lovelace. *Astarte: A Fragment of Truth Concerning George Gordon Byron, Sixth Lord Byron.* New ed. with additional letters edited by Mary, Countess of Lovelace. London: Christophers, 1921.

Miller, J. Hillis. *The Linguistic Moment from Wordsworth to Stevens.* Princeton: Princeton UP, 1985.

Milton, John. *Areopagitica. Complete Poems and Major Prose.* Ed. Merritt Y. Hughes. New York: Odyssey, 1957.

——. *Paradise Lost. A Poem in Twelve Books.* 2e. London: S. Simmons, 1674.

Mitford, Mary Russell. "Nutting." *Our Village: Sketches of Rural Character and Scenery.* New York: F. Bliss, 1828. 194–200.

Mole, Tom. *Byron's Romantic Celebrity: Industrial Culture and the Hermeneutic of Intimacy.* Basingstoke: Palgrave Macmillan, 2007.

Monthly Magazine 1 (March 1796): 117–18. [William Taylor], "Some Account of the Poems of G. A. Bürger."

—— 2 (July 1796): 453–56. "The Enquirer. No. VI. Question: *Is Verse Essential to Poetry?*" [William Enfield, attr. Owen and Smyser, *PrW*].

Monthly Review; or, Literary Journal ns 9 (December 1792): 406–13; on Charlotte Smith, *Desmond.* Curran identifies the reviewer as William Enfield (*Desmond* xvi).

—— ns 12 (December 1793) 375–76; on Charlotte Smith, *The Emigrants.*

Moore, Doris Langley. *The Late Lord Byron.* London: John Murray, 1961.

Moore, Thomas. *Letters and Journals of Lord Byron: With Notices of His Life.* 2 vs. London: John Murray, 1830. 2/e; *The Works of Lord Byron: With His Letters and Journals, and His Life.* 17 vs. London: John Murray, 1832–34.

More, Hannah. *Cœlebs in Search of a Wife; Comprehending Observations on Domestic Habits and Manners, Religion and Morals.* 1808; London: James Blackwood, 1809.

——. *Hints Towards Forming the Character of a Princess.* 1805. V. 6 of *Works* (1830).

——. *Essays on Various Subjects, Principally designed for Young Ladies.* London: J. Wilkie, 1777.

——. *A Prefatory Address to the Ladies, & c. of Great Britain and Ireland, in Behalf of the French Emigrant Clergy and Considerations on Religion and Public Education, with Remarks on the Speech of M. Dupont, Delivered in the National Convention of France.* April 1793; "First American Edition," Boston: Weld and Greenough, 1794; facsimile rpt., ed. Claudia Johnson, 1990.

——. *Remarks on The Speech of M. Dupont, Made in the National Convention of France, on the Subjects of Religion and Political Education,* with *A Prefatory Address to the Ladies, &c. of Great Britain, in Behalf of the French Emigrant Clergy.* London: T. Cadell, 1793.

——. *Strictures on the Modern System of Female Education; With a View of the Principles and Conduct Prevalent Among Women of Rank and Fortune.* 2 vs. London: T. Cadell Jr. and W. Davies, 1799.

——. *The Works of Hannah More.* 6 vs. London: H. Fisher, R. Fisher, and P. Jackson, 1833–35.

——. Correspondence. See Roberts, *Memoirs.*

Morley, Edith J., ed. *Henry Crabb Robinson on Books and their Writers*. 3 vs. London: J. M. Dent, 1938.

Murray, John. *The Letters of John Murray to Lord Byron*. Ed. Andrew Nicholson. Liverpool: Liverpool UP, 2007.

Murray, Lindley. *The English Reader: or, Pieces in Prose and Poetry, Selected from the Best Writers, Designed to Assist Young Persons to Read with Propriety and Effect; to Improve Their Language and Sentiments; and to Inculcate Some of the Most Important Principles of Piety and Virtue. With a Few Preliminary Observations on the Principles of Good Reading*. 2/e. London: T. N. Longman &c., 1799.

Myers, Mitzi. "Mary Wollstonecraft's literary reviews." Claudia L. Johnson, ed., *Cambridge Companion* 82–98.

Nabholz, John R. "Dorothy Wordsworth and the Picturesque." *Studies in Romanticism* 3 (1964): 118–28.

New Monthly Magazine and Literary Journal 16 (March 1826): 243–48. William West, "Lord Byron's Last Portrait, With Records of his Conversation, &c. during his sittings."

———. 22 (January 1828): 84–96. Notice of Leigh Hunt, *Lord Byron & c.*

New Monthly Magazine, and Universal Register 3/18 (1 July 1815): 527–30. "Some Account of the Right Hon. Geo. Gordon, Lord Byron."

———. 10/55 (September 1818): 156–62. Review of *Childe Harold's Pilgrimage, Canto the Fourth*.

Nicholson, Andrew, ed. *Byron: Complete Miscellaneous Prose*. See Byron.

———. *The Manuscripts of the Younger Romantics. Lord Byron, vol. IX: Don Juan, Cantos X, XI, XII and XVII*. New York: Garland, 1993.

Norton, Hon. Mrs. [Caroline]. *The True Story of Lady Byron. London Times*, 30 August 1869; in *The True Story*. 178–89.

Onorato, Richard J. *The Character of the Poet: Wordsworth in* THE PRELUDE. Princeton: Princeton UP, 1971.

Owen, W. J. B. "'The Thorn' and the Poet's Intentions." *The Wordsworth Circle* 8 (1977): 3–17.

———, and Jane Worthington Smyser, eds. See Wordsworth, *Prose Works*.

Page, Judith W. "'The weight of too much liberty': Genre and Gender in Wordsworth's Calais Sonnets." *Criticism* 30 (1988) 189–203.

Paine, Thomas. *Rights of Man, Being an Answer to Mr. Burke's Attack on the French Revolution*. London: J. S. Jordan, 1791.

Parker, Reeve. "Finishing Off 'Michael': Poetic and Critical Enclosures." *diacritics* (winter 1987): 523–64.

Parrish, Stephen Maxfield. *The Art of the* LYRICAL BALLADS. Cambridge: Harvard UP, 1973.

———, ed. *The Prelude, 1798–1799*. Ithaca: Cornell UP, 1977.

Paston, George, and Peter Quennell. *"To Lord Byron": Feminine Profiles based upon unpublished letters 1807–1824*. London: John Murray, 1939.

Peach, Annette. "Portraits of Byron." *The Walpole Society* 62 (2000): 1–144.

Peacock, Thomas Love. "Four Ages of Poetry." *Olliers Literary Miscellany in Prose and Verse*. London: C. and J. Ollier, 1820. 183–200.

Perkins, David. *Wordsworth and the Poetry of Sincerity*. Cambridge: Harvard UP, 1964.

Pinch, Adela. *Strange Fits of Passion: Epistemologies of Emotion*. Stanford: Stanford UP, 1996.

Pinion, F. B. *A Wordsworth Chronology*. Boston: G. K. Hall, 1988.

Piper, David. *The Image of the Poet: British Poets and Their Portraits*. Oxford: Clarendon P, 1982.

Piso, Carolus (Charles Lepois). *Selectiorum observationum et conciliorum de praeteretis*. Pont-à-Mousson, 1618.

Polwhele, Richard. *The Unsex'd Females: A Poem*. London: Cadell and Davies, 1798.

Poovey, Mary. *The Proper Lady and the Woman Writer*. Chicago: U Chicago P, 1984.

Pope, Alexander. *An Epistle from Mr. Pope, to Dr. Arbuthnot*. London: J. Wright, 1734.

——. *An Essay on Criticism*. 2/e. London: W. Lewis, 1713.

——. *An Essay on Man. Epistles to a Friend*. 1733; corrected 7/e. London: J. Wilford, 1733.

——. *The Iliad of Homer, translated by Alexander Pope*. 1743; 4 vs. London: Osborne &c., 1763.

——. *The Rape of the Lock, an Heroi-Comical Poem in Five Cantos*. London: Bernard Lintott, 1714.

——. *To a Lady, Of the Characters of Women. Moral Essays, in Four Epistles*. Glasgow: R. Urie, 1754.

——. *Windsor-Forest*. London: Bernard Lintott, 1713.

——. *The Works of Alexander Pope, Esq. in Verse and Prose, containing the principal notes of Drs. Warburton and Warton*. Ed. William Lisle Bowles. 10 vols. London: J. Johnson &c., 1806.

Portfolio, Political and Literary 1.4 (23 November 1816): 73–77. "Childe Harold's Pilgrimage. By Lord Byron. Canto III."

—— 1.6 (7 December 1816): 123–28. "Review: Literary Frauds."

Poston, Carol H., ed. *Mary Wollstonecraft, A Vindication of the Rights of Woman*. New York: Norton, 1988.

Pottle, Frederick A. "The Eye and the Object in the Poetry of Wordsworth." *Yale Review* 40 (1950): 27–42.

Pratt, Lynda, ed. *The Collected Letters of Robert Southey, Part One: 1791–1797.* Romantic Circles Electronic Edition. www.rc.umd.edu/editions/southey_letters/Part_One/.

——, ed. *Selected Shorter Poems c. 1793–1810.* V. 5 of *Robert Southey: Poetical Works 1793–1810.* London: Pickering and Chatto, 2004.

Praz, Mario. *La Casa della Vita.* 1958; tr. Angus Davidson, *The House of Life.* London: Methuen, 1964.

Priestley, Joseph. Lecture XVIII: *A general Account of the Pleasure we receive from Objects that occasion a moderate Exertion of our Faculties. A course of lectures on oratory and criticism.* London: J. Johnson, 1777. 136–45.

Prior, Matthew. *Hans Carvel. Poems on Several Occasions.* London: T. Johnson, 1720. 115–19.

Prothero, Rowland E., ed. *Letters and Journals. The Works of Lord Byron.* London: John Murray, 1900.

Quarterly Review 16 (October 1816): 172–208. [Walter Scott; named by Smiles 1: 374] on Byron, *Childe Harold's Pilgrimage, Canto III & c.* (pub. 11 February 1817 [Reiman, ed. B 5: 2028]).

—— 44 (January 1831): 168–226; on Thomas Moore, *Life of Byron.*

Rabelais, François. *Pantagruel.* 1532; tr. Samuel Putnam, *The Portable Rabelais.* New York: Viking P, 1946.

Radcliffe, Ann. *The Mysteries of Udolpho, A Romance.* 4 vs. London: G. G. and J. Robinson, 1794.

Rajan, Tilottama. *The Supplement of Reading.* Ithaca: Cornell UP, 1990.

Rand, Richard. "Hysteron Proteron, or 'Woman First.'" *Oxford Literary Review* 8 (1986) 51–56.

Reiman, Donald H. "Poetry of Familiarity: Wordsworth, Dorothy, and Mary Hutchinson." 1978; *Romantic Texts and Contexts.* Columbia: U Missouri P, 1987. 183–215.

——, ed. *The Romantics Reviewed: Contemporary Reviews of British Romantic Writers.* New York: Garland, 1972. Part B: *Byron and Regency Society Poets.*

Rich, Adrienne. *Snapshots.* New York: Harper & Row, 1963; 1967, 1970.

Richardson, Alan. "Romanticism and the Colonization of the Feminine." Mellor, ed., 13–25.

Ricks, Christopher. "Dryden's Triplets." *The Cambridge Companion to John Dryden.* Ed. Steven N. Zwicker. Cambridge: Cambridge UP, 2004. 92–110.

Roberts, William. *Memoirs of the Life and Correspondence of Mrs. Hannah More.* 2 vs. New York: Harper & Bros., 1834.

Roscoe, William. *The Life, Death and Wonderful Atchievements of Edmund Burke: a new ballad.* N.p.: 1791.

Ross, Marlon B. *The Contours of Masculine Desire: Romanticism and the Rise of Women's Poetry*. New York: Oxford UP, 1989.

———. "Naturalizing Gender: Woman's Place in Wordsworth's Ideological Landscape." *ELH* 53 (1986): 391–410.

———. "Romantic Quest and Conquest: Troping Masculine Power in the Crisis of Poetic Identity." Mellor, ed., 26–51.

Rowe, Nicholas. *The Fair Penitent*. 1728; *The fair penitent. A tragedy. Adapted for theatrical representation, as performed at the Theatres-Royal, Drury Lane, and Covent Garden, 1795*. Bell's British Theatre. London: Cawthorn, 1797.

Rowton, Frederic. *The Female Poets of Great Britain, Chronologically Arranged: With Copious Selections and Critical Remarks*. London: Longman &c., 1848.

Rutherford, Andrew, ed. *Byron: The Critical Heritage*. New York: Barnes and Noble, 1970.

Schama, Simon. *Citizens: A Chronicle of the French Revolution*. New York: Knopf, 1989.

Schor, Esther. *Bearing the Dead: The British Culture of Mourning from the Enlightenment to Victoria*. Princeton: Princeton University Press, 1994.

Schweickart, Patrocinio P. "Reading Ourselves: Toward a Feminist Theory of Reading." Flynn and Schweickart, eds., 31–62.

[Scott, John]. "Living Authors, No. IV: Lord Byron." *London Magazine* 3 (1821): 50–61.

Scott, Walter. *The Letters of Sir Walter Scott*. Ed. H. J. C. Grierson. 12 vs. London: Constable, 1932–37.

[———]. See *Quarterly Review*.

Scourge and Satirist 12 (July 1816): 60–72; on Coleridge, *Christabel & c.*

Segel, Elizabeth. "'As the Twig is Bent . . .': Gender and Childhood Reading." Flynn and Schweickart, eds., 165–86.

Sharp, William, ed. *Sonnets of this Century*. London: Walter Scott, 1886.

Sheats, Paul D. *The Making of Wordsworth's Poetry, 1785–1798*. Cambridge: Harvard UP, 1973.

[Shelley, Mary Wollstonecraft]. *Frankenstein; or, The Modern Prometheus*. 1818. Ed. Susan J. Wolfson. New York: Longman, 2006.

———. *Lodore*. London: Richard Bentley, 1835. Ed. Lisa Vargo. Ontario: Broadview P, 1997.

Shelley, Percy Bysshe. *A Defence of Poetry. Essays, Letters from Abroad, Translations and Fragments by Percy Bysshe Shelley*. Ed. Mrs. [Mary Wollstonecraft] Shelley. 2 vs. London: Edward Moxon, 1840. 1: 1–57.

———. "Dedication" [to] *Laon and Cythna; or, The Revolution of the Golden City: A Vision of the Nineteenth Century. In the Stanza of Spenser*. London: C & J. Ollier, 1818. Ed. Jack Donovan for *The Poems of Shelley. Volume 2: 1817–1819*, ed. Kelvin Everest and Geoffrey Matthews. Harlow, England: Pearson Education, 2000. 48–57.

Showalter, Elaine. *The Female Malady: Women, Madness, and English Culture, 1830–1980.* New York: Penguin, 1985.

——. *A Literature of Their Own: British Women Novelists from Brontë to Lessing.* Princeton: Princeton UP, 1977.

Simpson, David. *Irony and Authority in Romantic Poetry.* London: Macmillan, 1979.

Smiles, Samuel. *A Publisher and His Friends: Memoir and Correspondence of the Late John Murray with an Account of the Origin and Progress of the House, 1768–1843.* 2 vs. London: John Murray, 1891.

Smith, Adam. *The Theory of Moral Sentiments.* London: A. Millar, 1759.

Smith, Charlotte. *The Banished Man. A Novel.* 4 vs. London: T. Cadell Jr. and W. Davies, 1794. Ed. M. O. Grenby, v. 7 of *The Works of Charlotte Smith* (2005).

——. *Desmond, A Novel, in Three Volumes.* London: G. G. J. and J. Robinson, 1792.

——. *Elegiac Sonnets, and Other Poems.* 6/e. London: T. Cadell Jr. and W. Davies, 1792.

——. *Elegiac Sonnets, and Other Poems.* 8/e, 2s. London: T. Cadell Jr. and W. Davies, 1797.

——. *The Emigrants, A Poem, in Two Books.* London: T. Cadell, 1793.

——. *Emmeline, The Orphan of the Castle.* 4 vs. London: T. Cadell, 1788.

——. "The Female Exile. Written at Brighthelmstone, in Nov. 1792." *London Review and Literary Journal, European Magazine* 32 (October 1797), 264; *Scots Magazine* 59 (November 1797), 842.

——. Letter to James Dodsley. Neilson Campbell Hanney Collection of William Cooper, Manuscripts Division, Dept. of Rare Books and Special Collections, Princeton University Library.

——. *Collected Letters of Charlotte Smith.* Ed. Judith Phillips Stanton. Bloomington: Indiana UP, 2003.

[——]. "On the present unhappy Situation of the QUEEN of FRANCE, and her Son." *Universal Magazine of Knowledge and Pleasure* 23 (August 1793), 147–48; and *Gentleman's and London Magazine* (September 1793), 496.

——. *The Works of Charlotte Smith.* 14 vs. Gen. ed., Stuart Curran. London: Pickering Chatto, 2004–7.

Soboul, Albert. *La Révolution français.* 1965; tr. Geoffrey Symcox, *A Short History of the French Revolution 1789–1799.* Berkeley: U California P, 1977.

Soderholm, James. *Fantasy, Forgery, and the Byron Legend.* Lexington: U Kentucky P, 1996.

Southey, Robert. See Pratt, ed. See also *Critical Review* 2s 24.

Spence, Sarah. "A Fragment Taken from a Piece written about 28 Jan. 1793, and entitled THOUGHTS ON THE IMPENDING WAR." *Poems, and Miscellaneous Pieces.* London: J. Johnson, 1795. 87–92.

St. Cyres, Viscount. "The Sorrows of Mrs. Charlotte Smith." *Cornhill Magazine* ns 15.89 (1903): 683–96.

Steele, Sir Richard. *Tatler* no. 181. London: John Sharpe, 1804. 349–54.

Steevens, George. Advertisement. *The Plays of William Shakspeare.* 15s. 4/e, with "Notes by Samuel Johnson and George Steevens." London: T. Longman, 1793. 1. i–xxxvi.

Stewart, Susan. "Lyric Possession." *Critical Inquiry* 22 (Autumn 1995): 34–63.

Stillinger, Jack. *Multiple Authorship and the Myth of Solitary Genius.* New York: Oxford UP, 1991.

——, ed. *Wordsworth: Selected Poems and Prefaces.* Boston: Houghton Mifflin, 1965.

Stodart, M. A. *Female Writers: Thoughts on Their Proper Sphere, and on Their Powers of Usefulness.* London: R. B. Seeley and W. Burnside, 1842.

Stowe, Harriet Beecher. *My Wife and I: or, Harry Henderson's History.* New York J. B. Ford, 1871.

——. *Lady Byron Vindicated: A History of the Byron Controversy, From its Beginning in 1816 to the Present Time.* Boston: Fields, Osgood, 1870.

Sunstein, Emily. *A Different Face: The Life of Mary Wollstonecraft.* New York: Harper & Row, 1975.

Swann, Karen. "'Christabel': The Wandering Mother and the Enigma of Form." *Studies in Romanticism* 23 (1984): 533–53.

——. "Literary Gentlemen and Lovely Ladies: The Debate on the Character of *Christabel.*" *ELH* 52 (1985): 397–418.

——. "'Martha's Name,' or, the Scandal of 'The Thorn.'" *Dwelling in Possibility: Women Poets and Critics on Poetry.* Ed. Yopie Prins and Maeera Shreiber. Ithaca: Cornell UP, 1997. 61–79.

Swift, Jonathan. "Third Conversation." *A Compleat Collection of Genteel and Ingenious Conversation, & c. A Proposal for Correcting the English Tongue, Polite Conversation, Etc.* Dublin, 1738. Ed. Herbert Davis with Louis Landa. Oxford: Basil Blackwell, 1957. 193–201.

Sydenham, Thomas. *Dr. Sydenham's Compleat Method of Curing Almost All Diseases, and Description of their Symptoms.* 6e. London, T. Norris &c., 1724.

Tayler, Irene, and Gina Luria. "Gender and Genre: Women in British Romantic Literature." *What Manner of Woman.* Ed. Marlene Springer. New York: New York UP, 1977. 98–123.

Taylor, Isaac. *Saturday Evening.* Hingham: C. & E. B. Gill, 1833.

Taylor, William. See *Monthly Magazine*.

Thompson, E. P. *The Making of the English Working Class*. 1963; New York: Vintage, 1966.

Thompson, William [and Anna Doyle Wheeler]. *Appeal of One Half the Human Race, Women, Against the Pretensions of the Other Half, Men, To Retain Them in Political, and Thence in Civil And Domestic Slavery*. London: Longman, Hurst, Rees, Orme, Brown and Green, 1825.

Thomson, Douglass H. "Wordsworth's Lucy of 'Nutting.'" *Studies in Romanticism* 18 (1979) 287–98.

Thomson, James. *Coriolanus, A Tragedy* (1749, Covent Garden); *The Works of James Thomson*. 4 vs. London: A. Millar, 1766. 4: 209–86. *Epilogue Spoken by Mrs. Woffington* 287–88.

Throsby, Corin. "Flirting with Fame: Byron's Anonymous Female Fans." *Byron Journal* 32/2 (2004): 115–23.

Toulmin, Camille. "Angolina." *Heath's Book of Beauty for 1847*. Ed. Countess of Blessington. London: Longman &c., 1847. 79–87. Dated "June 1846."

The True Story of Lord & Lady Byron as told by Lord Macaulay, Thomas Moore, Leigh Hunt, Thomas Campbell, The Countess of Blessington, Lord Lindsay, The Countess Guiccioli, by Lady Byron, and by The Poet Himself, in Answer to Mrs. Beecher Stowe. London: John Camden Hotten, 1869. Assembled and introduced by J. M.

Vendler, Helen. *Invisible Listeners: Lyric Intimacy in Herbert, Whitman, and Ashbery*. Princeton: Princeton UP, 2005.

Veith, Ilza. *Hysteria: The History of a Disease*. 1965; Chicago: U Chicago P, 1970.

W. Q. *To the Editor of the Monthly Magazine*, April 1797. See *Wollstonecraft*.

Watts, Alaric Alfred. *Alaric Watts: A Narrative of His Life*. 2 vs. London: Richard Bentley & Son, 1884.

Weiner, Margery. *The French Exiles, 1789–1815*. London: John Murray, 1960.

Weiskel, Thomas. *The Romantic Sublime: Studies in the Structure and Psychology of Transcendence*. Baltimore: Johns Hopkins UP, 1976.

Westminster Review 3 (April 1825): 537–39; rev. of L.E.L., *The Improvisatrice*.

Whytt [Whyte], Robert. *Observations on the Nature, Causes, and Cure Of those Disorders which have been Commonly called Nervous, Hypochondriac, or Hysteric: To which are prefixed some Remarks on the Sympathy of the Nerves*. 2d corrected ed. London: T. Becket and P. A. De Hondt / Edinburgh: J. Balfour, 1765.

Williams, Helen Maria. *A Farewell, for Two Years, To England: A Poem*. London: T. Cadell, 1791.

———. *Letters from France: Containing a Great Variety of Interesting and Origi-*

nal Information Concerning the Most Important Events That Have Lately Occurred In That Country. 2/e. V. 4. London: G. G. and J. Robinson, 1796.

Willis, Thomas. *An Essay of the Pathology of the Brain and Nervous Stock in which convulsive Diseases are Treated of.* Trans. S. Pordage. London: Dring, Leigh, and Harper, 1684.

Wilson, Frances, ed. *Byromania.* New York: St. Martin's P, 1999.

Wilson, Harriette. *The Memoirs of Harriette Wilson Written by Herself.* 1825; rpt. 2 vs. London: private printing, 1924.

[Wilson, John]. *Edinburgh Review* 30 (June 1818): 87–120; on Byron, *Childe Harold's Pilgrimage, Canto the Fourth.* See also *Blackwood's.*

Wittreich, Joseph Anthony. *Feminist Milton.* Ithaca: Cornell UP, 1987.

Wolfson, Susan J. *Borderlines: The Shiftings of Gender in British Romanticism.* Stanford: Stanford UP, 2006.

——. "Hemans and the Romance of Byron." *Felicia Hemans: Reimagining Poetry in the Nineteenth Century.* Ed. Nanora Sweet and Julie Melnyk. New York: Palgrave P, 2001. 155–80.

——. *The Questioning Presence: Wordsworth, Keats, and the Interrogative Mode in Romantic Poetry.* Ithaca: Cornell UP, 1986.

Wollstonecraft, Mary. *The Collected Letters of Mary Wollstonecraft.* Ed. Janet Todd. New York: Columbia UP, 2003.

——. *The Female Reader; or Miscellaneous Pieces in Prose and Verse; Selected from the Best Writers, and Disposed Under Proper Heads; for the Improvement of Young Women; To Which is Prefixed a Preface, Containing Some Hints on Female Education.* By Mr. Cresswick, Teacher of Elocution. London: J. Johnson, 1789.

——. *Hints* [Chiefly to have been incorporated in the Second Part of The Vindication of the Rights of Woman]. *Posthumous Works* 4: 178–95.

——. *An Historical and Moral View of the French Revolution; and the Effect it Has Produced in Europe.* London: J. Johnson, 1794. *Works* 6: 1–235.

——. *Letters Written During a Short Residence in Sweden, Norway, and Denmark.* London: J. Johnson, 1796. Cited by letter and page.

——. *Letters* [to Gilbert Imlay]. *Posthumous Works* vs. 3–4. Cited by letter; then volume: page.

——. *Mary, A Fiction.* London: J. Johnson, 1788. Cited by chapter and page.

——. "On Poetry, and Our Relish for the Beauties of Nature." *Posthumous Works* 4: 159–75. See W. Q.

——. *Posthumous Works of the Author of a Vindication of the Rights of Woman.* Ed. William Godwin. 4 vs. London: J. Johnson, 1798.

——. *Thoughts on the Education of Daughters: with Reflections on Female Conduct, in the more important Duties of Life.* London: J. Johnson, 1787.

——. *Vindication of the Rights of Men, in a Letter to the Right Honourable Edmund Burke; Occasioned by his Reflections on the Revolution in France.* 2/e. London: Joseph Johnson, 1790.

——. *A Vindication of the Rights of Woman: with Strictures on Moral and Political Subjects.* 1792; 2/e. London: Joseph Johnson, 1792.

——. *A Vindication of the Rights of Woman: with Strictures on Moral and Political Subjects.* Ed. Lorne Macdonald and Kathleen Scherf. Peterborough, Ontario: Broadview P, 1997.

——. *The Works of Mary Wollstonecraft.* Ed. Janet Todd and Marilyn Butler. 7vs. New York: New York UP, 1989.

——. *The Wrongs of Woman: or, Maria. A Fragment.* 1798; *Posthumous Works* vs. 1–2. Cited by v., chapter, page.

[——]. Articles in *Analytical Review* (attr. by Mitzi Meyers, and by Butler and Todd, *Works* v. 7).

 I (June 1788): 207–8; on "a Sentimental Novel. By a Lady."

 II (December 1788): 431–39; on Samuel Stanhope Smith, *An Essay on the Causes of the Variety of Complexion and Figure in the Human Species. To which are added, Strictures on Lord Kames's Discourse on the original Diversity of Mankind.*

 —— 457–60; on Mr. Richardson, *Essays on Shakespeare's . . . Imitations of Female Characters.*

 III (January 1789): 73–74; on Amelia Pickering, *The Sorrows of Werter, a Poem.*

 V (December 1789): 484–46; on Charlotte Smith, *Ethelinde, or the Recluse of the Lakes.*

 ——. 488–89; on *The Fair Hibernian.*

 VI (April 1790): 466–68; on a novel based on Goethe's *Werther.*

 VII (July 1790): 299–301; on Anne Francis, *Miscellaneous Poems* (esp. "The Ghost of Charlotte at the Tomb of Werter").

 X (May 1791): 101–3; on Elizabeth Inchbald, *A Simple Story.*

 XIII (May 1792): 59–60; on Mr. Jerningham, *Abelard to Eloisa: A Poem.*

 —— (August 1792): 428–35; on Charlotte Smith, *Desmond.*

[W. Q.] [?Wollstonecraft Questioner]. *To the Editor of the Monthly Magazine.* *Monthly Magazine and British Register* 3 (April 1797): 279–82. The running head is "On Artificial Taste"; rpt. with some variants, by Godwin, *Posthumous Works* v. 4, as "On Poetry."

Woof, Pamela. "Dorothy Wordsworth, Writer." *The Wordsworth Circle* 17 (1986): 95–110.

Woolf, Virginia. "Dorothy Wordsworth" ("Four Figures," Essay IV). 1932; *The Second Common Reader. Collected Essays.* London: Hogarth, 1967. 3: 199–206.

——. *A Writer's Diary*. Ed. Leonard Woolf. New York: Harcourt Brace Jovanovich, 1954.

Wordsworth, Christopher. *The Memoirs of William Wordsworth*. 2 vs. London: Moxon, 1850.

Wordsworth, Dorothy. *Collected Poems of Dorothy Wordsworth*. Ed. Susan Levin, in Levin, *Dorothy Wordsworth*, Appendix One.

——. *The Alfoxden Notebook. DWLCE* 5–17.

——. *The Grasmere Journals*. Ed. Pamela Woof. New York: Oxford UP, 1991.

——. *A Narrative concerning George and Sarah Green of the Parish of Grasmere, addressed to a Friend*. The Clarkson's copy; *DWLCE* 124–44. Variants, from Joanna Hutchinson's copy, now at Dove Cottage, Grasmere, in the edition of Hilary Clark, based on de Selincourt's edition: Wolverhampton: Clark and Howard Books, 1987.

——. *Recollections of a Tour Made in Scotland A. D. 1803. Journals of Dorothy Wordsworth*. 2 vs. Ed. Ernest de Selincourt. 1941; Hamden, CT: Archon Books, 1970. 1: 195–409.

Wordsworth, Mary. *The Letters of Mary Wordsworth, 1800–1855*. Ed. Mary E. Burton. Oxford: Clarendon P, 1958.

Wordsworth, William. *Descriptive Sketches, in Verse. Taken During a Pedestrian Tour in the Italian, Grison, Swiss, and Savoyard Alps*. London: J. Johnson, 1793.

——. *An evening walk. An epistle; in verse. Addressed to a young lady, from the lakes of the north of England*. London: J. Johnson, 1793.

——. *The Excursion, Being a Portion of The Recluse, A Poem*. London: Longman &c., 1814.

——. *Home at Grasmere. Part First, Book First, of* THE RECLUSE *by William Wordsworth*. Ed. Beth Darlington. Ithaca: Cornell UP, 1971. Cited by ms. page; reading-text line number.

[——]. *Lyrical Ballads, With a Few Other Poems*. London: Longman, 1798.

——. *Lyrical Ballads, With Pastoral and Other Poems*. 2 vs. London, T. N. Longman and O. Rees, 1800; 1802.

——. *Poems*. 2 vs. London: Longman, Hurst, Rees, Orme, and Brown, 1815. Preface, 1: viii–xlii. *Essay, Supplementary to the Preface*, 1: 341–75.

——. *Poems, Chiefly of Early and Late Years*. London: Edward Moxon, 1842.

——. *Poems, in Two Volumes*. London: Longman, Hurst, Rees, and Orme, 1807.

——. POEMS IN TWO VOLUMES, *and Other Poems, 1800–1807*, by William Wordsworth. Ed. Jared Curtis. Ithaca: Cornell UP, 1983.

——. *"The Prelude": 1798–1799*. Ed. Stephen Parrish. Ithaca: Cornell University Press, 1977.

——. *The Fourteen-Book "Prelude."* Ed. W. J. B. Owen. Ithaca: Cornell UP, 1985. Cited as *1850*.

——. *The Thirteen-Book "Prelude."* Ed. Mark L. Reed. 2 vs. Ithaca: Cornell UP, 1991. Cited as *1805*.

——. *The Prose Works of William Wordsworth.* Ed. W. J. B. Owen and Jane Worthington Smyser. 3 vs. Oxford: Clarendon P, 1974.

——. *"The Ruined Cottage" and "The Pedlar."* Ed. James Butler. Ithaca: Cornell UP, 1979.

——. *The Sonnets of William Wordsworth.* London: Edward Moxon, 1838.

——. [An Unpublished Tour]. Appendix 2, *A Guide through the District of the Lakes. Prose* 2: 287–348.

——, and Dorothy Wordsworth. *The Letters of William and Dorothy Wordsworth.* Ed. Ernest de Selincourt. *The Early Years, 1787–1805;* rev. Chester L. Shaver. Oxford: Clarendon P, 1967. *The Middle Years, 1806–1820. Part 1, 1806–1811;* rev. Mary Moorman. Clarendon P, 1969. *Part 2, 1812–1820;* rev. Mary Moorman and Alan G. Hill. Clarendon P, 1970. *The Later Years, 1821–1853;* rev. Alan G. Hill. 4 parts. Oxford: Oxford UP, 1978–1988.

Wray, Mary. *The Ladies Library. Written by a Lady.* 3 vs. London: Steele, 1714.

Wu, Duncan. "Appropriating Byron: Lady Caroline Lamb's *A New Canto.*" *The Wordsworth Circle* 26 (1995): 140–46.

——. *Wordsworth's Reading, 1770–1799.* Cambridge; Cambridge UP, 1993.

——, ed. *Romantic Women Poets, An Anthology.* Oxford: Blackwell, 1997.

Young, Edward. *The Complaint: or, Night-Thoughts on Life, Death & Immortality. Night the Fourth. The Christian Triumph.* London, R. Dodsley, 1744.

Zimmerman, Sarah. "Charlotte Smith's Letters and the Practice of Self-Presentation." *Princeton University Library Chronicle* 8 (1991): 50–77.

INDEX

See *Works Cited* for full titles.

Bessborough, Countess of, 53–54
Bessborough, Lady, and Byron, 220,
326n13
Bewell, Alan, 308n8, 310n31
Blackwood, William, on Lord Byron, 226
Blackwood's, 3, 334n20; on Lord Byron,
221, 231–34, 270, 273–5, 334n19; on
the Byrons, 221–2, 335n27; on *Don
Juan*, 231
Blake, William: on Marie Antoinette,
297n45; on "Reason," 69, 300n12;
on Wollstonecraft, 80, 107, 300n9,
307n17
Blessington, M., 226; on Lady Byron,
287–88; on Lord Byron, 245, 282–84
Bloom, Harold: "anxiety of influence," 5,
170, 176; on "boy" poetics, 157, 315n9,
316n19
blue-stocking women, 178, 268, 329n32,
333n17
Book of Beauty, and the Byrons, 226,
271
Botting, Fred, 306n7
Bowles, William, 298n56. *See also under*
sonnets
Bowstead, Diana, 292n9
British Critic, on C. Smith, 34–35, 56,
294n22, 298n54
British Lady's Magazine, on *Christabel*,
131
Brontë, Emily, 6; [Ellis Bell], Byronic
Heathcliff / *Wuthering Heights*, 224,
327n19
Brownstein, Rachel, 317n32, 320n7
Brydges, Egerton, on Byron, 235
Bürger, G. A., ballads of, 121, 208n17,
309n18, 312n49
Burke, Edmund, 117; on French clergy,
25–27; *Revolution in France*, 20–21,
26, 29–30, 36, 43–45, 101, 117, 292n9,
293n14, 294–95nn23–24, 296n37,
303n29; *Sublime and Beautiful*, 75,
84–85, 137, 234; Wollstonecraft on,
61, 75, 84–85, 117–18, 296n37. *See also*
sentiment/sentimentality; *under*
Smith, C.
Burney, Charles, 298n56; on *Lyrical
Ballads*, 129
Burney, Frances, *Emigrant French
Clergy*, 27–30. *See also under* "Author"

Burns, Robert, 57, 295–96n31; on the
French monarchy, 48; "Is there for
honest poverty?" 34
Burton, Robert, *Anatomy of
Melancholy*, 132–36, 310n39
Byromania and Byronism, 12, 131, 215,
220, 226–47, 253–58, 263–65, 280,
288–89, 326n14, 326–27n17, 332n10;
Byronic heroine, 264–6, 329n30;
vampyrics, 236, 331n45
Byron, Lady, 217–18, 229–31, 246–47,
268; as Aurora Raby (*Don Juan*
XV–XVI), 286–88, 36nn34–35; *The
Byromania*, 242–43, 288–89; as
Donna Inez (*Don Juan* I), 231, 329n32;
Remarks (on Moore's *Byron*), 221–22,
268, 275, 326–27n17; Separation from
Lord Byron, 218–19, 222, 241–42, 280,
324n7, 326n12, 326n13, 328n24,
329n31, 331nn43–44, 333nn15–16,
334n19. *See also* Baillie: on the Byrons;
Blackwood's; Hunt, Leigh; John Bull;
Milbanke; Norton; portraits/portrai-
ture; Scott, W.; Stowe
Byron, Lord: as Apollo Belvedere, 214;
H. Brougham and, 225, 327n21; and
Coleridge, 327–28n23; courtship/
marriage/Separation, 213–32, 241–44,
256, 269, 280–83, 324–26nn8–10,
328nn24–26, 329nn29–30, 329–30n33,
330n34, 335–36n28; and masquerade, 271, 283, 324n4; and Napoleon,
325n9; and Shakespeare's tragic
heroes, 266, 285 (*see also* Shakespeare: Hamlet); and Southey, 333n13;
and Swift, 326n10; and Wordsworth,
132. WORKS: "And thou art dead,"
334n20; *Beppo*, 268; *Bride of Abydos*,
328n24; *Bright be the place*, 325n9;
Corsair, 224, 263–64, 335n28; *The
Dream*, 231–33, 270, 324–25n8,
329–30n33; *Fare thee well!*, 218,
224–30, 325n9, 327n20, 327n22,
328nn24–26, 329nn29–30; *Giaour*,
235, 266, 279; *Lara*, 239–40; *Lines,
on Hearing that Lady Byron was Ill*,
222; *Manfred*, 278, 334n20; *Marino
Faliero* (Angolina), 226; *Memoranda*
(his life), 247, 331nn43–44; *Poems*
(June 1816), 217–18, 225, 325n9,

327–28n23; *Prisoner of Chillon & c,* 215, 217–18, 230; *Sardanapalus,* 268, 329n29; *Sketch from Private Life,* 225, 282, 327n22, 328n24, 336n32; *Stanzas for Music,* 325n9; *Stanzas to———* (Augusta), 218, 230, 324n8, 333–34n18; "Thyrza" lyrics, 254–56, 332n5; *To———* (Augusta), 218, 269; *When we two parted,* 325n9. See also under *Blackwood's;* Byron, Lady; Milbanke; Moore; Murray, J.; portraits; Scott, W.

Byron, Lord, *Childe Harold's Pilgrimage / Childe Harold,* 228, 241, 258–9, 271, 326n12; *Cantos I–II,* 243, 252–56, 273; *Canto III,* 215, 217–18, 220, 228–29, 256, 266, 276, 324n6, 324–25n8, 334n20; *Canto IV,* 231–34, 263, 265, 267, 282, 330n35, 334n20

Byron, Lord, *Don Juan,* 268, 285–88, 329n31, 334n20, 336n34; Aurora Raby, 286–88, 336n34; Donna Inez, 231, 329n32; Donna Julia, 329n30; hysteria, 132; Lady Adeline, 279–80

Cadell, Thomas, Sr. / Thomas Cadell, Jr. (publishers), 24, 294n17, 299n60
canonicity, 291–92n1
Carlson, Julie, 303n35
Champion, on Lord Byron, 225, 327nn21–22, 328n25
charity: and French Emigrants, 20, 24–30, 33; and the poor, 129, 143
Chew, Samuel, 328n24
chivalry: language of, 56, 149; as lineage, 38; to the French Emigrant clergy, 26–27, 30, 33; masculine ethos, 66, 126–27, 149, 224, 267, 325–26n10
Christensen, Jerome, on Lord Byron, 328n28
"Christopher North" (*Blackwood's*), on the Byrons, 273–75. *See also* Wilson, J.
Clarke, Norma, 292n7, 333n14, 351
close reading, 8–9
Clubbe, John, on West's *Byron,* 331n49
Cobb, Richard, scorn of Wollstonecraft, 91
Coleridge, E. H., on the Byrons' Separation, 328n24
Coleridge, H. N., on female Byronism, 336n36

Coleridge, S. T., 149, 303n32, 311n41, 311n47, 313n55; *Aids to Reflection,* 119; on Bowles, 120, 308n16; and/on Byron, 212, 225, 263, 327–28n23; *Christabel,* 130–31, 310n34, 310n39, 327–28n23; and Crowe, 58, 299n59; on ghosts and credulity, 136, 140; and manliness, 118–20, 131, 310nn34–35; on "method," 123, 309n24; on passion, 113–14, 124, 133, 312n50; *Reflections on Having Left a Place of Retirement,* 119–20; and sensibility, 118–19, 133; and Shakespeare, 303n32; and sonnets, 120, 308n16; *Watchman,* 58, 105, 118, 299n59; on Wollstonecraft, 105, 108; and/on W. Wordsworth, 120, 124–25, 130–31, 139, 148–49, 304–5n41, 309n27, 310n35, 313–14nn62–63, 323n25, 327–28n23. *See also under* hysteria
Colley, Linda, 45, 47, 297nn40
Collins, William, *Fear,* 48–51, 298n48
Colls, J. H., *To Wollstonecraft,* 93–96, 306n5
commonplace books: female, 80, 181, 186, 301n14, 302n24, 321n12; male, 312n49
Cooke, Michael, on *Nutting,* 157–58
Cordé/Corday, Charlotte, 18, 103–5
Cornwall, Barry, on portraiture, 211
Courier, on Lord Byron, 225
Cowper, William, 80–81; *The Task,* 23, 41–42. *See also under* Smith, C.
Cox, Jeffrey, 1
Craciun, Adriana, 299n57
Crawford, Rachel, on D. Wordsworth, 315nn11–12
Critical Review: F. Burney, 30; Lord Byron, 228–29; Smith's *Desmond,* 23; Smith's *Emigrants,* 25, 34–5, 294n22, 295n27; Wollstonecraft's *Vindications,* 34, 306n10; Wordsworth, 129
Crompton, Louis, on Byron's homosexuality, 331n44
Crowe, William, 57–58, 299n59
Cruikshank, George and Isaac, cartoons of Lord Byron in 1816, 226–27
Culler, Jonathan, 311n42
Curran, Stuart, 6, 292–93n4, 292n9, 292–93n11, 293n15, 294n18, 295n29

121, 185, 300n6, 307n2, 308n17; and W. Wordsworth, 113–51, 165, 177, 307n2, 308n8, 314n3, 319n2, 320n8

masquerade, 270–71, 324n4

Mathias, T. J.: *Pursuits of Literature*, 98–99, 306nn7–8; *Shade of Alexander Pope*, 99

Matlak, Richard, 323n29

Mayne, Ethel, 243

Mayo, Robert, 312n49

McCann, W. E., spoofing Byronism, 229, 240, 264, 332n10

McDayter, Ghislaine, on Lord Byron, 328n28

McGann, Jerome J.: on Lord Byron, 229, 240, 324n4, 327n21, 329n29, 336n34; on L.E.L., 266

Melbourne, Lady, and the Byrons, 243–44

Mellor, Anne, 297n42; on Barbauld, 92, 306n4; on "Romanticism," 6, 291n8; on C. Smith, 19, 292n9; on women's poetry, 6, 291nn7–8; on D. Wordsworth, 321n8; on W. Wordsworth, 116, 158, 307n6, 315n10

meter: Smith and Shakespeare, 47; and vocation (Milton, Pope, W. Wordsworth), 184; and D. Wordsworth's poetry, 182–83, 190, 320n5, 320n7; and W. Wordsworth's passion-poetics, 113–14, 122–23, 140, 146, 155, 164–65, 169, 309n21

Meyer, Henry, profile of Byron, 216

Micale, Marc, on hysteria, 132, 310n31

Milbanke, Anne Isabella (*later* Lady Byron), 268; and Byron, 12, 213–24, 242–44, 278–79, 287–88, 326n12, 334n19. *See also* Byron, Lady

Miller, J. H., on W. Wordsworth, 182

Milton, John, 80, 293n14, 296n33, 296n35; Barbauld and, 305n45; Blake and, 300n12; *Comus*, 64–65; in "conduct" texts, 67, 70–75; H. More and, 71–75, 85, 301n17; *Ready and Easy Way*, 303n29; sonnets, 52, 171–72, 298n52, 308n16, 318n36; on Spenser, 315n13; Wray on, 77–78. *See also under* Smith, C.; Wollstonecraft; Wordsworth, W.

Milton, John, *Paradise Lost,* 19, 52, 63–65, 69, 78, 109, 189, 298n48, 301–2nn16–19; Adam, 67–68, 71, 75–77, 81, 84–86, 300n13, 301nn16–18, 303n35, 312n54; Eden, 68–69, 81; Eve, 67–80, 85–86, 152, 253–54, 302n21; Hell, 38; Milton blind, 82; Pandemonium, 40, 149; Satan, 9–10, 38–40, 62, 69, 82–83, 160–61, 296n33, 324n2; Sin, 67, 302n21

Mitford, M. R., 178; *Nutting,* 316n17

Mole, Tom, on Byron/celebrity, 328n28

Monthly Magazine, 299n1, 305n43; and Bürger, 121, 308n17, 312n49; and Coleridge, 119–20; and Wollstonecraft, 60–61, 109; and W. Wordsworth, 60, 129, 299n1

Monthly Review, C. Smith, 23, 294n16 298n54

Moore, Thomas, *Life of Byron,* 247, 264, 269–73, 278, 334n19; on Byron's appearance, 214, 251; on Byron's courtship, marriage, Separation, 213, 220–21, 224, 229–30, 232, 268–69, 279, 327n20, 328n24, 334nn18–19; and Byron's *Memoranda,* 246–47, 331n44; reception of, 215, 221, 239, 264, 273, 282, 328n27, 334n19. *See also* Baillie: on the Byrons; *under* Byron, Lady

More, Hannah, 306n4; on female education, 71, 303n33; on French emigrant clergy, 20, 27–28, 34, 53, 294n19, 295n25; on French Republic, 20, 27, 295n26; on gender and genre, 120–21; and Milton's Eve, 71–75, 85, 301n17; on sensibility, 119; and Wollstonecraft, 73, 304n38; on Wordsworth's "Harry Gill," 130. *See also under* "Author"

Morning Chronicle, 120, 126, 297n41, 327n22, 328n24

Murray, John: and Lady Byron, 275, 326–27n17, 331n43; and Lord Byron, 217–19, 225, 232, 238, 241, 246–47, 273, 324–25nn8–10, 327n23, 331n44, 333–34n18. See also *Quarterly Review*

Murray, Lindley, 81

Myers, Mitzi, 300nn5–6

Roscoe, William, 48, 297n45; on Burke and Wollstonecraft, 101
Ross, Marlon, 6, 320n8; on W. Wordsworth, 116, 165, 307n6, 314n3, 315nn9-10, 317n25
Rousseau, J.-J. *See under* Wollstonecraft
Rowe, Nicholas, *The Fair Penitent*, 63-64, 300nn3-4
Rowton, Frederic, on L.E.L./Byron, 265, 267

Schama, Simon, 295n24, 295n30, 297n45
Schor, Esther, 308n10
Schweickart, Patrocinio, 130, 310n33
Scott, John: on Byron, 223, 229, 256
Scott, Walter: and Byron, 12, 211-13, 215, 218-20, 223, 226-27, 232-33, 264, 325n8, 325-26nn10-11; portrait of, 211; and C. Smith, 293n14
Scourge and Satirist, on *Christabel*, 131
sensibility, and gender, 17, 116, 123, 131-32; and Burke, 308n10; and Burney, 30; Coleridge on, 118-20, 124, 131; Jewsbury on, 119; and C. Smith, 20, 31-35, 298-99n56; Wollstonecraft on, 61, 63-65, 109, 118-19, 304n39, 308n7; and D. Wordsworth, 177; and W. Wordsworth, 114, 124, 131
sentiment/sentimentality: as artifice, 60, 214-15, 228, 240-43, 329n31; as manly/moral sentiment, 26, 30-31, 48, 76, 117-18, 120-21, 196, 305n42; as unmanly, 21, 64, 86, 88, 105, 117-21, 123-24, 131, 181, 192, 304n39, 308n7
Shakespeare, William, characters: Antonio (*Merchant*), 323nn26-27; Cordelia, Imogen, Miranda, Portia, 81, 305n45; Desdemona, 161, 259; Hamlet, 10, 22, 67-68, 81-82, 84-85, 87, 95, 293n13, 302n27, 303nn33-34; Hamlet and Byron, 212, 215, 248, 266, 273; Iago, 84, 303n32; Lady Macbeth, 81, 96; Lear, 42-44, 68, 133, 285, 304n37, 310n37; and L.E.L., 266; Leontes, 266; Macbeth, 62, 68, 81, 302n28, 304n37; Nurse, Juliet's, 139; Ophelia, 84-85; Orlando, 81, 163-64, 317nn23-24; Othello, 161,

266; Prospero, 62, 81; Rosalind, 81, 305n45; Theseus, 61-62, 305n45
Shakespeare, William, plays: *As You Like It*, 22, 164, 293n13, 317nn23-24; 305n45; *Julius Caesar*, 46, 104, 305n45; *King John*, 81; *King Lear*, 42-44, 68, 81, 133, 285, 304n37, 305n45, 310n37; *Midsummer Night's Dream*, 86-87, 304n37; *Shrew*, 20; *2 Henry IV* and *Henry V*, 46-47. *See also under* Byron, Lord; sonnets; Wollstonecraft; Wordsworth, D.; Wordsworth, W.
Sheats, Paul, on Wordsworth, 309n26
Shelley, Mary Wollstonecraft, 4, 6, 107, 291n3; *Frankenstein* and Byron, 226, 256-57, 280-81, 332n8; and Godwin, 303n35; and Pope, 303n30
Shelley, P. B., 131, 331n45, 333n13, 334n20; *Defence*, v, 3-5, 8, 60-61; on Wollstonecraft and M. W. Shelley, 107-8
Showalter, Elaine: on female writing, 5-6, 291n5, 327n19; on hysteria and gender, 132, 136-37, 311n43
Siddons, Sarah, 55, 63
Simpson, David, on Wordsworth, 313n56
sisters / sororal poetics: Byron's, 269, 324-25nn8-9, 333-34n18, 334-35nn22-23; W. Wordsworth's, 4, 11, 152-252
Smith, Adam, *Theory of Moral Sentiments*, 76, 118, 308n9
Smith, Charlotte, 103; and Burke, 20-21, 26, 36, 43-44, 292n3, 292n9; and Burns, 34; and Cowper, 23-25, 296nn34-35, 298n56; and Crowe, 57-58; on French monarchs, 35, 47-48; and Gray, 298n53; and Milton, 39-42, 52, 293n13, 296n35, 298n52; and Pope, 49, 52; and Shakespeare, 22, 42-44, 46-47, 293n13; and Thomson, 37-38, 245n31; and Virgil, 38, 44, 49-51; and *Werter* (Goethe), 87, 304n39; and H. M. Williams, 298n51; and W. Wordsworth, 46-47, 58, 172, 192. WORKS: *Apostrophe to An Old Tree*,

109, 114, 117, 121–23, 138, 304n41, 317n23; *The Redbreast and the Butterfly*, 171; *Resolution and Independence* ("Leech Gatherer"), 166, 175, 185; *Songs of the Affections*, 126; *Sonnets of*, 172; *Sparrow's Nest*, 168–69; "Strange fits," 122–25, 134, 137, 146, 309nn20–22; "Three years she grew," 165; *Tintern Abbey*, 43, 125, 154–57, 186, 314–15nn6–8, 315n10; "'Tis said that some have died for love," 125, 309n25; *To a Butterfly*, 169–71; *Westminster Bridge*, 172; "A whirl-blast," 172–73, 194. *See also* Wordsworth, D., and William; *under* Coleridge, S. T.; De Quincey; hysteria; Jeffrey; "masculine" tradition and poetics

Wordsworth, William, *Poems on the Naming of Places*, 141–51, 312n52; "It was an April Morning," 145–46; "A narrow girdle of rough stones," 142–44, 313nn55–57; "There is an Eminence," 150–51; *To Joanna*, 142, 146–51, 313–14nn59–62; *To M. H.*, 142, 144–45

Wordsworth, William, *Prelude*, 193, 305n57; "island" poetics, 187–88; nest-robbing, 168–69; Sister, 153–57, 167–68; vocation, 120, 125, 181, 184, 189–90

Wordsworth, William, *The Thorn*, 124–26, 131–41, 146, 191–92, 311n42, 311nn45–46, 312n49; 1800 Note, 113, 136; Martha Ray, 139–41, 309n23, 311–12n48

Wordsworth family: Dora (DW's niece) and her poets' album, 182, 319n2; John (DW's brother), 193, 204–5; Johnny (DW's nephew), 180, 194; Mary (WW's wife / M. H.), 127, 175

Wray, Mary, on Milton's Adam, 77–78, 301n18

Wu, Duncan, 295n29, 299n1, 336n33

Young, Edward, *Night Thoughts*, 41, 63, 296n34. *See also under* Wollstonecraft

Zimmerman, Sarah, on C. Smith, 292n10